COLLECTOR'S ENCYCLOPEDIA OF
Hall China

THIRD EDITION
MARGARET & KENN WHITMYER

COLLECTOR BOOKS
A Division of Schroeder Publishing Co., Inc.

On the cover:
Top Right: "Columbia" teapot with Gold Medallion decoration.
Bottom Left: Autumn Leaf coffee pot, sugar, creamer, and metal tray.
Bottom Right: Red Poppy pretzel jar.

Cover design by Beth Summers
Book layout by Karen Smith

Searching for a Publisher?

We are always looking for knowledgeable people considered to be experts within their fields. If you feel that there is a real need for a book on your collectible subject and have a large comprehensive collection, contact Collector Books.

Collector Books
P.O. Box 3009
Paducah, Kentucky 42002-3009

www.collectorbooks.com

Dedication

To all the entusiastic Hall China collectors who dream about
that special piece of Hall at the end of the rainbow.
Without you this book would only be a dream.

CONTENTS

ACKNOWLEDGMENTS

The third edition of *The Collector's Encyclopedia of Hall China* has been made possible through the efforts of many faithful collectors and dealers who have been willing to share their knowledge and information with us. We want to thank all of our readers who have sent us pictures and other information which has helped to verify the existence of the many new pieces listed in this book. Due to the volume of mail, we have not been able to respond personally to all of your letters, but we have tried to answer as many as possible. We apologize if you have written to us and have not received an answer. However, we want you to know your letter has been read and the information or suggestions in it have been appreciated.

Several people again opened up their homes and allowed us to invade their privacy for our seemingly unending photography sessions. The contributions of Steve Cagle, Dave Period, Chris Shoemaker, Terry Bennet, Ron Gaumont, and Woody Griffith were especially appreciated. Without the thoughtfulness and dedication of these individuals many exciting pieces would be lacking from this update.

We are also very grateful to the following people who either helped with pricing, or supplied us with much needed information: Ken and Carol Baker, Dennis Bialek, Dennis and Rosemary Billings, Joyce and Parke Bloyer, Bob Brushaber, Jim and Kay Carpenter, Joe and Ramona Chance, Sam and Becky Collings, Carol Corn, Sally Davis, Don and Joyce DeJong, Ronald Durst, Ronald and Linda Ellis, Anne Fleming, Gene Florence, Peggy Halski, Jerry Harris, Don Haverstack, Linda and Elvin Heck, Mr. and Mrs. Johnson, Lorrie Kitchen and Mark Hunter, Joseph Lockard, Merle and Dee Long, Robert and Bernadette Ludwig, Nancy Maben, Jerry Macke, Janet and Wendell Martin, Dori McCrane, Paula Darden Moeller, Jerry and Connie Monarch, Mrs. W. H. Morgan, Benjamin Moulton, Naomi's Antiques To Go, Tom and Jean Niner, Harvey and Delores Pametickey, Mike and Karen Parkinson, Eugene and Jewel Payton, Bill and Sharon Phillips, Pansy and Billie Ramsey, Jim and Sharon Roberts, Ed Rutkowski, Bob Saunders, Patsy Schoemaker, Bonnie Scherrer, Dave Shupp, Millie Smith, Sue Switzer, Dan Tucker, Lee Wagner, Ray and Carolyn Wagner, Karen Wilhelm, Joel Wilson, Virginia Wilson, and Delmar and Mary Lou Youngen.

Hopefully, we have included everyone, but if someone's name has mysteriously been lost in our mountain of papers, please understand that we are not unappreciative of your co-operation. We do try to keep track of where the information is coming from, but sometimes finding names at the moment you need them is a problem.

INTERNET CONNECTIONS

Hall China collecting via the Internet has become a passion with some collectors. There are numerous antique and auction sites available for dealers to advertise and where collectors may learn more about their avocation. Marty Kennedy opereates a very informative website about Hall China collecting called Hall China Collectors Home Page at http://www.inter-services.com/HallChina. One of the more useful features of this site is a collector bulletin board where individuals may post questions or information that is responded to by other collectors. There are also announcements about upcoming Hall events hosted by collector organizations and links to collectors' web pages.

Anyone interested in learning more about Eva Zeisel or if you are interested in joining the Eva Zeisel Collectors Club more information may be found at http://www.evazeisel.org.

Collectors interested in learning more about current Hall China production may want to visit the Hall China Compoany website at http://hallchina.com.

There are also frequent chats among collectors about Hall China on the Delphi website. Times for the chats and directions for accessing this site are generally posted in advance on the bulletin board of the Hall China Collectors Home Page listed above.

INTRODUCTION

The purpose of this book is to provide collectors with a usable guide to the most popularly collected items produced by the Hall China Company of East Liverpool, Ohio. The greatest emphasis will be placed upon the most collectible patterns, but many of the more obscure pieces will also be identified and examined. Currently, the greatest collector interest in the production of the Hall China Company lies in the pieces produced between the early 1930s and the late 1960s. We have tried to illustrate and identify as many items from this period as possible.

In the eight years since the introduction of our first book, many new discoveries have been unearthed. We appreciate the efforts of the numerous collectors who have taken the time to share their discoveries and collections with us. Much of the new information in this book is a direct result of the efforts of these collectors who have been willing to share their knowledge with us.

Many of the articles from Hall's institutional line have not been included in this guide, since there is still not very much collector interest in most of these items. Some people, who like the superior durability of the ware, are currently buying some of these institutional pieces to use in their kitchens but most of these items have very little collectible value. The possible exceptions are institutional items with a colorful art glaze finish and the very large black tea servers which may be seen in some fast food chains and restaurants. Older tea servers, especially those embossed with unusual advertising, are finding homes with collectors.

Many metal, glass, and wooden items which match Hall patterns, but were not produced by Hall, are also included in this guide. A great number of collectors are now incorporating these matching accessory pieces into their collections.

To provide a more convenient reference, Hall collectibles have been divided into several major categories. Arrangement of patterns and items in each area is essentially alphabetical. The major divisions are as follows:

1. Dinnerware Patterns.
   A. Styles C, D, and ruffled-D dinnerware arranged alphabetically.
   B. E-shape dinnerware.
   C. Century shape dinnerware.
   D. Tomorrow's Classic shape dinnerware.
2. Kitchenware.
   A. Basic kitchenware shapes.
   B. Kitchenware colors and decorations.
   C. Kitchenware decal patterns.
3. Refrigerator Ware.
4. Teapots and Coffee Pots.
5. Teapots, Coffee Pots, and Accessories made for other companies.
6. Advertising and Specialty Items.
7. Reissues

To properly identify a piece of Hall China, more than one name is often necessary. Most items, especially if they have a decal, will have a pattern name, such as Autumn Leaf or Red Poppy. In addition to the pattern name, individual pieces in a pattern will also usually have a shape name. The shape name helps to distinguish like items in the same pattern from each other. For example, if someone tells you they have a teapot in the pattern Red Poppy, you still don't know exactly what they have since there are two different teapots in this pattern. Therefore, the shape name — Aladdin or New York — is used to distinguish between the two similar items in the same pattern. The items in the pictures will be identified by using the name of the pattern where necessary (when more than one pattern is shown in a single photo). This will be followed by the identifying name of the piece, followed by the shape name or color name. Examples are the following:

1. More than one pattern per photo: Acacia (pattern name), jug (item name), "Radiance" (shape name).
2. One pattern per photo: Jug (item name), "Radiance" (shape name).
3. Kitchenware shapes: Teapot (item name), Chinese red (color name).
4. Teapot section: Aladdin (shape name), green (color name).

A lot of the names for the colors, patterns, and shapes used in this book are the ones designated by Hall China. However, Hall did not have names for every piece they made. In the event an official Hall name could not be determined for an item, we have taken the liberty of providing one of our own. These new names we have used will be found in quotation marks. Also, over the years, other names have been introduced and accepted by collectors for the identification of some pieces. We have attempted to use those names in this book wherever possible. In some cases certain pieces have evolved with a dual identity. Therefore, a cross reference of multiple names has been included at the back of this book to aid collectors in their attempts to use other references.

PRICING

The prices in this book represent retail prices for mint condition pieces. Items which are excessively worn, chipped, or cracked will only bring a fraction of the listed price. A price range has been included to help account for regional differences in prices. Also, be aware that certain currently rare items, which are now valued at several hundred dollars, may prove hard to sell if a quantity of these items is discovered. The value of a few items, which are currently one-of-a-kind, may be omitted from the price guide if a retail value has not been established. In these cases, the letters "UND" for undetermined will be used to indicate an unestablished value.

All items are priced each, including shakers. Items which have lids are priced complete. Any exceptions to this will be noted in the individual listing. Prices of solid color kitchenware items, refrigerator items, teapots, and coffee pots may vary considerably according to color. Wherever possible, an attempt has been made to reflect these different valuations. However, any attempt to list and price the dozens of colors in which some of the pieces may be found is impossible in a guide of this type. An effort has been made to give the reader general guidelines about rarity and desirability of various pieces and colors. Thoughtful consideration of these guidelines should produce a qualitative value for most any item.

Pricing information has been obtained from dealer listings, flea market and show observations, trade publications, and from collectors. Remember, prices in this guide should only be used as a reference. Prices may vary in the marketplace and it is not the intention of the authors to establish or control prices.

REISSUES

Hall China introduced a new retail line to buyers at the Housewares Show held in Chicago in March 1985. The new line was called Hall American and was designed for the retail market to be sold through gourmet shops and department stores.

In addition to some casseroles, bakers, jugs, and teapots which were still in production, Hall revived some shapes from its past. The total number of new shapes available ranged to the mid-sixties, but only a few of these shapes which reflect the past are of particular interest to collectors. Noteworthy shapes, in the re-introduction, are the Airflow, Rhythm, and square T-Ball teapots; the Donut and Streamline jugs; a square-based "Sundial" batter bowl; and the "Nora" and "Hercules" water servers.

Generally, this new line was only available in six standard colors in the retail outlets. The new colors were red, black, white, Sandust (tan), Oxford Grey, and Marine Blue. However, any of Hall's colors could be special ordered, and some individual customers have had various pieces produced in their own unique colors. Therefore, do not be surprised to find new pieces in such colors as lavender, rose, or orange.

Fortunately, Hall has considered the concerns of collectors and all the new production was supposed to be marked with the rectangular backstamp which has been in use since 1970.

Hall China has produced a number of collector oriented limited edition items for several organizations or individuals over the last few years. Specifically, new items which are causing the most concern are in the Autumn Leaf, Orange Poppy, Red Poppy, Crocus, Cameo Rose, and "Silhouette" patterns. Also, new issues of some of the novelty teapots have been produced. Currently, all of the new items are being marked with special backstamps. However, it is possible to remove some of these backstamps, especially on the reissued novelty teapots. If an automobile or football teapot is found without a Hall backstamp, proceed cautiously and look for other distinguishing features of the new issues. For more information on new items see the chapter on Reissues at the back of this book.

COLORS

Hall China produced the widest variety of colored glazes of any china company. Many of the colors are very close, with some only varying by a shade. Due to this small difference, we have tried to reproduce some of the most frequently encountered colors in the accompanying color chart. Even with the help of the chart, it may still be difficult to identify some of the colors.

Ivory	Hi-white	Addison	Cobalt	Blue Turquoise	Turk Blue
Cadet	Delphinium	Dresden	Marine	Sandust	Tan
Stock Brown	Mahogany	Stock Green	Forest Green	Turquoise	Green Lustre
Emerald	Garden	Monterrey	Lettuce	Celadon	Seaspray
Old Rose	Rose	Pink	Sunset	Poppy	Indian Red
Camellia	Maroon	Chinese Red	Daffodil	Canary	Warm Yellow

HALL *Superior Quality* DINNERWARE

24 PIECE BREAKFAST SET

THE LOVELY 24 PIECE BREAKFAST SET

Consists of six dinner plates (No. 7) each 9¼ inches across; six fruit dishes (No. 3) each 5⅝ inches across; six cups (No. 1) each 3⅝ inches across; and six saucers. (No. 2) each 6⅛ inches across.

1 CUP
Measures 3⅝ inches across. (Shown in Breakfast Set)

2 SAUCER
Measures 6⅛ inches across. (Shown in Breakfast Set)

3 FRUIT DISH
Measures 5⅝ inches across. (Shown in Breakfast Set)

4 BREAD AND BUTTER PLATE
Measures 6⅛ inches across.

5 SALAD PLATE
Measures 7¼ inches across.

6 PIE PLATE
Measures 8¼ inches across.

7 DINNER PLATE
Measures 9¼ inches across. (Shown in Breakfast Set)

8 SMALL OVAL PLATTER
Length 11¼ inches. Width 8¾ inches.

9 ROUND VEGETABLE DISH
Family size. Measures 9⅛ inches across.

10 LARGE OVAL PLATTER
Length 13¼ inches. Width 10¼ inches.

11 COUPE SOUP DISH
Measures 8½ inches across.

12 CEREAL DISH
Measures 6 inches across.

LARGE DINNER PLATE
(Not illustrated) Measures 10" across.

SUGAR BOWL
(Not illustrated) Holds 16 ounces.

CREAM PITCHER
(Not illustrated) Holds 12 ounces.

GRAVY BOAT
(Not illustrated) Holds 16 ounces.

OVAL VEGETABLE DISH
(Not illustrated) Length 10¼ inches.

CARE OF HALL CHINA OVENWARE

Hall China Ovenware is easily and thoroughly cleaned with soap and water and is impervious to acids, alkalies and salt. Observance of the following simple rules assures long life, perfect service, and keeps the ware sparkling like new.

1. When baking, always use an asbestos pad.
2. Never place china over direct flame even with asbestos pad.
3. Never handle dish with a wet cloth.
4. Never run cold water on hot dish or hot water on cold dish.
5. Always preheat coffee server with warm water.
6. Always have a quantity of liquid in coffee server before placing on heat.
7. Always have china at room temperature before placing in oven or refrigerator.

THE HALL CHINA COMPANY

Printed in U. S. A.   1500-8-49

10

HISTORY OF THE HALL CHINA COMPANY

The Hall China Company was established on August 14, 1903, as a result of the dissolution of the East Liverpool Potteries Company. This company had been formed in 1901, as a result of the merger of six small East Liverpool area potteries. The six independent companies Included: The East End Pottery, The East Liverpool Pottery Company, The Globe Pottery, The George C. Murphy Pottery, Wallace and Chetwynd Pottery from East Liverpool, and the United States Pottery of Wellsville, Ohio. Robert Hall, a member of the board of directors of the East Liverpool Potteries Company, bought one of the companies — the former East Liverpool Pottery Company — located in the old West, Hardwick, and George building at Fourth and Walnut Streets in East Liverpool, Ohio. Initially, 38 potters were employed at three kilns to produce spittoons and combinets, and a limited amount of dinnerware. In 1904, Robert Hall died and his son, Robert Taggert Hall, became manager.

Robert T. Hall kept the plant operating by producing primarily toilet sets, jugs, and other white ware. At the same time he experimented endlessly to rediscover a lost process from the Ming Dynasty (A.D. 1368 – 1644) in China, which would allow him to produce non-lead glazed china with a single-fire process. This single-firing would allow the glaze to penetrate the unfired body, creating a craze-proof finish. Robert T. Hall experimented from 1904 until 1911 before he finally achieved success. His new process created a colorfully glazed china which was strong, non-porous, and craze-proof. The new technique fused together the white body, color, and glaze when it was fired at a temperature of 2400°F. The resulting product was very dense, did not absorb moisture, and held heat well.

Hall China experimented briefly with dinnerware from 1908 until 1911, but then chose to concentrate on institutional wares. As the company grew, and the institutional line expanded, two more plants were added in East Liverpool. The successful addition of their Gold Decorated Teapot Line in the 1920s pushed the capacity of these plants to the limit. By 1923, Hall claimed the title of "the largest manufacturer of fireproof cooking china in the world." In 1930, a new plant was built on the east side of East Liverpool and the three old plants were abandoned. This new plant enjoyed numerous expansions during the thirties and early forties as production boomed with the intense concentration on decal dinnerware and kitchenware patterns.

The Hall China Company is still operating in this plant today. Once again, production is targeted primarily at institutional and commercial customers. However, in 1985, Hall re-introduced some of Its old kitchenware and teapot shapes for the retail trade. Also, of great interest to many collectors are the limited edition Autumn Leaf pieces which are currently being made for both a private company and the National Autumn Leaf Collector's Club. In many ways Hall China has remained viable by adapting to meet the special needs of its customers.

The China Process

The manufacture of Hall China begins with a secret powdered mixture of flint, feldspar, and several different clays. These ingredients are mixed with water in a machine. The resulting slip is passed through separators which remove metals and other foreign objects.

The mixture is then pumped into presses which squeeze out the water, leaving clay in a cake form. The cakes of clay are then aged and pressed through pug mills which remove air from the clay.

The clay is then shaped by a "jiggerman" on a potter's wheel to form flat pieces and bowls. To produce pieces such as teapots or jugs, water is added to the clay, and the resulting slip is poured into a mold. The raw ware is allowed to dry for 24 hours at about 100°F. Then the special leadless glaze is applied by either spraying or hand dipping. The glazed items are placed on cars which move slowly through a kiln. The temperature of the ware is slowly increased to 2400°F. This intense heat causes chemical changes in the body and glaze materials which allows the color to set.

The fired china is then inspected for defects and the good pieces are sent on to the decorating department. Decorating is done by either hand painting or by transferring decals or prints to the ware. The finished product is then refired in a smaller oven at a lower temperature. Decals were a very popular method of decoration during the thirties and forties. Since only pieces of larger decals were sometimes used on smaller items in a pattern, it is sometimes difficult to associate these pieces with the rest of the items in the pattern. Careful comparison will usually result in a positive identification.

IDENTIFICATION OF HALL CHINA

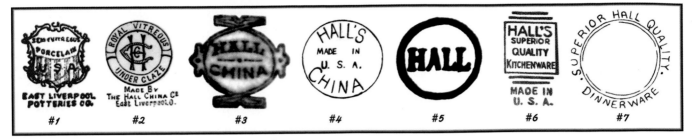

East Liverpool Potteries Co. #1 | Royal Vitreous, Made By The Hall China Co. East Liverpool, O. #2 | Hall China #3 | Hall's Made in U.S.A. China #4 | HALL #5 | Hall's Superior Quality Kitchenware, Made in U.S.A. #6 | Superior Hall Quality Dinnerware #7

Pictured here are the general backstamps which may be found on the bottom of most collectible Hall China pieces. Numerous other backstamps which are peculiar to a particular pattern or special application will be found illustrated in the sections portraying the individual patterns or specialty items.

Backstamp #1, the East Liverpool Potteries backstamp, is from the early 1900s. This company was a predecessor of Hall China and was used when Robert T. Hall was a principal in that company.

Backstamps #2 and #3 are a very early Hall marks. These marks were used until the early teens. Mark #2 has been found on some commemorative plates from that era. Mark #3 will be found on much of the utilitarian white ware and early dinnerware sets produced by Hall China. Examples of the type of wares found with this mark are shown on pages 14 and 15.

Backstamp #4 was used primarily from the early teens until the late twenties. "Made in U.S.A." is sometimes missing. Early Gold Decorated Line teapots produced during this period will often bear this mark.

Mark #5 is the backstamp which appears most frequently on items of interest to today's collector. The words "Made in U.S.A." will sometimes appear below the circle. Registration of the mark occurred on February 10, 1930, and use of the mark began in October 1930. This mark was used extensively from the early 1930s until the 1970s and will be found on most items except kitchenware and dinnerware. These two categories have special backstamps.

Mark #6 was used on kitchenware produced after 1932. This mark was usually stamped in gold, but will also be found in black, blue, green, and perhaps a few other colors. Occasionally a pattern name will also appear in conjunction with this mark.

Backstamp #7 was reserved for Hall dinnerware. This mark was modified slightly for use with the dinnerware produced for the Jewel Tea Company and for the Orange Poppy and Wildfire patterns of The Great American Tea Company. Autumn Leaf will have "Tested and

Approved by MARY DUNBAR — JEWEL HOMEMAKERS INSTITUTE" in the circle. Orange Poppy has the Great American Golden Key symbol inside the circle and the Wildfire mark acknowledges the 100th anniversary of Great American.

Fortunately for collectors, most of Hall's items have an identifying backstamp. With the exception of shakers, lamps, and some coffee pots, most of the unmarked pieces of Hall were seconds and never reached the decorating room.

In addition to the above printed backstamps, some items will be found with "Hall" impressed in large block letters. Many of the kitchenware pieces with this mark will date to the early 1930s or before. Many institutional pieces will also be marked in this manner.

Numerous other special identifying marks were reserved for certain pieces, patterns, or companies for which Hall produced china. We will show as many special marks as space permits throughout the book. Certain special marks have also been used on limited edition pieces of collector interest produced for such organizations as the National Autumn Leaf Collector's Club and private companies such as China Specialties. For more about these specific backstamps see the section on reissues at the back of this book.

Paper labels were also used for identification by Hall China. However, since most items were used heavily, not much Hall China is found with paper labels still intact. Paper labels are helpful in identifying lamps which Hall made for the White Lamp Company and others. The only way to identify these lamps as Hall is by their paper label, since there is no backstamp.

Much of the Hall China produced since the early 1970s has backstamp #8. Use of this mark began on January 6, 1969, and the mark was officially registered on February 20, 1969.

Hall #8

THE EAST LIVERPOOL POTTERIES COMPANY

In 1900, six independent East Liverpool area potteries formed an alliance called The East Liverpool Potteries Company. Member companies hoped to be better able to compete with the dominant potteries of the era such as Homer Laughlin and Harker. The unification was not very successful and the organization was dispersed in 1903. Robert Hall, a member of the board of directors of the East Liverpool Potteries Company, reorganized one of these companies — The East Liverpool Pottery Company — to form The Hall China Company.

Although examples are scarce today, some highly collectible pieces of china were made during the brief period The East Liverpool Potteries Company was in existence. All the items shown on this page bear the backstamp shown in the photo below.

The two large pitchers are part of chamber sets which were made by the East Liverpool Potteries Company shortly after the turn of the century. The pitcher at the bottom left is 12" tall and sets in a large bowl about 16" in diameter similar to the set shown at the top center. Other pieces in this type of set often included a smaller water pitcher, a toothbrush holder, and a covered soap dish.

The pitcher at the top left is 7½" tall. Although this example is decorated, other pitchers may be found without decoration. The colorful oval centerpiece exemplifies the beauty of early East Liverpool Potteries decorations.

Top Row	Value	Bottom Row	Value
Pitcher, 7½"	$65.00 – 85.00	Pitcher, 11½"	$80.00 – 90.00
Covered vegetable, 13"	$80.00 – 95.00	Pitcher, 12"	$90.00 – 125.00
Pitcher, 11½"	$80.00 – 90.00	Bowl, oval centerpiece	$80.00 – 90.00
Bowl, 14"	$30.00 – 35.00		

EARLY HALL CHINA

Collectors are finding it somewhat challenging to obtain good examples of Hall China that was manufactured between 1903 and 1920. Much of the early production consisted of spittoons, potties, commodes, and other utilitarian type items that were intended for use in hotels. Many of the commonly found pieces are plain whiteware and are not very attractive. However, a few patient and persistent collectors have been accumulating some very interesting decorated pieces from this era.

Notice the set of early dinnerware pictured on the next page. The early style shapes and decorations closely resemble that of Haviland and other major European makers of the period.

11 1/4" Oval Platter

8 1/4" Plate

9 1/4" Plate

Early Hall China Backstamp

Cup & Saucer

Oval Bowl

Gravy Boat

Butter Pat

13 1/4" Platter

Creamer Sugar and Lid

Butter or Cheese Dish

Relish

Waste Bowl

Flat Soup

5" Fruit Bowl

Covered Vegetable

Items on Page 14:

Item	Value	Item	Value
Bowl, 14"	$30.00 – 35.00	Plate, Pittsburgh Centennial	$120.00 – 140.00
Commode	$30.00 – 40.00	Potty, 6"	$20.00 – 30.00
Creamer, decorated	$35.00 – 45.00	Potty, large covered	$40.00 – 50.00
Pitcher, small decorated	$65.00 – 85.00	Vase/spooner, 5"	$60.00 – 70.00
Pitcher, large pink/white	$80.00 – 90.00	Waste bucket	$90.00 – 100.00

Dinnerware Set (above):

Item	Value	Item	Value
Bowl, 5" fruit	$8.00 – 10.00	Plate, 8¼"	$9.00 – 11.00
Bowl, flat soup	$16.00 – 18.00	Plate, 9¼"	$16.00 – 18.00
Bowl, oval	$45.00 – 55.00	Platter, 11¼"	$35.00 – 45.00
Butter pat	$12.00 – 15.00	Platter, 13¼"	$50.00 – 60.00
Butter/cheese dish with cover	$130.00 – 150.00	Relish dish	$35.00 – 45.00
Creamer	$20.00 – 25.00	Saucer	$2.00 – 3.00
Cup	$10.00 – 12.00	Sugar and lid	$30.00 – 35.00
Gravy boat	$45.00 – 50.00	Vegetable bowl and cover	$120.00 – 145.00
Plate, 6"	$6.00 – 8.00	Waste bowl	$25.00 – 30.00

Features of HALL CHINA OVENWARE

1. Crazeproof.
2. Stainproof.
3. Resists oven heat or refrigerator cold.
4. Extremely durable.
5. Holds the heat for serving.
6. Designed for perfect baking.
7. Ideal for storing.
8. Each item has many uses.
9. Easy to clean.
10. Beautiful pattern.
11. Approved by Good Housekeeping Institute.
12. Guaranteed against crazing.

(See back page for "CARE OF HALL CHINA")

® BOWL SET

Three bowls that can be used for four purposes—mixing, serving, baking, or storing. 1, 2 and 3½ qt. capacities; measure 6¼, 7½ and 8⅝ inches across, respectively. They nest conveniently.

Genuine HALL CHINA OVENWARE and DINNERWARE in the Lovely CROCUS PATTERN

The Perfect Drip Method
⑤ COFFEE MAKER
9 CUP FAMILY SIZE

The ideal combination for drip brewing of coffee—a nine cup family size Hall China server that never retains stale odor, keeps coffee hot and is supremely attractive for serving; and an aluminum dripper. China server is also available in four and six cup sizes. All servers have openings to fit any standard aluminum dripper.

COFFEE MADE BY THE DRIP METHOD IS HEALTHFUL

Leading authorities endorse the scientific drip method for it eliminates all guesswork, and retains the stimulating, aromatic coffee oils. The drip method is simplicity itself. First—preheat server with warm water. Second—boil water for coffee in sauce pan. Third—measure coffee into dripper. Fourth—pour hot water from sauce pan into dripper. Fifth—when dripping process is completed, remove dripper from pot and serve.

C-style D-style Ruffled-D Style

E-style Century Style Tommorow's Classic Style

Hall began producing large quantities of modern style decal pattern dinnerware in 1936 with the introduction of an Autumn Leaf breakfast set. During the next 20 years many different patterns and several different shapes of dinnerware were produced. The dinnerware patterns and shapes will be identified and evaluated in this section. Styles of dinnerware found in this guide include:

D-style. This was the most commonly used shape of dinnerware. The plates and bowls are round and the cups and gravy boat have ear-shaped handles. Although there are some minor modifications in the different patterns, the basic dinnerware service consists of the following pieces:

Bowl, 5¼" fruit	Plate, 6"
Bowl, 6" cereal	Plate, 8"
Bowl, 8½" flat soup	Plate, 9"
Bowl, 9" vegetable	Platter, 11¼" oval
Cup	Platter, 13¼" oval
Gravy boat	Saucer

Some patterns of D-style dinnerware will also have a 10" dinner plate.

C-style. The C-style pieces have the same round shape as the D-style. However, all the C-style dinnerware is embossed with the "Radiance" design. The cup does not have an ear-shaped handle and there is no gravy boat. The only pattern which has been found with this shape dinnerware is Orange Poppy.

Ruffled D-style. This is a modified D-style. The flat pieces and the bowls have a scalloped edge instead of just being plain round. Two additional sizes of plates — a 10" dinner and a 7¼" salad — were also included in the set. This shape is exclusive to the Autumn Leaf pattern.

E-style. The E-style dinnerware shape was designed by J. Palin Thorley and was produced during the 1940s and early 1950s. Many of the patterns which use this shape were produced for Sears, but several non-Sears products were also made.

Century shape. The Century shape was designed in the 1950s by Eva Zeisel. The shape of the plates is slightly oval with a prominent tab handle. Bowls and platters have two distinct tab handles.

Tomorrow's Classic shape. Tomorrow's Classic is another shape designed by Eva Zeisel in the 1950s. It is similar in style to the Century shape. However, the plates are slightly oval and lack a tab handle and the bowls and platters feature a single tab handle. There are other minor differences among the other serving pieces in the two shapes, but the butter dish and the gravy boat ladle are the same shape in both lines.

Arrangement of the dinnerware patterns in this chapter is alphabetical in three separate sections. The first section includes a combined listing of all C, D, and Ruffled D-shape dinnerware. This is followed by an alphabetical listing of the E-style dinnerware. The final section presents a listing of the Century and Tomorrow's Classic shapes designed by Eva Zeisel.

Will You Accept this 50-Piece Set as a Gift?

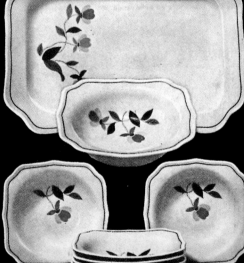

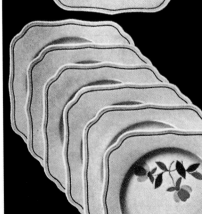

18

RUFFLED-D STYLE DINNERWARE
Autumn Leaf Introduction

Hall China with the Autumn Leaf decal first appeared in 1933 with the introduction of a large 9" mixing bowl. By Christmas of the same year, two smaller size bowls were added to complete the three-piece utility set. These three basic pieces remained in the line until Autumn Leaf was discontinued in 1976. Hall produced this pattern exclusively for the Jewel Tea Company of Barrington, Illinois. In the early years the pattern was referred to as the Autumn design and pieces were offered to Jewel customers as premiums for the purchase of other products.

Since Autumn Leaf developed as a premium line, new items were added regularly, and old pieces were discontinued periodically. This gave customers an incentive to buy more products to obtain the premiums while they were still available. Items which were not popular with the housewife of the day were short lived and are difficult for modern-day collectors to find. Metal shortages during World War II also caused the premature departure of some of the metal accessories associated with the line. As a result, collectors are having difficulty obtaining many pre-war tins. Although, all pieces of Autumn Leaf were discontinued in 1976, a number of items reappeared briefly in 1978. Items included in the reissue are the 10" plate, 7¼" plate, tea cup and saucer, 13½" oval platter, 5½" fruit bowl, 8½" flat soup, oval vegetable bowl, round 10 ounce French baker, two-handle bean pot, and Newport teapot. In addition, 106 of the long spout "Rayed" teapots were produced. These were given by Jewel as awards to outstanding sales people. Most pieces in this short re-introduction will have a backstamp shown to the right which includes the date 1978. Certain other premium pieces such as the newer Newport teapot and the two-handled bean pot also have slight decorative differences from the older versions which enable a knowledgeable collector to differentiate between the two issues.

In the last few years, limited edition pieces of Autumn Leaf have been made available to collectors. Thus far the new china pieces have been restricted to items which were not in the original Autumn Leaf line. For more information on these new items see the Reissues section at the back of this book.

As the hobby of collecting the Autumn Leaf pattern has matured, it has been possible to determine that certain items are truly rare. Pieces in this category are generally sample items submitted to Jewel by Hall. If the item was not approved for production, the few samples were offered for sale through Jewel's employee store. Many of these pieces have now reached the collectible market and some collectors are paying very high prices for them. As a word of caution, there are numerous private entrepreneurs who have made a variety of Autumn Leaf products over the years. Therefore, the authenticity of extremely expensive rarities should be carefully researched before any purchase is made. As a general guideline, most of the sample items we have seen have had the Mary Dunbar backstamp.

Although the Autumn Leaf decal became a Jewel Tea exclusive, other non-Hall china pieces may be found with this decal. Prior to 1933, the decal was used on a set of china which *Needlecraft* magazine promoted as a premium. This china was produced by the Crooksville China Company of Crooksville, Ohio, and is shown in the photo on page 18. The entire set could be obtained by selling 20 two-year subscriptions to the magazine for fifty cents each. Other companies which are known to have produced pieces using the Autumn Leaf decal include Columbia, Crown, Harker, American Limoges, Paden City, and Vernon of California. Although some items may have been submitted to Jewel by Hall's rivals in an attempt to gain their business, many of these pieces are far too common to have been mere samples. Most, like the ones in the *Needlecraft* ad, were probably made prior to 1933. A lot of the non-Hall items will not have a backstamp to identify the manufacturer. However, the shape of the piece will usually reveal the identity of the maker. Pieces of non-Hall Autumn Leaf are often crazed and discolored and do not generally approach the quality of Hall pieces. Today, some collectors are enthusiastically pursuing non-Hall items, and the prices are rising with the corresponding increased demand.

Autumn Leaf
Dinnerware Backstamp

Autumn Leaf
Kitchenware Backstamp

Autumn Leaf
1978 Dinnerware
Backstamp

Autumn Leaf Dinnerware

Abundant supplies of reasonably priced Autumn Leaf basic dinnerware pieces have enticed many people to begin collecting this pattern. Many collections have blossomed from the cheap acquisition of a few pieces at a garage sale, flea market, or auction. Other collectors have gotten their starts through the inheritance of a few pieces from a close relative. Natural curiosity and the thirst for knowledge have driven them to pursue the elusive Autumn Leaf motif. How many of them would have begun if they had realized the vast number of accessory pieces available and the enormous sums of money required to acquire them?

Most dinnerware articles were made for a long period of time — from the thirties and forties until the mid-seventies. Therefore, most of these items are readily available at a moderate price and collectors should expect to be able to purchase pieces which are in excellent condition. The only dinnerware pieces which appear to be in short supply are the cream soups and the 10" plates. Even these can be found by most collectors without extreme effort.

Although the crazing problem with this china is minimal, extensive use will result in abnormal wear and damage to the gold rim. Dinnerware which is scratched or dull will bring only a fraction of the listed prices. Some collectors, who want to use their china, buy these slightly worn pieces to use for everyday in order to preserve the value of the pieces in their collections.

Although Autumn Leaf kitchenware was made earlier, the first dinnerware appeared in 1936. Jewel ads of the time promoted this as the first dinnerware ever produced by Hall China and expounded on its beauty and durability. Perhaps these writers were not aware of the dinnerware produced by Hall almost 30 years earlier. The Jewel writers went on to exclaim the new dishes were "manufactured from the best imported and domestic clays. The china has been tested for an hour under 100 pounds of pressure at a temperature of 212 degrees and then doused with cold water. No cracks or crazes developed." The initial offering consisted of a 24-piece set which included six of each of the following: 9" breakfast plates, 5½" deep fruit bowls, and cups and saucers. The complete set sold for $4.95.

Some of the items shown here such as the cups and saucers and the small fruit bowls were essential items for the basic dinnerware set. Therefore, there is an ample supply of these pieces to supply the collector market and these prices have remained very reasonable. However, other items such as the cream soups, flat soups, and 10" dinner plates are becoming harder to find and prices for these items are gradually rising.

	Item	Introduced	Discontinued	Value
Row 1:	Cup, Ruffled D	1936	1976	$6.00 – 8.00
	Saucer, Ruffled D	1936	1976	$1.00 – 2.00
	Cream soup	1950	1976	$32.00 – 37.00
	Bowl, 6½" cereal	1938	1976	$14.00 –16.00
	Bowl, 8½" flat soup	1938	1976*	$15.00 – 18.00
Row 2:	Plate, 6"	1938	1976	$4.00 – 5.00
	Plate, 7¼"	1938	1976	$9.00 – 10.00
	Bowl, 5½", fruit	1936	1976*	$5.00 – 6.50
Row 3:	Plate, 10"	1938	1976*	$15.00 – 18.00
	Plate, 9"	1936	1976	$10.00 – 11.00
	Plate, 8"	1938	1976	$10.00 – 12.00

*Reissued in 1978.

Cup & Saucer

Cream Soup

Cereal Bowl

Flat Soup Bowl

6" Plate

7 1/4" Plate

Fruit Bowl

10" Plate

9" Plate

8" Plate

16-PIECE STARTER SET . . . ITEM NO. 307
Reflecting all the high quality for which its maker is famous, this charming 16-Piece Hall China Starter Set is a delightful asset to every home. The cheerful colors and attractive pattern are extremely popular. They blend well with many color schemes. If you like fine things, you will derive infinite pleasure from the Jewel 16-Piece Starter Set, consisting of four plates, four cups, four saucers, and four fruit dishes.

OPEN STOCK
Additional Pieces on Following Pages

Hall produced a number of special dinnerware pieces to complement Jewel's Autumn Leaf dinnerware line. Among the more interesting are the covered oval casserole, the divided oval bowl, and the tiered tidbit servers.

Jewel introduced the tiered serving tray in 1954. These trays were made from plates in the regular dinnerware line. However, plates which were selected for use in the trays do not have a backstamp in the normal position. The large 10¼" plates have an off-center backstamp so the holes for the center handle were not drilled through the backstamp. Also, the smaller plates which are used in the tidbit have no backstamp. The three-tiered tidbit offered in the 1960 catalog sold for $4.00. At various times a two-tiered tidbit was also available.

The new Ruffled D-style sugar and creamer replaced the original sugar and creamer in 1940. The shape of the handles on this later set matches the shape of the handles on the dinnerware pieces. The new sugar lid is sloped and has a "bud" knob which lacks rays on the surface of the lid. These lids are susceptible to having the buds broken off. Beware of buying lids that have had their knobs glued back. The older "Rayed" sugar and creamer set is pictured on page 31. This set was made for a much shorter period and is harder to find than the newer set.

The 9" round vegetable bowl is shown at the bottom right in the photo. This bowl was only made for a couple of years, between 1937 and 1939. Therefore, it is rather difficult to find and has become expensive.

The two styles of oval bowls are shown in the picture. The bowl on the left is divided and is much harder to find than the undivided style. The divided bowl was designed to serve two vegetables in the same bowl and was available from 1957 through 1976. In 1976, the oval bowl sold for $7.95 and the divided bowl sold for $10.95. Today, the value of the divided bowl is about four times that of the regular oval bowl.

Two sizes of oval platters were added to the dinnerware line in 1938. The 11½" platter sold for .65¢ and the 13½" platter was listed at $1.00.

The oval covered vegetable dish shown on the right side of the third row was introduced in 1940 and discontinued in 1976. Jewel's price for this piece in 1949 was $2.75. As with many other Jewel items, replacement of a damaged part was simple since the top and the bottom could be purchased separately.

The gravy boat was also introduced in 1940 and was discontinued in 1976. In 1949, the gravy boat was priced at $1.25. The 8½" oval pickle dish which also doubles as the underplate for the gravy boat was added to the line in 1942. The cost of the pickle dish was .75¢ in 1949.

	Item	Introduced	Discontinued	Value
Row 1:	Tidbit, 2-tier	1954	1969	$55.00 – 75.00
	Gravy boat	1940	1976	$30.00 – 35.00
	Platter, 11½", oval	1938	1976	$25.00 – 28.00
Row 2:	Bowl, oval divided	1957	1976	$100.00 – 130.00
	Tidbit, 3-tier	1954	1969	$95.00 – 135.00
	Bowl, oval	1939	1976*	$25.00 – 30.00
Row 3:	Platter, 13½", oval	1938	1976*	$25.00 – 32.00
	Vegetable dish, oval covered	1940	1976	$65.00 – 85.00
Row 4:	Pickle dish, 8½" (gravy boat liner)	1942	1976	$25.00 – 27.00
	Creamer, ruffled D	1934	1940	$12.00 – 16.00
	Sugar and lid, ruffled D	1940	1976	$15.00 – 27.00
	Bowl, 9" round	1937	1939	$95.00 – 125.00

Reissued in 1978.

2-tier Tidbit Tray

Gravy Boat

11 1/2" Oval Platter

Divided Oval Bowl

3-tier Tidbit Tray

Oval Bowl

13 1/2" Oval Platter

Oval Covered Vegetable Dish

8 1/2" Pickle Tray

Ruffled-D
Creamer, Sugar and Lid

9" Round Vegetable Bowl

Autumn Leaf Kitchenware

Two styles of Autumn Leaf bean pots are pictured in the photo on the opposite page — one handle and two handle. Of the two, the one handle variety is much harder to find. The two handle version was introduced in 1960, discontinued in 1976, and reissued in 1978. There are slight differences between the two issues. The major difference is in the gold decoration on top of the handles. The older one has three gold lines and the newer one has a single gold stripe on the handle. The newer two handle bean pot has closed the gap in price with the older one, but generally seems to be bringing about $20.00 to $25.00 less. Although the lids for both the one handle and two handle bean pots are the same size, they are not interchangeable. The lid to the two handle pot simply has a gold band around the knob, while the lid to the other one has the gold band plus an Autumn Leaf flower in the center of the knob.

The small 7 ounce custard cup shown in the center of the photograph was one of numerous items added to the Autumn Leaf line in 1936. The custard was Jewel's Item No. 303 and was sold as a set of six for one dollar.

An Autumn Leaf batter jug is shown at the left side of the third row. Not much is known about when this piece was made. It may have been a special promotion since it is quite rare to find one today.

Four different fluted bakers are shown in the photo. The largest holds three pints and sold for .85¢ in 1939. The medium size baker holds two pints and the smallest one holds ten ounces. The two pint fluted baker is not easy to find and the price of this size baker is rising

steadily. The small baker is commonly found and was reissued in 1978. The newer baker is about ¼" larger than the original baker.

The shallow oval bowl in the center near the bottom of the photo holds twelve ounces and is often called a Fort Pitt oval baker. It was a convenient item since it held individual size portions and allowed the food to be baked and served in the same dish. However, as the high price indicates, these are difficult to find today.

The oval baker pictured on the left side of the photo is similar in shape, but larger than the Fort Pitt baker. This baker holds two pints and measures 10" long by 7½" wide by 2½" deep. At the present time, the supply of these bowls is insufficient to meet the demand of collectors. Therefore the price for this bowl is on a continuously upward spiral.

The ball-shaped, beverage jug was an outstanding success for Jewel. This may be seen by the availability of this item today at shows and flea markets. It has a 5½ pint capacity and was designed with an ice lip to trap ice cubes while pouring.

The three-piece utility bowl set shown on the bottom row was introduced in 1939. If the number available today is any indication, this must have been one of Jewel's more successful offerings. The set cost $2.65 when it was introduced and had only increased to $4.95 by 1960. The three-piece set consisted of a large 3½ quart bowl, a medium-sized two quart bowl, and a small one quart bowl. They were advertised as being ideal for mixing, baking, serving, and storing.

	Item	Introduced	Discontinued	Value
Row 1:	Bean pot, 1-handle			$1,000.00 – 1,200.00
	Baker, French, 3 pint	1936	1976	$18.00 – 20.00
	Baker, French, 2 pint	1966	1976	$125.00 – 150.00
	Bean pot, 2 handle	1960	1976*	$225.00 – 265.00
Row 2:	Baker, 10" oval			$325.00 – 375.00
	Baker, French 4⅛"	1966	1976*	$10.00 – 12.00
	Baker, French 4½"	1978	1978	$30.00 – 32.00
	Bowl, salad	1937	1936	$18.00 – 20.00
Row 3:	Batter jug, "Sundial"			$2,000.00 – 3,000.00
	Custard, "Radiance"	1936	1976	$6.00 – 8.00
	Baker, Fort Pitt 12 oz.	1966	1976	$150.00 – 165.00
	Ball jug #3	1938	1976	$45.00 – 60.00
Row 4:	Bowl, 9", "Radiance"	1933	1976	$25.00 – 30.00
	Bowl, 7½", "Radiance"	1933	1976	$18.00 – 20.00
	Bowl, 6", "Radiance"	1933	1976	$14.00 – 18.00

*Reissued in 1978

1-handle Bean Pot

3 Pint French Baker

2-handle Bean Pot

2 Pint French Baker

10" Oval Baker

#499 4 1/2" French Baker

2 Quart Salad Bowl

4 1/8" French Baker

"Sundial" Batter Jug

"Radiance" Custard

Fort Pitt 12 Oz. Baker

No. 3 Ball Jug

9" "Radiance" Bowl

7 1/2" "Radiance" Bowl

6" "Radiance" Bowl

A few of the pieces pictured on the opposite page are among the scarcest in the Autumn Leaf pattern. These sample items came from former employees who got them from Jewel's employee store. A few other sample items have shown up in recent years, but it seems likely that most of these rarities are out of the attics now. Very few collectors have assembled complete four-piece canister sets. Among the examples that have been discovered, a few of the canisters have decals that are arranged differently from those in the photo.

Two sizes of butter dishes were made for Jewel by Hall — one pound and one-quarter pound. As may be seen from the photo, there are several different styles of each size butter. A quick glance at the prices indicates none of these butters is common. However, one style in each size will be obtainable for the average collector with a little diligent searching.

The first butter dish listed in the Jewel catalog was the one pound dish shown in the bottom center of the photo. It was introduced in 1959, and sold for $3.25. Its design proved to be inconvenient and this butter was discontinued after only one season. This style of pound butter was in very short supply until a quantity was discovered in a warehouse in the early 1980s. This find has been absorbed by collectors and the price of this butter has been steadily rising as its availability decreases.

The other two one pound butter dishes are probably experimental designs submitted by Hall as improvements to the original version. Both are the same shape as the original, but they have a knob which is easier to grip. The only difference between these two butters is the one on the right has a bud knob with rays and the one on the left has the same style knob without the rays. The lid without the rays is 5⁄16" taller than the one with the rays. The underplate for all three styles is the same.

The replacement for the pound butter was introduced in 1961 in the form of the one-quarter pound butter shown in the center of the top row of butterdishes. Another variety of one-quarter pound butter, the wings style, shown on the left side of the same row, was also introduced the same year. Judging from their availability today, this shape must not have been very popular. The other one-quarter pound butter with the smooth top grip is found frequently enough to suggest it was more than a mere sample item. It is possible this may have been a sales award item. The underplate for the first and third butters is the same, while the underplate for the wings style butter is more deeply curved.

The one pound butter in the center is an unusual Zephyr shape with the Autumn Leaf decal. It has not been confirmed that this butter was ever offered to Jewel customers and only a few examples are known.

Three different styles of condiment jars are pictured on the bottom row. In answer to a number of questions, no china spoons were provided for these jars by either Hall or Jewel. The larger jar on the right is a marmalade and the one on the left is a mustard. Both of these items made their appearance in 1938, and disappeared the following year. Even though both were only produced for a short time, collectors seem to have only moderate difficulty in obtaining them. Notice the underplates are different sizes. The diameter of the marmalade underplate is 6" and the diameter of the mustard underplate is 4¾". The 3½" tall condiment jar in the center is not commonly found. Very little is known about this jar. It is believed to have been a sample submitted by Hall in about 1941. Jewel must have rejected this design, since it was not put into regular production.

Item	Introduced	Discontinued	Value
Row 1: Canister, each			$1,200.00 – 1,500.00
ROw 2: Butter, ¼ pound, smooth top grip			$800.00 – 1,000.00
Butter, ¼ pound, regular	1961	1976	$220.00 – 250.00
Butter, ¼ pound, wings	1961		$1,800.00 – 2,200.00
Row 3: Butter, one pound Zephyr-shape			$2,500.00 – 3,000.00
Row 4: Butter, one pound, bud knob			$1,500.00 – 1,800.00
Butter, one pound, regular	1959	1960	$400.00 – 450.00
Butter, one pound, bud ray knob			$1,500.00 – 1,800.00
Row 5: Condiment, mustard	1938	1939	$85.00 – 95.00
Condiment, sample			$1,000.00 – 1,500.00
Condiment, marmalade	1938	1939	$100.00 – 125.00

SUGAR FLOUR TEA COFFEE

4-piece Canister Set

1/4 Pound Regular-style Butter

1/4 Pound Smooth-top Grip Butter

1/4 Pound "Wings" Butter

1 Pound "Zephyr" Shape Butter

1 Pound Bud-knob Butter

1 Pound Bud Ray-Knob Butter

1 Pound Regular-style Butter

Mustard

Sample-shape Condiment Jar

Marmalade

The Autumn Leaf clock shown in the center of the top row was introduced in 1956. A clock which still has its original movement will have the name "HALL" stamped on its face. Clocks could be hung on the wall or set upright on a shelf with the use of an attached wire stand. Two other styles of clocks, which have been produced from the regular Autumn Leaf cake plate may be found. One version is a salesman's award clock which was given as a prize to outstanding sales personnel by Jewel. This clock is pictured on the left side of the top row. The other type is a clock which is currently being produced for sale by a private individual. An easy way to tell the difference between the two cake plate-style clocks is to look at the size and placement of the numbers. The salesman's award clock has small numbers placed a few inches from the edge of the cake plate, similar in position to the standard Jewel clock. The numbers on the clock which is currently being made are larger and are arranged near the edge of the cake plate. The cost of this new clock is $65.00.

The candy and the cake stand with the metal base were both introduced in 1959. The metal base could be unscrewed from the china piece and used as a candle holder. Originally, each piece sold for $4.95. Today, the footed cake stand is found much more readily than the footed candy.

There is no proof the cake lifter shown in the second row was made by Hall. However, many Autumn Leaf collectors are searching for these accompanying pieces to enhance their collections. Although quite a few of the more advanced collectors own one, this cake lifter with the Autumn Leaf decal is not easily found. Another cake lifter with a large Autumn Leaf decal in the center and a long gold stripe on the handle may also be found. Since this lifter is usually found with Harker cake plates, this style lifter was probably made by Harker. Neither of these cake lifters bears an identifying backstamp and some confusion has resulted in distinguishing these two old lifters from the new ones which are being made by a private individual. The new lifters are thicker and more square at the area where the blade rises toward the handle. Another new cake lifter is currently being marketed by China Specialties. For more information see the Reissues section at the back of this book.

The round 9½" cake plate is one of the most commonly found pieces of Autumn Leaf. The cake plate was added to the line in 1937 and was discontinued in 1976. This was a truly multi-purpose item and was priced at .75¢ in 1937. It was designed to fit perfectly into the previously introduced metal cake carriers and could also be used as a serving plate or as a tile under the casseroles or coffee servers. In addition, the two raised rings on the underside allowed it to become a cover for the utility bowls.

The fork and candle holder shown in the second row and the covered candy jar at the bottom left are probably sample pieces. Sources have indicated these pieces were made by Hall and submitted to Jewel as samples. However, these items were not put into production.

The covered family casserole was introduced as a special premium for Jewel's 36th anniversary in 1935. The price of this item in 1939 was $1.75.

The old style cookie jar shown in the center of the bottom row was introduced for Christmas 1936. It was a dual purpose item since it could also be used as a bean pot. This cookie jar sold for $1.50 and was only offered for three years.

The modern-style cookie jar with the two big ear-like handles was added to the Autumn Leaf line in 1957. Jewel liked to call these handles "easy-grip" and sold the cookie jar for $3.00. The shape of the jar came from a line designed by Eva Zeisel.

Item	Introduced	Discontinued	Value
Row 1: Clock, saleman's award	1980	1980	$350.00 – 375.00
Clock	1956	1959	$650.00 – 850.00
Candy, metal base	1958	1969	$500.00 – 550.00
Row 2: Cake server			$550.00 – 600.00
Fork			$550.00 – 600.00
Candleholder, 4"			$1,000.00 – 1,250.00
Row 3: Cake plate	1937	1976	$20.00 – 25.00
Casserole, round, 2 quart	1935	1976	$37.00 – 40.00
Cake stand, metal base	1958	1969	$225.00 – 275.00
Row 4: Candy jar, sample			$2,500.00 – 3,000.00
Cookie jar, "Rayed"	1936	1939	$200.00 – 245.00
Cookie jar, Zeisel	1957	1969	$200.00 – 245.00

Salesman's Award Clock

Clock

Candy Comport
with Metal Base

Cake Server

Fork

Candleholder

Cake Plate

2-quart Round Casserole

Cake Plate
with Metal Base

Covered Candy Jar

"Rayed"-style Cookie Jar

Zeisel-style Cookie Jar

The ruffled base shakers were designed to be used with the Autumn Leaf dinnerware service. According to sources at Hall, the small-size version was introduced first. However, these were too small to be practical and they were soon replaced with the larger size shakers. The first pair of ruffled base shakers shown on the top row is the normal size pair. They were first offered in 1939, and were priced at four pairs for $1.00. The pair shown next to them is smaller — just 2" high — and only a few pairs of this size have been found. For a more distinct comparison between the two see the top row of the photo.

The demitasse cup and saucer on the right side of the top row was purchased by a Jewel employee at the employee store. Jewel never made this item available to the public.

The conic mug was listed in Jewel catalogs as a 10 ounce beverage mug. The introductory price was $6.95 for a set of four in 1966. This same 1966 catalog also heralded the introduction of the Irish coffee mugs which "let you serve coffee in a new and different way…eliminates use of saucers." The original price of these mugs was $7.95 for a set of four. When they were discontinued in 1976, beverage mugs were selling for $22.00 for a set of four, and four Irish coffee mugs cost $27.00. The Irish coffee mugs, which are now selling for more than ten times their last cost through Jewel, have appreciated considerably since they were discontinued.

The rare "Medallion" style shakers are shown on the right side of the second row.

The left side of the third row is occupied by the old style sugar and creamer. This sugar and creamer first appeared in 1936 with the No. 300 coffee set as pictured in the photo to the right. The handles and the vertical rays match the shape and style of the other kitchenware pieces from this period. Completing the third row is the large cup and saucer. This St. Denis cup and saucer is sometimes called the "he man" style since it is larger than the regular cup and saucer. It was introduced in 1942, and the original price was .45¢ for a cup and saucer. By the time these pieces were discontinued in 1976, the price of the cup had increased to $2.50 and the saucer was listed at $1.25.

The handled shakers and drip jar comprise the range set which was introduced in 1936. The price of the complete set in 1939 was $1.50. Many of the drip jars were used for other purposes, such as soup bowls or lidless butters. Therefore, a surplus of bottoms exists today. Notice both the left-handed and right-handed versions of the salt shaker in the photo.

Item	Introduced	Discontinued	Value
Row 1: Shaker, regular size, ruffled, ea.	1939	1976	$11.00 – 13.00
Shaker, miniature, ruffled, pr.	1939	1939	$650.00 – 800.00
Cup and saucer, demitasse			$500.00 – 600.00
Row 2: Mug, conic	1966	1976	$50.00 – 60.00
Mug, Irish coffee	1966	1976*	$90.00 – 125.00
Salt and pepper, "Medallion," pr			$1,800.0 – 2,000.00
Row 3: Creamer, "Rayed"	1934	1940	$18.00 – 22.00
Sugar and lid, "Rayed"	1934	1940	$30.00 – 35.00
Cup, St. Denis	1942	1976	$20.00 – 25.00
Saucer, St. Denis	1942	1976	$10.00 – 12.00
Row 4 Shaker, range, ea.	1936	1976	$15.00 – 20.00
Drip jar	1936	1976	$25.00 – 30.00
Shaker, left hand range			$18.00 – 22.00
Above: Metal tray, 18¾" oval	1934	1938	$90.00 – 125.00

* Reissued in 1978

Regular-size
Ruffled-D Shakers

Miniature-size
Ruffled-D Shakers

Demitasse Cup & Saucer

Conic Mug

Irish Coffee Mug

"Medallion" Salt & Pepper

"Rayed" Creamer, Sugar & Lid

St. Denis Cup & Saucer

Pepper Range Shaker

Drip Jar

Left Hand Salt

Right Hand Salt

The pie baker, which is shown on the left side of the top row held a 9½" pie and was guaranteed to heat evenly. This resulted in a perfectly baked pie with "no burnt crusts." This pie baker was also promoted as "easy to clean" and had the added advantage of being a convenient size to fit into the metal cake safe. Jewel priced this item at .75¢ in 1941.

The round warmer shown in the center of the top row was used with the coffee servers or the round casserole. The oval warmer to the right side of the second row was designed for use with the Aladdin shape teapot. It was introduced for the 1955 Christmas season and was produced until 1960. Both shapes contain a built-in candleholder in the center and came boxed with four candles. The selling price of both warmers in 1960, the year they were discontinued, was $2.25.

The Autumn Leaf bud vase is shown in the top right of the photo. Collectors may expect to find variations in size and location of the decal on these vases, These variations are common occurrences for some pieces of the Autumn Leaf pattern.

The 2½ pint utility pitcher was introduced in 1937. It was a multi-purpose kitchen item which was convenient for either beverages or batter.

An Autumn Leaf salt box with a wooden lid is pictured in the center of the second row. This rare piece is a sample item that was never placed in production. Other salt box examples in Chinese red and Rose Parade have been found in the morgue at the Hall China plant.

A rare two-cup Boston-shape teapot is pictured to the left of the third row. So few of these have been found that it is almost certain this was never in the Jewel line.

The coaster in the center of the photo was purchased by a Jewel employee at the employee store. Jewel never made coasters available to the public.

The two large vases shown in the bottom row have no backstamp to indicate they were made by Hall. There is also not any evidence to associate them with Jewel Tea. However, they are striking examples of pieces with the Autumn Leaf decal and exhibit the same excellent quality in both pottery and glaze which other Hall pieces possess.

The Autumn Leaf four-piece stack set is pictured on the right side of the bottom row. It was called the stackette set in Jewel's ads and consists of three separate stacking containers and one lid. Each of the stacking units is a different size. The bottom one holds 34 ounces; the center one 24 ounces; and the top one 18 ounces. The complete set sold for $5.25 in 1960.

Items shown below include a holiday fruit tin from the 1970s and an old wooden bowl. The wooden bowl shows a lot of age and the enameled design appears to be original. However no information is available on its history.

Holiday Fruit Cake Tin   *Hand Painted Wooden Bowl*

Item	Introduced	Discontinued	Value
Row 1: Pie baker	1937	1976	$40.00 – 45.00
Warmer, round	1956	1960	$155.00 – 175.00
Vase, bud	1940		$195.00 – 225.00
Row 2: Jug, 2½ pint, "Rayed"	1937	1976	$20.00 – 30.00
Salt box			UND
Warmer, oval	1955	1960	$165.00 – 185.00
Row 3: Teapot, 2-cup, Boston			UND
Coaster			$450.00 – 550.00
Vase (sample)			UND
Row 4: Vase, 7¾" (sample)			$950.00 – 1,000.00
Vase, 11" (sample)			$950.00 – 1,000.00
Stack set	1951	1976	$100.00 – 125.00
Photo above:			
Tin, holiday fruit cake			$15.00 – 18.00
Wooden bowl			$300.00 – 350.00

Pie Baker

Round Warmer

Bud Vase

Utility Jug

Salt Box

Oval Warmer

2--cup Boston Teapot

Coaster

Vase (Sample)

7 3/4" Vase (Sample)

11" Vase (Sample)

Stack Set

Autumn Leaf Coffee Pots and Teapots

The first Autumn Leaf coffee pot appeared in 1934. It was a nine-cup server introduced as part of a complete coffee service set which also included the oval 18¾" metal tray, an asbestos hot pad, and the old style sugar and creamer. The price of the complete set was $5.25 in 1937. The coffee server was also sold with an optional metal dripper made by the West Bend Aluminum Company. This nine-cup server remained in the line until 1949.

In November 1936, Jewel added a coffee server with an open dripper to the Autumn Leaf line. This was an eight-cup maker and was lauded in their ads as being "improved for the making of perfect coffee and modernized in appearance." The lid of this pot would not fit the metal dripper. The dripper for this coffee pot was designed to "aid in the flow of water and to simplify coffee making." Apparently this new concept was short-lived. Ads for the eight-cup coffee server from late 1937 indicate the dripper was redesigned. The new dripper had the Autumn Leaf motif and was made so the cover of the coffee server also fit the dripper. On occasion, glass drippers will be found with some coffee servers. Coffee servers with glass drippers are illustrated in Jewel News publications during the early 1940s. The wartime restrictions during World War II necessitated this alteration. In later years, the eight-cup coffee pot came complete with a measuring spoon and an asbestos pad.

The introduction of another coffee maker was prompted by wartime restrictions. The five-cup all-china coffee maker appeared in 1942. The new design was implemented to meet the government's request to conserve coffee and also eliminated the need for the use of any metal in its manufacture.

The ultimate in automation in coffee brewing was achieved in 1957 when the automatic electric percolator was added to the line. It featured a safety-lock top, switched automatically to warming heat after brewing, and was guaranteed for a full year against any defects in workmanship. The price of this marvel was only $19.95.

Teapots played an important role in the early development of the Autumn Leaf line. The Newport shape was introduced in 1933. It was a square seven-cup teapot which sold for $1.50. Two years later, it was replaced by a combination tea/coffee pot. This was the familiar long-spout pot which could be used to make either seven cups of tea or four cups of coffee. A small metal dripper was provided to institute the conversion from a teapot to a coffee pot. This new pot was also priced at $1.50. In 1978, a special issue of 106 long spout teapots was made by Hall China for Jewel to be given as sales awards. The Newport teapot was reissued in 1978. There are several differences between the two versions The old teapot has no gold around the tip of the spout and the decal is larger than the decal on the later teapot. The teapot from 1978 has gold around the tip of the spout and has a decal with a pink leaf. The two lids are also different. The lid of the newer teapot only has gold on the very tip of the knob.

The seven-cup Aladdin teapot, introduced in 1942, with a china tea strainer eliminated the need for the metal tea ball. Judging from the number of Aladdins seen today, the success of this teapot must have been phenomenal. Autumn Leaf purists collect two different versions of this teapot — long spout and short spout. The difference here was probably not intentional. Instead, the variation appears to be the result of slight mold variations. The Aladdin teapot was listed in a 1960 catalog for $4.25.

The rare Autumn Leaf morning tea set is pictured at the bottom right of the photo. So few morning tea sets have been found that it can be assumed they were never a regular production item. This set is the same style as other morning sets which were made in some of Hall's kitchenware patterns. The teapot is identical to the teapot used in the No. 1 tea set. However the sugar was restyled and features the addition of handles. Also new is a lid for the sugar which matches the style of the teapot lid.

	Item	Introduced	Discontinued	Value
Row 1:	Drip coffee, "Jordan," all-china	1942	1945	$300.00 – 350.00
	Teapot, Aladdin	1942	1976	$65.00 – 85.00
	Teapot, "Rayed" long spout	1935	1942	$75.00 – 85.00
Row 2:	Coffee pot, 9-cup, "Rayed"	1934	1949	$60.00 – 70.00
	Coffee pot, 8-cup, "Rayed" with open drip (not shown)	1936	1937	$70.00 – 75.00
	Coffee pot, 8-cup, "Rayed"	1937	1976	$55.00 – 65.00
	Electric Percolator	1957	1969	$350.00 – 400.00
Row 3.	Teapot, Newport, 1978	1978	1978	$200.00 – 225.00
	Teapot, Newport, 1930s	1933	1935	$225.00 – 285.00
	Teapot, Morning Set			$1,500.00 – 1,800.00
	Creamer, sugar and lid, Morning style			$900.00 – 1,000.00

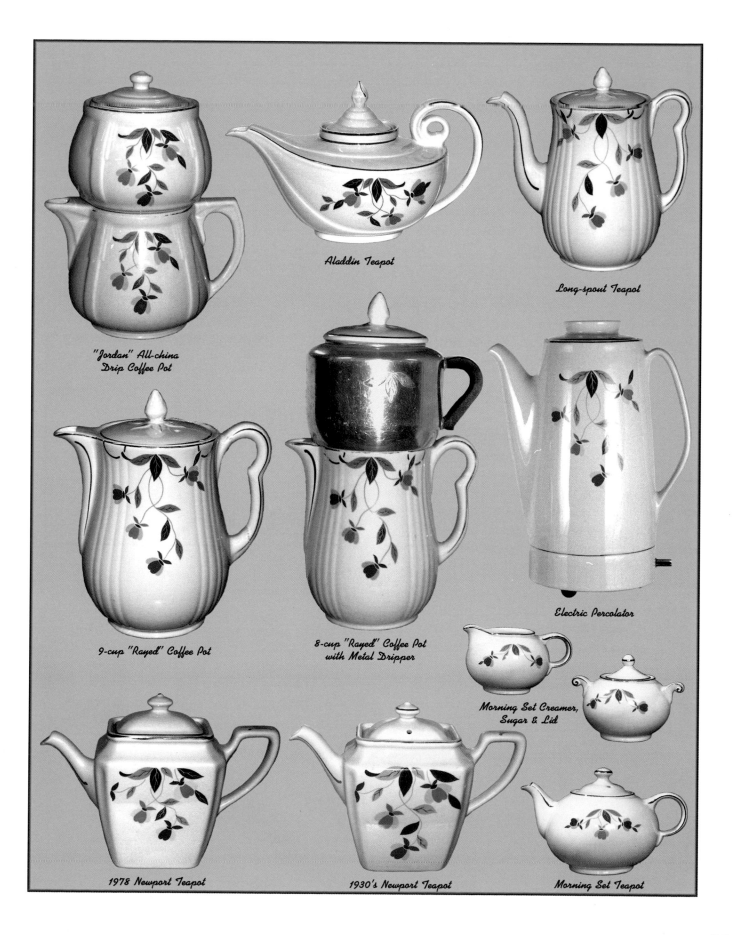

"Jordan" All-china
Drip Coffee Pot

Aladdin Teapot

Long-spout Teapot

9-cup "Rayed" Coffee Pot

8-cup "Rayed" Coffee Pot
with Metal Dripper

Electric Percolator

Morning Set Creamer,
Sugar & Lid

1978 Newport Teapot

1930's Newport Teapot

Morning Set Teapot

Autumn Leaf Paper and Plastic Articles

Jewel made a short-lived attempt to market Melmac with an Autumn Leaf pattern in 1960. Many of the pieces offered in the Melmac Autumn Leaf sets lacked the pattern. For example, in the 16-piece starter set only the 10" dinner plates and the saucers had the pattern; the cups and fruit dishes were plain Melmac pieces. Also, in the larger 45-piece service, the sugar, creamer, soups, cups, and vegetable dish lacked decoration. The only decorated pieces of Melmac which collectors will find available are 10" dinner plates, 8" salad plates, saucers, and a 14" platter.

The insulated mug and tumbler were sample items which were bought in Jewel's employee store. Undoubtedly, there were some advantages to working for Jewel, even if the former employees did not realize it at the time.

Several different styles of hotpads have been found associated with the Autumn Leaf pattern. Some are readily identifiable with the pattern and some which Jewel supplied with the coffee servers lack the pattern and are not commonly thought of as Autumn Leaf. The black asbestos hotpad shown in the right center of the photo was supplied with coffee service sets during the 1930s. A cream color cardboard hotpad with a tin back was introduced in 1937. Another type of hotpad with a creamy wax-like coating and a green or red felt backing was introduced later.

Plastic covers for appliances and bowls were introduced in 1950. An eight-piece set of bowl covers in assorted sizes with a drawstring holder sold for $1.00 in 1950. In 1960 a seven-piece set which included a toaster cover and six bowl covers in assorted sizes sold for .98¢. The bowl covers ranged in size from five inches to thirteen inches. Other plastic covers included a Mary Dunbar mixer cover and a standard-size mixer cover.

Two styles of playing cards were introduced in 1943. Attractively boxed sets of pinochle decks or regular double deck sets were available. The price of a box of regular cards in 1943 was $1.50. Collectors should be aware that new decks of playing cards are currently on the market. Careful examination of these cards will reveal an almost microscopic date on the reverse side of each card. Also new decks are complete with a 1992 calendar card.

The Linoettes (placemats) are from the early 1940s. They have scalloped edges and the Autumn Leaf pattern in the corners.

Place Mats

Item	Introduced	Discontinued	Value
Coaster, 3⅛"			$6.00 – 8.00
Hotpad, 10¾", oval			$15.00 – 18.00
Hotpad, 7¼", felt back	1946		$18.00 – 20.00
Hotpad, 7¼", tin back	1937		$15.00 – 18.00
Mixer cover, standard	1950	1961	$50.00 – 65.00
Mixer cover, Mary Dunbar	1950	1961	$50.00 – 65.00
Place mat	1940		$40.00 – 55.00
Plastic bowl covers, 8 pc. set	1950	1961	$200.00 – 250.00
Playing cards, regular deck	1943	1946	$140.00 – 160.00
Playing cards, pinochle deck	1943	1946	$150.00 – 175.00
Toaster cover	1950	1961	$60.00 – 65.00

Melmac (1960)	Value	Melmac (1960)	Value
Bowl, fruit (no pattern)	$5.00 – 7.00	Plate, 7" salad	$20.00 – 22.00
Bowl, soup (no pattern)	$5.00 – 7.00	Plate, 10" dinner	$20.00 – 25.00
Creamer (no pattern)	$7.00 – 9.00	Platter, 14"	$35.00 – 45.00
Cup/saucer	$20.00 – 22.00	Sugar (no pattern)	$7.00 – 9.00

Autumn Leaf Cloth, Paper, Plastic, and Flatware

An Autumn Leaf blanket was released by Jewel in 1979. It was made by Martex and came in three sizes and two colors. The twin size retailed for $22.99; the full size for $29.99; and the queen/king size for $46.99. Another version, in addition to the standard color, is shown in the picture. This one has green leaves and lilac Autumn Leaf-style flowers.

Shelf paper was a premium which was offered in 1945. This issue of shelf paper had the pattern only on the edge and was available in sheets nine feet long and 9¼ inches wide. In 1956 shelf paper was again offered. This newer shelf liner was 13 inches wide. It was made of plastic, came in rolls 12 feet long, and had an allover design.

Mary Dunbar cookbooks are a favorite collectible of many Autumn Leaf collectors. They were produced for many years. Besides the excellent recipes, they feature many pieces of Autumn Leaf.

An 18" x 30" rubber backed fatigue mat was listed in a 1958 catalog. This was intended to be used by the busy housewife to stand on while ironing or doing dishes. To date only a few of these have been reported.

In 1958, Jewel offered a silver-plate flatware service made by the International Silver Company. The sets were offered in a 24-piece service for six and a 50-piece service for eight. Serving pieces including a gravy ladle, meat fork, berry spoon, and sugar shell were also available as open stock items. Autumn silver-plate pieces were no longer offered after 1959, but 1960 catalogs indicate special orders would still be accepted. In the photo on page 39, the silver-plate knife and fork are on the right side; the silver-plate spoon is positioned horizontally at the top of the picture. Notice the silver-plate pieces have square ends at the handle and the stainless ends are curved. The other items in a horizontal position are stainless serving pieces.

Autumn pattern stainless steel tableware made by the International Silver Company craftsmen became available in 1960. Sets were available in both 24-piece and 50-piece services. A 24-piece service sold for $19.95 in 1960. A six-piece place setting included a teaspoon, a soup spoon, a tablespoon, a dinner knife, a dinner fork, and a salad fork. Open stock items included a sugar shell, a solid serving spoon, a slotted serving spoon, and a butter knife. Recently, a private company has revived the Autumn pattern stainless. A five-piece place setting of stainless tableware has been produced from the old International Silver silver-plate dies. Thus, the new stainless differs in style from that of the old. Also, the backstamp on the new stainless is "C & C Collectible® 93."

Item	Introduced	Discontinued	Value
Blanket, standard color, twin-size	1979	1979	$175.00 – 190.00
Blanket, standard color, full-size	1979	1979	$200.00 – 225.00
Blanket, standard color, king-size	1979	1979	$225.00 – 250.00
Blanket, lilac color, full-size	1979	1979	$125.00 – 150.00
Cookbook, Mary Dunbar			$15.00 – 25.00
Shelf paper, pattern on edge, sheet	1945		$35.00 – 45.00
Shelf paper, allover pattern, roll	1956	1957	$125.00 – 150.00
Flatware			
Silverware, 5-piece silver-plate setting	1958	1959	$150.00 – 175.00
Silverware, silver-plate serving items	1958	1959	$60.00 – 65.00
Silverware, 6-piece stainless setting	1960	1968	$145.00 – 165.00
Silverware, stainless serving items	1960	1968	$60.00 – 65.00
Item not pictured:			
Fatigue mat	1958		$450.00 – 550.00

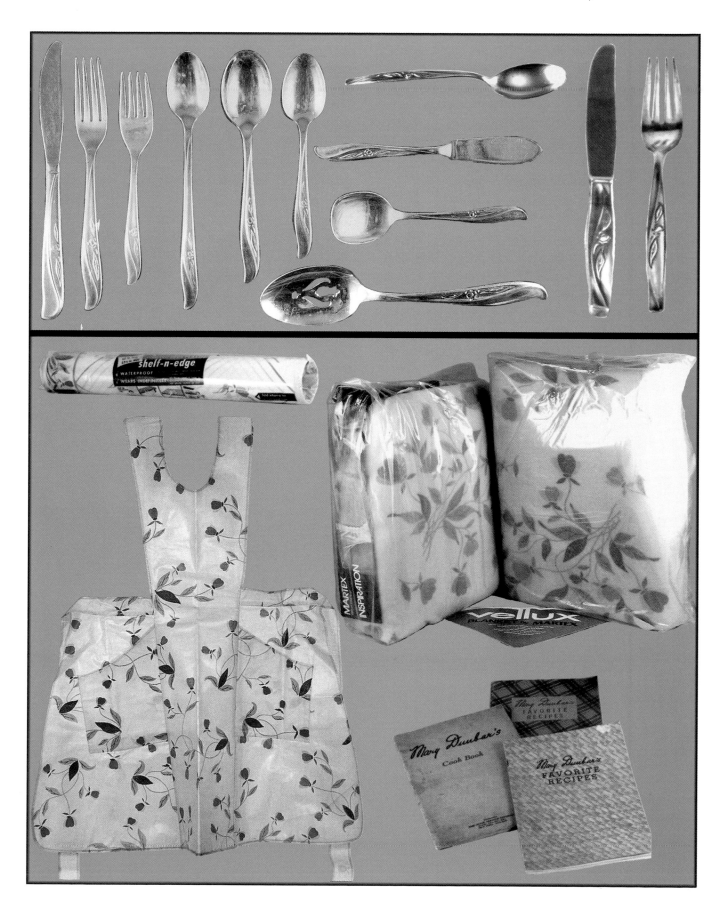

Autumn Leaf Linens

The items shown here were not made by Hall. However they are the Autumn Leaf design and were made for the Jewel Company to complement their existing china pattern. Many collectors of Autumn Leaf china are finding these accessories attractive additions to their collections.

Most Autumn Leaf linens, like many other collectible linens, have been subjected to many years of daily use and abuse. As a result, the availability of quality Autumn Leaf linens is limited, and prices are slowly creeping upward as more collectors are striving to add these treasures to their collections. Pieces which are stained, torn, or badly faded will only bring a fraction of the prices listed below.

The muslin tablecloth was introduced as a premium for the 1937 Christmas season. The Autumn Leaf design ran just above a row of stripes along the edge and was repeated again in the center of the cloth. This set was discontinued in 1942.

Napkins that match the muslin table cloth were also made during the same time period. The napkins are about 16" square and have Autumn Leaf bud clusters in the four corners. The cloth is bordered by an exterior brown band, a middle orange band, and an interior gold band.

In 1950, another tablecloth was offered. This tablecloth was plastic-coated cotton and came in two sizes — 54" x 54" and 54" x 72". Both sizes had an allover Autumn Leaf design and were discontinued in 1953. The smaller retailed for $4.50 and the larger one cost $5.50.

The last tablecloth introduced was made of cotton sailcloth and appeared in 1955. There were two official sizes — 54" x 54" and 54" x 72". However, a 54" x 62" tablecloth also is appearing frequently. These were decorated with a border design featuring a gold stripe below an Autumn Leaf motif.

The history of the tablecloth with the aqua, purple, and yellow colors is unknown. It is an interesting find and only a few of these have been reported.

A cotton tea towel produced by Startex that was 16 inches wide and 33 inches long was sold by Jewel in 1956 and 1957.

Curt towels replaced the regular tea towels and were made from 1957 through 1959. These towels were 20 inches wide and 35 inches long and served a dual purpose. They could be used as dish towels, or curtain rods could be inserted in their wide hems to produce cafe curtains. These linens were made from a blend of cotton, rayon, and linen to maximize softness and absorbency. A set of two sold for $1.69. In the photo the curt towel is the article with the Autumn Leaf design, the cup and saucer, and the clock.

A Jewel tablecloth with a modernistic design using Autumn Leaf colors is shown right at the bottom of the photo. Due to the color similarities, some Autumn Leaf collectors are beginning to search for this style tablecloth.

Item	Introduced	Discontinued	Value
Curt towel, 20" x 35"	1957	1959	$40.00 – 50.00
Napkin, 16" x 16"	1937	1942	$40.00 – 60.00
Tablecloth, 56" x 81", muslin	1937	1942	$160.00 – 180.00
Tablecloth, 54" x 54", plastic	1950	1953	$130.00 – 165.00
Tablecloth, 54" x 72", plastic	1950	1953	$130.00 – 165.00
Tablecloth, 54" x 54", sailcloth	1955	1958	$95.00 – 120.00
Tablecloth, 54" x 62", sailcloth			$110.00 – 135.00
Tablecloth, 54" x 72", sailcloth	1955	1958	$125.00 – 150.00
Tea towel, 16" x 33"	1956	1957	$35.00 – 40.00
Tablecloth, modernistic			UND

Autumn Leaf Tin Accessories

During the last several years many new Autumn Leaf collectors have joined the ranks. These new collectors have joined with the more advanced collectors in focusing more attention on non-Hall and non-china Autumn Leaf pieces. As a result the demand for tin accessories has increased dramatically. Collectors still prefer to buy pieces in mint condition, so care should be exercised when attempting to clean metal items with a lacquered finish. The finish practically dissolves when subjected to washing with water. Dealers should also remember that any pricing labels which are placed on the lacquered surface will cause damage to the finish.

The round four-piece canister set introduced in 1960 had a "chip-resistant baked enamel finish" and Coppertone finished lids with black plastic knobs. The sugar and flour each hold five pounds and the coffee and tea hold 1½ pounds. The set retailed for $3.98 when it was introduced.

The picnic thermos is hard to find in good condition. This item dates to 1941 and many have been destroyed by rust through the negligence of an uncaring owner. This, coupled with a war-shortened production of only one year due to the scarcity of tin, has caused many collectors to search a long time to obtain one. The thermos has an outer jacket made of tin with a lacquered finish bearing the Autumn Leaf motif. The heavy weight of the thermos is due to the thick stoneware lining which is used for insulation.

The tin canister set in the center consists of three different size canisters. The large canister appeared in 1935, and the other two sizes followed the next year. The introduction of the smallest canister preceded the arrival of the medium-size canister by a few months. The original canister was designed to hold three pounds of coffee and sold for .50¢ in 1936. The price of the three-piece set was $1.00 in 1939. None of the canisters has a label to designate its contents. There are two slight variations of these sets. One style is marked "TINDECO" on the bottom and has gold lacquered insides and gold bottoms. The other style is unmarked and has a gold bottom and silver insides. The smallest canister is the most plentiful.

The rectangular canisters on the bottom row are a four-piece set. The set consists of two large canisters for sugar and flour and two smaller canisters for coffee and tea. The canisters have plastic handles on their lids which are easily damaged. The so-called "chip resistant baked on enamel finish" is a little tougher than the coating on some of the earlier tinware, but it can also be damaged if handled carelessly.

The cleanser can is quite a prize. Any of these which are offered for sale seem to find a new home immediately.

Jewel customers remember the metal canisters below with the plastic lids coming filled with old fashioned hard Christmas candy.

Item	Introduced	Discontinued	Value
Row 1: Canister, round, tall (copper-color lid)	1960	1962	$45.00 – 55.00
Canister, round, short (copper-color lid)	1960	1962	$40.00 – 47.00
Thermos	1941	1941	$400.00 – 450.00
Row 2: Canister, round, 8¼"	1935	1942	$45.00 – 55.00
Canister, round, 7"	1935	1942	$40.00 – 47.00
Canister, round, 6"	1935	1942	$40.00 – 45.00
Sifter			$400.00 – 500.00
Row 3: Canister, 8¼", sugar	1959		$45.00 – 65.00
Canister, 8¼", flour	1959		$40.00 – 60.00
Canister, 4", tea	1959		$35.00 – 47.00
Canister, 4", coffee	1959		$35.00 – 47.00
Cleanser can			$500.00 – 600.00
Above: Canister, brown/gold			$18.00 – 22.00
Canister, white plastic lid			$25.00 – 28.00

4-piece Round Canister Set with Copper Lids

Thermos

3-piece Round Canister Set

Sifter

4-piece Rectangular Canister Set

Cleanser Can

The lacquer finish on metal accessories was easily damaged through use and by washing. Any damage drastically reduces the desirability and value of a piece. Most collectors are seeking these metal items in almost mint condition.

Glass serving trays are difficult to find in good condition. They were only made for a short time, therefore they only turn up infrequently. However, to complicate matters, the design, which is painted on the reverse side of the glass, is easily damaged by water. If care is not taken in cleaning these trays, and water gets between the glass and the backing, the paint will become wrinkled and the value of the tray will decrease substantially.

According to Jewel ads the metal coffee dispenser "released the exact measure for one cup of coffee with each pull of the lever." The price of the dispenser was $2.50 in 1942, when it was discontinued. The dispenser was designed to be wall mounted and featured a glass window so the remaining quantity of coffee could be determined easily. Its war curtailed production has caused a short supply today.

The bread box is a very desirable item for an Autumn Leaf collector to own. It was introduced in 1936, and was a casualty of the tin shortages of World War II. Bread boxes were designed to hold three regular-size loaves or two larger sandwich loaves. Since they opened conveniently from the front they could be easily fit between two cabinet shelves. In 1938, the price of the bread box was $1.45.

Two different styles of cake safes are available to the collector. The older one was released in 1935, and has the Autumn Leaf pattern on top as well as on the side of the lid. It sold for $1.25 in 1936. The newer one was issued in 1950, and lacks the pattern on the top of the lid. Both cake safes were equipped with a locking handle and were designed to carry a standard 9" cake placed on the matching Jewel Autumn Leaf cake plate. Notice also, the lighter color of the older cake safe, which is characteristic of the pre-war tinware.

A metal kitchen chair with a folding step was listed in a 1941 catalog. The retail price was $2.75. The chair had a baked enamel finish with the Autumn Leaf decal on the front of the backrest. Wartime restrictions on the use of metals probably resulted in the production of very few of these chairs.

	Item	Introduced	Discontinued	Value
Row 1:	Glass tray			$135.00 – 150.00
	Coffee dispenser	1941	1941	$400.00 – 450.00
Row 2:	Bread box	1937	1941	$500.00 – 600.00
Row 3:	Cake safe	1950	1953	$35.00 – 40.00
	Cake safe	1935	1941	$65.00 – 75.00
Photo Below:				
	Waste basket	1951	1951	$225.00 – 250.00
	Chair, kitchen	1939	1942	$500.00 – 550.00
	Tray, 17¾" x 12 ¾" red trim	1951	1951	$85.00 – 95.00

Waste Basket   *Red Border Tray*

Rectangular Glass Tray

Bread Box

MEAS
-O-
MATIC
THE AUTOMATIC
COFFEE DISPENSER
3-½ LB. CAPACITY

MANUFACTURED BY
WEST BEND ALUMINUM CO.
WEST BEND, - WIS.

Coffee Dispenser with Box

Early Cake Safe

1950's Cake Safe

Autumn Leaf Porcelain-Clad and Glasbake

Autumn design porcelain-clad steel cookware was a Jewel exclusive introduced in 1979. The cookware set consisted of seven pieces. It included a 1½-quart covered saucepan, a two-quart covered saucepan, a five-quart covered Dutch oven, and a 9½" open skillet. The Dutch oven cover also fits the skillet. Retail price for this set was $59.95. Also, offered at the same time was a matching tea kettle which sold for $16.95. By the next year the price of the tea kettle had increased to $18.99.

In 1980, Jewel added three new sets to complement its original offering. All were made of the familiar enameled porcelain metal which was supposed to be chip resistant and easy to clean.

A three-piece mixing bowl set consisted of bowls in the 1⅓-quart, 2-quart, and 2⅔-quart sizes. This set and a two-quart fondue set were priced at $29.99 each. The fondue set consisted of a two-quart pot with a brown metal cover, a metal rack with a fork stand, six color-coded forks, a chrome-plated burner, and a brown metal tray.

The rectangular pieces of the bakeware/casserole set came in one-quart, two-quart, and three-quart sizes. They were conveniently designed so the same dish could be utilized for cooking, serving, and storing leftovers. The casseroles had tab handles for easy handling and featured plastic storage lids which snapped on tightly to ensure the safekeeping of leftovers.

The Royal Glasbake articles shown below are part of a short-lived bakeware set introduced in 1961. The set consists of a divided oval bowl, two sizes of covered casseroles, and a four-piece mixing bowl set. These items were not very popular and were only offered for one season.

Cookware/Bakeware	Value
Row 1: Saucepan, 2-quart	$100.00 – 125.00
Dutch oven, 5-quart	$140.00 – 160.00
Row 2: Fondue set	$200.00 – 225.00
Mixing bowl, 2⅔-quart	$25.00 – 30.00
Row 3: Mixing bowl, 1⅓-quart	$35.00 – 45.00
Saucepan, 1½-quart	$90.00 – 110.00
Saucepan	$50.00 – 60.00
Row 4: Bakeware/casserole set,	
3-piece	$180.00 – 225.00
Mixing bowl, 2-quart	$40.00 – 50.00
Tea kettle	$225.00 – 250.00
Skillet, 9½"	$85.00 – 95.00

Royal Glasbake	Value
Row 1: Casserole, 2 quart	$150.00 – 175.00
Bowl, divided vegetable	$140.00 – 175.00
Casserole, 1 quart	$140.00 – 170.00
Row 2: Mixing bowl set (4-pc.)	
Bowl, 4 quart	$80.00 – 90.00
Bowl, 2½ quart	$50.00 – 70.00
Bowl, 1½ quart	$50.00 – 70.00
Bowl, 1 quart	$60.00 – 75.00

Autumn Leaf Glass and Metal Accessories

Glassware with the Autumn Leaf motif continues to be popular among collectors. The most desirable items are those pictured on the top row. However, the Douglas pieces are becoming increasingly collectible although many collectors are finding them prohibitively expensive.

The exciting news in this area is the discovery of a new style frosted tumbler. It is a 6½" tall pilsner-shaped tumbler with frosted sides and a clear bottom. The bottom has the Libbey "L" mark and the sides have the all-over Autumn design. The bad news for collectors is that this is a sample item which was never offered for sale by Jewel. Therefore, only a handful of collectors can ever hope to own one of these pieces.

The frosted tumblers on the first row were made for Jewel by Libbey. The tumbler with the bands at the bottom is the hardest to find. Of the two frosted tumblers with the Autumn Leaf motif, the large one is the easiest to find. A set of six of the large tumblers sold for $1.98 in 1949.

The clear tumblers on the top shelf with the Autumn-like design were made by Brockway. The tumblers were offered in three sizes and disappeared quickly from Jewel's catalog after a short trial in the mid-seventies. As a result of the short run, these tumblers are not easy to find and they are expensive for a newer item.

The clear tumblers in the second row were made for Jewel by Libbey in the early sixties. These tumblers were advertised as having "an all-over Autumn pattern in 22K gold and etched frost motif with Safedge Gold rims which defy chipping." The four pieces offered consisted of two sizes of heavy bottom tumblers, a footed goblet, and a footed sherbet. A set of eight tumblers sold for $3.98, and sets of sherbets or goblets for $5.98.

The first Autumn pattern Douglas piece shown in a catalog reprint at the bottom right — a combination coffee percolator, carafe, and candle warmer — appeared in Jewel's 1960 catalog. It had a 22K gold fused design, a Bakelite handle, and an anodized aluminum lid and collar. Like many other Jewel items this was a multi-purpose piece. It was presented as an eight-cup percolator, or a 12-cup instant coffee maker, tea maker, or beverage server. Other Douglas pieces introduced the following year included a sauce dish and hurricane lamp with a goldtone metal base. Several collectors have reported finding an unlisted ice-lip style pitcher similar in shape and size to the eight-cup coffee maker. This pitcher is shown in the bottom center of the photo. To positively identify the Douglas Autumn pattern items look for the name Douglas stamped in gold near the bottom of the piece.

The goldtone candlesticks pictured at the right side of the second row are also used as the base for the footed cake plate and footed candy shown on page 29.

Item	Introduced	Discontinued	Value
Row 1: Tumbler, banded			$40.00 – 45.00
Tumbler, 5½", frosted	1940	1949	$20.00 – 25.00
Tumbler, 3¾", frosted	1950	1953	$27.00 – 32.00
Tumbler, 16 oz., Brockway	1975	1976	$50.00 – 55.00
Tumbler, 13 oz., Brockway	1975	1976	$42.00 – 47.00
Tumbler, 9 oz., Brockway	1975	1976	$42.00 – 47.00
Row 2: Sherbet, 6½ oz., Libbey	1960	1961	$50.00 – 55.00
Tumbler, 10 oz., Libbey	1958	1961	$40.00 – 45.00
Tumbler, 15 oz., Libbey	1960	1961	$50.00 – 55.00
Goblet, 10 oz., Libbey	1960	1961	$50.00 – 55.00
Tumbler, pilsner-style			UND
Candlestick, pair			$60.00 – 70.00
Row 3: Hurricane lamp, Douglas	1961	1962	$250.00 – 300.00
Sauce dish, Douglas	1961	1962	$300.00 – 350.00
Warmer base	1960	1962	$25.00 – 30.00
Pitcher, Douglas, ice lip			$500.00 – 600.00
Percolator, Douglas	1960	1962	$500.00 – 600.00

SAVE Today! FLAMEPROOF GLASSWARE

Autumn Pattern
PERCOLATOR CARAFE
• Perks 8 cups of Coffee!
• Holds 12 cups Instant Coffee or Tea!
• Gold Plated Warmer with 2 Candles!
4030 reg. $7.95

SPECIAL TODAY!
$6.95
SAVE $1.00

Autumn Pattern
HURRICANE LAMPS
• Gold Plated Bases!
• 4 candles included!
4042 reg. $5.98 pair

SPECIAL TODAY!
$4.98 PAIR
SAVE $1.00

Autumn Pattern
SERVING SAUCE DISH
• Warms & Serves sauces, vegetables, etc.!
• Graduated 1-Quart Size!
4043 reg. $2.98

SPECIAL TODAY!
$2.68
SAVE 10%

BUY ALL 3 ITEMS AND SAVE MORE!
Complete Set SPECIAL TODAY!
$13.45
4044 reg. $14.95

D 7.95

D – Autumn Leaf Pattern Coffee Percolator-Carafe and Candle Warmer by Douglas. It's an 8-cup percolator or 12-cup instant coffee maker, tea maker and beverage server! 22 Karat Gold fused design with gleaming brass candle warmer. You'll add a subtle air of excitement when you serve coffee or tea in this stunning new carafe...and it stays piping hot! Cool bakelite handle; anodized aluminum lid and collar.
4D 30. Incl. Tea Ball, 2 Candles........7.95

C- AND D- STYLE DINNERWARE
Blue Bouquet

Hall China produced the Blue Bouquet decal line for the Standard Coffee Company of New Orleans, therefore, this is a pattern which is found more frequently in the southeastern states. Production began in the early fifties and continued into the mid-sixties. All pieces of the D-style dinnerware can be found. Many china kitchenware pieces also exist, and there is a limited number of metal accessories available.

Among the more frequently found pieces are the large salad bowl, the drip jar, the handled shakers, sugars and creamers, and the #3 "Medallion" jug. Hard-to-find pieces include the New England bean pot, the pretzel jar, the electric percolator, both leftovers, the soup tureen, and the spoon. Notice the special heating element on the electric percolator which fits between the base and the china dripper.

Metal kitchen items with the Blue Bouquet decal include canisters, coasters, shakers, a coffee dispenser, and a rectangular tray.

The photo below shows tumbler prototypes with the Blue Bouquet decal. These tumblers were found in the Toledo area which is the home of Libbey. Yellow markings on the tumblers suggest their former home may have been in the company's sample department. The two tumblers to the left are frosted. However, the one on the left has a narrow clear band around the top. The tumbler in the center is clear and the one on the right is frosted on the bottom half and clear on the top. Since other tumblers are not being found it is probably safe to assume these samples did not meet with approval and were never put into production.

The photo on page 52 pictures a "Kadota" style all-china coffee pot, a six-cup Boston teapot, and a "Radiance #3 jug. All of these pieces are hard to find. Rare items include the "Sundial" batter bowl, the "Five Band" cookie jar.

D-style Dinnerware	Value
Bowl, 5½", fruit	$9.00 – 11.00
Bowl, 6", cereal	$18.00 – 22.00
Bowl, 8½", flat soup	$25.00 – 30.00
Bowl, 9¼", round vegetable	$35.00 – 45.00
Cup	$18.00 – 20.00
Gravy boat	$50.00 – 65.00
Plate, 6"	$4.00 – 6.00
Plate, 7¼"	$8.00 – 10.00
Plate, 8¼"	$10.00 – 11.00
Plate, 9"	$18.00 – 22.00
Platter, 11¼", oval	$24.00 – 30.00
Platter, 13¼", oval	$30.00 – 50.00
Saucer	$2.50 – 4.00

Prototype Blue Bouquet tumblers made by Libbey

Left to right: 1. Lower ¾ frosted, top ¼ clear; 2. Entire tumbler frosted;
3. Entire tumbler clear; 4. Bottom ½ frosted with clear bands, top ½ clear.

Boston Creamer Sugar & Lid

Modern Creamer Sugar & Lid

9" Salad Bowl

Cup and Saucer

"Radiance" Drip Jar

"Thick Rim" Drip Jar

Handled Salt & Pepper

6" Plate

8 1/2" Soup Bowl

6" Cereal Bowl

5 1/4" Fruit Bowl

11 1/4" Oval Platter

7 3/4" Flared Bowl

"Thick Rim" Custard

13 1/4" Oval Platter

8 1/4" Plate

Blue Bouquet

Kitchenware	Value
Baker, French, fluted	$18.00 – 20.00
Ball jug, #3	$100.00 – 150.00
Batter bowl, "Sundial"	$2,000.00 – 2,500.00
Bean pot, New England, #4	$180.00 – 225.00
Bowl, 7¾", flared	$35.00 – 45.00
Bowl, 9", salad	$17.00 – 20.00
Bowl, 6", "Radiance"	$14.00 – 18.00
Bowl, 7½", "Radiance"	$20.00 – 25.00
Bowl, 9", "Radiance"	$27.00 – 32.00
Bowl, straight-sided, 6"	$16.00 – 18.00
Bowl, straight-sided, 7½"	$28.00 – 32.00
Bowl, straight-sided, 9"	$30.00 – 35.00
Bowl, 6", "Thick Rim"	$18.00 – 22.00
Bowl, 7½", "Thick Rim"	$22.00 – 28.00
Bowl, 8½", "Thick Rim"	$30.00 – 35.00
Cake plate	$40.00 – 45.00
Casserole, "Radiance"	$40.00 – 45.00
Casserole, "Thick Rim" (2 sizes)	$45.00 – 50.00
Coffee pot, "Five Band"	$70.00 – 85.00
Coffee pot, "Terrace"	$90.00 – 110.00
Cookie jar, "Five Band"	$350.00 – 400.00
Creamer, Boston	$25.00 – 28.00
Creamer, modern	$25.00 – 30.00
Custard, "Thick Rim"	$25.00 – 30.00
Drip coffee pot, "Kadota,"	

Kitchenware	Value
all china	$450.00 – 550.00
Drip jar, "Radiance"	$150.00 – 200.00
Drip jar, "Thick Rim"	$50.00 – 60.00
Electric percolator	$500.00 – 700.00
Jug, "Medallion," #3	$32.00 – 35.00
Jug, "Radiance"	$80.00 – 100.00
Leftover, rectangular	$100.00 – 125.00
Leftover, square	$150.00 – 170.00
Pie baker	$60.00 – 70.00
Pretzel jar	$200.00 – 240.00
Shakers, teardrop, ea.	$18.00 – 22.00
Shakers, handled, ea.	$20.00 – 25.00
Spoon	$125.00 – 135.00
Soup tureen	$290.00 – 320.00
Sugar and lid, Boston	$37.00 – 42.00
Sugar and lid, modern	$45.00 – 55.00
Teapot, Aladdin	$165.00 – 185.00
Teapot, Boston	$200.00 – 225.00

Metal Accessories	
Canister, 6" rnd.	$20.00 – 25.00
Coaster	$12.00 – 15.00
Coffee dispenser	$40.00 – 45.00
Shakers, ea.	$20.00 – 25.00
Tray, rectangular	$50.00 – 60.00

"Thick Rim" Casserole   Boston Teapot

Square Leftover   "Kadota" all-china Coffee Pot   "Radiance" #3 Jug

Pretzel Jar

Soup Tureen

"Terrace" Coffee Pot

Ball Jug #3

New England #4
One Handle Bean Pot

"Five Band" Coffee Pot

"Medallion" #3 Jug

Aladdin Teapot

Fluted French Baker

Spoon

Metal Canisters

Coffee Dispenser

All-china Electric Percolator

Crocus

Crocus is a Hall dinnerware pattern which was introduced in the mid-thirties. Assembling the multitude of pieces available in this pattern presents a challenge to even the most dedicated collector. Obtaining basic dinnerware pieces, which appear to be in short supply, is frustrating to some of the collectors who do not have access to major shows or flea markets. The 10" dinner plate has become virtually extinct.

The list of kitchenware shapes appearing with the Crocus decal is almost endless. Even some veteran Hall collectors have been astounded by some of the discoveries in this pattern. Some of the more interesting pieces include the "Radiance" canister set, "Five Band" shakers, and a "Deco" style coffee pot. The canisters shown in the photo have the decals in an upright position. Other canisters have been found with the decal positioned higher on the canisters and inverted, similar to the mug and Streamline teapot below. Other unusual pieces of high desirability include the Donut shape teapot, the "Teardrop"-style shakers, the Aladdin teapot, the Streamline teapot, and the "Meltdown" sugar and creamer. In addition, just to keep collectors interested and to add a little confusion, there are three styles of all-china drip coffee pots, two different shape beverage mugs, and at least five different shapes of coffee pots with the Drip-O-lator backstamp. One is a shape called "Kadota" which we have only seen with a china dripper. The other

four have a metal dripper which usually has the Crocus decal embossed on it. The "Five Band" coffee pot also will be found with a glass dripper which contains an electric heating element. The "Arthur" shape coffee pot and melody teapot are new listings in this edition. The "Arthur" shape is shown with the coffee pots pictured on page 309. The small-size "Terrace" has also been found with a china dripper.

The New York teapot is most commonly found in the six-cup size, but it has also been found in the two-cup, four-cup, eight-cup, and 12-cup sizes with the Crocus decal.

Several "Zephyr" style one-pound butter dishes and leftovers have been reported since the last book, but these pieces are still lacking from many collections. The matching water bottle is not being found as frequently. Notice the two different shapes of beverage mugs — eight ounce flagon and tankard style. The tureen may be found smooth or with an embossed clover shape.

Metal pieces include a coffee dispenser, a soap dispenser, a round canister set, a bread box, a cake safe, and an oval tray.

Hall is making special limited edition pieces with the Crocus decal for a private company. All of the new issue is clearly marked with a special backstamp and no old shapes are being reproduced. For more information see the section on Reissues in the back of this book.

D-style Dinnerware	Value
Bowl, 5½", fruit	$9.00 – 10.00
Bowl, 6", cereal	$18.00 – 20.00
Bowl, 8½", flat soup	$30.00 – 35.00
Bowl, 9¼", round vegetable	$40.00 – 45.00
Bowl, oval	$35.00 – 40.00
Cup	$12.00 – 15.00
Gravy boat	$32.00 – 37.00
Plate, 6"	$6.00 – 8.00

D-style Dinnerware	Value
Plate, 7¼"	$9.00 – 12.00
Plate, 8¼"	$9.00 – 12.00
Plate, 9"	$18.00 – 20.00
Plate, 10"	$90.00 – 110.00
Platter, 11¼", oval	28.00 – 32.00
Platter, 13¼", oval	$30.00 – 35.00
Saucer	$1.50 – 2.50
Tidbit, 3-tier	$75.00 – 85.00

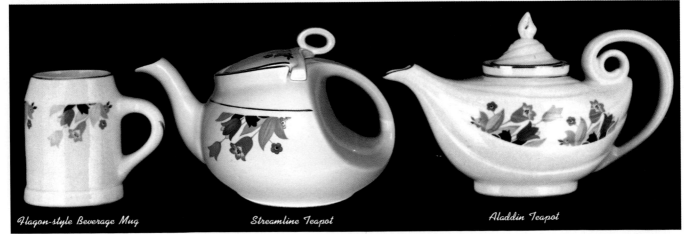

Flagon-style Beverage Mug   *Streamline Teapot*   *Aladdin Teapot*

"Teardrop" Salt & Pepper

Square Leftover

Cup & Saucer

"Radiance" Custard

11 1/4" Oval Platter

"Radiance" Canister Set

5 1/2" Fruit Bowl

Art Deco Style Creamer, Sugar & Lid

9" Plate

8 1/2" Flat Soup Bowl

Oval Bowl

"Kadota" All-china Coffee Pot

"Meltdown" Coffee Pot   "Jordan" All-china Drip Coffee Pot   "Terrace" Coffee Pot

"Medallion" Teapot   Donut Teapot   "Waverly" Coffee Pot

Kitchenware	Value	Kitchenware	Value
Baker, French, fluted	$35.00 – 40.00	Leftover, rectangular	$65.00 – 95.00
Ball jug, #3	$180.00 – 200.00	Leftover, square	$100.00 – 120.00
Bean pot, New England, #4	$285.00 – 300.00	Leftover, "Zephyr"-style	$350.00 – 450.00
Bowl, 9", salad	$18.00 – 22.00	Mug, flagon style	$80.00 – 90.00
Bowl, 6", "Radiance"	$18.00 – 22.00	Mug, tankard style	$60.00 – 75.00
Bowl, 7½", "Radiance"	$22.00 – 27.00	Pie baker	$85.00 – 95.00
Bowl, 9", "Radiance"	$35.00 – 40.00	Pretzel jar	$180.00 – 200.00
Butter, one-pound, "Zephyr"-style	$900.00 – 1,100.00	Saucer, St. Denis	$8.00 – 10.00
Cake plate	35.00 – 42.00	Shakers, "Five Band," ea.	$50.00 – 60.00
Canister, "Radiance"	$800.00 – 1,000.00	Shakers, handled, ea. (salt, pepper)	$22.00 – 25.00
Casserole, "Radiance"	$27.00 – 32.00	Shakers, handled, ea. (sugar, flour)	$75.00 – 85.00
Coffee pot, "Arthur"	UND	Shakers, "Teardrop," ea.	$20.00 – 25.00
Coffee pot, "Deco"	$700.00 – 850.00	Soup tureen, "Thick Rim" or Clover	$275.00 – 300.00
*Coffee pot, "Five Band"	$60.00 – 75.00	Stack set, "Radiance"	$250.00 – 350.00
Coffee pot, "Medallion"	$55.00 – 65.00	Sugar and lid, Art Deco	$40.00 – 45.00
Coffee pot, "Meltdown"	$90.00 – 110.00	Sugar and lid, "Medallion"	$30.00 – 40.00
**Coffee pot, "Terrace" (two sizes)	$50.00 – 65.00	Sugar and lid, "Meltdown"	$55.00 – 65.00
Coffee pot, "Waverly" (Drip-O-lator)	$65.00 – 75.00	Sugar and lid, modern	$25.00 – 30.00
Creamer, Art Deco	$30.00 – 35.00	Sugar and lid, New York	$27.00 – 32.00
Creamer, "Medallion"	$22.00 – 27.00	Teapot, Aladdin	$1,500.00 – 1,800.00
Creamer, "Meltdown"	$35.00 – 40.00	Teapot, Boston	$190.00 – 225.00
Creamer, modern	$18.00 – 20.00	Teapot, Donut	$1,800.00 – 2,000.00
Creamer, New York	$18.00 – 20.00	Teapot, "Medallion"	$95.00 – 110.00
Cup, St. Denis	$35.00 – 40.00	Teapot, Melody	UND
Custard	$27.00 – 32.00	Teapot, New York, 2 or 4 cup	$175.00 – 200.00
Drip coffee pot, "Jordan"	$450.00 – 500.00	Teapot, New York, 6 cup	$135.00 – 185.00
Drip coffee pot, "Kadota"	$400.00 – 450.00	Teapot, New York, 8 or 12 cup	$200.00 – 225.00
Drip jar, #1188, open	$40.00 – 47.00	Teapot, Streamline	$1,500.00 – 1,800.00
Drip jar and lid, "Radiance"	$35.00 – 40.00	Teapot, two cup, "Terrace"	$200.00 – 250.00
Jug and cover, "Radiance," #3, #4	$200.00 – 250.00	Water bottle, "Zephyr"-style	$850.00 – 1100.00
Jug and cover, "Radiance," #5, #6	$250.00 – 300.00	*With glass dripper	$110.00 – 125.00
Jug, "Simplicity"	$300.00 – 350.00	**Small-size with china dripper	$600.00 – 800.00

New England No. 4 Bean Pot

"Radiance" 9" Bowl

"Radiance" 7 1/2" Bowl

Rectangular Leftover

"Zephyr" Shape Leftover

"Zephyr" Shape Butter

SALT PEPPER FLOUR SUGAR

Handled 4-piece Shaker Set

"Radiance" Drip Jar

Beverage Mug

New York Teapot

"Thick Rim" Soup Tureen

Gravy Boat

Clover-style Soup Tureen

"Radiance" No. 5 Covered Jug

3-tier Tidbit

Metal Accessories	Value	Metal Accessories	Value
Bread box	$110.00 – 130.00	Coffee dispenser with glass window	$35.00 – 45.00
Cake safe	$50.00 – 65.00	Soap dispenser	$100.00 – 125.00
Canister set, round, 4-piece	$125.00 – 150.00	Tray, oval	$60.00 – 75.00
Coffee dispenser	$25.00 – 35.00	Tray, round	$50.00 – 60.00

Bread Box

Canister Set

Cake Safe

"Five Band" Coffee Pot

"Meltdown" Sugar & Lid

"Five Band" Shakers

Coffee Dispenser

"Meltdown" Creamer

No. 3 Ball Jug

"Simplicity" Jug

8" Salad Bowl

"Deco" Shape Coffee Pot

French Baker

Gaillardia

Gaillardia is a scarce decal pattern about which little is known at this time. More pieces of both dinnerware and kitchenware are sure to appear, but it will take a very persistent collector to amass any quantity of this pattern.

D-style Dinnerware	Value	Kitchenware	Value
Bowl, 5¼", fruit	$6.00 – 8.00	Casserole, "Radiance"	$30.00 – 35.00
Bowl, 8½", flat soup	$12.00 – 14.00	Coffee pot, "Terrace"	$45.00 – 55.00
Cup	$10.00 – 12.00	Creamer, Art Deco	$18.00 – 22.00
Plate, 6"	$3.00 – 5.00	Creamer, "Medallion"	$18.00 – 22.00
Plate, 7¼"	$8.00 – 10.00	Drip jar, "Radiance	$27.00 – 32.00
Plate, 9"	$12.00 – 15.00	Jug, "Radiance" #5	$28.00 – 35.00
Saucer	$1.00 – 2.00	Leftover, rectangular	$75.00 – 85.00
Kitchenware	**Value**	Leftover, square	$100.00 – 125.00
Baker, French fluted	$25.00 – 30.00	Mug, beverage (tankard style)	$35.00 – 45.00
Ball jug #3	$140.00 – 160.00	Pretzel jar	$125.00 – 150.00
Bowl, 6", "Radiance"	$16.00 – 18.00	Shaker, handled	$20.00 – 25.00
Bowl, 7½", "Radiance"	$18.00 – 22.00	Sugar & lid, Art Deco	$27.00 – 30.00
Bowl, 9", Radiance"	$25.00 – 30.00	Teapot, Boston	$175.00 – 195.00

9" Plate

6" Plate

"Medallion" Creamer

Pretzel Jar

Rectangular Leftover

Square Leftover

Rectangular Leftover

5 1/4" Fruit Bowl

French Baker

Beverage Mug

"Terrace" Coffee Pot

Art Deco Sugar

"Radiance" Casserole

Cup and Saucer

"Radiance" Mixing Bowl

Boston Teapot

Golden Oak

Hall's Golden Oak D-line dinnerware pattern has a gold leaf decoration on a white body. This is a hard-to-find pattern that is new to this edition. The following listing has been compiled from a grouping that was found in eastern Ohio and sold to a collector in Michigan. It is possible that more kitchenware pieces will be found.

D-style Dinnerware	Value	Kitchenware	Value
Bowl, 5¼" fruit	$4.00 – 5.00	Ball jug, #3	$100.00 – 125.00
Bowl, 6" cereal	$6.00 – 8.00	Bowl, 6", straight-sided	$10.00 – 12.00
Bowl, 8½" flat soup	$7.00 – 9.00	Bowl, 7½", straight-sided	$14.00 – 16.00
Bowl, 9¼" round vegetable	$12.00 – 15.00	Bowl, 9", straight-sided	$18.00 – 20.00
Cup	$5.00 – 6.00	Bowl, salad	$10.00 – 12.00
Gravy boat	$15.00 – 18.00	Coffee pot, "Kadota" (bottom)	$65.00 – 85.00
Plate, 6"	$2.00 – 2.50	Creamer, modern	$10.00 – 12.00
Plate, 7¼"	$5.00 – 6.00	Custard, straight-sided	$6.00 – 8.00
Plate, 9"	$8.00 – 10.00	Shaker, handled	$16.00 – 18.00
Saucer	$1.00 – 1.50	Sugar and lid, modern	$18.00 – 20.00
		Teapot, E-style	$90.00 – 125.00
		Teapot, French	$175.00 – 195.00

9 1/4" Round Vegetable Bowl

French Teapot

Custard

"Kadota" Coffee Pot

5 1/4" Fruit Bowl

6" Cereal Bowl

Cup and Saucer

GOLDEN OAK PATTERN
HALL'S SUPERIOR QUALITY OVENWARE
MADE IN U. S. A.

8 1/2" Flat Soup

9" Plate

7 1/4" Plate

Gravy Boat

Modern Creamer, Sugar and Lid

E-style Teapot

Homewood

The Homewood pattern was made for the Eureka Tea Company of Chicago. The availability of pieces in this pattern is limited to a few kitchenware pieces and some of the D-style dinnerware.

D-style Dinnerware	Value
Bowl, 5½", fruit	$5.00 – 6.00
Bowl, 8½", flat soup	$12.00 – 14.00
Cup	$7.00 – 8.00
Plate, 9"	$10.00 – 12.00
Saucer	$1.00 – 1.50

Kitchenware	Value
Bowl, 6", "Radiance"	$14.00 – 16.00
Bowl, 7½", "Radiance"	$18.00 – 20.00
Bowl, 9", "Radiance"	$20.00 – 25.00
Coffee pot, "Terrace"	$60.00 – 75.00
Creamer, Art Deco	$22.00 – 25.00
Drip coffee pot, "Kadota"	$125.00 – 150.00
Drip jar, "Radiance"	$30.00 – 35.00
Sugar, Art Deco	$25.00 – 30.00
Shakers, handled, ea.	$20.00 – 22.00
Teapot, New York	$150.00 – 175.00

"Kadota" Drip Coffee Pot

Handled Shakers

"Radiance" Drip Jar

"Terrace" Coffee Pot

Mums

Mums is a pink floral decal which appears to be most prevalent in the Wisconsin and Minnesota areas. The earliest references to this decal date to the late 1930s. Many people seem to be confusing this decal with another similar decal — Pastel Morning Glory. There are substantial differences between the two decals if care is taken to look at them closely. Even if the obvious difference between the two types of flowers is ignored, Mums does not have the sprigs of blue flowers which are present on the Pastel Morning Glory pieces.

The dinnerware is D-shape. Although the kitchenware listing is continuing to expand, this pattern is almost impossible to collect unless you live in one of the two states mentioned above.

Choice pieces include "Radiance" canisters, the "Medallion" coffee pot, and a large-size "Terrace" coffee pot. Also, the New York six-cup teapot, the "Simplicity" jug, and the pretzel jar are difficult pieces for many collectors to find. The large-size "Medallion" teapot is shown in the photograph. We have not heard any reports of the smaller one appearing with this decal.

D-style Dinnerware	Value
Bowl, 5½", fruit	$6.50 – 8.00
Bowl, 6", cereal	$12.00 – 14.00
Bowl, 8½", flat soup	$22.00 – 25.00
Bowl, 9¼", round	$40.00 – 45.00
Bowl, 10¼", oval	$40.00 – 45.00
Cup	$11.00 – 13.00
Gravy boat	$30.00 – 35.00
Plate, 6"	$4.00 – 5.50
Plate, 8¼"	$6.50 – 8.00
Plate, 9"	$10.00 – 14.00
Platter, 11¼", oval	$30.00 – 35.00
Platter, 13¼", oval	$35.00 – 45.00
Saucer	$1.50 – 2.50

Kitchenware	Value
Baker, French	$30.00 – 40.00
Bowl, 9", salad	$22.00 – 27.00
Bowl, 6", "Radiance"	$20.00 – 22.00
Bowl, 7½", "Radiance"	$25.00 – 27.00
Bowl, 9", "Radiance"	$35.00 – 40.00
Bowl, 9½", ruffled, tab handled, "Medallion"	$75.00 – 90.00
Canister, "Radiance"	$500.00 – 600.00
Casserole, "Medallion"	$45.00 – 50.00
Casserole, "Radiance"	$45.00 – 50.00
Coffee pot, "Medallion"	$100.00 – 125.00

Kitchenware	Value
Coffee pot, "Meltdown"	$125.00 – 150.00
Coffee pot, "Terrace"	$100.00 – 120.00
Creamer, Art Deco	$22.00 – 25.00
Creamer, "Medallion"	$22.00 – 25.00
Creamer, New York	$22.00 – 25.00
Custard, "Medallion"	$25.00 – 30.00
Custard, "Radiance"	$22.00 – 25.00
Drip jar, #1188, open	$40.00 – 45.00
Drip jar and cover, "Medallion"	$40.00 – 45.00
Jug, #3, "Medallion"	$50.00 – 55.00
Jug, "Simplicity"	$200.00 – 220.00
Mug, beverage	$50.00 – 60.00
Pie baker	$45.00 – 55.00
Pretzel jar	$200.00 – 250.00
Shakers, handled, ea.	$20.00 – 25.00
Stack set, "Radiance"	$100.00 – 150.00
Sugar and lid, Art Deco	$28.00 – 35.00
Sugar and lid, "Medallion"	$28.00 – 35.00
Sugar and lid, New York	$28.00 – 35.00
Teapot, Boston	$225.00 – 300.00
Teapot, "Medallion"	$180.00 – 200.00
Teapot, New York	$185.00 – 200.00
Teapot, "Rutherford"	$200.00 – 250.00

"Medallion" Teapot

"Terrace" Coffee Pot

"Rutherford" Teapot

Handled Shakers

"Medallion" Casserole

"Medallion" 9 1/4" Round Bowl

New York Covered Sugar and Creamer

Cup & Saucer

"Medallion" Covered Sugar and Creamer

Gravy Boat

9" Round Vegetable

No. 1188 Open Drip Jar

"Radiance" Drip Jar

Beverage Mug

"Simplicity" Jug

Pretzel Jar

Oval Bowl

Numerous kitchenware shapes with this decal and the discovery of the existence of Hall dinnerware have made this pattern more attractive to collect. All of the dinnerware seems to be concentrated in the Wisconsin and Minnesota areas, while kitchenware seems to be found both there and in eastern Pennsylvania. Although it is not rare, a complete set of dinnerware will be difficult to assemble.

The "Teardrop" shakers may be difficult to identify since they only have a small part of the No. 488 decal. The lids to all the sizes of "Radiance" jugs exist, but it will take diligent searching to find both the largest and the smallest.

The handled shakers may be found on either an ivory or an eggshell body. We have only seen the salad bowl on an eggshell body. The Tom & Jerry punch bowl is difficult to find, but the mugs have been appearing more frequently. An interesting new kitchenware find is the "Zephyr" water bottle. Other items which have been rapidly disappearing into collections include the "Zephyr" butter, "Radiance" condiment jar, and the all-china drip coffee pots.

D-style Dinnerware	Value
Bowl, 5½", fruit	$7.00 – 8.50
Bowl, 8½", flat soup	$30.00 – 35.00
Bowl, 9¼", round	$50.00 – 60.00
Cup	$18.00 – 20.00
Plate, 7"	$10.00 – 12.00
Plate, 8¼"	$10.00 – 12.00
Plate, 9"	$18.00 – 20.00
Platter, 11¼", oval	$30.00 – 35.00
Platter, 13¼", oval	$45.00 – 50.00
Saucer	$1.50 – 2.50

"Radiance" Teapot

"Radiance" Drip Jar

"Radiance" Casserole

"Zephyr" Water Bottle

"Zephyr" 1# Butter

"Radiance All-china Drip Coffee Pot

"Radiance #6 Jug

"Radiance #5 Jug

"Radiance" #4 Jug

"Radiance" #3 Jug

"Radiance" #2 Jug

"Radiance" Stack Set

Square Leftover

"Thick Rim" Casserole

Pretzel Jar

"Sundial" #4 Casserole

"Radiance" 7 1/2" Bowl

"Five Band" Cookie Jar

SALT   PEPPER   SUGAR   FLOUR

"Novelty Radiance" 4-piece Shaker Set

"Radiance" Custard   "Radiance" Condiment Jar

Kitchenware	Value	Kitchenware	Value
Baker, French	$35.00 – 45.00	Drip coffee pot, "Radiance"	$400.00 – 500.00
Ball jug, #3	$150.00 – 185.00	Drip jar, #1188, open	$40.00 – 45.00
Bean pot, New England, (#3, #4, #5)	$200.00 – 250.00	Drip jar and cover, "Medallion"	$40.00 – 45.00
Bowl, 9", salad	$35.00 – 40.00	Drip jar and cover, "Radiance"	$40.00 – 45.00
Bowl, 5", "Radiance"	$20.00 – 25.00	Jug, "Medallion"	$85.00 – 100.00
Bowl, 6", "Radiance"	$20.00 – 25.00	Jug and cover, "Radiance" (#1, #2, #3)	$125.00 – 140.00
Bowl, 7½", "Radiance"	$25.00 – 27.00	Jug and cover, "Radiance" (#4, #5, #6)	$175.00 – 225.00
Bowl, 9", "Radiance"	$30.00 – 32.00	Jug, "Rayed"	$65.00 – 75.00
Bowl, 10", "Radiance"	$45.00 – 50.00	Jug, "Simplicity"	$250.00 – 300.00
Bowl, 8½", "Thin Rim"	$45.00 – 50.00	Leftover, square	$150.00 – 185.00
Butter, 1 lb., "Zephyr"	$500.00 – 650.00	Mug, Tom & Jerry	$25.00 – 30.00
Canister, "Radiance"	$300.00 – 400.00	Pretzel jar	$250.00 – 300.00
Casserole, "Five Band"	$50.00 – 75.00	Punch bowl, Tom & Jerry	$800.00 – 950.00
Casserole, "Medallion"	$45.00 – 55.00	Shakers, handled, ea.	$20.00 – 25.00
Casserole, "Radiance"	$40.00 – 45.00	Shakers, "Medallion," ea.	$40.00 – 47.00
Casserole, "Sundial"	$45.00 – 55.00	Shakers, "Novelty Radiance," ea.	$45.00 – 50.00
Casserole, "Thick Rim"	$45.00 – 55.00	Shakers, "Teardrop," ea.	$22.00 – 25.00
Cocotte, handled	$45.00 – 55.00	Shirred egg dish	$35.00 – 40.00
Coffee pot, "Meltdown"	$100.00 – 125.00	Soup tureen	$300.00 – 350.00
Coffee pot, "Terrace"	$100.00 – 125.00	Stack set, "Radiance"	$100.00 – 150.00
Condiment jar, "Radiance"	$400.00 – 500.00	Sugar and lid, Art Deco	$40.00 – 50.00
Cookie jar, "Five Band"	$250.00 – 300.00	Sugar and lid, "Meltdown"	$40.00 – 50.00
Creamer, Art Deco	$20.00 – 25.00	Sugar and lid, modern	$40.00 – 50.00
Creamer, "Meltdown"	$27.00 – 32.00	Sugar and lid, New York	$40.00 – 50.00
Creamer, modern	$20.00 – 25.00	Teapot, New York	$250.00 – 300.00
Creamer, New York	$20.00 – 25.00	Teapot, "Radiance"	$200.00 – 250.00
Custard "Radiance"	$20.00 – 25.00	Water bottle, "Zephyr"	$700.00 – 900.00
Drip coffee pot, #691	$400.00 – 500.00		

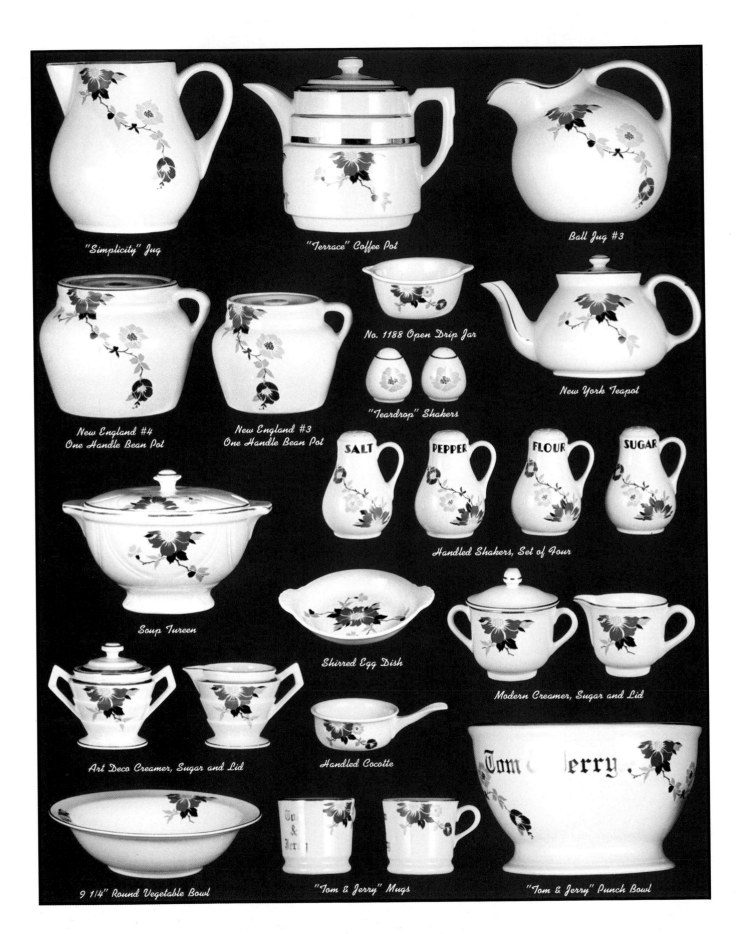

"Simplicity" Jug

"Terrace" Coffee Pot

Ball Jug #3

New England #4
One Handle Bean Pot

New England #3
One Handle Bean Pot

No. 1188 Open Drip Jar

"Teardrop" Shakers

New York Teapot

SALT **PEPPER** **FLOUR** **SUGAR**

Handled Shakers, Set of Four

Soup Tureen

Shirred Egg Dish

Modern Creamer, Sugar and Lid

Art Deco Creamer, Sugar and Lid

Handled Cocotte

9 1/4" Round Vegetable Bowl

"Tom & Jerry" Mugs

"Tom & Jerry" Punch Bowl

Orange Poppy

Orange Poppy is a decal dinnerware line which was introduced in 1933. This pattern was originally used as a premium for the Great American Tea Company. However, Great American discontinued offering this pattern in 1940 and it was offered by Hall as open stock until 1953.

Until recently, C-style dinnerware appeared to be abundant, but newer collectors are reporting shortages of plates, cups, and saucers. One problem collectors of this pattern encounter is crazing of the dinnerware pieces. Items which are hardest to find include the canister style shakers and the Bellevue shape teapot and coffee pot. Other desirable pieces which many collectors are still seeking are the canister set and the Melody and Donut teapots. Items which are rapidly disappearing into collections are the Streamline, Boston, and Windshield teapots.

The few metal accessories available in this pattern are not abundant, but most collectors, who are patient and persistent, will be able to find these items. Notice there are three different canister sets shown in the photo on page 70. The cake safe has a metal cover and a wooden base.

The teardrop shaped salt and pepper have been dropped from the listing. There does not appear to be any evidence that this style shaker was made in Orange Poppy. An oval bowl has been added to the dinnerware listing, but only one of these has been reported. In addition D-style cups have been sighted, but this style cup is scarce.

Dinnerware in Orange Poppy is particularly susceptible to crazing. Collectors are having a difficult time finding examples of dinnerware without discoloration and the prices for mint pieces have risen dramatically.

Additional items in Orange Poppy are currently being made by China Specialties. For more information see the Reissues section at the back of this book.

C-style Dinnerware	Value
Bowl, 5½", fruit	$7.50 – 8.50
Bowl, 6", cereal	$22.00 – 25.00
Bowl, 8½", flat soup	$30.00 – 35.00
Bowl, 9¼", round vegetable	$45.00 – 50.00
Bowl, 10¼" oval	UND
Cup	$25.00 – 30.00

C-style Dinnerware	Value
Plate, 6"	$6.00 – 8.00
Plate, 7¼"	$12.00 – 14.00
Plate, 9"	$25.00 – 30.00
Platter, 11¼", oval	$30.00 – 35.00
Platter, 13¼", oval	$40.00 – 45.00
Saucer	$3.00 – 5.00

Oval Bowl

9 1/4" Round Vegetable Bowl

9" Plate

5 1/4" Fruit Bowl

Flat Soup

Cup & Saucer

Kitchenware	Value	Kitchenware	Value
Baker, French, fluted	$20.00 – 25.00	Custard, "Radiance"	$7.00 – 9.00
Ball jug, #3	$100.00 – 125.00	Drip jar and cover, "Radiance"	$30.00 – 35.00
Bean pot, New England, #4	$125.00 – 145.00	Fork	UND
Bowl, 6", "Radiance"	$20.00 – 22.00	Jug #4, "Radiance"	$55.00 – 60.00
Bowl, 7½", "Radiance"	$22.00 – 25.00	Jug #5, "Radiance"	$40.00 – 45.00
Bowl, 9", "Radiance"	$30.00 – 35.00	Leftover, loop handle	$100.00 – 125.00
Bowl, 10", "Radiance"	$40.00 – 50.00	Mustard and liner	$125.00 – 145.00
Bowl, 9", salad	$18.00 – 20.00	Pie baker	$45.00 – 55.00
Cake plate	$40.00 – 45.00	Pretzel jar	$100.00 – 150.00
Cake server	UND	Shakers, handled, ea.	$20.00 – 25.00
Canister, "Radiance"	$400.00 – 500.00	Shakers, canister-style, "Radiance," ea.	$100.00 – 125.00
Casserole, 8", oval	$60.00 – 65.00	Shakers, "Novelty Radiance," ea.	$40.00 – 50.00
Casserole, 11¾", oval	$65.00 – 75.00	Spoon	$100.00 – 120.00
Casserole, 13", oval	$120.00 – 150.00	Sugar and lid, "Great American"	$30.00 – 35.00
Casserole, #76, round	$35.00 – 40.00	Teapot, 2-cup, Bellevue	$1,500.00 – 1,800.00
Coffee pot, 2-cup, Bellevue	$1,600.00 – 1,800.00	Teapot, Boston	$200.00 – 250.00
Coffee pot, "Great American"	$55.00 – 65.00	Teapot, Donut	$350.00 – 425.00
Coffee pot, S-lid	$65.00 – 75.00	Teapot, Melody	$260.00 – 360.00
Condiment jar, "Radiance"	$800.00 – 900.00	Teapot, Streamline	$260.00 – 350.00
Creamer, "Great American"	$18.00 – 20.00	Teapot, Windshield	$250.00 – 350.00

Loop Handle Leftover
Handled Salt
"Radiance" Drip Jar
Handled Pepper
No. 5 "Radiance" Jug
Mustard
"Novelty Radiance" Shakers
"Radiance" 6" Bowl
"Radiance" 7 1/2" Bowl
"Radiance" 9" Bowl
"Radiance" Canister Set
"Radiance" Shakers

"Radiance" Custard

"Great American" Creamer, Sugar and Lid

Spoon

S-lid Coffee Pot

Pretzel Jar

New England #4 Bean Pot

"Great American" Coffee Pot

Melody Teapot

Donut Teapot

No. 3 Ball Jug

Bellvue Coffee Pot

Streamline Teapot

Boston Teapot

Windshield Teapot

Bellvue Teapot

"Radiance" Casserole

No. 76 Round Casserole

8" Oval Baker

French Baker

Cakeplate

9" Salad Bowl

13" Oval Casserole

Metal Accessories	Value
Bread box	$100.00 – 150.00
Cake safe	$45.00 – 60.00
Canister set, round, 4-piece	$80.00 – 100.00
Canister set, square, 4-piece	$80.00 – 100.00
Coffee dispenser	$40.00 – 50.00
Match safe	$85.00 – 100.00
Shakers, ea.	$13.00 – 16.00
Sifter	$60.00 – 80.00
Soap dispenser	$145.00 – 185.00
Tray, 14¼" x 18½"	$40.00 – 50.00
Waste basket	$85.00 – 100.00
Waste can w/foot pedal	$125.00 – 150.00

Canister Set, 4-pc., Square

Bread Box

Cake Safe

Sifter

Matchholder

Canister Set, 4-pc., Round

Coffee Dispenser

Shakers, Round

Waste Can

Oval Platter

Canister Set, 4-pc., Round
with Glass Knobs

Pastel Morning Glory

The Pastel Morning Glory pattern provides an attractive dinnerware service. The decal features a prominent pink morning glory accented with tiny blue floral sprigs and green leaves. This decal appears to be of late thirties origin and the pattern was distributed primarily in upper Michigan, Wisconsin, and Minnesota. Collectors living in these areas seem to find an ample supply of items; those in other parts of the country have trouble finding even the most common pieces.

Among the more interesting items are the "Radiance" canister set, the "Radiance" teapot, and the round tea tile. The Donut jug, which is rarely found with any decal, and the square and rectangular leftovers are also prize pieces. Covered "Radiance" jugs are still in short supply, but more are turning up.

Recent new finds in this pattern include an all-china drip "Radiance" coffee pot on a Hi-white body and a set of "Thick Rim" mixing bowls with a black exterior featuring the pink morning glory decal on a Hi-white interior. Reasonable prices for these items are still undetermined.

D-style Dinnerware	Value
Bowl, 5½", fruit	$6.00 7.50
Bowl, 6", cereal	$12.00 – 15.00
Bowl, 8½", flat soup	$22.00 – 25.00
Bowl, 9¼", round	$40.00 – 45.00
Bowl, oval	$40.00 – 45.00
Cup	$11.00 – 13.00
Gravy boat	$30.00 – 35.00
Plate, 6"	$4.00 – 5.00
Plate, 7¼"	$6.00 – 8.00
Plate, 8¼"	$6.00 – 8.50
Plate, 9"	$10.00 – 15.00
Plate, 10"	$60.00 – 85.00
Platter, 11¼"	$30.00 – 35.00
Platter, 13¼"	$35.00 – 45.00
Saucer	$1.50 – 2.50

New England No. 4 Bean Pot

New York Teapot

"Radiance" All China Coffee Pot

Square Leftover

Rectangular Leftover

"Terrace" Coffee Pot

No. 1188 Open Drip Jar

PEPPER   SALT

Handled Salt & Pepper

"Medallion" Teapot

8" Luncheon Plate

Kitchenware	Value	Kitchenware	Value
Ball jug, #3 & #4	$175.00 – 210.00	Jug, Donut	$255.00 – 350.00
Bean pot, New England, #4	$185.00 – 220.00	Jug and cover, #4, #5, #6, "Radiance"	$160.00 – 190.00
Bowl, 9", salad	$30.00 – 35.00	Leftover, rectangular	$90.00 – 120.00
Bowl, 6", "Radiance"	$20.00 – 22.00	Leftover, square	$120.00 – 150.00
Bowl, 7½", "Radiance"	$25.00 – 27.00	Petite marmite	$55.00 – 65.00
Bowl, 9", "Radiance"	$35.00 – 40.00	Pie baker	$40.00 – 50.00
Bowl, 10", "Radiance"	$40.00 – 47.00	Pretzel jar	$195.00 – 225.00
Cake plate	$40.00 – 45.00	Saucer, St. Denis	$6.00 – 7.50
Canister, "Radiance"	$400.00 – 450.00	Shakers, handled, ea.	$20.00 – 25.00
Casserole, "Medallion"	$45.00 – 50.00	Shakers, "Novelty Radiance," ea.	$60.00 – 75.00
Casserole, #76 round	$65.00 – 75.00	Shakers, "Teardrop," ea.	$20.00 – 22.00
Casserole, "Radiance"	$40.00 – 45.00	Stack set, "Radiance"	$100.00 – 150.00
Coffee pot, "Terrace"	$100.00 – 125.00	Sugar and lid, Art Deco	$25.00 – 35.00
Creamer, Art Deco	$22.00 – 25.00	Sugar and lid, modern	$25.00 – 35.00
Creamer, modern	$22.00 – 25.00	Sugar and lid, New York	$25.00 – 35.00
Creamer, New York	$22.00 – 25.00	Teapot, Aladdin	$500.00 – 700.00
Condiment jar, "Radiance"	$200.00 – 250.00	Teapot, Boston	$250.00 – 300.00
Cup, St. Denis	$35.00 – 40.00	Teapot, "Medallion"	$195.00 – 225.00
Custard, "Radiance"	$25.00 – 30.00	Teapot, New York	$200.00 – 260.00
Drip coffee, "Radiance" all-china	UND	Teapot, "Radiance"	$250.00 – 300.00
Drip jar and lid, "Radiance"	$40.00 – 45.00	Teapot, "Rutherford"	$200.00 – 250.00
Drip jar, #1188, open	$40.00 – 45.00	Tea tile	$90.00 – 120.00

No. 3 Ball Jug

10 1/2" Oval Vegetable

"Radiance" Casserole

9" Round Vegetable Bowl

"Radiance" Custard

Gravy Boat

8 1/2" Flat Soup

Tea Tile

Cup & Saucer

"Radiance" 6" Bowl

Modern Creamer, Sugar & Lid

"Teardrop" Salt & Pepper

Pretzel Jar

Red Poppy

Hall's Red Poppy pattern consists of a red floral decal accented with black leaves using an ivory body as a background. Additionally, each piece is highlighted with a narrow silver band. Production of this pattern began in the mid-thirties and continued for about twenty years. The Grand Union Tea Company, which used this pattern as a premium, was the primary recipient of this lengthy production.

With the exception of the 10" dinner plate, the D-style dinnerware pieces are generally available for moderate prices, although both the quantity and quality of available items appear to be shrinking. The serving pieces have become especially popular and usually sell very quickly. The gravy boat lacks an underplate and is not an easily found item. Cups may be found with their decal on either the inside or on the outside. Collectors should also be aware some of the dinnerware was decorated with gold trim. Cups, saucers, and plates are found easily with this color trim. The 9" dinner plate is the most commonly found size of plate.

D-style Dinnerware	Value
Bowl, 5½", fruit	$7.50 – 9.00
Bowl, 6", cereal	$15.00 – 17.00
Bowl, 8½", flat soup	$18.00 – 20.00
Bowl, 9¼", round	$35.00 – 45.00
Bowl, 10¼", oval	$45.00 – 55.00
Cup	$12.00– 14.00
Gravy boat	$35.00 – 40.00
Plate, 6"	$4.00 – 5.00
Plate, 7¼"	$8.00 – 9.50
Plate, 8¼"	$9.00 – 10.50
Plate, 9"	$12.00 – 14.00
Plate, 10"	$65.00 – 85.00
Platter, 11¼"	$24.00 – 28.00
Platter, 13¼"	$28.00 – 32.00
Saucer	$2.00 – 3.00

9" Plate

7" Plate

11 1/4" Platter

Cup & Saucer (Pattern Outside)

Cup & Saucer (Pattern Inside)

8 1/2" Flat Soup

9 1/4" Round Vegetable

5 1/2" Fruit

13 1/4" Platter

6" Cereal

6" Plate

China kitchenware accessory pieces in Red Poppy appear to be limited to the "bare essentials." There is not the variety of shapes and sizes of such premium articles like coffee pots, teapots, or cookie jars which are found in some other popular Hall patterns. Also, while interesting pieces are being uncovered in other patterns, new items are not surfacing in this pattern.

In the photo to the right there are two sizes of "Daniel" cream pitchers. The taller one is sometimes called a milk jug or syrup by collectors. Notice the slight difference in color of the Aladdin teapot and the French baker in comparison to the other pieces in the photo. On these two articles, the Red Poppy decal has been placed on a Hi-white body. This deviation from the use of an ivory body may indicate that these two items were made for some company other than Grand Union. A set of "Thin Rim" mixing bowls with a black exterior and a Hi-white interior has also been found. See the photo below.

See the Reissues section at the back of this book for new items made by Hall for a private company.

Kitchenware	Value
Baker, French, fluted	$24.00 – 26.00
Ball jug, #3	$100.00 – 120.00
Bowl, 9", salad	$18.00 – 22.00
Bowl, 6", "Radiance"	$18.00 – 20.00
Bowl, 7½", "Radiance"	$20.00 – 22.00
Bowl, 9", "Radiance"	$22.00 – 27.00
Cake plate	$45.00 – 55.00
Casserole, "Radiance"	$30.00 – 35.00
Coffee pot, "Daniel"	$55.00 – 62.00
Creamer, "Daniel"	$18.00 – 22.00
Creamer, modern	$22.00 – 25.00
Custard	$18.00 – 20.00
Drip jar, #1188, open	$40.00 – 45.00

Kitchenware	Value
Drip jar and cover, "Radiance"	$32.00 – 37.00
Jug, 4", "Daniel," milk or syrup	$42.00 – 47.00
Jug, #5, "Radiance"	$35.00 – 45.00
Leftover, rectangular	$150.00 – 200.00
Leftover, square	$200.00 – 250.00
Pie baker	$40.00 – 50.00
Pretzel jar	$500.00 – 600.00
Shakers, "Teardrop," ea.	$18.00 – 22.00
Shakers, handled, ea.	$18.00 – 22.00
Sugar and lid, "Daniel"	$22.00 – 25.00
Sugar and lid, modern	$22.00 – 25.00
Teapot, Aladdin	$125.00 – 155.00
Teapot, New York	$110.00 – 130.00

"Thin Rim" 8 1/2" Bowl with Black Exterior

"Thin Rim" 6" Bowl with Black Exterior

"Thin Rim" 7 1/2" Bowl with Black Exterior

"Daniel" Coffee Pot

Pie Baker

Pretzel Jar

Metal Teapot Shaped Clock

Cakeplate

Aladdin Teapot

"Teardrop" Shakers

"Radiance" Custard

No. 5 "Radiance" Jug

"Radiance" Casserole

New York Teapot

Gravy Boat

Salad Bowl

Modern Creamer

French Baker

Handled Shaker

"Radiance" Covered Drip Jar

Handled Shaker

No. 1188 Open Drip Jar

"Daniel Creamer Sugar & Lid

9" "Radiance" Bowl

7 1/2" "Radiance" Bowl

6" "Radiance" Bowl

"Daniel Syrup or Milk Pitcher

Glass accessory items in the Red Poppy pattern consist of a 10 ounce frosted tumbler with two styles of decal, a clear tumbler, and a one gallon canister. Of these glass items, the clear tumbler is the hardest to find. The gallon canister is a square clear glass jar with a screw lid and red poppies painted on the outside with enamel. This jar is also sometimes found with green enameled poppies. Two styles of frosted tumblers are shown in the picture on page 78. One style is slightly taller than the other, the flower is a little different and the bands around the top are different colors — one has red bands, the other has black.

Metal accessories with the Red Poppy decal are relatively abundant. Many were available through Montgomery Ward mail order catalogs in the 1940s. Metal pieces are subject to dents through abuse and damage to their enamel finish from improper cleaning. Most collectors are still resisting the temptation to buy metal items which are in poor condition. Three different styles of bread boxes have been reported. None of these is easy to find. Other hard-to-find items include the dustpan and soap dispenser. There are two different styles of coffee dispensers. One type has a glass window like the Autumn Leaf dispenser and the other style has no window.

Plastic accessories include an eight-piece bowl cover set, appliance covers, a teapot-shaped clock, and a tablecloth.

Reports of a waffle iron produced in the Red Poppy pattern always seem to lead to a decal which is similar to and goes well with Hall's Red Poppy decal. This decal has red poppy-like flowers which are much smaller than the ones on Hall pieces. Also, the stem of the flower on the waffle iron has both black and green leaves. The Hall Red Poppy decal has only black leaves. The waffle iron has a metal base and metal lid which contains the decaled china insert. The back of the waffle iron is marked "SAMSON NO E128; Samson United Corp., Rochester, NY." A picture of this waffle iron is shown in the photo at the top of page 78. A dinnerware set with this decal also exists. The set was made by AVCO China Co. of Alliance, Ohio.

Glass Accessories	Value
Canister, gallon	$45.00 – 55.00
Tumbler, clear	$35.00 – 40.00
Tumbler, frosted, 2 styles	$22.00 – 25.00

Metal Accessories	Value
Bread box, three styles	$100.00 – 125.00
Cake safe	$40.00 – 45.00
Cake safe w/gold trim	$55.00 – 65.00
Canister set (glass knobs)	$45.00 – 55.00
Canister set, round, 5 pc.	$90.00 – 110.00
Canister set, square, 4 pc.	$60.00 – 85.00
Clock, metal, teapot shape	$125.00 –175.00
Coffee dispenser	$35.00 – 45.00
Coffee dispenser with glass window	$45.00 – 55.00
Dust pan	$100.00 – 140.00
Hot pad	$18.00 – 22.00
Match safe (2 styles)	$130.00 – 145.00
Recipe box	$60.00 – 75.00
Shaker, ea.	$12.00 – 15.00
Sifter (2 styles)	$65.00 – 85.00

Metal Accessories	Value
Soap dispenser	$140.00 – 185.00
Tray, rectangular	$35.00 – 50.00
Tray, round	$40.00 – 55.00
Waste can, 12½", oval	$65.00 – 80.00
Waste can, round, 15½" tall	$85.00– 100.00
Waste can, step-on pedal	$125.00– 140.00
Wax paper dispenser	$100.00 – 125.00

Plastic Accessories	Value
Bowl covers, 8-pc set	$120.00 – 145.00
Clock, teapot shape	$110.00 – 135.00
Mixer cover	$35.00 – 45.00
Tablecloth, 54" x 100"	$90.00 – 110.00
Toaster cover	$35.00 – 45.00

Miscellaneous Accessories	Value
Cutting board, wooden	$40.00 – 55.00
Hotpot	$16.00 – 18.00
Napkin, linen	$20.00 – 25.00
Silverware box, wooden	$60.00 – 80.00
Tablecloth, cotton	$110.00 –135.00

Round 15 1/2" Tall Waste Can ·*Round 15 1/2" Tall Waste Can* *Oval Waste Can*

Round Canister Set

Cutting Board

Soap Dispenser

Square Canister Set

Match Safe

Coffee Dispenser

Round Canister Set

Hot Pad

Wax Paper Dispenser

Cotton Tablecloth

Recipe Box

Round Metal Tray

Rectangular Metal Tray

Red Poppy

Round Canisters

10 Oz. Frosted Tumbler

10 Oz. Frosted Tumbler

Look-alike Waffle Iron

Cake Safe

Bread Box

Soap Dispenser

Cake Safe

Sifter

Sifter

Serenade

No. 3 Ball Jug

Aladdin Teapot

Fork

New York Teapot

"Kadota" All-china Coffee Pot

SALT   PEPPER

Handled Shakers

Serenade

The autumn-colored floral Serenade pattern was made for the Eureka Tea Company of Chicago. The complete D-style dinnerware is available, although most pieces are not easy to find. A growing list of kitchenware pieces has sparked collectors' interest, but availability is still a problem. The "Kadota" style all-china drip coffee maker is pictured. In addition the "Jordan" shape all-china coffee pot has been found. This is the same shape as the one found in the Autumn Leaf pattern. Interesting new discoveries include a fork and an Aladdin teapot. Other hard-to-find items include the pretzel jar, New York teapot, New England bean pot, and the all-china drip coffee pots. Basic kitchenware items such as mixing bowls, bakers, casseroles, and handled shakers are found frequently.

D-style Dinnerware	Value
Bowl, 5½", fruit	$4.50 – 5.50
Bowl, 6", cereal	$7.50 – 8.50
Bowl, 8½", flat soup	$12.00 – 14.00
Bowl, 9¼", round	$20.00 – 25.00
Bowl, oval	$20.00 – 25.00
Cup	$8.00 – 9.00
Gravy Boat	$25.00 – 30.00
Plate, 6"	$3.00 – 4.00
Plate, 8¼"	$6.00 – 8.50
Plate, 9"	$9.00 – 11.00
Platter, 11¼"	$18.00 – 20.00
Platter, 13¼"	$22.00 – 25.00
Saucer	$1.00 – 2.00

Kitchenware	Value
Baker, French, fluted	$16.00 – 18.00
Ball jug, #3	$125.00 – 150.00
Bean pot, New England, #4	$120.00 – 145.00
Bowl, 9", salad	$14.00 – 16.00
Bowl, 6", "Radiance"	$12.00 – 14.00
Bowl, 7½", "Radiance"	$14.00 – 16.00

Kitchenware	Value
Bowl, 9", "Radiance"	$18.00 – 20.00
Casserole, "Radiance"	$30.00 – 40.00
Coffee pot, "Terrace"	$65.00 – 75.00
Creamer, Art Deco	$18.00 – 22.00
Creamer, modern	$14.00 – 16.00
Creamer, New York	$14.00 – 16.00
Custard, "Radiance"	$12.00 – 14.00
Drip coffee pot, "Jordan," all-china	$300.00 – 400.00
Drip coffee pot, "Kadota," all-china	$135.00 – 150.00
Drip jar and cover, "Radiance"	$28.00 – 32.00
Fork	$110.00 – 125.00
Pie baker	$35.00 – 40.00
Pretzel jar	$125.00 – 150.00
Shaker, handled, ea.	$16.00 – 18.00
Spoon	$110.00 – 125.00
Sugar and lid, Art Deco	$27.00 – 32.00
Sugar and lid, modern	$22.00 – 27.00
Sugar and lid, New York	$22.00 – 27.00
Teapot, Aladdin	$250.00 – 300.00
Teapot, New York	$120.00 – 150.00

9 1/4" Round Vegetable Bowl

11 1/4" Oval Platter

9" Plate

10 1/4" Oval Bowl

Pie Baker

Gravy Boat

"Silhouette"

The "Silhouette" pattern was introduced in the 1930s. This all-black decal contains two figures seated at a table on two high-back, bench-like chairs. Individual pieces are highlighted with silver trim. Both Hall China and Taylor, Smith, and Taylor produced numerous items with this decal for Cook Coffee and Standard Coffee to use as premiums.

D-style dinnerware was produced in this pattern. Collectors are finding a general lack of availability of all pieces of Hall "Silhouette" dinnerware. Therefore, some collectors are mixing Hall and non-Hall pieces in their collections.

Collectors have the opportunity to obtain two all-china drip coffee pots in this pattern — "Medallion" and "Kadota." Some other items which are unusual and of particular interest to collectors include the handled shak-ers, the "Radiance" stack set, and the St. Denis cup and saucer.

In addition to the two companies listed above, Harker also made some items with the same "Silhouette" decal. Two of their most popular pieces with collectors include the china rolling pin and pie lifter. A similar decal was used by the Crooksville China Company. However, this decal featured a seated dog at the foot of the table. The Hall items do not contain a dog in the decal.

Glass, metal, and wooden accessories are numerous, but many of these are not easily found. A gallon-size screw lid jar with green enameled figures may be found.

Information on new items being made by Hall for a private company may be found in the Reissues chapter at the back of this book.

D-style Dinnerware	Value
Bowl, 5½", fruit	$6.50 – 8.00
Bowl, 6", cereal	$14.00 – 16.00
Bowl, 8½", flat soup	$18.00 – 20.00
Bowl, 9¼", round vegetable	$30.00 – 32.00
Bowl, oval	$27.00 – 32.00
Cup	$12.00 – 14.00
Gravy Boat	$25.00 – 30.00

D-style Dinnerware	Value
Plate, 6"	$5.00 – 6.50
Plate, 8¼"	$7.00 – 8.50
Plate, 9"	$16.00 – 18.00
Platter, 11¼", oval	$18.00 – 22.00
Platter, 13¼", oval	$25.00 – 30.00
Saucer	$1.50 – 2.50

9" Plate

"Five Band" Shakers

Cup & Saucer

11 1/4" Oval Platter

9" Salad Bowl

Handled Shakers

French Baker

Kitchenware	Value	Kitchenware	Value
Baker, French, fluted	$16.00 – 18.00	Drip coffee pot, "Medallion"	$250.00 – 300.00
Ball jug, #3	$95.00 – 125.00	Drip jar and cover, "Medallion"	$22.00 – 28.00
Bean pot, New England, #4	$125.00 150.00	Drip jar and cover, "Radiance"	$35.00 – 40.00
Bowl, 3⅝", flared	$10.00 – 12.00	Jug, #2, "Medallion"	$18.00 – 22.00
Bowl, 7¾", flared	$30.00 – 35.00	Jug, #3, "Medallion"	$22.00 – 27.00
Bowl, 9", salad	$16.00 – 18.00	Jug, #4, "Medallion"	$25.00 – 30.00
Bowl, 6", "Medallion"	$12.00 – 14.00	Jug, "Simplicity"	$130.00 – 150.00
Bowl, 7½", "Medallion"	$14.00 – 16.00	Leftover, rectangular	$45.00 – 55.00
Bowl, 8½", "Medallion"	$18.00 – 22.00	Leftover, square	$55.00 – 65.00
Bowl, 6", "Radiance"	$13.00 – 15.00	Mug, beverage	$42.00 – 45.00
Bowl, 7½", "Radiance"	$16.00 – 18.00	Pie baker	$25.00 – 30.00
Bowl, 9", "Radiance"	$20.00 – 22.00	Pretzel jar	$100.00 – 125.00
Casserole, "Medallion"	$30.00 – 40.00	Saucer, St. Denis	$8.00 – 10.00
Casserole, "Radiance"	$35.00 – 45.00	Shakers, "Five Band," ea.	$16.00 – 18.00
Coffee pot, "Five Band"	$45.00 – 55.00	Shakers, "Medallion," ea	$25.00 – 30.00
Coffee pot, "Five Band," (glass dripper)	$90.00 – 110.00	Shakers, handled, ea.	$40.00 – 50.00
Coffee pot, "Medallion"	$90.00 – 110.00	Shakers, "Teardrop" ea.	$20.00 – 25.00
Creamer, "Medallion"	$12.00 – 15.00	Sugar and lid, "Medallion"	$22.00 – 25.00
Creamer, modern	$12.00 – 15.00	Sugar and lid, modern	$22.00 – 25.00
Cup, St. Denis	$30.00 – 35.00	Teapot, "Medallion"	$60.00 – 80.00
Custard, "Medallion"	$22.00 – 27.00	Teapot, New York	$225.00 – 250.00
Drip coffee pot, "Kadota," all-china	$200.00 – 250.00	Teapot, Streamline	$250.00 – 285.00
		Tea tile, 6"	$85.00 – 95.00

"Medallion" Teapot

New England #4 Bean Pot

Rectangular Leftover

Pretzel Jar

"Medallion" Drip Jar

Flared Bowl

"Medallion" Casserole

"Simplicity" Jug

"Medallion" Drip Coffee Pot

*"5 Band" Coffee Pot
with Glass Dripper*

Beverage Mug

*"Kodota" Drip
Coffee Pot*

"5 Band" Coffee Pot

"New York" Teapot

"Medallion" No. 3 Jug

"Medallion" Teapot

"Streamline" Teapot

"Medallion" 8 1/2" Bowl

"Medallion" 7 1/2" Bowl

One Gallon Glass Canister

Electric Clock

"Medallion" 6" Bowl

Flared Custard

"Medallion" Shakers

Tea Tile

Rectangular Metal Tray

Other Accessories	Value	Other Accessories	Value
Bread box	$65.00 – 75.00	Pitcher, crystal, Federal	$100.00 – 120.00
Cake safe	$30.00 – 35.00	Pitcher, crystal, Macbeth-Evans style	$110.00 – 125.00
Canister, one gallon glass		Rolling pin, china, (not Hall)	$110.00 – 120.00
with green decal	$22.00 – 27.00	Sifter	$45.00 – 55.00
Canister set, 4-pc., metal	$50.00 – 60.00	Soap dispenser	$35.00 – 45.00
Clock, electric	$70.00 – 75.00	Shakers, lg. metal, ea.	$12.00 – 14.00
Coffee dispenser	$70.00 – 75.00	Shelf paper (30 ft pack)	$50.00 – 55.00
Coaster	$5.00 – 6.00	Silverware box	$60.00 – 65.00
Double boiler, enamel	$45.00 – 55.00	Tumbler, 9 oz., crystal	$30.00 – 35.00
Kitchen utensils, wooden handled, ea.	$10.00 – 12.00	Tumbler, 10 oz., crystal	$27.00 – 30.00
Match safe	$35.00 – 40.00	Waffle iron	$125.00 – 150.00
Metal tray, oval	$28.00 – 32.00	Waste basket	$55.00 – 65.00
Metal tray, rectangular	$25.00 – 28.00	Wax paper dispenser	$45.00 – 55.00
Mirror	$65.00 – 75.00		

Springtime

The Springtime decal consists of a floral sprig with a prominent grayish-white flower accented by numerous smaller red and yellow flowers. All pieces in the pattern are also trimmed with a silver band. The dinnerware line is comprised of the entire number of D-style items. However, some pieces of dinnerware appear to be eluding the efforts of some collectors to obtain them within a reasonable amount of time. This appears to be true for the small platter, cereal bowls, and the round vegetable bowls. The once plentiful supplies in eastern Pennsylvania appear to be dwindling.

Some of the Springtime kitchenware items appear on the market quite frequently. Among these are the cake plate, covered drip jar, and the casserole. However, teapot collectors also are tapping into the supply of French teapots and the small platter is not seen very often. A new discovery in this pattern is the E-style creamer shown in the photo below.

Items produced in recent years with the Springtime decal include several sizes of the Washington shape coffee pot.

D-style Dinnerware	Value	Kitchenware	Value
Bowl, 5½", fruit	$4.50 – 5.50	Bowl, 6", "Thick Rim"	$9.00 – 11.00
Bowl, 6", cereal	$7.00 – 8.00	Bowl, 7½", "Thick Rim"	$12.00 – 14.00
Bowl, 8½", flat soup	$11.00 – 13.00	Bowl, 8½", "Thick Rim"	$15.00 – 17.00
Bowl, 9¼", round	$22.00 – 25.00	Cake plate	$14.00 – 16.00
Bowl, oval	$20.00 – 22.00	Casserole, "Thick Rim"	$22.00 – 27.00
Cup	$6.00 – 7.50	Coffee pot, "Kadota," bottom only	$55.00 – 65.00
Gravy boat	$22.00 – 25.00	Coffee pot, Washington	$35.00 – 40.00
Plate, 6"	$3.00 – 4.00	Creamer, E-style	$25.00 – 27.00
Plate, 7¼"	$5.00 – 6.00	Creamer, modern	$9.00 – 11.00
Plate, 8¼"	$5.00 – 6.00	Custard	$11.00 – 14.00
Plate, 9"	$7.50 – 9.50	Drip jar and cover, "Thick Rim"	$18.00 – 22.00
Platter, 11¼", oval	$30.00 – 35.00	Jug, #6, "Radiance"	$20.00 – 25.00
Platter, 13¼", oval	$28.00 – 32.00	Pie baker	$18.00 – 20.00
Saucer	$1.50 – 2.50	Shakers, handled, ea.	$12.00 – 14.00
Ball jug, #3	$45.00 – 55.00	Sugar and lid, modern	$16.00 – 18.00
Bowl, 9", salad	$12.00 – 14.00	Teapot, French	$75.00 – 85.00

E-style Creamer   *Gravy Boat*

French Teapot

Oval Bowl

"Thick Rim" Drip Jar

7 1/4" Plate

No. 3 Ball Jug

Cakeplate

Cup & Saucer

"Thick Rim" Casserole

9 1/4" Round Vegetable Bowl

8 1/2" Flat Soup

5 1/4" Fruit Bowl

9" Dinner Plate

Handled Salt & Pepper

SALT

S&PEPPER

Tulip

The Tulip decal is a budding lavender and pink floral representation on an ivory body with platinum trim. This pattern was used as a premium by the Cook Coffee Company. The dinnerware shape is D-style with the addition of a 10" dinner plate and the omission of the 8¼" plate. Other potteries such as Harker, Paden City, and Universal Cambridge also used this same decal on some of their wares.

The "Perk" coffee pot pictured at the center right and the "Kadota" all-china drip coffee pot both have the Drip-O-Lator backstamp of Enterprise Aluminum Company. The "Perk" coffee pot will also be found with the "Shaggy Tulip" decal and in colored glazes without a decal. Notice the tab-handled casserole at the top right.

This piece is a new discovery since the last book. The Aladdin teapot shown in the center of the photo was reported a few years ago. Since that time only a handful have surfaced.

Collectors seem to be having some trouble finding the "Radiance" stack set and the St. Denis cups and saucers. Obtaining Hall dinnerware also seems to be more difficult than finding Harker dinnerware. Although there are numerous Hall kitchenware shapes to collect in this pattern, many collectors are mixing in pieces made by other companies. The rolling pin and pie server made by Harker are especially desirable.

Metal accessories include a non-Hall waffle iron and a four-piece canister set with glass knobs.

D-style Dinnerware	Value
Bowl, 5½", fruit	$6.50 – 8.00
Bowl, 6", cereal	$14.00 – 16.00
Bowl, 8½", flat soup	$16.00 – 18.00
Bowl, 9¼", round	$30.00 – 35.00
Bowl, oval	$32.00 – 37.00
Cup	$11.00 – 13.00
Gravy boat	$32.00 – 37.00
Plate, 6"	$4.00 – 5.00
Plate, 7"	$6.00 – 7.00
Plate, 9"	$11.00 – 13.00
Plate 10"	$55.00 – 65.00
Platter, 11¼", oval	$25.00 – 30.00
Platter, 13¼", oval	$30.00 – 35.00
Saucer	$1.50 – 2.50
Tidbit, 3-tier	$55.00 – 65.00

Kitchenware	Value
Baker, French, fluted	$20.00 – 22.00
Bowl, 9", salad	$18.00 – 20.00
Bowl, 6", "Radiance"	$14.00 – 16.00
Bowl, 7½", "Radiance"	$17.00 – 20.00
Bowl, 9", "Radiance"	$25.00 – 30.00

Kitchenware	Value
Bowl, 6", "Thick Rim"	$16.00 – 18.00
Bowl, 7½", "Thick Rim"	$19.00 – 24.00
Bowl, 8½", "Thick Rim"	$30.00 – 35.00
Casserole, "Radiance"	$35.00 – 45.00
Casserole, tab-handled	$100.00 – 125.00
Casserole, "Thick Rim"	$40.00 – 45.00
Coffee pot, "Perk"	$55.00 – 65.00
Creamer, modern	$18.00 – 22.00
Cup, St. Denis	$30.00 – 35.00
Custard, "Thick Rim"	$16.00 – 20.00
Drip coffee pot, "Kadota," all-china	$125.00 – 150.00
Drip jar and cover, "Thick Rim"	$30.00 – 35.00
Jug, #3 "Medallion"	$65.00 – 85.00
Saucer, St. Denis	$8.00 – 9.00
Shakers, handled, ea.	$18.00 – 22.00
Stack set, "Radiance"	$95.00 – 110.00
Sugar and lid, modern	$22.00 – 27.00
Teapot, Aladdin	$600.00 – 850.00

Metal Accessories	Value
Canister set, 4-pc	$100.00 – 120.00
Waffle iron	$100.00 – 125.00

Modern Creamer,
Sugar and Lid

Tab-handled Casserole

French Baker

"Kadota" Drip Coffee Pot

Cup & Saucer

"Perk" Coffee Pot

8 1/2" Flat Soup

Aladdin Teapot

St. Denis Cup & Saucer

13 1/4" Oval Platter

6" Plate

9" "Radiance" Bowl

10 1/4" Oval Bowl

7 1/2" "Radiance" Bowl

6" "Radiance" Bowl

Wildfire

The Wildfire pattern was used as a premium by the Great American Tea Company during the 1940s and 1950s. The dinnerware is D-style, but the 8¼" plate was not used and a 10" dinner plate, a 7¼" salad plate, a three-tier tidbit, and an oval bowl were added.

A sunken handle "Thick Rim" casserole and a "Thick Rim" drip jar with a cadet base have been found to go along with the cadet "Thick Rim" bowl in the picture. The bases do not have the Wildfire pattern and are inter-changeable with those of other patterns such as Royal Rose and Morning Glory. Sets of utility bowls in both the straight-sided and "Thick Rim" styles have been found with cadet exteriors and white interiors. On these bowls the decal is on the hi-white interior.

Two styles of Aladdin teapots with the Wildfire decal have been reported — round opening and oval opening. Infusors may be obtained for both styles. The S-lid coffee pot has been found with an electric heating element and glass dripper. Rarely found pieces include the Sani-Grid jugs, Sani-Grid teapot, and Boston teapot.

The exciting news in this pattern is the discovery of a Streamline teapot a few years ago and the recent appearance of a tab-handled bean pot.

The cake plate has been deleted from the listing since numerous Wildfire collectors have expressed doubts about its existence.

D-style Dinnerware	Value
Bowl, 5½", fruit	$5.00 – 6.00
Bowl, 6", cereal	$11.00 –13.00
Bowl, 8½", flat soup	$13.00 –16.00
Bowl, 9¼", round	$27.00–30.00
Bowl, oval	$22.00 – 28.00
Cup	$12.00 – 14.00
Gravy boat	$22.00 – 25.00
Plate, 6"	$4.00 – 5.00
Plate, 7"	$8.50 – 9.50
Plate, 9"	$10.00 – 12.00
Plate 10"	$50.00 – 65.00
Platter, 11¼", oval	$22.00 – 25.00
Platter, 13¼", oval	$25.00 – 28.00
Saucer	$1.50 – 2.50
Tidbit, 3-tier	$60.00 – 70.00

Kitchenware	Value
Baker, French, fluted	$18.00 – 22.00
Bean pot, tab-handled	$250.00 – 300.00
Bowl, 9", salad	$15.00 – 18.00
Bowl, 6", straight-sided	$16.00 – 18.00
Bowl, 7½", straight-sided	$20.00 – 22.00
Bowl, 9", straight-sided	$27.00 – 32.00
Bowl, 6", "Thick Rim"	$16.00 – 18.00
Bowl, 7½", "Thick Rim"	$18.00 – 22.00
Bowl, 8½", "Thick Rim"	$27.00 – 32.00
Casserole, tab-handled	$30.00 – 35.00
Casserole, "Thick Rim"	$45.00 – 50.00
Coffee pot, S-lid	$65.00 – 75.00
Coffee pot, S-lid (glass dripper)	$95.00 – 125.00
Creamer, modern	$16.00 – 18.00
Creamer, Sani-Grid	$25.00 – 30.00

Kitchenware	Value
Custard, straight-sided	$22.00 – 25.00
Drip jar and cover, tab-handled	$45.00 – 55.00
Drip jar and cover, "Radiance"	$75.00 – 95.00
Drip jar and cover, "Thick Rim"	$28.00 – 32.00
Jug, 5", Sani-Grid	$55.00 – 65.00
Jug, 6", Sani-Grid	$70.00 – 75.00
Jug, 7½", Sani-Grid	$80.00 – 90.00
Jug #5, "Radiance"	$50.00 – 60.00
Pie baker	$45.00 – 55.00
Shaker, handled, ea.	$20.00 – 22.00
Shaker, Sani-Grid, ea.	$25.00 – 30.00
Shaker, "Teardrop," ea.	$18.00 – 22.00
Sugar and lid, modern	$28.00 – 32.00
Sugar, Sani-Grid	$25.00 – 30.00
Teapot, Aladdin	$120.00 – 140.00
Teapot, Boston	$250.00 – 300.00
Teapot, 6-cup, Sani-Grid	$300.00 – 350.00
Teapot, Streamline	$500.00 – 600.00

Kitchenware (Blue Parts)	Value
Bowl, 6", straight-sided	$20.00 – 22.00
Bowl, 7½", straight-sided	$25.00 – 30.00
Bowl, 9", straight-sided	$32.00 – 37.00
Bowl, 6", "Thick Rim"	$20.00 – 22.00
Bowl, 7½", "Thick Rim"	$25.00 – 30.00
Bowl, 8½", "Thick Rim"	$32.00 – 37.00
Casserole, "Thick Rim"	$35.00 – 40.00
Drip jar and cover, "Thick Rim"	$35.00 – 40.00

Metal Accessories	Value
Coffee dispenser	$25.00 – 30.00

Sani-Grid 5" Jug

Streamline Teapot

Aladdin Teapot

Sani-Grid Teapot

Sani-Grid Salt & Pepper

Sani-Grid Sugar & Creamer

"Teardrop" Salt & Pepper

Tab Handled Bean Pot

Boston Teapot

S-lid Coffee Pot

"Radiance" No. 5 Jug

Modern Creamer, Sugar & Lid

Cup & Saucer

"Thick Rim" Drip Jar

"Radiance" Drip Jar

SALT

Handled Salt Shaker

9 1/4" Round Vegetable Bowl

6" Cereal Bowl

Pie Baker

Oval Bowl

7 1/4" Plate

Straight-sided 6" Bowl

"Thick Rim" 6" Bowl with Blue Exterior

Yellow Rose

Yellow Rose was produced for the Eureka Tea Company of Chicago. Distribution of this pattern was regional, and collectors are having very little success finding any outside of the northern midwest area.

The "Norse" shape coffee pot, sugar, and creamer are found frequently in this pattern, but this shape has not been found in other decal lines. A new item in the listing below is the "Kadota" coffee pot with a "Jordan" dripper. Enough of these strange all-china drip coffee pot combinations have been found that we must conclude this was an intentional combination by some seller.

D-style Dinnerware	Value
Bowl, 5½", fruit	$4.50 – 5.50
Bowl, 6", cereal	$9.50 – 11.50
Bowl, 8½", flat soup	$16.00 – 18.00
Bowl, 9¼", round vegetable	$30.00– 35.00
Cup	$8.00 – 10.00
Gravy boat	$30.00 – 35.00
Plate, 6"	$3.50 – 4.50
Plate, 8¼"	$8.00 – 9.00
Plate, 9"	$12.00 – 14.00
Platter, 11¼", oval	$22.00 – 25.00
Platter, 13¼", oval	$28.00 – 32.00
Saucer	$1.50 – 2.00

Kitchenware	Value
Baker, French, fluted	$22.00 – 27.00
Bowl, 9", salad	$22.00 – 27.00

Kitchenware	Value
Bowl, 6", "Radiance"	$14.00 – 16.00
Bowl, 7½", "Radiance"	$18.00 – 22.00
Bowl, 9", "Radiance"	$25.00 – 30.00
Casserole, "Radiance"	$35.00 – 40.00
Coffee pot, "Kadota" bottom	$50.00 – 60.00
Coffee pot, "Norse"	$75.00 – 85.00
Coffee pot, "Waverly"	$40.00 – 50.00
Creamer, "Norse"	$18.00 – 22.00
Custard	$14.00 – 16.00
Drip coffee pot, "Kadota/Jordan"	$300.00 – 350.00
Drip jar and cover, "Radiance"	$35.00 – 40.00
Shakers, handled, ea.	$18.00 – 22.00
Special marmite	$35.00 – 42.00
Stack set, "Radiance"	$95.00 – 110.00
Sugar and lid, "Norse"	$27.00 – 32.00
Teapot, New York	$150.00 – 200.00

11 1/4" Oval Platter

8 1/2" Flat Soup

8 1/4" Plate

6" Cereal Bowl

9" Plate

9" Round Vegetable Bowl

5 1/4" Fruit Bowl

"Radiance" Custard

"Norse" Coffee Pot

"Kodota Coffee Pot
With "Jorden" Dripper

Special Marmite

"Waverly" Coffee Pot

PEPPER SALT

Handled Shakers

New York Teapot

"Radiance" Casserole

French Baker

"Norse" Sugar & Lid

"Norse" Creamer

E-STYLE DINNERWARE
Cameo Rose

Cameo Rose is an E-style dinnerware pattern which was made exclusively for the Jewel Tea Company. According to their catalog, the pattern "features a single rose, framed by a rosebud and leaf wreath, accented in gold." It was lauded as a "superior quality hand fired semi-porcelain dinnerware that would never fade or craze." Cameo Rose was first offered in the fifties and remained available until the early seventies.

Services were offered as a 16-piece "breakfast starter set," a 16-piece "dinner starter set," and a "53-piece service for eight." Individual pieces could also be bought from open stock.

Today most pieces of Cameo Rose can be readily found. However, a few items require diligent searching. With the exception of the sample items, the piece we have found to be the hardest to acquire is the cream soup. This is followed by the 15½" oval platter and the butter. These last two pieces were not made for the entire time and this may explain their scarcity.

A decal variation of most of the dinnerware pieces has been reported. The commonly found style is pictured in the reprint on the next page. Another form exists with only the the large rosebud decal in the center of each piece. This style lacks the border design.

Several rare pieces have been reportedly purchased from a former Jewel employee. These were probably one-of-a-kind sample items which found their way to the employee's home through the employee store. These items include a clock fashioned from a dinner plate and a covered round vegetable bowl with tab handles on both the base and the lid. Another scarce piece is the "wings" style butter dish.

Cameo Rose	Value
Bowl, 5¼", fruit	$5.00 – 6.50
Bowl, 6¼", tab-handle cereal	$14.00 – 16.00
Bowl, 5", cream soup	$85.00 – 90.00
Bowl, 8", flat soup	$12.00 – 14.00
Bowl, covered vegetable	$50.00 – 65.00
Bowl, 9", round vegetable	$20.00 – 25.00
Bowl, 10½", oval	$20.00 – 25.00
Butter, quarter pound	$400.00 – 500.00
Butter, quarter pound, "wings" top	$900.00 – 1,200.00
Clock	UND
Creamer	$9.00 – 11.00
Cup	$7.50 – 8.50
Gravy boat and underplate	$27.00 – 32.00

Cameo Rose	Value
Plate, 6½"	$3.00 – 4.00
Plate, 7¼"	$7.50 – 8.50
Plate, 8"	$8.00 – 9.50
Plate, 9¼"	$8.00 – 9.50
Plate, 10"	$19.00 – 25.00
Platter, 11¼", oval	$16.00 – 18.00
Platter, 13¼", oval	$20.00 – 22.00
Platter, 15½", oval	$25.00 – 30.00
Saucer	$1.00 – 1.50
Shakers, pr	$40.00 – 45.00
Sugar and lid	$18.00 – 20.00
Teapot, 8-cup	$85.00 – 95.00
Tidbit tray, 3-tier	$65.00 – 75.00

Clock   Cereal Bowl   Cream Soup

Salt & Pepper   "Wings" 1/4 Pound Butter   3-tier Tidbit

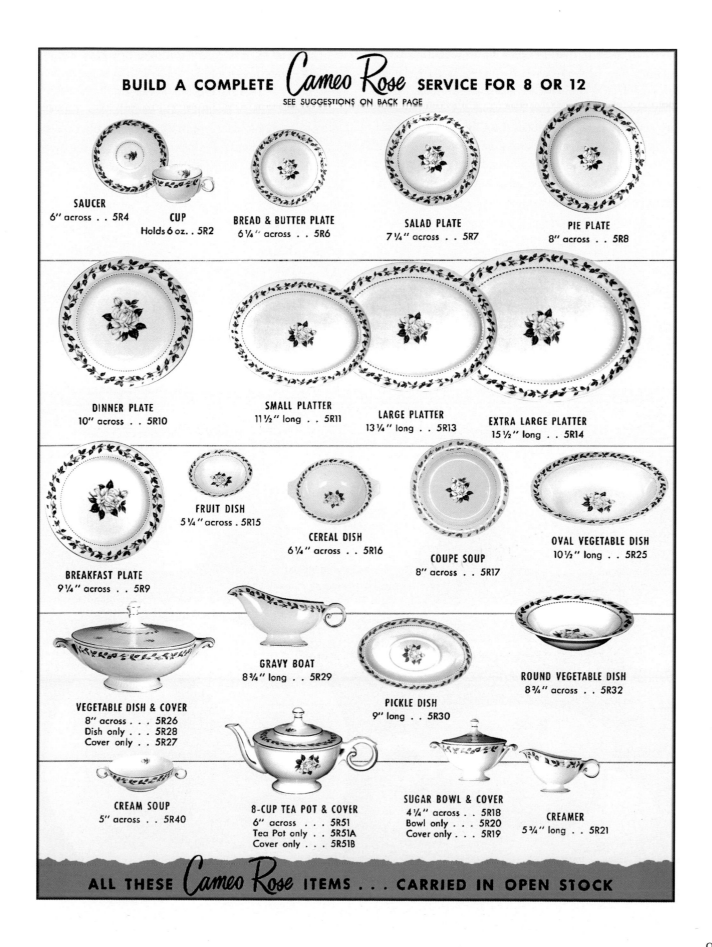

BUILD A COMPLETE *Cameo Rose* SERVICE FOR 8 OR 12

SEE SUGGESTIONS ON BACK PAGE

SAUCER
6" across . . 5R4

CUP
Holds 6 oz. . 5R2

BREAD & BUTTER PLATE
6¼" across . . 5R6

SALAD PLATE
7¼" across . . 5R7

PIE PLATE
8" across . . 5R8

DINNER PLATE
10" across . . 5R10

SMALL PLATTER
11½" long . . 5R11

LARGE PLATTER
13¼" long . . 5R13

EXTRA LARGE PLATTER
15½" long . . 5R14

FRUIT DISH
5¼" across . 5R15

CEREAL DISH
6¼" across . . 5R16

COUPE SOUP
8" across . . 5R17

OVAL VEGETABLE DISH
10½" long . . 5R25

BREAKFAST PLATE
9¼" across . . 5R9

GRAVY BOAT
8¾" long . . 5R29

PICKLE DISH
9" long . . 5R30

ROUND VEGETABLE DISH
8¾" across . . 5R32

VEGETABLE DISH & COVER
8" across . . . 5R26
Dish only . . . 5R28
Cover only . . 5R27

CREAM SOUP
5" across . . 5R40

8-CUP TEA POT & COVER
6" across . . . 5R51
Tea Pot only . . 5R51A
Cover only . . . 5R51B

SUGAR BOWL & COVER
4¼" across . . 5R18
Bowl only . . . 5R20
Cover only . . . 5R19

CREAMER
5¾" long . . 5R21

ALL THESE *Cameo Rose* ITEMS . . . CARRIED IN OPEN STOCK

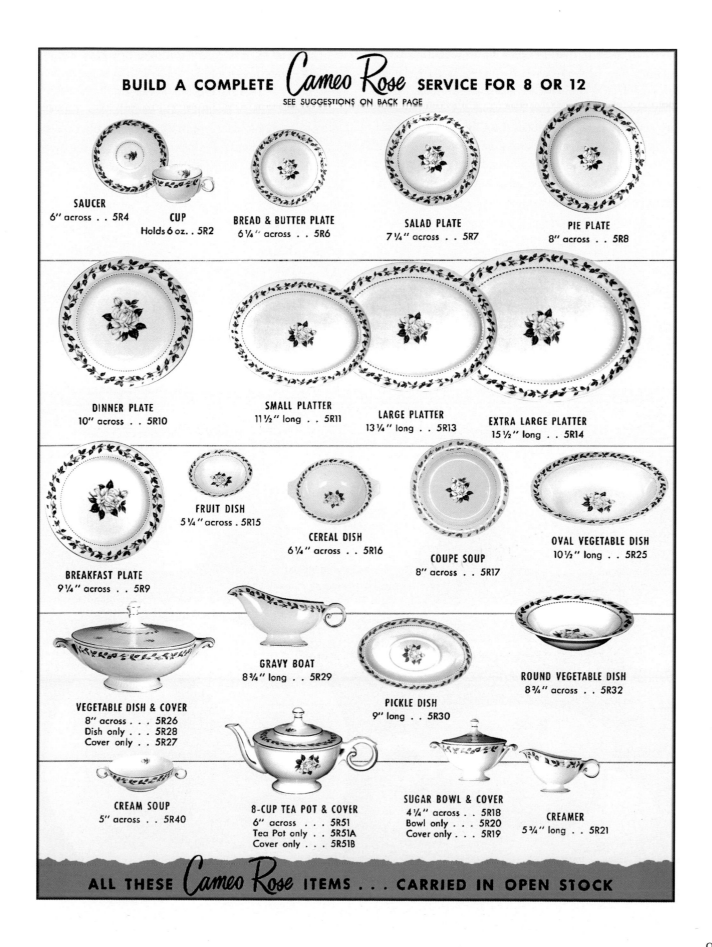

Christmas Tree and Holly

The discovery of dinnerware with this decorative holiday pattern has peaked collector interest. E-style dinnerware and selected kitchenware items are available in this combination of Christmas tree and holly decals. Plates and serving pieces will generally bear the Christmas tree decal. The cups, saucers, sugar and creamer, and some of the kitchenware pieces are decorated with the holly decal. In some cases, as with the coffee pot shown, a piece may be found decorated with either decal.

The #1091, 4½" plum pudding bowl will often be found decorated with a holly decal with light green leaves. These bowls usually have gold lettering on the reverse side which reads "Keen's English Chop House, New York City." Notice two variations of the holly decal on the coffee set sugars and creamers in the photo on the opposite page. A second Christmas Tree decal is also shown in the photo below.

Dinnerware	Value
Bowl, oval	$55.00 – 60.00
Cup	$18.00 – 22.00
Plate, 7¼"	$18.00 – 22.00
Plate, 10"	$35.00 – 45.00
Platter, 15½"	$55.00 – 65.00
Saucer	$3.00 – 4.00
Tidbit, 2-tier	$100.00 – 125.00

Accessories	Value
Bowl, 4½", plum pudding	$25.00 – 30.00
Coffee pot, coffee set	$200.00 – 250.00
Cookie jar, Zeisel	$300.00 – 350.00
Creamer, coffee set	$40.00 – 45.00
Mug, 3 oz..A.D coffee	$40.00 – 45.00
Sugar, coffee set	$40.00 – 45.00

Keen's English Chop House Plum Pudding Bowls

No. 1091 4 1/2" Plum Pudding Bowls

Christmas Decal Variations

"Holly" Christmas Cup and Saucer

7 1/4" Christmas Tree with Presents Decoration

Coffee Set Coffee Pot w/Holly Decal

Coffee Set Coffee Pot w/Christmas Tree Decal

Zeisel-style Cookie Jar

10" Dinner Plate

Cup & Saucer

7 1/4" Salad Plate

Oval Bowl

2-tier Tidbit

3 Oz. Irish Coffee Mug

Coffee Set Sugar & Creamer

Coffee Set Sugar & Creamer

Game Bird

The Game Bird pattern consists of four different decals featuring scenes with several different birds. One decal depicts an ascending male and female pheasant. Another shows a pair of geese in flight. Still another decal depicts a covey of grouse. Some pieces will have only one decal while other pieces may have two different decals — one on each side. Notice the small fruit bowls at the bottom of the photo. Each bowl has a different decal.

This decal is more commonly associated with the electric percolator than with a dinnerware pattern. However, some pieces of E-style dinnerware are surfacing. It has been reported that this pattern dinnerware was sold by Swan's in the Chicago area.

The most popular pieces found with this decal are the New York and Windshield teapots.

A matching metal saucepan has been found with the Ernest Sohn backstamp. Ernest Sohn was a Hall China customer and a picture of an electric percolator marketed by Sohn will be found in the section on electric percolators.

Dinnerware	Value
Bowl, 5½", fruit	$12.00 – 14.00
Bowl, oval	$55.00 – 65.00
Cup	$22.00 – 27.00
Plate, 6½"	$10.00 – 11.00
Plate, 7¼"	$20.00 – 25.00
Plate, 9¼"	$35.00 – 45.00
Plate, 10"	$60.00 – 75.00
Platter, 13¼" oval	$65.00 – 75.00
Saucer	$3.00 – 4.00

China Accessories	Value
Ball Jug, #3	$250.00 – 300.00
Bowl, 6", "Thick Rim"	$25.00 – 30.00
Bowl, 7½", "Thick Rim"	$27.00 – 32.00
Bowl, 8½", "Thick Rim"	$35.00 – 45.00
Casserole, #65, round, 16 oz.	$30.00 – 40.00
Casserole, "MJ"	$65.00 – 85.00
Cookie jar, Zeisel	$250.00 – 300.00
Creamer, New York	$35.00 – 40.00
Mug, Tom & Jerry	$22.00 – 27.00
Mug, Irish coffee	$60.00 – 75.00
Percolator, electric	$100.00 – 120.00
Sugar and lid, New York	$45.00 – 55.00
Teapot, "Grape," Thorley	$250.00 – 300.00
Teapot, New York	$170.00 – 195.00
Teapot, Windshield	$255.00 – 315.00

"Pheasants" Windshield Teapot

"Pheasants"
Electric Percolator

"Quail"
Tom & Jerry Mug

"Ducks" "Grape"
Thorely Teapot

"Geese" Electric Percolator

"Ducks" 6" Plate

"Quail" No, 3 Ball Jug

"Quail" Zeisel-style Cookie Jar

"Geese" Tom & Jerry Mug

"Pheasants" Irish
Coffee Mug

"Quail" 8 1/2" "Thick
Rim" Bowl

"Geese" 7 1/2" "Thick
Rim" Bowl

"Ducks" 6" "Thick
Rim" Bowl

"Pheasants" 5 1/4" Bowl

"Geese" 5 1/4" Bowl

"Ducks" 5 1/4" Bowl

"Pheasants" New York Teapot

Heather Rose

The Heather Rose decal dinnerware used the same E-style blanks used for the Granitetone dinnerware which Hall produced for Sears starting in the 1940s. The decal is a pink rose with green leaves which are interspersed with delicate white baby's breath. Although this dinnerware pattern dates to the fifties and sixties, it is not plentiful. However, most pieces can be found with diligent searching. Cream soups could exist, but we have not seen any and the E-style covered casserole is not plentiful.

Several shapes, other than E-style, sporting this decal include the New York teapot, the Irish coffee mug, the Washington coffee pot, the "Rayed" jug, the "Terrace" coffee pot, and several Flare-shape items. The New York teapot with the Heather decal is probably hard enough to find that it should be considered rare. The Washington coffee pots are of recent vintage and still may be made on occasion if Hall desires. Two sizes are commonly found. The smaller 12 ounce size can be found with either a knob lid or a sunken lid. The larger six cup coffee pot has only been found with the knob-style lid. The Irish coffee mug is also a newer piece, but we have not seen many. Another new piece is the small open teapot which is Hall's London shape. The "Rayed" jug is one of the more common Heather Rose pieces.

Flare-shape pieces do not appear to be common, but there are probably enough of these out there to satisfy the demand. Three sizes of bowls, a three-pint casserole, a teapot, and a cookie jar have been found. Other Flare-shape pieces with this decal are pictured on page 150.

Some dealers and collectors are confusing this pattern with a similar Hall pattern — Primrose. Both patterns utilize the same E-style shape and a very similar rose decal, but Primrose does not have the dainty white sprigs of baby's breath.

Heather Rose	Value
Bowl, 5¼", fruit	$3.50 – 5.00
Bowl, 6¼", cereal	$7.50 – 10.00
Bowl, 8", flat soup	$10.00 – 12.00
Bowl, 9", salad	$14.00 – 16.00
Bowl, 9¼", oval	$22.00 – 25.00
Bowl, 6¾", Flare-shape	$10.00 – 12.00
Bowl, 7¾", Flare-shape	$14.00 – 16.00
Bowl, 8¾", Flare-shape	$18.00 – 20.00
Bowl, covered vegetable	$35.00 – 40.00
Cake plate	$15.00 – 18.00
Casserole, Flare-shape	$35.00 – 45.00
Coffee pot, Flare-shape	$40.00 – 45.00
Coffee pot, "Terrace"	$40.00 – 45.00
Coffee pot, 30 oz., Washington	$45.00 – 55.00
Coffee pot, 12 oz., Washington	$25.00 – 35.00
Cookie jar, Flare-shape	$75.00 – 85.00
Creamer	$8.00 – 10.00
Cup	$6.00 – 7.00

Heather Rose	Value
Gravy boat and underplate	$27.00 – 32.00
Jug, "Rayed"	$20.00 – 25.00
Mug, Irish coffee	$18.00 – 20.00
Pickle dish, 9"	$9.00 – 11.00
Pie baker	$22.00 – 25.00
Plate, 6½"	$2.50 – 3.50
Plate, 7¼"	$5.50 – 7.00
Plate, 9¼"	$8.00 – 10.00
Plate, 10"	$9.50 – 12.50
Platter, 11¼", oval	$16.00 – 18.00
Platter, 13¼", oval	$22.00 – 27.00
Platter 15½", oval	$25.00 – 30.00
Saucer	$1.00 – 2.00
Sugar and lid	$15.00 – 18.00
Teapot, Flare-shape	$35.00 – 45.00
Teapot, London	$20.00 – 25.00
Teapot, New York	$125.00 – 135.00

"Terrace" Coffee Pot

New York Teapot

30 Oz. Washington Coffee Pot

London Coffee Pot

Irish Coffee Mug

Sugar & Lid

Creamer

Cup & Saucer

5 1/4" Fruit Bowl

7 1/4" Flare-shape Bowl

Covered Vegetable Bowl

"Rayed" Jug

6 1/4" Cereal Bowl

15 1/2" Oval Platter

Pie Baker

Gravy Boat & Underplate

9" Salad Bowl

Oval Bowl

Flare-Shape Casserole

10" Dinner Plate

Prairie Grass

Prairie Grass, sometimes called "Sea Oats" is an E-style dinnerware line with a wild grain style decal. Not very much is known about this pattern at the present time, however, more pieces are beginning to appear on the secondary market. Collectors are also beginning to report the appearance of pieces of this pattern in the Tomorrow's Classic shape.

Prairie Grass Dinnerware	Value
Bowl, 5¼", fruit	$4.50 – 5.50
Bowl, 6¼", cereal	$8.50 – 10.00
Bowl, 8", flat soup	$12.00 – 14.00
Bowl, 9¼", oval	$22.00 – 25.00
Creamer	$8.00 – 10.00
Cup	$6.00 – 8.00
Plate, 6½"	$4.00 – 5.00
Plate, 7¼"	$5.50 – 7.50
Plate, 8"	$8.50 – 10.00
Plate, 9¼"	$8.50 – 11.00
Plate, 10"	$11.00 – 14.00
Platter, 11¼", oval	$18.00 – 22.00
Platter, 13¼", oval	$25.00 – 30.00
Saucer	$1.00 – 2.00
Sugar and lid	$15.00 – 18.00
Tidbit, 3-tier	$65.00 – 75.00

3-tier Tidbit Tray
8" Salad Plate
6 1/2" Plate
10" Dinner Plate

Primrose

Primrose is an E-style dinnerware line with a rose decal very similar to that of Heather Rose. However, Primrose lacks the sprigs of baby's breath. Primrose was made for Grand Union during the fifties and early sixties.

In addition to the regular E-style dinnerware, a few other pieces have been found. The cake plate, pie baker, and "Rayed" jug are seen most often.

Primrose Backstamp

Primrose	Value
Ashtray	$8.00 – 10.00
Baker, French fluted	$14.00 – 16.00
Bowl, 5¼", fruit	$3.50 – 5.00
Bowl, 6¼", cereal	$7.50 – 8.50
Bowl, 8", flat soup	$10.00 – 12.00
Bowl, 9", salad	$14.00 – 16.00
Bowl, 9¼", oval	$22.00 – 25.00
Cake plate	$15.00 – 18.00
Creamer	$7.00 – 9.00
Cup	$6.00 – 7.00
Jug, "Rayed"	$18.00 – 22.00
Pie baker	$22.00 – 25.00
Plate, 6½"	$2.50 – 3.50
Plate, 7¼"	$5.00 – 6.50
Plate, 9¼"	$7.00 – 8.50
Plate, 10"	$10.00 – 12.00
Platter, 13¼", oval	$22.00 – 25.00
Saucer	$1.00 – 1.50
Sugar and lid	$14.00 – 16.00

Creamer

Sugar & Lid

Pie Baker

Cakeplate

Oval Bowl

Sears own
Granitone
Fine Dinnerware

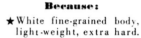

A Four Star Feature Because:

★ White fine-grained body, light-weight, extra hard.

★ Exquisite beauty for your table in a specially designed shape after the ever-popular, clean-cut Duncan Phyfe style.

★ Clear Alabastrone glaze (glass-like outer coating) is extra hard and will not crack.

★ Exclusive at Sears. Almost as fine as True China, yet priced to fit every income. Suitable for any meal—everyday or company.

Granitone was created for Sears by the noted designer, J. Palin Thorley, and made exclusively for Sears by the Hall China Co. Although it was introduced only a year ago, its big public acceptance proves its popularity with homemakers who like to set a beautiful table with dinnerware they know will give good service.

Mount Vernon

Monticello

Richmond

Mount Vernon

● Combination border and wreathed center floral spray
● Costlier because of finer all-over decorations
● Antique 22K Gold trim on every piece

$6.79 32-piece set

Richest of these three patterns. Conventionalized leaf border in blue-green and tan. Inner wreath encircles dainty pink roses in center of plate. Every piece edged, and all handles, knobs and feet trimmed with antique 22K Coin Gold. Dinnerware of outstanding quality!

35 D 04465—State size of set. Mailable.
32-piece set—service for six. Shipping weight, 19 pounds....**$6.79**
Sugar and Creamer Set. Shipping weight, 3 pounds........... 1.93
53-piece set—service for eight. Shipping weight, 37 pounds. 12.95
35 DM 4465—Not mailable.
95-piece set—service for twelve. Shipping weight, 68 pounds. 23.95

Monticello

● Expensive floral border decoration
● All cups and serving dishes fully decorated for dainty beauty

$5.79 32-piece set

Named after Thomas Jefferson's Virginia home. Delicate sprigs of flowers scattered in profusion on each piece. Dainty blue, blue green, pink and yellow colors. A gracious pattern, easy to live with, day after day.

35 D 04464—State size of set. Mailable.
32-piece set—service for six. Shipping weight, 19 pounds....**$5.79**
Sugar and Creamer Set. Shipping weight, 3 pounds............. 1.59
53-piece set—service for eight. Shipping weight, 37 pounds. 10.95
35 DM 4464—Not mailable.
95-piece set—service for twelve. Shipping weight, 68 pounds. 20.95

Richmond

● Dewy fresh cluster of meadow flowers form center decoration

$4.79 32-piece set

For everyday or company. Pink, yellow, blue, brown and green in the spray. Colors selected from fabrics used on Duncan Phyfe furniture.

35 D 04463—State size of set. Mailable.
32-piece set—service for six. Shipping weight, 19 pounds....**$4.79**
Sugar and Creamer Set. Shipping weight, 3 pounds............. 1.44
53-piece set—service for eight. Shipping weight, 37 pounds.. 9.49
35 DM 4463—Not mailable.
95-piece set—service for twelve. Shipping weight, 68 pounds. 17.95
Note: Sugar and Creamer included only in 53- and 95-pc. sets.

Granitone Candle-Sticks

Gleaming white. Gracefully balanced and fluted to match the Granitone shape and patterns. Height, 8½ inches.
35 D 04467—Shipping weight, 4 pounds. ....Pair.**$1.69**

102

Sears' Arlington

9 1/4" Plate

8" Flat Soup

Gravy Boat

5 1/4" Fruit Bowl

Covered Vegetable Bowl

10" Plate

Oval Bowl

Sugar & Lid

Creamer

Cup & Saucer

Arlington is an E-style dinnerware pattern that Hall produced for Sears during the 1950s. Currently, not much of this pattern appears at shows or flea markets. The pattern is characterized by a series of three blue parallel brushstrokes which alternately intersect a winding golden vine. Pieces are nicely accented with gold trim. An example of the backstamp is shown below.

Arlington Dinnerware	Value
Bowl, 5¼", fruit	$3.50 – 4.50
Bowl, 6¼", cereal	$6.50 – 7.50
Bowl, 8", flat soup	$8.00 – 10.00
Bowl, 9¼", oval	$18.00 – 20.00
Bowl, covered vegetable	$30.00 – 35.00
Creamer	$7.00 – 9.00
Cup	$4.00 – 5.00
Gravy boat and underplate	$22.00 – 25.00
Plate, 6½"	$3.00 – 3.50
Plate, 7¼"	$4.50 – 5.50
Plate, 8"	$4.50 – 6.00
Plate, 9¼"	$5.00 – 7.50
Plate, 10"	$6.00 – 8.00
Platter, 11¼", oval	$14.00 – 16.00
Platter, 13¼", oval	$18.00 – 22.00

Arlington Dinnerware	Value
Platter, 15½", oval	$20.00 – 25.00
Saucer	$1.00 – 1.50
Sugar and lid	$14.00 – 16.00

Arlington Backstamp

103

Sears' Fairfax

Fairfax was produced for Sears by Hall during the 1950s and it was sold under the Harmony House label. Fairfax has a white floral pattern with brown leaves in the center of the piece and the pattern is repeated in a narrow band along the edge. A new item in the listing is the covered vegetable bowl.

Fairfax Dinnerware	Value	Fairfax Dinnerware	Value
Bowl, 5¼", fruit	$3.50 – 4.50	Plate, 7¼"	$4.50 – 5.50
Bowl, 6¼", cereal	$6.50 – 8.00	Plate, 8"	$4.50 – 5.50
Bowl, 8", flat soup	$9.00 – 11.00	Plate, 9¼"	$6.50 – 7.50
Bowl, 9¼", oval	$22.00 – 25.00	Plate, 10"	$7.00 – 9.00
Bowl, covered vegetable	$35.00 – 40.00	Platter, 11¼", oval	$14.00 – 16.00
Creamer	$6.00 – 8.00	Platter, 13¼", oval	$22.00 – 24.00
Cup	$4.00 –5.00	Saucer	$1.00 – 2.00
Gravy boat and underplate	$22.00 – 25.00	Sugar and lid	$12.00 – 14.00
Plate, 6½"	$2.50 – 3.50		

Covered Vegetable Bowl

Sugar & Lid

8" Flat Soup

Creamer

Cup & Saucer

Gravy Boat and Underplate

9 1/4" Oval Bowl

10" Plate

13 1/4" Oval Platter

Sears' Monticello

5 1/4" Fruit Bowl

Covered Vegetable Bowl

Cream Soup

Oval Bowl

Cup & Saucer

8" Soup Bowl

Sugar & Lid

Creamer

Gravy Boat & Underplate

6 1/4" Cereal Bowl

11 1/4" Oval Platter

Monticello was introduced in 1941, as a pattern of the Harmony House Granitetone dinnerware line by Sears. This pattern was discontinued in 1959. Granitetone was created for Sears by the noted designer, J. Palin Thorley. The pattern utilized Hall's E-style dinnerware and was named after Thomas Jefferson's Virginia home. According to Sears' ads, it features "flower sprigs in dainty blue, blue-green, pink, and yellow colors scattered in profusion on each piece." A 32-piece service for six sold for $5.79 and was designed to provide the fine china look for a modest price.

Matching style white Granitetone candlesticks without the pattern could also be added to the set. These tall candles sold for $1.69 a pair. Of interest to collectors is a listing in a 1954 Sears' catalog for handled cream soups for $6.25 each. Cream soups are definitely the scarcest item in the Monticello pattern. One of these is shown in the photo above.

Monticello Dinnerware	Value
Bowl, 5¼", fruit	$4.00 – 5.00
Bowl, 6¼", cereal	$7.50 – 9.00
Bowl, 5", cream soup	$80.00 – 90.00
Bowl, 8", flat soup	$10.00 – 12.00
Bowl, 9¼", oval	$22.00 – 25.00
Bowl, covered vegetable	$35.00 – 40.00
Creamer	$7.00 – 9.00
Cup	$5.00 – 6.00
Gravy boat and underplate	$25.00 – 28.00
Plate, 6½"	$3.00 – 4.00
Plate, 8"	$6.50 – 7.50
Plate, 9¼"	$8.00 – 9.00

Monticello Dinnerware	Value
Plate, 10"	$9.00 – 11.00
Platter, 11¼", oval	$18.00 – 20.00
Platter, 13¼", oval	$20.00 – 24.00
Platter, 15½", oval	$25.00 – 30.00
Saucer	$1.00 – 1.50
Sugar and lid	$15.00 – 18.00

Monticello Backstamp

Sears' Mount Vernon

Water Goblet

Cream Soup Bowl

Cup & Saucer

8" Soup Bowl

5 1/4" Fruit Bowl

All-china Coffee Pot

10" Dinner Plate

Sugar & Lid

6 1/4" Cereal Bowl

15 1/2" Oval Platter

Creamer

The Mount Vernon pattern was sold under Sears' Harmony House label. This pattern was offered in the catalog from 1941 through 1959. The style was created by designer J. Palin Thorley and the decoration was the most exquisite of the contemporary designs which Hall produced for Sears. The plate design consists of a blue-green and tan leaf border with an inner wreath of pink roses. Edges, handles, knobs, and feet are trimmed in 22K coin gold.

The eight-cup all-china drip coffee maker shown in the center of the photo was available in this pattern from 1942 to 1948. The coffee maker and 100 paper filters were available for $2.89. Also, a three-piece hostess set which included a creamer and covered sugar with the coffee maker could be purchased for $4.65. Plain white 8½" tall candlesticks which matched the style of the dinnerware were available for $1.69 a pair. There is a listing for a two-handled cream soup bowl in this pattern in a 1954 Sears' catalog. These cream soups are slowly showing up on the secondary market. Mount Vernon pattern crystal could also be ordered from the Sears' catalog.

Dinnerware	Value
Bowl, 5¼", fruit	$4.00 – 6.00
Bowl, 6¼", cereal	$8.00 – 10.00
Bowl, 5", cream soup	$80.00 – 90.00
Bowl, 8", flat soup	$11.00 – 13.00
Bowl, 9¼", oval	$20.00 – 22.00
Casserole and cover	$37.00 – 42.00
Coffee pot, all-china	$200.00 – 225.00
Creamer	$8.00 – 9.00
Cup	$6.00 – 7.00
Gravy boat and underplate	$22.00 – 27.00
Plate, 6½"	$3.50 – 4.50
Plate, 8"	$5.00 – 6.00
Plate, 9¼"	$6.50 – 8.50
Plate, 10"	$11.00 – 13.00
Platter, 11¼", oval	$18.00 – 22.00
Platter, 13¼", oval	$20.00 – 25.00
Platter 15½", oval	$25.00 – 30.00
Saucer	$1.00 – 2.00
Sugar and lid	$15.00 – 18.00

Sears' Richmond/Brown-Eyed Susan

Aladdin Teapot

Sugar & Lid

French Baker

9" Round Vegetable Bowl

Creamer

Covered Vegetable Bowl

8 1/2" "Thick Rim" Bowl

7 1/2" "Thick Rim" Bowl

6" "Thick Rim" Bowl

Richmond and Brown-Eyed Susan are two names for Hall dinnerware with the same decal. The decal consists of a cluster of brown, pink, and yellow meadow flowers which are used as a center decoration. The beauty of the design is enhanced by the use of 22K gold trim. The Richmond design, as selected by Sears, was intended to match the floral decoration of some of the Duncan Phyfe fabric of the period. Richmond had a relatively short life with Sears. It was introduced in 1941 and disappeared from their catalog in 1946.

Later, in the 1960s, this pattern was revived by Hall under the name Brown-Eyed Susan for use by trading stamp companies. Pieces from this later issue will not bear the Harmony House backstamp. During this period, Hall also used this decal on some kitchenware shapes. These additional kitchenware items made later in only the Brown-Eyed Susan era will be indicated by (BES) in the listing below.

Richmond/Brown-Eyed Susan	Value
Baker, French, flute (BES)	$14.00 – 18.00
Bowl, 5¼", fruit	$3.50 – 4.50
Bowl, 6¼", cereal	$7.00 – 8.00
Bowl, 8", flat soup	$7.00 – 9.00
Bowl, 9", salad (BES)	$14.00 – 18.00
Bowl, 9", round, vegetable	$18.00 – 22.00
Bowl, 9¼", oval	$18.00 – 22.00
Bowl, 6", "Thick Rim" (BES)	$10.00 – 12.00
Bowl, 7½", "Thick Rim" (BES)	$12.00 – 14.00
Bowl, 8½", "Thick Rim" (BES)	$15.00 – 18.00
Creamer	$7.00 – 9.00
Cup	$5.00 – 6.50

Richmond/Brown-Eyed Susan	Value
Gravy boat and underplate	$22.00 – 25.00
Jug, "Rayed" (BES)	$16.00 – 19.00
Plate, 6½"	$3.00 – 3.50
Plate, 7¼"	$4.00 – 5.00
Plate, 9¼"	$5.00 – 6.50
Plate, 10"	$7.00 – 9.00
Platter, 11¼", oval	$16.00 – 18.00
Platter, 13¼", oval	$18.00 – 22.00
Platter 15½", oval	$22.00 – 27.00
Saucer	$1.00 – 1.50
Sugar and lid	$13.00 – 15.00
Teapot, Aladdin (BES)	$200.00 – 250.00

EVA ZEISEL SHAPES
Eva Zeisel Designs

Eva Zeisel designed the Tomorrow's Classic and Century shapes which were produced by Hall China. She was essentially working as a free-lance designer while she held a teaching position at Pratt Institute in the early fifties. In 1952, nine decal patterns were created by Zeisel and her associates and students. The ensuing years resulted in the addition of more patterns. However, production problems at Hall led to the acquisition of the molds by the Hollydale Pottery of California in 1957.

The Century shape consists of a dinnerware service which includes 24 pieces. The latest addition to the list of known items is a snack plate with an off-center cup ring. There are four different patterns — white and three decal patterns. Plates consist of slightly distended ovals which are elongated into gently arching tips which also serve as handles. Platters and bowls are slightly elongated with the upward sloping tips forming double handles. The shapes of the teapots, jugs, casseroles, and other accessories are equally modernistic.

The Tomorrow's Classic shape consists of 40 different pieces which comprise a futuristic-looking dinner-ware service. The pieces differ only slightly in style from that used in the Century line. Plates are slight ovals which lack any elongated tips and bowls are essentially ovals which distend to a single elongated tip which forms a handle.

Hallcraft Century Backstamp

CENTURY AND TOMMOROW'S CLASSIC DINNERWARE
Century Fern

The Hallcraft Century Fern pattern consists of 24 pieces of stylized china. The decal is comprised of leaf-like shapes in mulberry, green, and pastel blue set on a lace-like gray background. The interiors of the jugs and cups and the tops of the casserole lids, sugar lids, and teapot lids are glazed in pastel blue. Cups may be found both with the decal and without.

Fern	Value	Fern	Value
Ashtray	$6.00 – 8.00	Ladle	$18.00 – 22.00
Bowl, 5¾", fruit	$5.00 – 6.50	Plate, 6"	$4.00 – 5.00
Bowl, 8", soup/cereal	$7.50 – 8.50	Plate, 8"	$6.50 – 8.00
Bowl, 11¾", salad	$25.00 – 30.00	Plate, snack (with off-center indent)	UND
Bowl, 10½", vegetable	$18.00 – 22.00	Plate, 10¼"	$12.50 – 14.00
Bowl, divided vegetable	$28.00 – 32.00	Platter, 13¾"	$24.00 – 28.00
Butter dish	$85.00 – 125.00	Platter, 15"	$28.00 – 35.00
Casserole	$50.00 – 60.00	Relish, 4-part	$35.00 – 42.00
Creamer	$8.00 – 10.00	Saucer	$1.00 – 1.50
Cup	$6.00 – 7.00	Shaker, ea.	$12.00 – 15.00
Gravy boat	$25.00 – 30.00	Sugar and cover	$14.00 – 16.00
Jug	$28.00 – 32.00	Teapot, 6-cup	$150.00 – 185.00

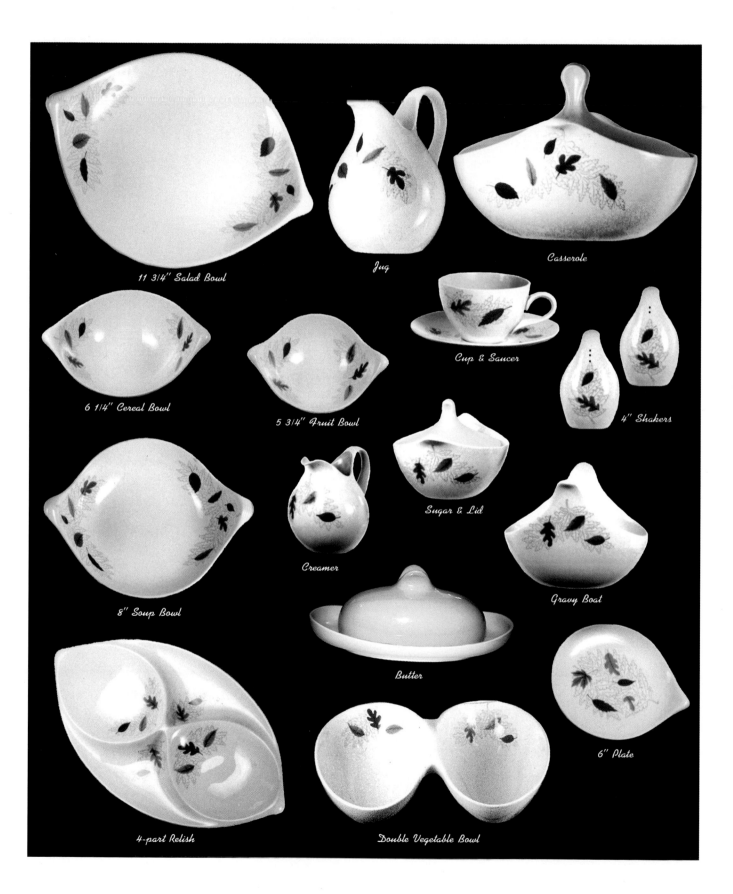

11 3/4" Salad Bowl

Jug

Casserole

6 1/4" Cereal Bowl

5 3/4" Fruit Bowl

Cup & Saucer

4" Shakers

8" Soup Bowl

Creamer

Sugar & Lid

Gravy Boat

Butter

6" Plate

4-part Relish

Double Vegetable Bowl

Garden Of Eden

Butter

Linen Tea Towel

Sunglow

Butter

Although some Century patterns are beginning to appear on the secondary market with regularity, Garden of Eden appears to be in hibernation. This pattern is very scarce in all the parts of the country we frequent. The catalog best describes the decal as "an Oriental fantasy of exotic foliage and tropical birds in warm shades of grey."

The Sunglow pattern of the Hallcraft Century shape consists of a decal that features a thin tree dotted with brilliant yellow leaves. Randomly dispersing yellow leaves also generously adorn the otherwise stark exterior surfaces. The interiors of the jugs and cups and the tops of the casseroles, teapots, and sugar lids are also finished in a matching yellow glaze. Some cups will be found with only the interior yellow glaze, while others will also sport the decal decoration.

Item	Sunglow	Garden of Eden
Ashtray	$7.00 – 9.00	$7.50 – 8.50
Bowl, 5¾", fruit	$6.50 – 7.50	$6.00 – 7.00
Bowl, 8", soup/cereal	$8.00 – 10.00	$8.00 – 10.00
Bowl, 11¾", salad	$28.00 – 32.00	$25.00 – 30.00
Bowl, 10½", vegetable	$22.00 – 27.00	$22.00 – 25.00
Bowl, divided vegetable	$35.00 – 40.00	$30.00 – 35.00
Butter dish	$90.00 – 125.00	$110.00 – 140.00
Casserole	$55.00 – 65.00	$45.00 – 55.00
Creamer	$9.00 – 11.00	$9.00 – 11.00
Cup	$6.50 – 7.50	$6.00 – 7.00
Gravy boat	$32.00 – 37.00	$28.00 – 32.00
Jug	$30.00 – 35.00	$28.00 – 32.00
Ladle	$18.00 – 22.00	$18.00 – 20.00
Plate, 6"	$4.00 – 5.50	$4.00 – 5.00
Plate, 8"	$7.50 – 9.50	$7.00 – 9.00
Plate, snack (with off-center indent)	UND	UND
Plate, 10¼"	$12.00 – 14.00	$11.00 – 13.00
Platter, 13¾"	$25.00 – 30.00	$20.00 – 25.00
Platter, 15"	$32.00 – 37.00	$30.00 – 35.00
Relish, 4-part	$35.00 – 42.00	$30.00 – 35.00
Saucer	$1.00 – 1.50	$1.00 – 1.50
Shaker, ea.	$14.00 – 16.00	$12.00 – 15.00
Sugar and cover	$16.00 – 18.00	$14.00 – 15.00
Teapot, 6-cup	$155.00 – 195.00	$120.00 – 160.00

Teapot

4" Shakers

15" Large Platter

13 3/4" Platter

Gravy Boat

1 1/4 Quart Jug

Ladle

Creamer

Cup & Saucer

10 1/4" Dinner Plate

Vegetable Bowl

Relish Dish

6" Plate

Double Vegetable Bowl

Tomorrow's Classic Arizona and Buckingham

Tomorrow's Classic Arizona pattern features a decal with rust colored leaves set against a white background with traces of fine black lines. The design was originated by Charles Seliger who was an associate of Eva Zeisel. Designer Erik Blegvad was responsible for the creation of the Buckingham pattern. Pieces in this pattern exhibit an iron grill-work fence. The design varies slightly among the various items in the pattern as may be seen in the photograph. The shape of the fence is different and trees will be interspersed in some fences and lacking in others.

Item	Arizona	Buckingham
Ashtray	$7.00 – 9.00	$8.00 – 10.00
Bowl, 5¾", fruit	$6.00 – 7.00	$7.00 – 8.00
Bowl, 6", cereal	$8.00 – 10.00	$8.00 – 10.00
Bowl, 9", coupe soup	$8.50 – 10.00	$9.00 – 11.00
Bowl, 8¾", sq. open vegetable	$22.00 – 25.00	$26.00 – 28.00
Bowl, 14½", large salad	$32.00 – 37.00	$35.00 – 45.00
Bowl, 11 oz., open baker	$18.00 – 22.00	$20.00 – 24.00
Bowl, oval, celery	$18.00 – 22.00	$22.00 – 24.00
Bowl, large, ftd. fruit	$35.00 – 40.00	$40.00 – 45.00
Butter dish	$145.00 – 175.00	$160.00 –190.00
Candlestick, 4½"	$28.00 – 32.00	$30.00 – 35.00
Candlestick, 8"	$35.00 – 40.00	$40.00 – 45.00
Casserole, 1¼ qt	$32.00 – 37.00	$35.00 – 40.00
Casserole, 2 qt.	$45.00 – 55.00	$55.00 – 65.00
Coffee pot, 6-cup	$90.00 – 110.00	$100.00 – 120.00
Creamer	$10.00 – 12.00	$12.00 – 14.00
Creamer, a.d.	$10.00 – 12.00	$14.00 – 16.00
Cup	$8.00 – 10.00	$9.00 – 11.00
Cup, a.d.	$22.00 – 25.00	$22.00 – 27.50
Egg cup	$45.00 – 47.00	$50.00 – 55.00
Gravy boat	$35.00 – 40.00	$42.00 – 45.00
Jug, 1¼ qt.	$25.00 – 32.00	$32.00 – 37.00
Jug, 3 qt	$30.00 – 37.00	$40.00 – 47.00
Ladle	$18.00 – 22.00	$20.00 – 25.00
Marmite and cover	$27.00 – 32.00	$32.00 – 35.00
Onion soup and cover	$35.00 – 37.00	$37.00 – 42.00
Plate, 6"	$4.00 – 5.50	$4.50 – 6.00
Plate, 8"	$7.50 – 8.50	$8.50 – 9.50
Plate, 11"	$11.00 – 13.00	$12.00 – 14.00
Platter, 12¼"	$20.00 – 22.00	$22.00 – 27.00
Platter, 15"	$30.00 – 35.00	$32.00 – 37.00
Platter, 17"	$34.00 – 38.00	$35.00 – 40.00
Saucer	$1.00 – 1.50	$1.50 – 2.50
Saucer, a.d.	$3.00 – 3.50	$4.00 – 4.50
Shaker, ea.	$14.00 – 16.00	$15.00 – 18.00
Sugar and cover	$18.00 – 20.00	$20.00 – 22.00
Sugar, open a.d.	$10.00 – 12.00	$14.00 – 16.00
Teapot, 6-cup	$175.00 – 195.00	$195.00 – 210.00
Vase	$65.00 – 75.00	$80.00 – 95.00
Vinegar bottle	$65.00 – 75.00	$80.00 – 95.00

Arizona

Marmite & Cover

Ashtray

Gravy Boat

1 1/4 Quart Jug

Buckingham

Teapot

Egg Cup

1 1/4 Quart Jug

Square Open Vegetable Bowl

Coupe Soup Bowl

Tomorrow's Classic Bouquet

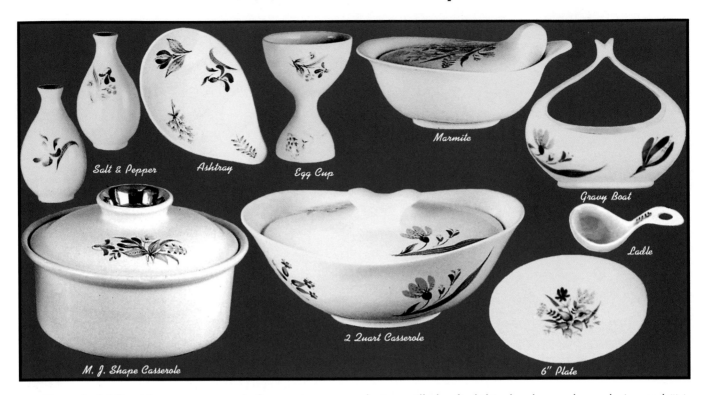

Salt & Pepper   Ashtray   Egg Cup   Marmite   Gravy Boat   Ladle

M. J. Shape Casserole   2 Quart Casserole   6" Plate

The colorful floral Bouquet pattern is the most popular of the Eva Zeisel designs among collectors. This pattern is also the most readily available of all the Hallcraft designs. In addition to the 40 pieces of Classic shape, collectors will also find this decal on a shape designated "M. J." by some researchers. The "M. J." casserole and electric percolator are shown in the photographs.

Bouquet	Value
Ashtray	$11.00 – 13.00
Bowl, 5¾", fruit	$6.00 – 7.00
Bowl, 6", cereal	$8.50 – 10.00
Bowl, 9", coupe soup	$14.00 – 16.00
Bowl, 8¾", sq. open vegetable	$25.00 – 30.00
Bowl, 14½", large salad	$35.00 – 45.00
Bowl, 11 oz., open baker	$20.00 – 25.00
Bowl, oval, celery	$25.00 – 30.00
Bowl, large, ftd. fruit	$60.00 – 75.00
Butter dish	$185.00 – 210.00
Candlestick, 4½"	$35.00 – 45.00
Candlestick, 8"	$40.00 – 50.00
Casserole, 1¼ qt.	$40.00 – 45.00
Casserole, 2 qt.	$55.00 – 65.00
Casserole, "M. J."	$45.00 – 50.00
Coffee pot, 6-cup	$95.00 – 120.00
Creamer	$12.00 – 14.00
Creamer, a.d.	$14.00 – 16.00
Cup	$9.00 – 11.00
Cup, a.d.	$20.00 – 25.00
Egg cup	$55.00 – 60.00
Gravy boat	$40.00 – 45.00

Bouquet	Value
Jug, 1¼ qt.	$30.00 – 35.00
Jug, 3 qt.	$40.00 – 45.00
Ladle	$20.00 – 25.00
Marmite and cover	$32.00 – 37.00
Mug, Tom & Jerry	$18.00 – 22.00
Onion soup and cover	$40.00 – 45.00
Percolator, electric "M. J."	$140.00 – 165.00
Plate, 6"	$4.50 – 5.00
Plate, 8"	$8.00 – 9.50
Plate, 11"	$14.00 – 16.00
Platter, 12¼"	$28.00 – 30.00
Platter, 15"	$30.00 – 35.00
Platter, 17"	$40.00 – 45.00
Saucer	$1.50 – 2.50
Saucer, a.d.	$2.00 – 3.00
Shaker, ea.	$15.00 – 20.00
Sugar and cover	$18.00 – 22.00
Sugar, open a.d.	$14.00 – 16.00
Teapot, 6-cup	$185.00 – 215.00
Teapot, Thorley "Grape"	$225.00 – 250.00
Vase	$80.00 – 95.00
Vinegar bottle	$80.00 – 95.00

Coffee Pot

Electric Percolator

Teapot

Creamer

Sugar & Lid

1 1/4 Quart Jug

8 3/4" Square Vegetable Bowl

A. D. Sugar

A. D. Creamer

Butter

5 3/4" Fruit Bowl

Cup & Saucer

4 1/2" Candleholder

11" Dinner

Celery

Coupe Soup

15" Platter

Tomorrow's Classic Caprice and Dawn

Caprice is a Tomorrow's Classic leaf and floral design. The colors are pastel pinks, grays, and yellows. Discerning the pattern on some of the smaller pieces is sometimes confusing since only one part of the pattern often appears on the piece. Dawn is an interesting creation featuring a sunburst with thin black lines adorned with speckles of coral.

Item	Caprice	Dawn
Ashtray	$7.50 – 9.00	$8.00 – 10.00
Bowl, 5¾", fruit	$6.00 – 7.00	$7.00 – 8.00
Bowl, 6", cereal	$8.00 – 10.00	$8.00 – 10.00
Bowl, 9", coupe soup	$8.50 – 10.00	$9.00 – 11.00
Bowl, 8¾", sq. open vegetable	$22.00 – 25.00	$26.00 – 28.00
Bowl, 14½", large salad	$32.00 – 37.00	$35.00 – 45.00
Bowl, 11 oz., open baker	$18.00 – 22.00	$20.00 – 24.00
Bowl, oval, celery	$18.00 – 22.00	$22.00 – 24.00
Bowl, large, ftd. fruit	$35.00 – 40.00	$40.00 – 45.00
Butter dish	$140.00 – 160.00	$160.00 –190.00
Candlestick, 4½"	$28.00 – 32.00	$30.00 – 35.00
Candlestick, 8"	$35.00 – 40.00	$40.00 – 45.00
Casserole, 1¼ qt.	$32.00 – 37.00	$35.00 – 40.00
Casserole, 2 qt.	$45.00 – 55.00	$55.00 – 65.00
Coffee pot, 6-cup	$90.00 – 110.00	$100.00 – 120.00
Creamer	$10.00 – 12.00	$12.00 – 14.00
Creamer, a.d.	$10.00 – 12.00	$14.00 – 16.00
Cup	$8.00 – 10.00	$9.00 – 11.00
Cup, a.d.	$22.00 – 25.00	$22.00 – 27.50
Egg cup	$45.00 – 47.00	$50.00 – 55.00
Gravy boat	$35.00 – 40.00	$42.00 – 45.00
Jug, 1¼ qt.	$25.00 – 32.00	$32.00 – 37.00
Jug, 3 qt.	$30.00 – 37.00	$40.00 – 47.00
Ladle	$18.00 – 22.00	$20.00 – 25.00
Marmite and cover	$27.00 – 32.00	$32.00 – 35.00
Onion soup and cover	$35.00 – 37.00	$37.00 – 42.00
Plate, 6"	$4.00 – 5.50	$4.50 – 6.00
Plate, 8"	$7.50 – 8.50	$8.50 – 9.50
Plate, 11"	$11.00 – 13.00	$12.00 – 14.00
Platter, 12¼"	$20.00 – 22.00	$22.00 – 27.00
Platter, 15"	$30.00 – 35.00	$32.00 – 37.00
Platter, 17"	$34.00 – 38.00	$35.00 – 40.00
Saucer	$1.00 – 1.50	$1.50 – 2.50
Saucer, a.d.	$3.00 – 3.50	$4.00 – 4.50
Shaker, ea.	$14.00 – 16.00	$15.00 – 18.00
Sugar and cover	$18.00 – 20.00	$20.00 – 22.00
Sugar, open a.d.	$10.00 – 12.00	$14.00 – 16.00
Teapot, 6-cup	$175.00 – 195.00	$195.00 – 210.00
Vase	$65.00 – 75.00	$80.00 – 95.00
Vinegar bottle	$65.00 – 75.00	$80.00 – 95.00

Caprice

3 Quart Jug

1 1/4" Jug

Teapot

Sugar & Lid

Creamer

A.D. Creamer

5 3/4" Fruit

6 " Cereal

A.D. Sugar

Cup & Saucer

Coupe Soup

11" Dinner Plate

4 1/2" Candleholder

Salad Plate

Vinegar Bottle

Celery

Dawn

Ladle

Gravy Boat

15" Platter

117

Tomorrow's Classic Fantasy and Flair

Fantasy is a Hallcraft Tomorrow's Classic design expounding thin line intertwined parabolas to produce a modernistic effect. The design was created by Douglas Kelley, W. Katavolos, and Ross Littell who were Pratt Institute students of Eva Zeisel.

The Hallcraft Flair design features intertwining delicate turquoise blossoms with a gray scroll-like design. Obtaining this pattern is challenging for collectors.

Item	Fantasy	Flair
Ashtray	$7.00 – 9.00	$8.00 – 10.00
Bowl, 5¾", fruit	$6.00 – 7.00	$7.00 – 8.00
Bowl, 6", cereal	$8.00 – 10.00	$8.00 – 10.00
Bowl, 9", coupe soup	$8.50 – 10.00	$9.00 – 11.00
Bowl, 8¾", sq. open vegetable	$22.00 – 25.00	$26.00 – 28.00
Bowl, 14½", large salad	$32.00 – 37.00	$35.00 – 45.00
Bowl, 11 oz., open baker	$18.00 – 22.00	$20.00 – 24.00
Bowl, oval, celery	$18.00 – 22.00	$22.00 – 24.00
Bowl, large, ftd. fruit	$35.00 – 40.00	$40.00 – 45.00
Butter dish	$165.00 – 185.00	$170.00 – 190.00
Candlestick, 4½"	$28.00 – 32.00	$30.00 – 35.00
Candlestick, 8"	$35.00 – 40.00	$40.00 – 45.00
Casserole, 1¼ qt.	$32.00 – 37.00	$35.00 – 40.00
Casserole, 2 qt.	$45.00 – 55.00	$55.00 – 65.00
Coffee pot, 6-cup	$80.00 – 100.00	$100.00 – 120.00
Creamer	$10.00 – 12.00	$12.00 – 14.00
Creamer, a.d.	$10.00 – 12.00	$14.00 – 16.00
Cup	$8.00 – 10.00	$9.00 – 11.00
Cup, a.d.	$22.00 – 25.00	$22.00 – 27.50
Egg cup	$45.00 – 47.00	$50.00 – 55.00
Gravy boat	$35.00 – 40.00	$42.00 – 45.00
Jug, 1¼ qt.	$25.00 – 32.00	$32.00 – 37.00
Jug, 3 qt.	$30.00 – 37.00	$40.00 – 47.00
Ladle	$18.00 – 22.00	$20.00 – 25.00
Marmite and cover	$27.00 – 32.00	$32.00 – 35.00
Onion soup and cover	$35.00 – 37.00	$37.00 – 42.00
Plate, 6"	$4.00 – 5.50	$4.50 – 6.00
Plate, 8"	$7.50 – 8.50	$8.50 – 9.50
Plate, 11"	$11.00 – 13.00	$12.00 – 14.00
Platter, 12¼"	$20.00 – 22.00	$22.00 – 27.00
Platter, 15"	$30.00 – 35.00	$32.00 – 37.00
Platter, 17"	$34.00 – 38.00	$35.00 – 40.00
Saucer	$1.00 – 1.50	$1.50 – 2.50
Saucer, a.d.	$3.00 – 3.50	$4.00 – 4.50
Shaker, ea.	$14.00 – 16.00	$15.00 – 18.00
Sugar and cover	$18.00 – 20.00	$20.00 – 22.00
Sugar, open a.d.	$10.00 – 12.00	$14.00 – 16.00
Teapot, 6-cup	$175.00 – 195.00	$195.00 – 210.00
Vase	$65.00 – 75.00	$80.00 – 95.00
Vinegar bottle	$65.00 – 75.00	$80.00 – 95.00

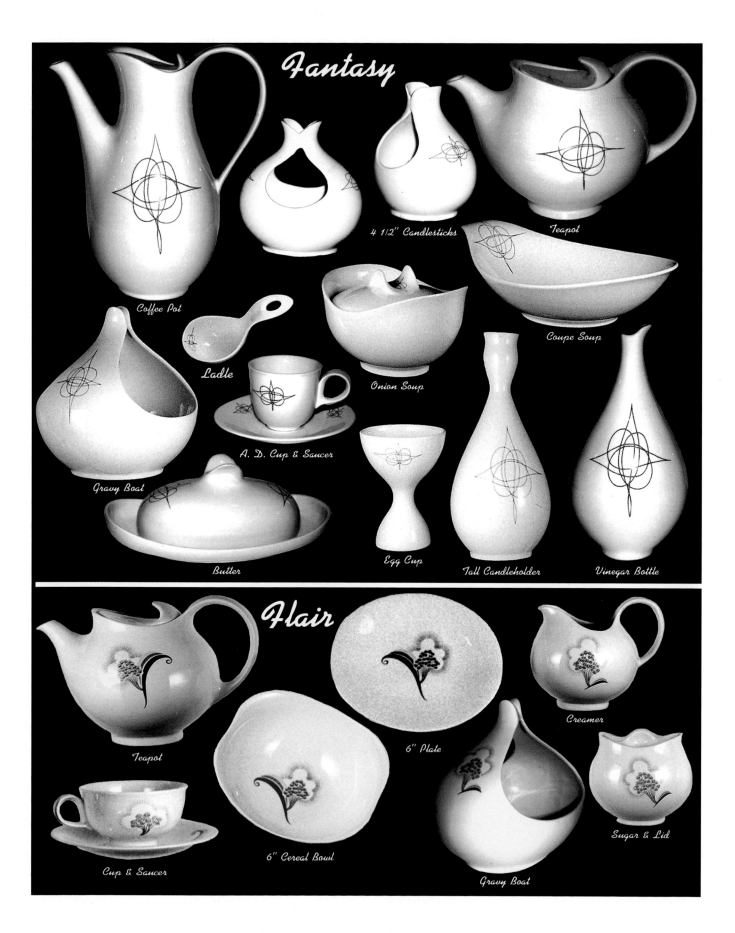

Fantasy

Coffee Pot

4 1/2" Candlesticks

Teapot

Ladle

Onion Soup

Coupe Soup

Gravy Boat

A. D. Cup & Saucer

Butter

Egg Cup

Tall Candleholder

Vinegar Bottle

Flair

Teapot

6" Plate

Creamer

Cup & Saucer

6" Cereal Bowl

Gravy Boat

Sugar & Lid

Tomorrow's Classic Frost Flowers and Harlequin

Coffee Pot

11" Plate

Teapot

Cup & Saucer

5 1/4" Fruit Bowl

Celery

6" Plate

Gravy Boat

Onion Soup

2 Quart Covered Casserole

The Tomorrow's Classic Frost Flowers pattern shown above consists of a generous adornment of sprigs of blue flowers. The design was created by Eva Zeisel's assistant, Irene Haas.

The Harlequin pattern shown on the next page uses a series of abstract pink, gray, and black lines to produce a decoration. Notice in the photograph other shapes than those associated with Hallcraft will be found with this decoration.

Item	Frost Flowers	Harlequin
Ashtray	$7.50 – 9.00	$8.00 – 10.00
Ball jug, #3		$160.00 – 190.00
Bowl, 5¾", fruit	$6.00 – 7.00	$7.00 – 8.00
Bowl, 6", cereal	$8.00 – 10.00	$8.00 – 10.00
Bowl, 9", coupe soup	$8.50 – 10.00	$9.00 – 11.00
Bowl, 8¾", sq. open vegetable	$22.00 – 25.00	26.00 – 28.00
Bowl, 14½", large salad	$32.00 – 37.00	$35.00 – 45.00
Bowl, 11 oz., open baker	$18.00 – 22.00	$20.00 – 24.00
Bowl, oval, celery	$18.00 – 22.00	$22.00 – 24.00
Bowl, large, ftd. fruit	$35.00 – 40.00	$40.00 – 45.00
Butter dish	$140.00 – 160.00	$160.00 – 190.00
Candlestick, 4½"	$28.00 – 32.00	$30.00 – 35.00
Candlestick, 8"	$35.00 – 40.00	$40.00 – 45.00
Casserole, 1¼ qt.	$32.00 – 37.00	$35.00 – 40.00
Casserole, 2 qt.	$45.00 – 55.00	$55.00 – 65.00

Item	Frost Flowers	Harlequin
Coffee pot, 6-cup	$90.00 – 110.00	$100.00 – 120.00
Cookie jar, Zeisel-style		$250.00 – 300.00
Creamer	$10.00 – 12.00	$12.00 – 14.00
Creamer, a.d.	$10.00 – 12.00	$14.00 – 16.00
Cup	$8.00 – 10.00	$9.00 – 11.00
Cup, a.d.	$22.00 – 25.00	$22.00 – 27.50
Egg cup	$45.00 – 47.00	$50.00 – 55.00
Gravy boat	$35.00 – 40.00	$42.00 – 45.00
Jug, 1¼ qt.	$25.00 – 32.00	$32.00 – 37.00
Jug, 3 qt.	$30.00 – 37.00	$40.00 – 47.00
Ladle	$18.00 – 22.00	$20.00 – 25.00
Marmite and cover	$27.00 – 32.00	$32.00 – 35.00
Onion soup and cover	$35.00 – 37.00	$37.00 – 42.00
Plate, 6"	$4.00 – 5.50	$4.50 – 6.00
Plate, 8"	$7.50 – 8.50	$8.50 – 9.50
Plate, 11"	$11.00 – 13.00	$12.00 – 14.00
Platter, 12¼"	$20.00 – 22.00	$22.00 – 27.00
Platter, 15"	$30.00 – 35.00	$32.00 – 37.00
Platter, 17"	$34.00 – 38.00	$35.00 – 40.00
Saucer	$1.00 – 1.50	$1.50 – 2.50
Saucer, a.d.	$3.00 – 3.50	$4.00 – 4.50
Shaker, ea.	$14.00 – 16.00	$15.00 – 18.00
Sugar and cover	$18.00 – 20.00	$20.00 – 22.00
Sugar, open a.d.	$10.00 – 12.00	$14.00 – 16.00
Teapot, 6-cup	$175.00 – 195.00	$195.00 – 210.00
Teapot, Thorley		$250.00 – 300.00
Vase	$65.00 – 75.00	$80.00 – 95.00
Vinegar bottle	$65.00 – 75.00	$80.00 – 95.00

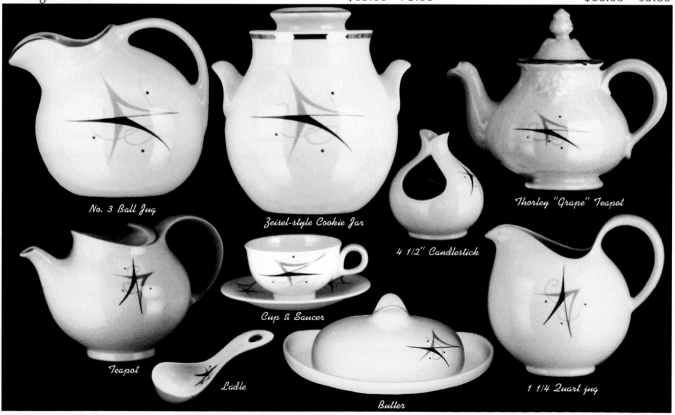

No. 3 Ball Jug

Zeisel-style Cookie Jar

Thorley "Grape" Teapot

4 1/2" Candlestick

Cup & Saucer

Teapot

Ladle

Butter

1 1/4 Quart Jug

Tomorrow's Classic Holiday

The Holiday pattern features an almost gaudy combination of red and black colors used to produce a leaf-like design.

Holiday	Value
Ashtray	$8.00 – 11.50
Bowl, 5¾", fruit	$8.00 – 10.00
Bowl, 6", cereal	$9.00 – 11.00
Bowl, 9", coupe soup	$10.00 – 12.00
Bowl, 8¾", sq. open vegetable	$26.00 – 28.00
Bowl, 14½", large salad	$35.00 – 40.00
Bowl, 11 oz., open baker	$20.00 – 25.00
Bowl, oval, celery	$22.00 – 25.00
Bowl, large, ftd. fruit	$40.00 – 45.00
Butter dish	$180.00 – 210.00
Candlestick, 4½"	$30.00 – 35.00
Candlestick, 8"	$40.00 – 45.00
Casserole, 1¼ qt.	$35.00 – 40.00
Casserole, 2 qt.	$50.00 – 60.00
Coffee pot, 6-cup	$100.00 – 120.00
Creamer	$12.00 – 14.00
Creamer, a.d.	$14.00 – 16.00
Cup	$9.00 – 11.00
Cup, a.d.	$22.00 – 27.00
Egg cup	$50.00 – 60.00
Gravy boat	$40.00 – 45.00
Jug, 1¼ qt.	$32.00 – 35.00
Jug, 3 qt.	$37.00 – 40.00
Ladle	$18.00 – 22.00
Marmite and cover	$32.00 – 35.00
Onion soup and cover	$37.00 – 40.00
Plate, 6"	$4.00 – 5.00
Plate, 8"	$8.00 – 9.00
Plate, 11"	$10.00 – 12.00
Platter, 12¼"	$22.00 – 25.00
Platter, 15"	$30.00 – 35.00
Platter, 17"	$35.00 – 40.00
Saucer	$1.00 – 2.00
Saucer, a.d.	$2.50 – 3.50
Shaker, ea.	$15.00 – 18.00
Sugar and cover	$20.00 – 22.00
Sugar, open a.d.	$12.00 – 14.00
Teapot, 6-cup	$195.00 – 225.00
Vase	$80.00 – 90.00
Vinegar bottle	$80.00 – 90.00

Gravy Boat

11" plate

1 1/4 Quart Covered Casserole

6" Cereal Bowl

8" Plate

Teapot

Cup & Saucer

Sugar & Lid

Coupe Soup

5 3/4" Fruit Bowl

A. D. Cup & Saucer

A. D. Creamer

8 3/4" Square Open Vegetable

6" Plate

Coffee Pot

Ladle

12 1/4" Platter

Tomorrow's Classic Lyric and Mulberry

Mulberry

3 Quart Jug

Celery

Cup and Saucer

Coffee Pot

1 1/4 Quart Casserole

Salt & Pepper

11" Plate

Coupe Soup

Covered Onion Soup

5 3/4" Fruit Bowl

Sugar & Lid

Creamer

Gravy Boat

Ladle

8 3/4" Square Open Vegetable

Ashtray

15" Platter

Teapot

Lyric is a Hallcraft pattern which features an abstract chartreuse and black border design. It is proving to be one of the harder-to-find Hallcraft patterns.

The Hallcraft Mulberry pattern decal consists of a branch with green leaves laden with purple mulberries.

Collectors should be able to find most pieces of this pattern with a bit of diligent searching.

Item	Lyric	Mulberry
Ashtray	$8.50 – 10.00	$8.00 – 10.00
Bowl, 5¾", fruit	$6.00 – 7.00	$7.00 – 8.00
Bowl, 6", cereal	$8.00 – 10.00	$8.00 – 10.00
Bowl, 9", coupe soup	$8.50 – 11.00	$9.00 – 11.00
Bowl, 8¾", sq. open vegetable	$24.00 – 28.00	$26.00 – 28.00
Bowl, 14½", large salad	$35.00 – 42.00	$35.00 – 45.00
Bowl, 11 oz., open baker	$20.00 – 22.00	$20.00 – 24.00
Bowl, oval, celery	$20.00 – 24.00	$22.00 – 24.00
Bowl, large, ftd. fruit	$40.00 – 45.00	$40.00 – 45.00
Butter dish	$150.00 – 170.00	$150.00 –175.00
Candlestick, 4½"	$28.00 – 32.00	$28.00 – 32.00

Item	Lyric	Mulberry
Candlestick, 8"	$35.00 – 40.00	$37.00 – 42.00
Casserole, 1¼ qt.	$32.00 – 37.00	$35.00 – 40.00
Casserole, 2 qt.	$45.00 – 55.00	$45.00 – 55.00
Coffee pot, 6-cup	$90.00 – 110.00	$90.00 – 110.00
Creamer	$11.00 – 13.00	$12.00 – 14.00
Creamer, a.d.	$11.00 – 13.00	$14.00 – 16.00
Cup	$8.00 – 10.00	$9.00 – 11.00
Cup, a.d.	$22.00 – 25.00	$22.00 – 27.50
Egg cup	$50.00 – 55.00	$50.00 – 55.00
Gravy boat	$35.00 – 40.00	$35.00 – 40.00
Jug, 1¼ qt.	$25.00 – 32.00	$32.00 – 35.00
Jug, 3 qt.	$30.00 – 37.00	$37.00 – 42.00
Ladle	$18.00 – 22.00	$20.00 – 22.00
Marmite and cover	$27.00 – 32.00	$32.00 – 35.00
Onion soup and cover	$35.00 – 37.00	$37.00 – 42.00
Plate, 6"	$4.00 – 5.50	$4.50 – 6.00
Plate, 8"	$7.50 – 8.50	$8.50 – 9.50
Plate, 11"	$11.00 – 13.00	$11.00 – 13.00
Platter, 12¼"	$20.00 – 22.00	$22.00 – 25.00
Platter, 15"	$30.00 – 35.00	$32.00 – 37.00
Platter, 17"	$34.00 – 38.00	$35.00 – 40.00
Saucer	$1.00 – 1.50	$1.50 – 2.50
Saucer, a.d.	$3.00 – 3.50	$4.00 – 4.50
Shaker, ea.	$14.00 – 16.00	$15.00 – 18.00
Sugar and cover	$18.00 – 20.00	$20.00 – 22.00
Sugar, open a.d.	$11.00 – 13.00	$14.00 – 16.00
Teapot, 6-cup	$175.00 – 195.00	$195.00 – 210.00
Vase	$65.00 – 75.00	$70.00 – 80.00
Vinegar bottle	$65.00 – 75.00	$70.00 – 80.00

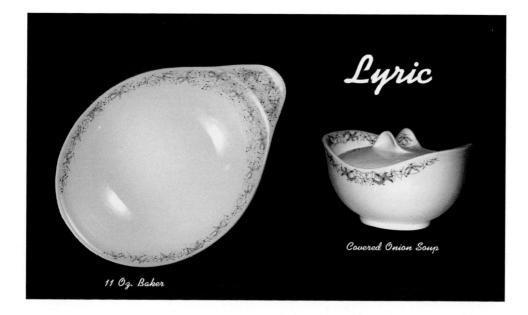

11 Oz. Baker

Lyric

Covered Onion Soup

Tomorrow's Classic Peach Blossom

The Peach Blossom decal is a branch-like decal which has green leaves and pastel pink flowers and flower buds. E-style dinnerware has also been found in this pattern. An example is the E-style oval bowl shown in the picture.

Peach Blossom E-Style Dinnerware	Value
Bowl, 5¼", fruit	$5.50 – 6.50
Bowl, 9", round vegetable	$22.00 – 27.00
Bowl, oval	$22.00 – 27.00
Cup	$9.00 – 11.00
Plate, 6"	$3.50 – 4.00
Plate, 7¼"	$5.50 – 6.50
Plate, 9¼"	$8.50 – 9.50
Platter, 11¼"	$22.00 – 25.00
Saucer	$1.00 – 1.50

Peach Blossom—Tomorrow's Classic	Value
Ashtray	$7.50 – 9.00
Bowl, 5¾", fruit	$5.50 – 6.50
Bowl, 6", cereal	$8.00 – 10.00
Bowl, 9", coupe soup	$9.00 – 11.00
Bowl, 8¾", sq. open vegetable	$22.00 – 25.00
Bowl, 14½", large salad	$30.00 – 35.00
Bowl, 11 oz., open baker	$18.00 – 22.00
Bowl, oval, celery	$20.00 – 24.00
Bowl, large, ftd. fruit	$35.00 – 40.00
Butter dish	$140.00 – 180.00
Candlestick, 4½"	$28.00 – 30.00
Candlestick, 8"	$35.00 – 40.00
Casserole, 1¼ qt.	$32.00 – 35.00
Casserole, 2 qt.	$45.00 – 50.00
Coffee pot, 6-cup	$85.00 – 105.00

Peach Blossom—Tomorrow's Classic	Value
Creamer	$11.50 – 13.00
Creamer, a.d.	$11.00 – 13.00
Cup	$6.00 – 7.00
Cup, a.d.	$22.00 – 27.50
Egg cup	$42.00 – 45.00
Gravy boat	$32.00 – 35.00
Jug, 1¼ qt.	$25.00 – 28.00
Jug, 3 qt.	$30.00 – 35.00
Ladle	$18.00 – 22.00
Marmite and cover	$25.00 – 27.00
Onion soup and cover	$32.00 – 35.00
Plate, 6"	$4.50 – 5.50
Plate, 8"	$7.50 – 9.50
Plate, 11"	$11.00 – 13.00
Platter, 12¼"	$22.00 – 28.00
Platter, 15"	$28.00 – 32.00
Platter, 17"	$32.00 – 38.00
Saucer	$1.50 – 2.00
Saucer, a.d.	$2.00 – 3.00
Shaker, ea.	$17.00 – 19.00
Sugar and cover	$20.00 – 22.00
Sugar, open a.d.	$11.00 – 13.00
Teapot, 6-cup	$170.00 – 190.00
Vase	$65.00 – 75.00
Vinegar bottle	$65.00 – 75.00

Tomorrow's Classic Pinecone

Teapot

Flagon-style Mug

Gravy Boat

A.D. Creamer

A.D. Sugar

Coupe Soup

Demi Cup & Saucer

2 Quart Casserole

8 3/4" Square Open Vegetable

Pinecone E-style dinnerware was produced for Grand Union during the fifties. A 16-piece starter set was available for only $7.95. In addition, the decal was also used on Hallcraft Tomorrow's Classic shape pieces. The mug shown in the picture is an accessory piece which may be found in this pattern. Notice the gold trim around the top and at the base.

Pinecone — E-style Dinnerware	Value
Bowl, 5¼", fruit	$5.50 – 6.50
Bowl, 9", round vegetable	$22.00 – 27.00
Cup	$9.00 – 11.00
Plate, 6"	$3.50 – 4.00
Plate, 7¼"	$5.50 – 6.50
Plate, 9¼"	$8.50 – 9.50
Platter, 11¼"	$22.00 – 25.00
Saucer	$1.00 – 1.50
Tidbit, 3-tier	$55.00 – 65.00
Mug	$22.00 – 27.00

3 Tiered Tidbit

Coffee Pot

Cup & Saucer

Marmite

11" Platter

Pinecone—Tomorrow's Classic	Value	Pinecone—Tomorrow's Classic	Value
Ashtray	$7.50 – 9.00	Gravy boat	$32.00 – 35.00
Bowl, 5¾", fruit	$5.50 – 6.50	Jug, 1¼ qt.	$25.00 – 28.00
Bowl, 6", cereal	$8.00 – 10.00	Jug, 3 qt.	$30.00 – 35.00
Bowl, 9", coupe soup	$9.00 – 11.00	Ladle	$18.00 – 22.00
Bowl, 8¾", sq. open vegetable	$22.00 – 25.00	Marmite and cover	$25.00 – 27.00
Bowl, 14½", large salad	$30.00 – 35.00	Onion soup and cover	$32.00 – 35.00
Bowl, 11 oz., open baker	$18.00 – 22.00	Plate, 6"	$4.50 – 5.50
Bowl, oval, celery	$20.00 – 24.00	Plate, 8"	$7.50 – 9.50
Bowl, large, ftd. fruit	$35.00 – 40.00	Plate, 11"	$11.00 – 13.00
Butter dish	$140.00 – 180.00	Platter, 12¼"	$22.00 – 28.00
Candlestick, 4½"	$28.00 – 30.00	Platter, 15"	$28.00 – 32.00
Candlestick, 8"	$35.00 – 40.00	Platter, 17"	$32.00 – 38.00
Casserole, 1¼ qt.	$32.00 – 35.00	Saucer	$1.50 – 2.00
Casserole, 2 qt.	$45.00 – 50.00	Saucer, a.d.	$2.00 – 3.00
Coffee pot, 6-cup	$85.00 – 105.00	Shaker, ea.	$17.00 – 19.00
Creamer	$11.50 – 13.00	Sugar and cover	$20.00 – 22.00
Creamer, a.d.	$11.00 – 13.00	Sugar, open a.d.	$11.00 – 13.00
Cup	$6.00 – 7.00	Teapot, 6-cup	$170.00 – 190.00
Cup, a.d.	$22.00 – 27.50	Vase	$65.00 – 75.00
Egg cup	$42.00 – 45.00	Vinegar bottle	$65.00 – 75.00

Tomorrow's Classic Spring and Studio 10

Tomorrow's Classic Spring pattern features a pastel color floral arrangement. Pink, turquoise, and green are deftly interwoven to provide a soft pleasing pattern.

Studio 10 is an elusive pattern that incorporates modernistic shapes in shades of gray.

Spring/Studio 10	Value	Spring/Studio 10	Value
Ashtray	$7.50 – 9.00	Gravy boat	$32.00 – 35.00
Bowl, 5¾", fruit	$5.50 – 6.50	Jug, 1¼ qt.	$25.00 – 28.00
Bowl, 6", cereal	$8.00 – 10.00	Jug, 3 qt.	$30.00 – 35.00
Bowl, 9", coupe soup	$9.00 – 11.00	Ladle	$18.00 – 22.00
Bowl, 8¾", sq. open vegetable	$22.00 – 25.00	Marmite and cover	$25.00 – 27.00
Bowl, 14½", large salad	$30.00 – 35.00	Onion soup and cover	$32.00 – 35.00
Bowl, 11 oz., open baker	$18.00 – 22.00	Plate, 6"	$4.50 – 5.50
Bowl, oval, celery	$20.00 – 24.00	Plate, 8"	$7.50 – 9.50
Bowl, large, ftd. fruit	$35.00 – 40.00	Plate, 11"	$11.00 – 13.00
Butter dish	$140.00 – 180.00	Platter, 12¼"	$22.00 – 28.00
Candlestick, 4½"	$28.00 – 30.00	Platter, 15"	$28.00 – 32.00
Candlestick, 8"	$35.00 – 40.00	Platter, 17"	$32.00 – 38.00
Casserole, 1¼ qt.	$32.00 – 35.00	Saucer	$1.50 – 2.00
Casserole, 2 qt.	$45.00 – 50.00	Saucer, a.d.	$2.00 – 3.00
Coffee pot, 6-cup	$85.00 – 105.00	Shaker, ea.	$17.00 – 19.00
Creamer	$11.50 – 13.00	Sugar and cover	$20.00 – 22.00
Creamer, a.d.	$11.00 – 13.00	Sugar, open a.d.	$11.00 – 13.00
Cup	$6.00 – 7.00	Teapot, 6-cup	$170.00 – 190.00
Cup, a.d.	$22.00 – 27.50	Vase	$65.00 – 75.00
Egg cup	$42.00 – 45.00	Vinegar bottle	$65.00 – 75.00

Tomorrow's Classic Satin Black and Hi-White

Hall sold Tomorrow's Classic in Hi-White without any decal or gold decoration and in Satin Black. The Satin Black teapot and coffee pot have Hi-White lids. Both colors are difficult to find.

The butter pictured at the top right is an unknown decal that collectors are calling "Poinciana." Note the base has a matching decal.

Satin Black/Hi-White	Value
Ashtray	$11.00 – 13.00
Bowl, 5¾", fruit	$6.00 – 7.00
Bowl, 6", cereal	$8.50 – 10.00
Bowl, 9", coupe soup	$14.00 – 16.00
Bowl, 8¾", sq. open vegetable	$25.00 – 30.00
Bowl, 14½", large salad	$35.00 – 45.00
Bowl, 11 oz., open baker	$20.00 – 25.00
Bowl, oval, celery	$25.00 – 30.00
Bowl, large, ftd. fruit	$60.00 – 75.00
Butter dish	$185.00 – 210.00
Candlestick, 4½"	$35.00 – 45.00
Candlestick, 8"	$40.00 – 50.00
Casserole, 1¼ qt.	$40.00 – 45.00
Casserole, 2 qt.	$55.00 – 65.00
Coffee pot, 6-cup	$95.00 – 120.00
Creamer	$12.00 – 14.00
Creamer, a.d.	$14.00 – 16.00
Cup	$9.00 – 11.00
Cup, a.d.	$20.00 – 25.00
Egg cup	$55.00 – 60.00
Gravy boat	$40.00 – 45.00

Satin Black/Hi-White	Value
Jug, 1¼ qt.	$30.00 – 35.00
Jug, 3 qt.	$40.00 – 45.00
Ladle	$20.00 – 25.00
Marmite and cover	$32.00 – 37.00
Mug, Tom & Jerry	$18.00 – 22.00
Onion soup and cover	$40.00 – 45.00
Plate, 6"	$4.50 – 5.00
Plate, 8"	$8.00 – 9.50
Plate, 11"	$14.00 – 16.00
Platter, 12¼"	$28.00 – 30.00
Platter, 15"	$30.00 – 35.00
Platter, 17"	$40.00 – 45.00
Saucer	$1.50 – 2.50
Saucer, a.d.	$2.00 – 3.00
Shaker, ea.	$15.00 – 20.00
Sugar and cover	$18.00 – 22.00
Sugar, open a.d.	$14.00 – 16.00
Teapot, 6-cup	$185.00 – 215.00
Vase	$80.00 – 95.00
Vinegar bottle	$80.00 – 95.00

Tomorrow's Classic Miscellaneous

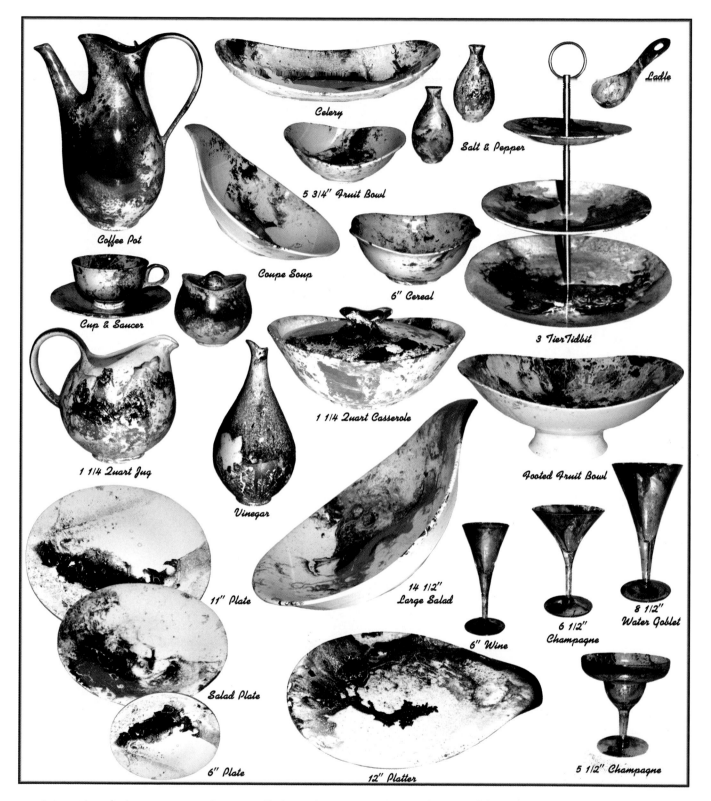

Coffee Pot

Celery

5 3/4" Fruit Bowl

Salt & Pepper

Ladle

Coupe Soup

6" Cereal

3 Tier Tidbit

Cup & Saucer

1 1/4 Quart Jug

Vinegar

1 1/4 Quart Casserole

Footed Fruit Bowl

11" Plate

14 1/2" Large Salad

6" Wine

6 1/2" Champagne

8 1/2" Water Goblet

Salad Plate

6" Plate

12" Platter

5 1/2" Champagne

Interesting designs are sometimes applied to pieces of Hall China by independent artists. The Eva Zeisel items shown above have a backstamp indicating they were decorated by Dixie Rett of Coral Gables, Florida. The pieces are decorated with a platinum color spatter design depicting the strong modernistic feelings that were characteristic of some of the artists during the 1950s. In addition to the Hall Eva Zeisel pieces, some other items of pottery and glass stemware were included with the set. Matching ashtrays, a butter, relishes, and several serving pieces were not made by Hall China.

KITCHENWARE
Shapes

Hall introduced its first modern era kitchenware line — "Medallion" — in 1932. The two initial colors were ivory and lettuce. Successful marketing in this venture soon led to the addition of other colors and the introduction of new shapes. Decals were also applied to both ivory and cobalt bodies and new patterns of kitchenware were developed. In addition to creating new kitchenware patterns, the kitchenware shapes were decorated with the appropriate decals and were incorporated into the dinnerware lines shown in Part I.

The desirability of the solid color kitchenware has increased remarkably over the past few years since many collectors have learned that Hall kitchenware is very ser-viceable as well as attractive. The Chinese red and cobalt colors have been especially popular. Other interesting colors would probably also be popular with collectors if enough pieces could be found to put together meaningful sets. The appearance of pieces in red, yellow, and blue art glaze colors has proven especially interesting.

The kitchenware section of this book is divided into three separate sections — basic kitchenware shapes, kitchenware shapes with gold decorated or painted decorations, and kitchenware shapes with decal designs. Patterns in each area will appear in alphabetical order.

The photo below shows some interesting pieces with some different color and decoration variations.

"Medallion" Jug

"Radiance" Casserole

"Medallion" Custard

"Medallion" Drip Coffee Pot

"Radiance" Jug & Lid

"Sundial" Individual Sugar & Creamer

"Radiance" Jug & Lid

"Radiance" Jug & Lid

Sani-Grid Sugar & Lid

"Ribbed" Bean Pot

"Sundial" Cookie Jar w/Surfside Gold Design

"Sundial" Casserole w/Surfside Gold Design

"Five Band"

Carafe
Cookie Jar
Cookie Jar
6 1/4" Jug
8 3/4" Bowl
7 1/4" Bowl
6" Bowl
Batter Bowl
Casserole
5" Jug
Salt & Pepper
5" Jug
Syrup

The "Five Band" kitchenware line was introduced in 1936. Chinese red was the most popular color then and is still the most collectible color today. Other colors including cobalt, Indian red, marine, cadet, ivory, and canary are often found. Some items in the "Five Band" shape will also be found decorated with numerous decals in both dinnerware and kitchenware patterns. The casserole had two different types of lids — knob handle and loop-shaped handle. To date the carafe has not been found with a decal decoration. However, a cobalt example without a handle has been discovered. This could possibly have been a prototype designed for use with a metal or wooden handle.

Item	Red/Cobalt	Other Colors
Batter bowl	$50.00 – 60.00	$40.00 – 50.00
Bowl, 6"	$12.00 – 14.00	$10.00 – 12.00
Bowl, 7¼"	$16.00 – 19.00	$12.00 – 14.00
Bowl, 8¾"	$22.00 – 27.00	$18.00 – 20.00
Carafe	$180.00 – 225.00	$130.00 – 180.00
Casserole, 8"	$30.00 – 40.00	$27.00 – 32.00
Coffee pot		$45.00 – 55.00
*Cookie jar	$125.00 – 145.00	$90.00 – 125.00
Jug, 5"	$27.00 – 32.00	$20.00 – 25.00
Jug, 6¼"	$35.00 – 45.00	$28.00 – 35.00
Shakers, ea.	$11.00 – 13.00	$10.00 – 12.00
Syrup	$65.00 – 75.00	$60.00 – 70.00

*Cobalt and Art Glaze Blue $145.00 – 185.00

"Medallion"

"Medallion," which was introduced in 1932, was Hall's first kitchenware line. The original issue consisted of the square leftover, the teapot, the casserole, the four sizes of jugs, and the six-piece bowl set. These were made initially in the ivory and lettuce colors. The #1 size bowl is the same as the custard and the #1 size jug is the same as the creamer. Later other colors and pieces were added, but the only other color appearing with any frequency is Chinese red. Unusual pieces include the all-china drip coffee pot, the stack set, the square leftover, and the reamer. The ruffled tab-handled bowl is a scarcely found serving piece which has also been found in a few decal patterns.

The orange reamers in this pattern probably attract the most attention and certainly command the highest prices. Notice the glazing difference in the reamers. The Art Glaze Yellow (Citrus or Screaming Yellow) reamer also has the colored glaze on the interior surface of the reamer. A similar reamer without the exterior embossing has been made recently in several decal patterns for a private company. For more information see the Reissues section at the back of this book.

"Medallion"	*Lettuce	**Chinese Red	Other Colors
Bowl, #2, 5¼"	$10.00 – 12.00	$13.50 – 15.00	$11.00 – 14.00
Bowl, #3, 6"	$11.00 – 13.00	$14.00 – 16.00	$11.00 – 14.00
Bowl, #4, 7¼"	$14.00 – 16.00	$16.00 – 20.00	$12.00 – 16.00
Bowl, #5, 8½"	$18.00 – 20.00	$22.00 – 27.00	$15.00 – 18.00
Bowl, #6, 10"	$25.00 – 32.00	$28.00 – 35.00	$25.00 – 30.00
Bowl, 9¼", ruffled	$125.00 – 145.00		
Casserole	$30.00 – 35.00	$35.00 – 45.00	$25.00 – 30.00
Creamer	$15.00 – 18.00	$20.00 – 25.00	$12.00 – 16.00
Custard	$16.00 – 18.50	$25.00 – 30.00	$16.00 – 18.00
Drip coffee pot	$200.00 – 250.00	$350.00 – 400.00	$200.00 – 225.00
Drip jar	$35.00 – 40.00	$45.00 – 55.00	$28.00 – 32.00
Jug, ice lip, 4 pt.	$32.00 – 37.00	$37.00 – 45.00	$30.00 – 35.00
Jug, ice lip, 5 pt.	$42.00 – 47.00	$45.00 – 55.00	$35.00 – 45.00
Jug, 4¼", 5", 5½"	$27.00 – 35.00	$35.00 – 42.00	$27.00 – 32.00
Jug, 6½", 7"	$40.00 – 45.00	$42.00 – 52.00	$40.00 – 45.00
Leftover, square	$55.00 – 65.00	$75.00 – 85.00	$55.00 – 65.00
Reamer	$350.00 – 400.00	$400.00 – 500.00	$475.00 – 625.00
Shakers, ea.	$45.00 – 50.00	$50.00 – 60.00	$40.00 – 50.00
Stack set	$95.00 – 125.00	$110.00 – 130.00	$90.00 – 120.00
Sugar and lid	$25.00 – 30.00	$30.00 – 40.00	$20.00 – 25.00
Teapot, 40 oz.	$185.00 – 210.00	$250.00 – 300.00	$195.00 – 250.00
Teapot, 64 oz.	$180.00 – 220.00	$250.00 – 350.00	$200.00 – 250.00

*Ivory prices are about 50% of Lettuce.

**Art Glaze colors are about 50% higher than Chinese red.

Custard

5" Jug

40 Oz. Teapot

Drip Coffee Pot

Casserole

Square Leftover

Reamer

Reamer

Ruffled 9 1/4" Tab-handled Bowl

Reamer

Reamer

7" Jug

Ice Lip Jug

8 1/2" Bowl

10" Bowl

7 1/4" Bowl

6" Bowl

5 1/4" Bowl

"Radiance"

Following the success of the first kitchenware line, Hall introduced a second shape — "Radiance" — in 1933. "Radiance" will be found in a variety of colors, but Chinese red is the most common and the most desirable to today's collectors. The easiest pieces to find are the mixing bowls and the medium-size jugs. However, the lids to most sizes of the jugs are not easily found. Jugs without lids will generally bring about one-third of the prices listed below. The hardest items to locate are the condiment jar, the reamer, and the all-china drip coffee pot. The condiment jar is not turning up in the solid colors, although it is beginning to show up in several of the decal lines.

Although many cereal sets, which include four canisters and two matching shakers, have found their way into collectors hands, the demand for these sets has remained strong. The cereal set was introduced in 1938, and was produced in numerous colors. Many "Radiance" shape kitchenware items will be found in the various decal lines.

A shape which is very similar to "Radiance" is the "Rayed" shape commonly associated with the Autumn Leaf pattern. "Rayed" shape pieces have a similar style and the same vertical line in their body. The most significant difference is in the ear-shaped handles which are present on such items as the "Rayed" jugs, teapots, and coffee pots.

The #2 mixing bowl and drip jar bottom are similar enough to cause some confusion among dealers and collectors. The following measurements should help to clarify the problem. The #2 bowl measures 5⅛" across the top and the base is about 2¼" in diameter. The drip jar bottom is 2⅝" in diameter at the top and has a 3¾" diameter base.

"Radiance"	Red/Cobalt	Ivory	Other Colors
Bowl, #1, 3½" (custard)	$18.00 – 22.00	$5.00 – 6.00	$16.00 – 20.00
Bowl, #2, 5¼"	$16.00 – 18.00	$5.00 – 6.50	$12.00 – 15.00
Bowl, #3, 6"	$14.00 – 16.00	$6.00 – 7.50	$12.00 – 14.00
Bowl, #4, 7¼"	$16.00 – 18.00	$6.00 – 7.50	$13.00 – 15.00
Bowl, #5, 8½"	$18.00 – 22.00	$7.00 – 9.00	$16.00 – 18.00
Bowl, #6, 10"	$27.00 – 32.00	$9.00 – 11.00	$20.00 – 25.00
Canister, 2 qt.	$200.00 – 230.00	$50.00 – 70.00	$190.00 – 210.00
Casserole	$50.00 – 65.00	$20.00 – 25.00	$40.00 – 50.00
Condiment jar	UND	UND	UND
Drip coffee pot	$350.00 – 400.00	$125.00 – 150.00	$350.00 – 400.00
Drip jar	$47.00 – 52.00	$10.00 – 12.00	$38.00 – 42.00
*Jug, 3¼", #1; 4¼", #2	$125.00 – 145.00	$25.00 – 30.00	$100.00 – 120.00
*Jug, 4¾", #3; 5¼", #4	$140.00 – 170.00	$32.00 – 34.00	$120.00 – 150.00
*Jug, 6¼", #5; 6¾", #6	$165.00 – 200.00	$35.00 – 40.00	$160.00 – 175.00
Reamer	UND	UND	UND
Shaker, canister style	$100.00 – 110.00	$15.00 – 22.00	$80.00 – 100.00
Stack set	$115.00 – 145.00	$30.00 – 42.00	$95.00 – 115.00
Teapot, 6-cup	$300.00 – 350.00	$50.00 – 65.00	$280.00 – 320.00

*With lid

Canister Set

6 1/4" Covered Jug

Canister-style
Salt & Pepper

6-cup Teapot

Condiment Jar

5 1/4" Covered Jug

Drip Jar

4 1/4" Covered Jug

Stack Set

6-cup Teapot

Drip Coffee Pot

Casserole

"Ribbed"

"Ribbed" kitchenware was introduced in 1935 under the name Russetware. The line was originally named for its russet color. Later, Chinese red was produced and it became the predominate color in the line. Today, all colors of this shape, including Chinese red are hard to find. The bakers, ramekins, and custards were made in assorted sizes which are listed in the price guide below.

The 12 ounce covered onion soup (sometimes called a marmite) is listed in a 1935 Sears' catalog. Original prices included a set of six custard cups for $1.79, the bean pot for $1.15, and the individual onion soup for .49¢. According to the ad, the casserole was a truly multi-purpose item. It could be used as an open baker, a pie plate (the cover inverted), a two-unit baker (the casserole with the cover inverted), or as a covered baker. Russetware was heralded as "an inexpensive reproduction of expensive imported china" and was also listed by the Good Housekeeping Institute.

The "Rutherford" shape teapot will also be found in some of the decal lines without ribbing. The handled shakers will be found with black lettering and with raised letters. A four-piece set which includes salt, pepper, sugar, and flour is available. The two shapes of teapots and the side-handled casserole are not often seen.

"Ribbed"	Chinese Red	Russet	Other Colors
Baker, 8, 10 & 12 oz., diag. rib	$12.00 – 14.00	$8.00 – 10.00	$12.50 – 14.00
Baker, 1, 1½ & 2 pt., diag. rib	$18.00 – 22.00	$14.00 – 16.00	
Baker, 2 & 3 qt., diag. rib	$24.00 – 28.00	$19.00 – 21.00	
Baker, 2½ & 3 pt., vert. rib	$18.00 – 22.00	$14.00 – 16.00	
Baker, 2 & 3 qt., vert. rib	$24.00 – 28.00	$19.00 – 21.00	
Bean pot	$125.00 – 150.00	$60.00 – 90.00	
Bowl, 8¾" salad	$20.00 – 22.00	$18.00 – 20.00	
Bowl, 9¾" salad	$20.00 – 25.00	$18.00 – 22.00	
Bowl, 6¼"	$12.00 – 14.00	$9.00 – 11.00	
Bowl, 7¼"	$13.00 – 15.00	$10.00 – 12.00	
Bowl, 8¼"	$18.00 – 20.00	$14.00 – 16.00	
Bowl, 9½"	$18.00 – 22.00	$16.00 – 20.00	
Casserole, 8"	$32.00 – 35.00	$24.00 – 28.00	
Casserole, 9"	$35.00 – 45.00	$28.00 – 32.00	
Casserole, 5¼" or 6¼", side handle	$45.00 – 50.00	$25.00 – 30.00	
Casserole, 7¼", side handle	$45.00 – 55.00	$30.00 – 35.00	
Casserole, 8¼" or 9¼", side handle	$60.00 – 75.00	$50.00 – 60.00	
Custard, 3½, 5 & 7 oz.	$7.00 – 10.00	$5.00 – 8.00	
Onion soup and cover	$35.00 – 45.00	$22.00 – 24.00	$30.00 – 40.00
Ramekin, 2 & 2¾ oz.	$5.00 – 6.00	$4.00 – 5.50	
Ramekin, 4 & 4½ oz.	$6.00 – 7.00	$4.00 – 5.50	
Ramekin, 6 oz.	$7.50 – 8.50	$5.00 – 6.00	
Ramekin, 4 oz., scalloped	$5.00 – 6.50	$4.00 – 5.50	
Shaker, handled, ea.	$15.00 – 18.00	$14.00 – 17.00	
Teapot, Globe shape	$225.00 – 255.00		
Teapot, "Rutherford"	$225.00 – 250.00		

"Rutherford" Teapot

Globe-shape Teapot

Bean Pot

Handled 4-piece Shaker set

Covered Onion Soup

9" Casserole

Side-handle French Casserole

Side-handle French Casserole

Diagonal-rib Baker

10" Salad Bowl

Embossed Handled Shakers

8 1/4" Bowl

7 1/4" Bowl

6 1/4" Bowl

Custard

Sani-Grid, Tab-Handled, and Straight-Sided

The Sani-Grid kitchenware shape was introduced in 1941. It is most commonly found in the colors Chinese red/white and cadet/white. These pieces have solid colored bodies with contrasting Hi-white handles and knobs. Bowls in this shape are straight-sided with a series of interior rings near the top edge. Usually, the cadet/white colored items are found decorated with a floral decal such as Rose Parade. White bodied pieces in this shape also exist and they are usually decorated with a decal of one of the kitchenware patterns.

A lid to the Sani-Grid sugar has appeared. The limited number of lids which have surfaced indicate that a lid was not a regular feature for this style sugar. The rounded oval shape of this lid is significantly different from that of the two sizes of teapot lids. For a comparison of the three lids see the photo below.

The tab-handled and straight-sided shapes are frequently found in Chinese red or cadet with contrasting Hi-white features, and are associated with the Sani-Grid line. Tab-handled items easily found are a casserole, drip jar, and bean pot. Straight-sided pieces that complement Sani-Grid kitchenware are a custard cup and four sizes of mixing bowls.

Notice the salt box in the photo below. This is a sample item that was recently discovered in Hall's morgue. Other unique examples have been found in the Autumn Leaf and Rose Parade patterns.

Kitchenware	Chinese Red	Cadet
Bean pot, tab-handled	$90.00 – 110.00	$37.00 – 42.00
Bowl, 6" Sani-Grid	$14.00 – 16.00	$13.00 – 15.00
Bowl, 7½" Sani-Grid	$16.00 – 18.00	$14.00 – 16.00
Bowl, 8¾" Sani-Grid	$18.00 – 22.00	$18.00 – 20.00
Bowl, 5¼", straight-sided	$12.00 – 14.00	$9.00 – 11.00
Bowl, 6", straight-sided	$14.00 – 16.00	$10.00 – 12.00
Bowl, 7½", straight-sided	$16.00 – 18.00	$12.00 – 14.00
Bowl, 9", straight-sided	$18.00 – 22.00	$16.00 – 18.00
Casserole, tab-handled	$35.00 – 45.00	$22.00 – 28.00
Creamer, Sani-Grid	$14.00 – 16.00	$8.00 – 10.00
Custard, straight-sided	$17.00 – 20.00	$4.00 – 5.00
Drip jar, tab-handled	$30.00 – 35.00	$10.00 – 12.00
Jug, 5", Sani-Grid	$20.00 – 25.00	$8.00 – 9.00
Jug, 6½", Sani-Grid	$28.00 – 32.00	$9.00 – 11.00
Jug, 7½", Sani-Grid	$35.00 – 40.00	$11.00 – 13.00
Shakers, Sani-Grid, ea.	$12.00 – 15.00	$5.00 – 7.00
Sugar, Sani-Grid	$14.00 – 16.00	$8.00 – 10.00
Sugar lid, Sani-Grid	$225.00 – 275.00	UND
Teapot, 3-cup, Sani-Grid	$35.00 – 45.00	$14.00 – 16.00
Teapot, 6-cup, Sani-Grid	$47.00 – 52.00	$18.00 – 20.00

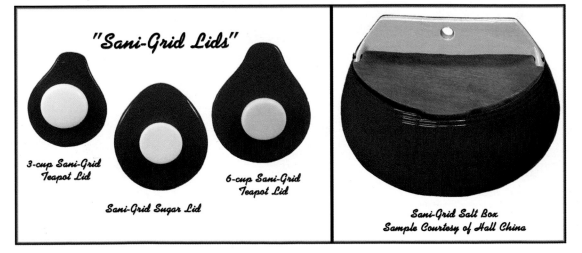

"Sani-Grid Lids"

3-cup Sani-Grid Teapot Lid

Sani-Grid Sugar Lid

6-cup Sani-Grid Teapot Lid

Sani-Grid Salt Box
Sample Courtesy of Hall China

Sani-Grid

Sugar

Creamer

7 1/2" Jug

6 1/2" Jug

5" Jug

6-cup Teapot

3-cup Teapot

Salt & Pepper

Tab-handled

Bean Pot

Casserole

Drip Jar

Straight-sided

Custard

9" Bowl

7 1/2" Bowl

6" Bowl

5" Bowl

"Sundial"

The "Sundial" kitchenware shape was introduced in 1938. The most commonly found color is Chinese red. The casseroles, sugars and creamers, individual teapots, and coffee pots will be found in a number of sizes and some of these pieces are still available. Look at the Hall backstamp on these pieces to help in determining age. The batter jug was reissued in the 1980s as part of the Hall American line. The easiest way to distinguish the difference between the old and new jugs is to look at the base. Old batter jugs have a round base and the newer jugs have a square base.

The hardest pieces to find are the coffee server and the cookie jar. The wholesale price of the cookie jar in 1940 was $2.00. Today, a cookie jar in cobalt or red will bring over $200.00.

Some pieces have been found in Canary with a Surfside teapot style gold decoration. The cookie jar and casserole are pictured on page 132.

"Sundial"	Red/Cobalt	Art Glaze Colors	Other Colors
Batter jug	$170.00 – 210.00	$200.00 – 250.00	$150.00 – 200.00
*Casserole, #1, 4¾"	$25.00 – 30.00	$27.00 – 32.00	$20.00 – 25.00
Casserole, #2, 5¼"	$32.00 – 35.00	$32.00 – 35.00	$22.00 – 27.00
Casserole, #3, 6½"	$32.00 – 37.00	$32.00 – 37.00	$27.00 – 30.00
Casserole, #4, 8"	$35.00 – 40.00	$40.00 – 45.00	$32.00 – 37.00
Coffee pot, individual	$85.00 – 95.00	$95.00 – 120.00	$80.00 – 90.00
*Creamer	$10.00 – 1200	$12.00 – 15.00	$10.00 – 12.00
Coffee server	$500.00 – 600.00	$500.00 – 700.00	$400.00 – 500.00
Cookie jar	$200.00 – 230.00	$225.00 – 275.00	$200.00 – 225.00
Sugar	$15.00 – 18.00	$20.00 – 25.00	$15.00 – 18.00
Syrup	$150.00 – 190.00	$200.00 – 220.00	$150.00 – 170.00
Teapot, individual	$85.00 – 95.00	$95.00 – 120.00	$80.00 – 90.00
Teapot, six cup	$185.00 – 225.00	$225.00 – 275.00	$175.00 – 200.00

*Currently being produced in various colors and sizes.

Canary with Surfside Gold Decoration	Price
Batter bowl	$150.00 – 175.00
Cookie Jar	$200.00 – 250.00
Casserole, 8"	$50.00 – 60.00

Cookie Jar

Coffee Server

Cookie Jar

Batter Jug

Individual Sugar & Creamer

Six-cup Teapot

Batter Jug

Individual 5 1/4" Casserole

Batter Jug

Syrup

Batter Jug

1 Oz. Creamer

Individual Coffee Pot

Syrup

8" Casserole

KITCHENWARE COLORS AND DECORATIONS
Black and White with Gold Decorations

From the late 1940s through the early 1950s Hall selected a number of special items for their No. 05 Kitchenware Assortment. The bodies of these pieces are matte black and white. Decoration consists of a wide gold band with gold sprigs on handles. Although the colledction has been dubbed "Black Gold," many collectors are not particularly charmed by the satin black finish; therefore the only pieces that are attracting significant interest are the Aladdin and French teapots and the ball jug.

Kitchenware	Value
Ball jug, #3	$55.00 – 65.00
Bean pot, New England, #4	$55.00 – 65.00
Bowl, 9", salad	$12.00 – 14.00
Bowl, 6¼", "Thick Rim"	$10.00 – 12.00
Bowl, 7½", "Thick Rim"	$12.00 – 15.00
Bowl, 8½", "Thick Rim"	$16.00 – 19.00
Casserole, #71, #75, round	$20.00 – 25.00
Casserole, #76, #78, round	$20.00 – 25.00
Casserole, #100, #101, #103, oval	$20.00 – 25.00
Casserole, French, side handle	$18.00 – 22.00
Casserole, "Thick Rim"	$30.00 – 35.00
Coffee pot, Washington	$95.00 – 115.00

Kitchenware	Value
Creamer, Boston	$12.00 – 15.00
Drip jar, "Thick Rim"	$25.00 – 30.00
Jug, "Five Band"	$22.00 – 25.00
Jug, loop handle	$50.00 – 60.00
Jug, Princeton	$65.00 – 75.00
Shaker, handled	$12.00 – 15.00
Shirred egg dish	$20.00 – 25.00
Sugar and lid, Boston	$18.00 – 22.00
Teapot, Aladdin	$150.00 – 170.00
Teapot, French	$95.00 – 115.00
Tea tile, round	$25.00 – 30.00
Warmer, round	$35.00 – 40.00

Golden White Jug Set

The white gold decorated three jug series that comprises this set was designed in the 1950s by J. Palin Thorley.

This set was introduced into the Hall line in mid-1959.

Golden White Jug	Value
Jug, #1536-6 oz.	$15.00 – 20.00
Jug, #1538-1½ pint	$20.00 – 25.00
Jug, # 1540-1 quart	$27.00 – 32.00

1540-12uart   1538-1 1/2 Pint   1536-6 Ounce

Golden White HALL CHINA JUG SET

3 SIZES—1 SET

ONE 1536—6 oz. • ONE 1538—1½ Pints • ONE 1540—1 Quart

22 CARAT BRIGHT GOLD DECORATION

SHIPPING WEIGHT 18 POUNDS • PACKED 1 SET TO CARTON, 6 SETS TO SHIPPER

HALL KITCHENWARE

SECRET PROCESS FIREPROOF CHINA

1376

398

1377

633

1411

1378

3 PIECE BOWL SET

988

3 PIECE RANGE SET

1187

1186

NO. 05 KITCHENWARE ASSORTMENT

BLACK AND WHITE
BLACK GOLD DECORATION

Quantity	Item	Capacity	Height Inches	Diam. Top Inches
2 only	**3 Piece Bake Bowl Set**			
	1376—Bowl	2 pts.	3¼"	6⅜"
	1377—Bowl	3 ½ pts.	3⅞"	7½"
	1378—Bowl	2 ⅔ qts.	4½"	8⅝"
2 only	**3 Piece Range Set**			
	1186—Salt	8 oz.	4¾"	
	1187—Pepper	8 oz.	4¾"	
	988—Grease Pot	16 oz.	2½"	5⅜"
2 only	**398—Casserole**	3 pts.	3⅛"	8¼"
2 only	**3078—Salad or Bake Dish**	4 pts.	3⅛"	9⅛"
2 only	**1411 Aladdin Teapot**	6 cup	6½"	
2 only	**633—Jug**	2 qts.	7"	

Guaranteed by Good Housekeeping — Replacement or refund of money if not as advertised therein

Shipping Weight of Assortment—50 pounds
Guaranteed against breakage in oven heat

3078

Eggshell Buffet Service

Hall's Eggshell Buffet Service with the Dot, Plaid, and Swag designs is a line with a large number of pieces. The most frequently found color of Dot is red, but other color dots such as green, blue, and orange will also be seen. Generally, the dots are found on an eggshell body, but some pieces with an ivory body are also available. Examples of the ivory body are the set of handled shakers and the pretzel jar with green dots at the bottom left of the photo on on page 148. The pretzel jar has a Half-Dot design. When the lid and bottom are lined up correctly a whole dot pattern is created.

As may be seen from the listing, the Dot design appears on some kitchenware shapes which are not usually found in other decorated patterns. Examples of these are the handled cocotte, the #691 Drip coffee, and the buffet style round and oval casseroles. The "Thin Rim"

bowls and the custard may be found either smooth or with vertical ribs. The 13½" fish-shaped salad is part of the set even though it only has matching trim and does not have any dots. This platter is still being made in numerous colors and now comes in two different sizes.

The pieces appearing most often are the handled shakers. Many teapot collectors are still eagerly waiting to acquire the "Rutherford" teapot. Another hard-to-find piece is the Tom and Jerry bowl.

In addition to the Dot pattern illustrated in the photo on page 148, some pieces of the Buffet Service in the Plaid and Swag patterns are shown in the photo below. Some elusive examples of the "Swag" pattern include the #691 all-china drip coffee pot and the "Rutherford" teapot. The pattern which is illustrated on the fish platter and the oval buffet casserole below is called Plaid.

Fish-shape Baker

Fish-shape Baker

No. 691 All-china Drip Coffee Pot

SALT   PEPPER

Oval Buffet Casserole

FLOUR   SUGAR

"Rutherford" Teapot

Handled 4-piece Shaker Set

Round Buffet Casserole

7 1/4" "Ribbed" Bowl

6" "Ribbed" Bowl

Oval Handled Casserole

Covered Onion Soup

8 1/2" "Ribbed" Bowl

8 1/2" "Thin Rim" Bowl

7 1/4" "Thin Rim" Bowl

6" "Thin Rim" Bowl

Kitchenware	Dot	"Plaid" or "Swag" Patterns
Baker, 13½", fish-shape	$50.00 – 65.00	$70.00 – 85.00
Bean pot, New England, #3	$95.00 – 110.00	$110.00 – 145.00
Bean pot, New England, #4	$95.00 – 125.00	
Bowl, 8¾", salad	$28.00 – 32.00	
Bowl, 9¾", salad	$32.00 – 35.00	$40.00 – 45.00
Bowl, 15½" salad	$45.00 – 55.00	
Bowl, 6", "Ribbed"	$18.00 – 22.00	$22.00 – 25.00
Bowl, 7¼", "Ribbed"	$26.00 – 30.00	$28.00 – 32.00
Bowl, 8½", "Ribbed"	$30.00 – 35.00	$35.00 – 45.00
Bowl, 6", "Thin Rim"	$18.00 – 22.00	$22.00 – 25.00
Bowl, 7¼", "Thin Rim"	$25.00 – 30.00	$28.00 – 32.00
Bowl, 8½", "Thin Rim"	$30.00 – 35.00	$35.00 – 45.00
Bowl, ftd., Tom & Jerry	$225.00 – 250.00	
Casserole, oval handled	$45.00 – 55.00	$50.00 – 60.00
Casserole, 9¾", oval	$45.00 – 55.00	$50.00 – 60.00
Casserole, 8½", 9¼", round	$45.00 – 55.00	$50.00 – 60.00
Cocotte, 4", handled	$22.00 – 25.00	$24.00 – 28.00
Custard	$20.00 – 22.00	$20.00 – 26.00
Custard, "Ribbed"	$20.00 – 25.00	
Drip, #188, open	$30.00 – 35.00	$37.00 – 42.00
Drip coffee, #691	$225.00 – 270.00	$300.00 – 350.00
Jug and cover, "Radiance," #1	$85.00 – 100.00	
Jug and cover, "Radiance," #2	$95.00 – 110.00	
Jug and cover, "Radiance," #3	$125.00 – 145.00	
Jug and cover, "Radiance," #5	$150.00 – 170.00	
Jug, room service	$90.00 – 110.00	
Mug, Tom & Jerry	$12.00 – 15.00	
Mustard	$70.00 – 95.00	$90.00 – 110.00
Onion soup	$40.00 – 50.00	$45.00 – 55.00
Shakers, (4) handled, ea.	$18.00 – 22.00	$22.00 – 25.00
Shirred egg dish	$27.00 – 32.00	$35.00 – 40.00
Teapot, "Rutherford"	$220.00 – 250.00	$275.00 – 325.00

Kitchenware	Dot with an Ivory Body
Casserole, "Radiance"	$45.00 – 55.00
Custard	$20.00 – 25.00
Pretzel jar	$155.00 – 190.00
Shakers, handled, ea.	$18.00 – 22.00

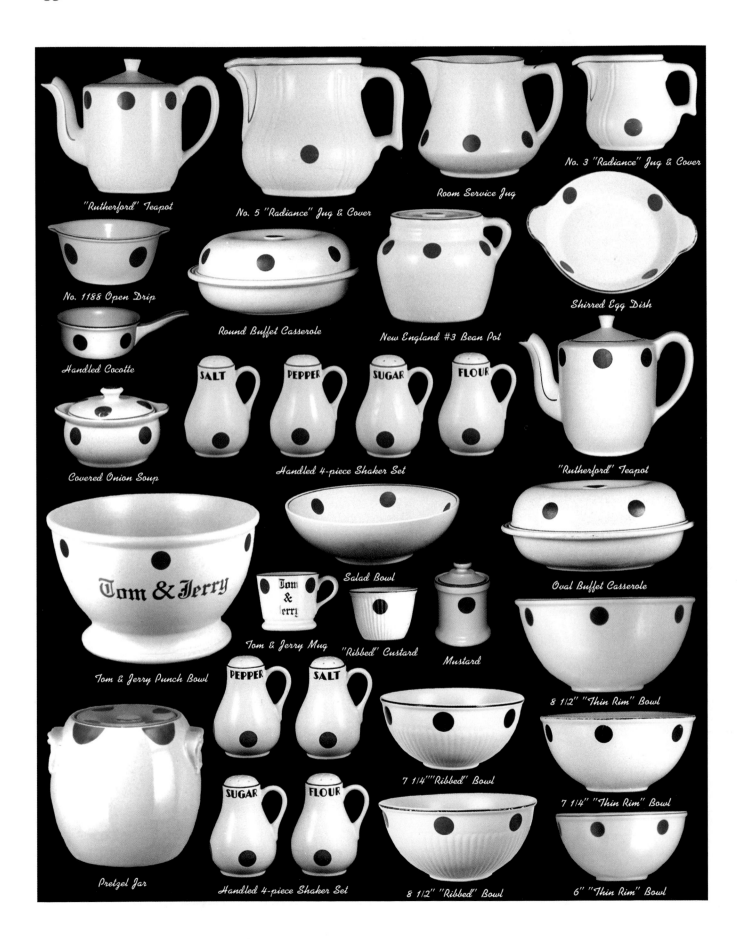

"Rutherford" Teapot

No. 5 "Radiance" Jug & Cover

Room Service Jug

No. 3 "Radiance" Jug & Cover

No. 1188 Open Drip

Round Buffet Casserole

New England #3 Bean Pot

Shirred Egg Dish

Handled Cocotte

SALT   PEPPER   SUGAR   FLOUR

Covered Onion Soup

Handled 4-piece Shaker Set

"Rutherford" Teapot

Salad Bowl

Oval Buffet Casserole

Tom & Jerry Mug

"Ribbed" Custard

Mustard

Tom & Jerry Punch Bowl

8 1/2" "Thin Rim" Bowl

PEPPER   SALT

7 1/4" "Ribbed" Bowl

7 1/4" "Thin Rim" Bowl

Pretzel Jar

SUGAR   FLOUR

Handled 4-piece Shaker Set

8 1/2" "Ribbed" Bowl

6" "Thin Rim" Bowl

#1768 Covered Casserole
SUNNYVALE DECORATION

#1768 Covered Casserole
MYNAH DECORATION

HALL CHINA
FOR PERFECT BAKING
HOLDS THE HEAT

TEFLON
FOR EASY CLEANING
FOOD WON'T STICK

Flare-Ware ®
BY
HALL CHINA
MADE IN U·S·A

Fireproof HALL CHINA Casserole
Lined with NON-STICK TEFLON*

MYNAH DECORATION · SUNNYVALE DECORATION · PLAIN WHITE

#1768 COVERED CASSEROLE—3 pint capacity. Each item individually boxed. Packed ½ dozen to shipping carton. Shipping weight, dozen—54 pounds.

THE FOLLOWING MATCHING PIECES ARE AVAILABLE WITHOUT TEFLON LINING

#1756 TEAPOT	**#1766 COOKIE JAR**	**#1769 COV'D CASSEROLE**	**3-piece BOWL SET**
6 cup capacity. Each item individually boxed. Packed ½ dozen to shipping carton. Shipping weight, dozen — 36 pounds.	3 quart capacity. Each item individually boxed. Packed ½ dozen to shipping carton. Shipping weight, dozen — 66 pounds.	2 quart capacity. Each item individually boxed. Packed ½ dozen to shipping carton. Shipping weight, dozen — 90 pounds.	**#1776** — 1 quart capacity **#1777** — 1½ quart capacity **#1778** — 2½ quart capacity Each set individually boxed. Packed ½ dozen sets to shipping carton. Shipping weight, dozen sets — 100 pounds.

Flare-Ware

Heather Rose
6" Bowl

Heather Rose
Cookie Jar

Autumn Leaf
Cookie Jar

Radial Casserole

Flareware is essentially a serving type kitchenware line which was offered by Hall in the early 1960s. Basic decorations were Autumn Leaf, Gold Lace, Chestnut, and Radial. Today the only decoration found in any quantity is Gold Lace. A common variation of the Gold Lace decoration includes pieces found with the Heather Rose decal used in combination with the star-like Gold Lace design. The Flareware Autumn Leaf has nothing in common with the Autumn Leaf dinnerware pattern shown earlier in this book which was distributed by Jewel Tea. An example of the pattern may be seen on the cookie jar to the right in the picture. The Radial design has thin black vertical lines over a white base. Pieces of the Chestnut pattern have an all-over brown glaze.

The coffee server was designed to be used with the brass and wooden three-legged candle warmer. Another multi-purpose three-legged warmer, made of china, was used with the teapot, coffee urn, and casserole. The coffee urn is shaped like the cookie jar and has a spigot to dispense the coffee instead of a pour spout. The brass warmer has no design and was used with all the patterns. Therefore, it will only be listed once in the price guide below.

Hall also produced a three-pint casserole with a Teflon coating in plain white and with the Sunnyvale and Mynah decorations during the mid 1960s. Additional matching pieces without the Teflon coating included a teapot, cookie jar, two-quart casserole, and a three-piece bowl set. Examples are shown in the reprint pictured on page 149.

Kitchenware	Gold Lace	Autumn Leaf	Heather Rose	Radial
Bowl, 6¾"	$6.00 – 8.00	$6.00 – 7.00	$10.00 – 12.00	$5.00 – 6.00
Bowl, 7¾"	$7.00 – 8.00	$6.00 – 7.00	$14.00 – 16.00	$5.00 – 6.00
Bowl, 8¾"	$9.00 – 10.00	$8.00 – 9.00	$18.00 – 20.00	$6.00 – 7.00
Bowl, 5", salad	$8.00 – 10.00	$7.00 – 9.00	$10.00 – 12.00	$6.00 – 7.00
Casserole, 3 pt.	$18.00 – 22.00	$18.00 – 22.00	$22.00 – 27.00	$17.00 – 19.00
Casserole, 2 qt.	$20.00 – 25.00	$20.00 – 25.00	$35.00 – 45.00	$18.00 – 22.00
Coffee server, 15-cup	$35.00 – 55.00	$30.00 – 40.00	$40.00 – 45.00	$30.00 – 40.00
Coffee urn, 15-cup	$40.00 – 45.00	$22.00 – 28.00		$18.00 – 22.00
Cookie jar	$32.00 – 37.00	$32.00 – 37.00	$75.00 – 85.00	$30.00 – 35.00
Teapot, 6-cup	$35.00 – 40.00	$35.00 – 40.00	$35.00 – 45.00	$35.00 – 40.00
Trivet, china	$11.00 – 13.00			
Warmer, brass	$20.00 – 25.00			

GOLD LACE DECORATION—WHITE BODY

#1756 TEAPOT
6 cup capacity. Packed ½ dozen in shipping carton.
Packed weight of carton 18 pounds.

#1758 TRIVET
complete with #1757 Holder and Candle.
Fits #1759 Coffee Urn, #1765 Coffee Server,
#1766 Cookie Jar, #1768 Casserole,
#1769 Casserole and #1778 Bowl.
Packed ½ dozen in shipping carton.
Packed weight of carton 18 pounds.

#1759 COFFEE URN
complete with Faucet and
#1758 Trivet including
#1757 Holder and Candle.
15 cup capacity. Packed in individual carton.
Packed weight of carton 10 pounds.

#1765 COFFEE SERVER
complete with Brass Warmer including Candle.
15 cup capacity. Packed in individual carton.
Packed weight of carton 5 pounds.

#1766 COOKIE JAR
3 quart capacity. Packed ½ dozen in shipping carton.
Packed weight of carton 33 pounds.

#1768 COVERED CASSEROLE
3 pint capacity. Packed ½ dozen in shipping carton.
Packed weight of carton 27 pounds.

Each item individually boxed.

#1769 COVERED CASSEROLE
complete with
#1758 Trivet including
#1757 Holder with Candle.
2 quart capacity. Packed in individual carton.
Packed weight of carton 8½ pounds.

#1775 SALAD BOWL
1 pint capacity. Packed 1 dozen in shipping carton.
Packed weight of carton 20 pounds.

3-piece BOWL SET
#1776—6" Bowl, 1 quart capacity.
#1777—7" Bowl, 1½ quart capacity.
#1778—8" Bowl, 2½ quart capacity.
Packed ½ dozen in shipping carton.
Packed weight of carton 50 pounds.

French Flower

Although the French Flower gold decoration is most often found on the French shape teapot, it was also used on other kitchenware shapes. Therefore, the design has been added to the kitchenware section of this book. Several other teapots such as the Aladdin, Boston, New York, Cube, and McCormick have been found with this gold decoration. Also an interesting discovery new to this edition is the French Coffee Biggin coffee pot. The one that has been reported is in the warm yellow color. The large brown teapot shown below is the same shape as the "Crown" that Hall produced for the Tricolator Company. This is an early teapot and has a round Hall backstamp instead of a Tricolator backstamp.

Kitchenware	Value
Ashtray, #683	$22.00 – 25.00
Ball jug, #3	$150.00 – 170.00
Coffee pot, French Coffee Biggin	$300.00 – 350.00
Coffee pot, Washington	$65.00 – 75.00
Creamer, Bellevue	$20.00 – 25.00

Kitchenware	Value
Creamer, Boston	$22.00 – 27.00
Drip jar, "Tootsie"	$30.00 – 35.00
Jug, Donut	$125.00 – 145.00
Jug, loop handle	$115.00 – 135.00
Jug, room service	$55.00 – 65.00
Shaker, handled	$20.00 – 25.00
Sugar and lid, Boston	$32.00 – 37.00
Teapot, Airflow	$200.00 – 225.00
Teapot, Aladdin	$270.00 – 320.00
Teapot, Boston	$100.00 – 120.00
Teapot, buffet service	$85.00 – 105.00
Teapot, "Crown"	$175.00 – 225.00
Teapot, Cube	$165.00 – 200.00
Teapot, French	$55.00 – 65.00
Teapot, Los Angeles	$190.00 – 220.00
Teapot, McCormick	$170.00 – 210.00
Teapot, New York	$90.00 – 115.00
Teapot, Parade	$115.00 – 150.00

Washington Coffee Pot

Loop Handle Jug

2 oz. Creamer

Crown Teapot

Donut Jug

Donut Jug

French 2-cup Teapot

No. 683 Ash Tray

Buffet Service Teapot

New York 6-cup Teapot

French 6-cup Teapot

No. 3 Ball Jug

Bellvue Creamer

Cube Teapot

Gold Label Kitchenware

Hall selected 12 teapot shapes from the Gold Decorated line in the mid-1950s and added additional gold decoration to produce the Gold Label line. Teapots in this new line have an extensive gold decoration and may be identified through a gold code number on the bottom followed by the letters "GL." The handles, spouts, and knobs of the lids to these teapots are covered with gold.

In addition to the teapots, eight kitchenware shapes were also selected for use in the Gold Label line. Included were the 9" salad bowl, "Terrace" coffee pot, Zeisel cookie jar, "Rayed" jug, the #76 round casserole, and the three-piece "Thick Rim" bowl set. As may be seen in the photograph, a French baker also exists in the squiggle design, but we have not seen this piece in the other gold designs.

The following listing provides the names of the teapots and the names associated with the design as assigned by researchers. Prices of the teapots may vary greatly according to color and size. Therefore, a detailed color and size breakdown for prices of these gold decorated teapots has been provided in the teapot section of this book. For specific prices refer to the color under the Gold Label column for each particular style teapot.

Teapots	Design
Aladdin	Squiggle
Aladdin	Swag
Albany	Reflection
Baltimore	Nova
Boston	Fleur-de-lis
French	Daisy
Hollywood	Grid
Hook Cover	Star
Los Angeles	Medallion
New York	Flower
Parade	Squiggle
Philadelphia	Basket
Windshield	Dot

Kitchenware Accessories	Value
Baker, French	$14.00 – 18.00
Bowl, 6", "Thick Rim"	$10.00 – 12.00
Bowl, 7½", "Thick Rim"	$14.00 – 16.00
Bowl, 9", "Thick Rim"	$16.00 – 20.00
Bowl, 9", salad	$15.00 – 18.00
Casserole, #76, round	$30.00 – 32.00
Coffee pot, "Terrace"	$45.00 – 55.00
Cookie jar, Zeisel	$60.00 – 85.00
Jug, "Rayed"	$18.00 – 22.00

Star Design Zeisel Cookie Jar

Squiggle Design No. 76 Casserole

Basket Design Zeisel Cookie Jar

Squiggle Design 9" Salad Bowl

Medallion Design Los Angeles Teapot

Squiggle Design Aladdin Teapot

Basket Design Philadelphia Teapot

Swag Design Aladdin Teapot

Nova Design Baltimore Teapot

Fleur-de-lis Design Boston Teapot

Reflection Design Albany Teapot

Squiggle Design "Rayed" Jug

Squiggle Design Parade Teapot

Daisy Design "Thick Rim" Bowl

Squiggle Design French Baker

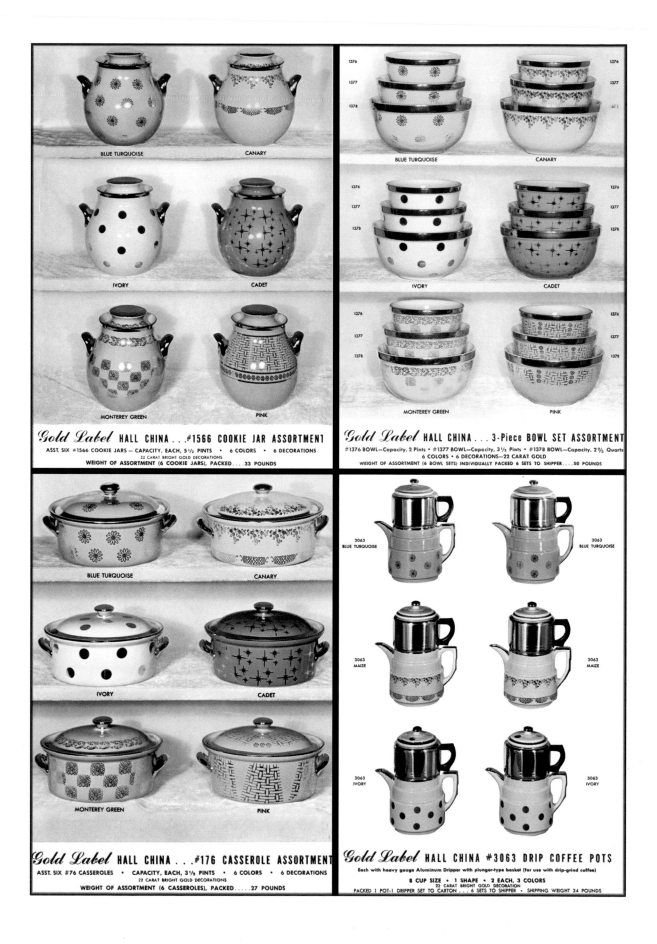

Gold Label HALL CHINA...#1566 COOKIE JAR ASSORTMENT
ASST. SIX #1566 COOKIE JARS — CAPACITY, EACH, 5½ PINTS • 6 COLORS • 6 DECORATIONS
22 CARAT BRIGHT GOLD DECORATIONS
WEIGHT OF ASSORTMENT (6 COOKIE JARS), PACKED....33 POUNDS

BLUE TURQUOISE · CANARY · IVORY · CADET · MONTEREY GREEN · PINK

Gold Label HALL CHINA...3-Piece BOWL SET ASSORTMENT
#1376 BOWL—Capacity, 2 Pints • #1377 BOWL—Capacity, 3½ Pints • #1378 BOWL—Capacity, 2⅔ Quarts
6 COLORS • 6 DECORATIONS—22 CARAT GOLD
WEIGHT OF ASSORTMENT (6 BOWL SETS) INDIVIDUALLY PACKED 6 SETS TO SHIPPER....50 POUNDS

Gold Label HALL CHINA...#176 CASSEROLE ASSORTMENT
ASST. SIX #76 CASSEROLES • CAPACITY, EACH, 3½ PINTS • 6 COLORS • 6 DECORATIONS
22 CARAT BRIGHT GOLD DECORATIONS
WEIGHT OF ASSORTMENT (6 CASSEROLES), PACKED.....27 POUNDS

Gold Label HALL CHINA #3063 DRIP COFFEE POTS
Each with heavy gauge Aluminum Dripper with plunger-type basket (for use with drip-grind coffee)
8 CUP SIZE • 1 SHAPE • 2 EACH, 3 COLORS
22 CARAT BRIGHT GOLD DECORATION
PACKED 1 POT-1 DRIPPER SET TO CARTON...6 SETS TO SHIPPER • SHIPPING WEIGHT 34 POUNDS

3063 BLUE TURQUOISE · 3063 MAIZE · 3063 IVORY

155

Golden Glo

Golden Glo is a Hall kitchenware line which dates back to the 1940s and is still in production today. As a result of this long period of production, many different pieces have been subjected to this gold treatment. The gold color top glaze is normally applied over a Hi-white base. An example of the gold color backstamp used on older Golden Glo pieces is shown in the photo on the next page. Pieces made after 1970 will have the new square backstamp. According to information contained in its backstamp, the oval casserole with the basketweave pattern was made for Bump's of San Francisco. The following listing has been compiled with the aid of a 1967 catalog offering.

Golden Glo Kitchenware	Value	Golden Glo Kitchenware	Value
Ashtray, #615, 4½"	$6.00 – 8.00	Casserole, hen on nest	$40.00 – 50.00
Ashtray, shell shape, 4", 5", 6"	$6.00 – 9.00	Casserole, French side	
Baking shell, 4"	$6.00 – 9.00	handle, 8, 12 oz.	$20.00 – 25.00
Baker, French, 7¼"	$18.00 – 22.00	Casserole, French side	
Baker, French, 8½"	$18.00 – 22.00	handle, 1½, 2½, 4 pint	$25.00 – 30.00
Bean pot, New England, ½ pint		Casserole, French side	
no cover	$18.00 – 20.00	handle, 6, 7, 8 pint	$35.00 – 45.00
Bean pot, New England, 5 pint	$65.00 – 85.00	Casserole, oval, #99,#100, #101	$25.00 – 30.00
Bean pot, New England, 6 pint	$65.00 – 85.00	Casserole, #102, #103, 7 pint	$30.00 – 45.00
Bowl, Medallion, #3, #4, #5	$18.00 – 25.00	Casserole, #65 rnd16 oz. no handle	$20.00 – 25.00
Bowl, 24 oz. salad	$8.00 – 10.00	Casserole, round, #75, #76, #77, #78	$25.00 – 35.00
Bowl, 4 pint salad	$18.00 – 20.00	Coffee pot, demi coffee set	$80.00 – 95.00
Bowl, 4 quart salad	$25.00 – 30.00	Coffee pot, Fr. Coffee Biggin	
Bowl, 2 gallon salad	$40.00 – 50.00	3, 4, 6, and 10 cup	$85.00 – 100.00
Casserole, basketweave	$40.00 – 50.00	Coffee pot, # 53½ 6-cup	
Casserole, duck knob	$40.00 – 50.00	Creamer, #321 Boston	$12.00 – 15.00

Golden Glo Kitchenware	Value	Golden Glo Kitchenware	Value
Creamer, demi coffee set	$16.00 – 20.00	Shaker, handled	$22.00 – 25.00
Creamer, #1395 morning set	$16.00 – 20.00	Souffle, 10, 12 oz.	$8.00 – 12.00
Creamer, Sani-Grid	$16.00 – 20.00	Souffle, 1, 1½, 2, 2½, 3 pint	$16.00 – 20.00
Cup, #1270 hndl, Turkish coffee	$12.00 – 14.00	Souffle, 2, 3 quart	$20.00 – 25.00
Custard, fluted, 3½, 5, 7 oz.	$10.00 – 12.00	Souffle, 2½, 3-pint, French	$16.00 – 20.00
Custard, #352	$10.00 – 12.00	Souffle, 2, 3-quart, French	$20.00 – 25.00
Dish, #1149, 9" fondue	$22.00 – 25.00	Souffle, round fluted, 16 oz.	$10.00 – 12.00
Dish, shirred egg, 7, 8, 12, 14 oz.	$16.00 – 22.00	Souffle, oval fluted 4, 5, 7½ oz.	$8.00 – 12.00
Jug, "Five Band"	$18.00 – 22.00	Sugar and lid, #320, Boston	$20.00 – 25.00
Jug, #247, 5-pint	$25.00 – 30.00	Sugar, demi coffee set	$16.00 – 20.00
Jug, #625, 3-pint	$18.00 – 22.00	Sugar #1394 morning set	$16.00 – 20.00
Jug, #626, 2-quart	$32.00 – 37.00	Sugar, Sani-Grid	$16.00 – 20.00
Jug, #2633, 4¾-pint	$35.00 – 40.00	Teapot, Airflow	$150.00 – 185.00
Marmite, 1½, 2, 3 pt.	$20.00 – 22.00	Teapot, Aladdin	$175.00 – 225.00
Mug, #1272, 7 oz., hndl coffee	$8.00 – 10.00	Teapot, Boston	$150.00 – 175.00
Mug, #1273, 10 oz., hndl coffee	$16.00 – 20.00	Teapot, Hollywood	$180.00 – 225.00
Mug, #343	$10.00 – 12.00	Teapot, McCormick	$140.00 – 160.00
Mug, #1310, hndl conic	$10.00 – 12.00	Teapot, Sani-Grid	$125.00 – 140.00
Onion soup, 8, 14 oz.	$16.00 – 20.00	Teapot, #1393 morning set	$150.00 – 175.00
Ramekin, #831, 4 oz., scalloped	$6.00 – 8.00	Tumbler, #343 handled chocolate	$10.00 – 12.00
Ramekin, fluted 2, 2¾, 3, 4½, 6 oz.	$7.00 – 11.00	Welsh rarebit, 8, 12, 15 oz.	$20.00 – 25.00

Aladdin Teapot

Sani-Grid Creamer

Hollywood Teapot

Sani-Grid Sugar

McCormick Creamer

French Coffee Biggin Coffee Pot

McCormick Creamer

Sani-Grid Teapot

McCormick Teapot

Basketweave Casserole

Hen on Nest Casserole

Coffee Pot Made for Forman Brothers

GOLDEN GLO
HALL
MADE IN U.S.A.
WARRANTED 22 CARAT GOLD
783

Hand-painted Kitchenware

Some, but not all, hand-painted pieces were decorated by artists at Hall. Hand-decorated pieces produced at the Hall factory will usually bear the Hall backstamp and reflect the quality resulting from professional decoration. Many blanks were also sold for decoration by independent artists. The quality and beauty of the finished product is a reflection of the ability of the individual artist. As a result prices depend on how well the piece is decorated and may vary widely. Decorated wide body Aladdin teapots are especially popular among today's collectors.

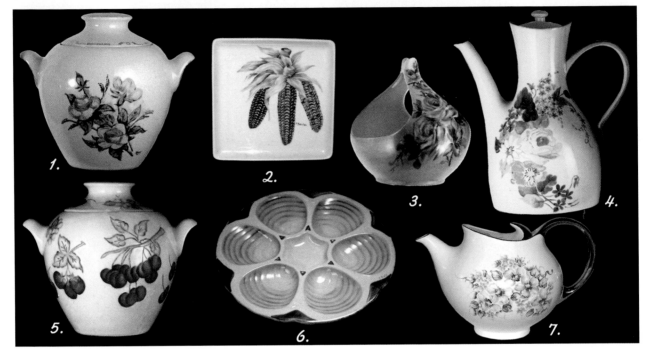

Photo above:

	Value
1. Cookie jar, signed "Kay '79"	$180.00 – 200.00
2. Plate, 6" x 6" with Indian corn, signed "Sanden"	$65.00 – 75.00
3. Tomorrow's Classic gravy boat with hand-painted flowers	$40.00 – 50.00
4. Carafe, signed "Jean Alpert"	$185.00 – 210.00
5. Zeisel cookie jar with hand-painted cherries, signed "Wood"	$180.00 – 200.00
6. Hand-painted oyster plate	$100.00 – 125.00
7. Floral decorated Zeisel-shape teapot	$170.00 – 190.00

Photo on page 159:

	Value
1. Teapot, Aladdin with pink hand painted roses	$400.00 – 600.00
2. Teapot, Aladdin, signed "E. L. Cross"	$500.00 – 625.00
3. Aladdin teapot with painted floral design and gold trim	$400.00 – 525.00
4. Teapot, Sani-Grid with pink hand-painted flowers	$175.00 – 200.00
5. Teapot, Aladdin, signed "To my sister Esther and Bob, from Marie and John	$500.00 – 750.00
6. Teapot, Sani-Grid with hand-painted floral design and silver trim	$175.00 – 200.00
7. Handled shakers with Southwestern scene signed "Edith Payment," pr.	$100.00 – 125.00
8. Teapot, Boston, signed "Edith Payment"	$225.00 – 300.00
9. Teapot, Boston with hand-painted white daisies	$225.00 – 275.00
10. Syrup, "Sundial," signed "Eita"	$100.00 – 125.00
11. Drip-O-lator coffee pot with floral painting signed "Nan '54"	$200.00 – 250.00
12. Sani-Grid creamer and sugar with painted leaves, unsigned	$60.00 – 75.00
13. "Rayed" creamer, sugar, and lid with floral painting unsigned	$65.00 – 75.00
14. Coffee pot, "Five Band" with hand-painted flowers and gold trim	$200.00 – 250.00

Oyster White and Red Cooking China

The reprint to the right shows some examples of the shapes of china Hall was producing during the mid-1950s.

The refrigerator items shown at the bottom right could be bought individually, but were also marketed as a set.

Oyster White and Red	Value
Bean pot, New England, 6 pint	$100.00 – 125.00
Bowl, #1215, 8 oz., dessert	$10.00 – 12.00
Bowl, 8 oz, sq. salad	$12.00 – 14.00
Bowl, 28 oz. sq. salad	$22.00 – 27.00
Bowl, #5120, 6" covered	$20.00 – 25.00
Bowl, #5121, 7" covered	$25.00 – 30.00
Bowl, #5122, 8" covered	$35.00 – 40.00
Bowl, 2 pint "Thin Rim"	$14.00 – 16.00
Bowl, 3½ pint, "Thin Rim"	$16.00 – 18.00
Bowl, 2⅔ quart, "Thin Rim"	$18.00 – 22.00
Casserole, 9 oz., round handled	$18.00 – 20.00
Casserole, 2 pint, round handled	$22.00 – 27.00
Casserole, 3½ pint, round handled	$22.00 – 27.00
Casserole, 6 pint, round handled	$30.00 – 35.00
Casserole, 3½ pint, oval handled	$22.00 – 27.00
Casserole, 5 pint, oval handled	$30.00 – 35.00
Casserole, 7 pint, oval handled	$35.00 – 45.00

Oyster White and Red	Value
Casserole, side handle, French, 8 oz	$20.00 – 22.00
Casserole, side handle, French, 4 pint	$27.00 – 32.00
Casserole, side handle, French, 7 pint	$35.00 – 45.00
Coffee pot, Washington, 15 cup	$95.00 – 115.00
Creamer, Boston	$16.00 – 18.00
Jar, 4 oz., horseradish	$60.00 – 80.00
Jar, 4 oz., mustard	$60.00 – 80.00
Jug, 1½ pint, "Five Band"	$22.00 – 27.00
Jug, 2 quart, Princeton	$85.00 – 95.00
Jug, #5118, 2 quart, covered	$125.00 – 150.00
Leftover, #5119, 1 quart, covered	$37.00 – 42.00
Mug, #535, 8 oz.	$10.00 – 12.00
Shaker, handled	$18.00 – 22.00
Sugar and cover, Boston	$25.00 – 35.00
Warmer, oval	$35.00 – 45.00
Warmer, round	$35.00 – 45.00

Rainbow Bowl Set

Hall produced a set of four bowls for the Jewel Tea Company in the 1940s. The brightly colored bowls were Jewel's Item No. 320, known as the Rainbow bowl set and have the following backstamp: "Hall Radiant Ware." Each bowl will be found in a single color. The diameters of the bowls from smallest to largest are: 5½", 6½", 7½", and 9".

Bowl	Value
Red	$50.00 – 65.00
Blue	$50.00 – 55.00
Yellow	$40.00 – 47.00
Green	$35.00 – 45.00

7 1/2" Bowl

9" Bowl

5 1/2" Bowl

6" Bowl

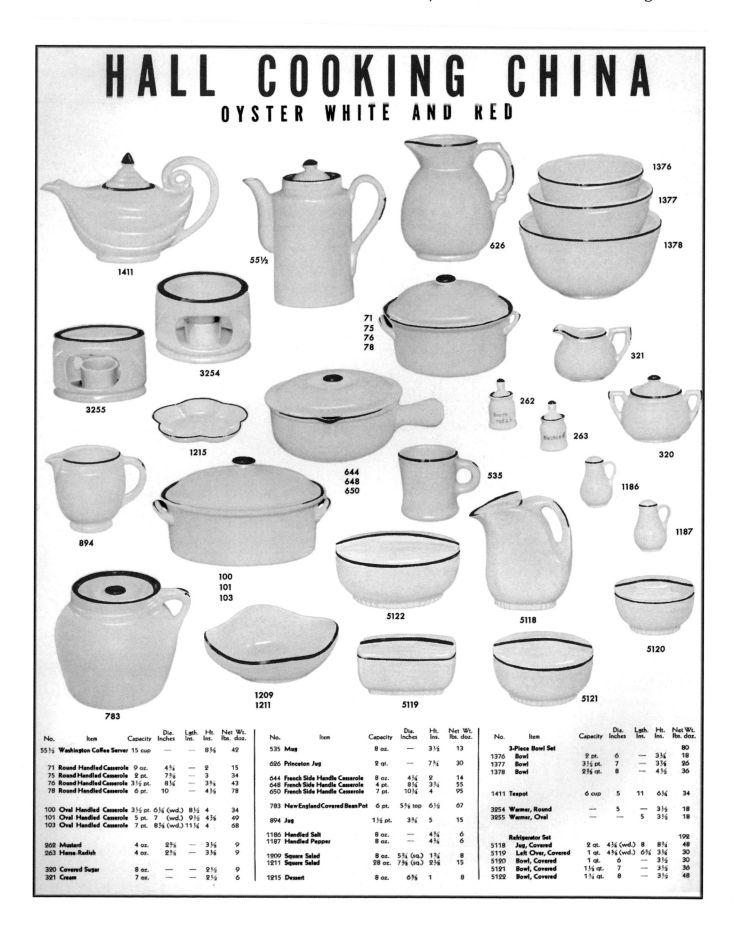

HALL COOKING CHINA
OYSTER WHITE AND RED

No.	Item	Capacity	Dia. Inches	Lgth. Ins.	Ht. Ins.	Net Wt. lbs. doz.
55½	Washington Coffee Server	15 cup	—	—	8¼	42
71	Round Handled Casserole	9 oz.	4¾	—	2	15
75	Round Handled Casserole	2 pt.	7⅜	—	3	34
76	Round Handled Casserole	3½ pt.	8¼	—	3⅜	43
78	Round Handled Casserole	6 pt.	10	—	4⅛	78
100	Oval Handled Casserole	3½ pt.	6¼ (wd.)	8½	4	34
101	Oval Handled Casserole	5 pt.	7 (wd.)	9½	4⅜	49
103	Oval Handled Casserole	7 pt.	8⅜ (wd.)	11¼	4	68
262	Mustard	4 oz.	2⅜	—	3⅝	9
263	Horse-Radish	4 oz.	2⅜	—	3⅝	9
320	Covered Sugar	8 oz.	—	—	2½	9
321	Cream	7 oz.	—	—	2½	6

No.	Item	Capacity	Dia. Inches	Ht. Ins.	Net Wt. lbs. doz.
535	Mug	8 oz.	—	3½	13
626	Princeton Jug	2 qt.	—	7¾	30
644	French Side Handle Casserole	8 oz.	4¼	2	14
648	French Side Handle Casserole	4 pt.	8¼	3¾	55
650	French Side Handle Casserole	7 pt.	10¼	4	95
783	New England Covered Bean Pot	6 pt.	5⅜ top	6½	67
894	Jug	1½ pt.	3¾	5	15
1186	Handled Salt	8 oz.	—	4¾	6
1187	Handled Pepper	8 oz.	—	4¾	6
1209	Square Salad	8 oz.	5¾ (sq.)	1¾	8
1211	Square Salad	28 oz.	7⅜ (sq.)	2⅝	15
1215	Dessert	8 oz.	6⅝	1	8

No.	Item	Capacity	Dia. Inches	Lgth. Ins.	Ht. Ins.	Net Wt. lbs. doz.
	3-Piece Bowl Set					80
1376	Bowl	2 pt.	6	—	3¾	18
1377	Bowl	3½ pt.	7	—	3¾	26
1378	Bowl	2⅝ qt.	8	—	4½	36
1411	Teapot	6 cup	5	11	6¼	34
3254	Warmer, Round	—	5	—	3½	18
3255	Warmer, Oval	—	—	5	3½	18
	Refrigerator Set					192
5118	Jug, Covered	2 qt.	4¾ (wd.)	8	8¾	48
5119	Left Over, Covered	1 qt.	4⅝ (wd.)	6¾	3¼	30
5120	Bowl, Covered	1 qt.	6	—	3½	30
5121	Bowl, Covered	1½ qt.	7	—	3½	36
5122	Bowl, Covered	1¾ qt.	8	—	3½	48

Red Kitchenware

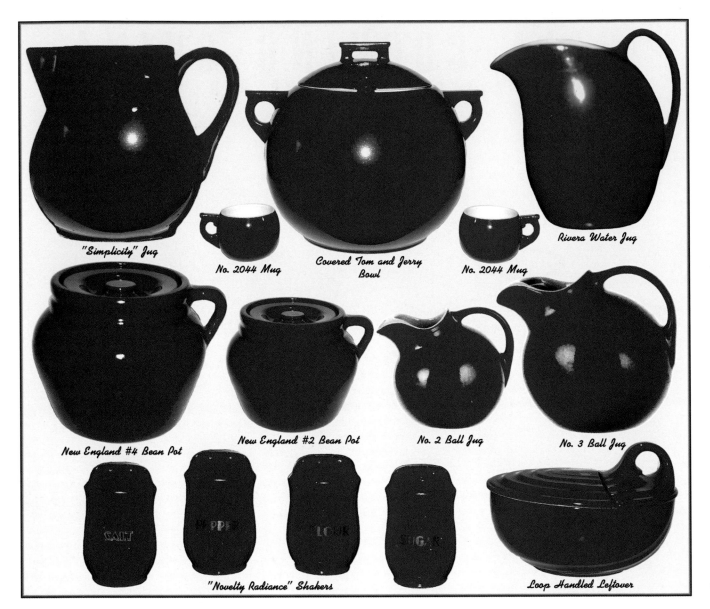

"Simplicity" Jug

No. 2044 Mug

Covered Tom and Jerry Bowl

No. 2044 Mug

Rivera Water Jug

New England #4 Bean Pot

New England #2 Bean Pot

No. 2 Ball Jug

No. 3 Ball Jug

"Novelty Radiance" Shakers

Loop Handled Leftover

Kitchenware		Value
Row 1:	Jug, "Simplicity"	$200.00 – 225.00
	Bowl, covered Tom & Jerry	$250.00 – 300.00
	Mug, Tom & Jerry #2044	$10.00 – 12.00
	*Jug, Rivera	$65.00 – 85.00
Row 2:	Bean pot, New England, #4	$100.00 – 125.00
	Bean pot, New England, #2	$100.00 – 125.00
	Ball jug, #2	$50.00 – 65.00
	Ball jug, #3	$50.00 – 65.00
Row 3:	Salt or pepper, "Novelty Radiance"	$65.00 – 75.00
	Flour or sugar, "Novelty Radiance"	$100.00 – 110.00
	Leftover, loop handle	$55.00 – 65.00
	*With new mark	

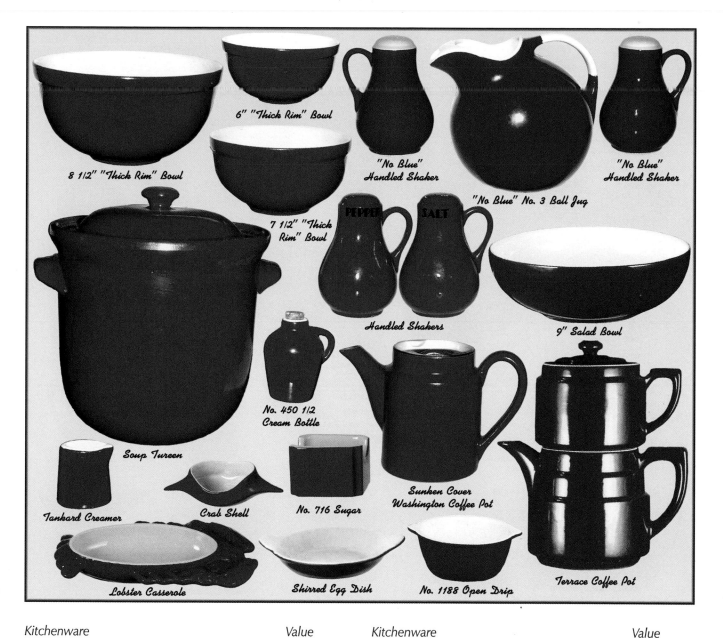

8 1/2" "Thick Rim" Bowl

6" "Thick Rim" Bowl

"No Blue" Handled Shaker

"No Blue" No. 3 Ball Jug

"No Blue" Handled Shaker

7 1/2" "Thick Rim" Bowl

PEPPER   SALT

Handled Shakers

9" Salad Bowl

Soup Tureen

No. 450 1/2 Cream Bottle

Sunken Cover Washington Coffee Pot

Tankard Creamer

Crab Shell

No. 716 Sugar

Terrace Coffee Pot

Lobster Casserole

Shirred Egg Dish

No. 1188 Open Drip

Kitchenware	Value	Kitchenware	Value
Row 1: Bowl, "Thick Rim," 8½", "No Blue"	$22.00 – 27.00	Row 4: Casserole, lobster shape	$32.00 – 37.00
Bowl, "Thick Rim," 7½", "No Blue"	$16.00 – 20.00	Shirred egg dish	$22.00 – 25.00
Bowl, "Thick Rim," 6", "No Blue"	$14.00 – 16.00	Drip jar, #1188 open	$27.00 – 32.00
Handled shaker, "No Blue"	$20.00 – 22.00	Coffee pot, "Terrace," small	
Ball jug, #3, "No Blue"	$80.00 – 95.00	size	$150.00 – 225.00
Row 2: Soup tureen	$250.00 – 350.00		
Cream bottle, #650½	$25.00 – 35.00	*Other "No Blue" Kitchenware not shown:*	
Shaker, handled (black letters)	$18.00 – 20.00	Casserole, "Thick Rim," w/knob lid	$50.00 – 55.00
Bowl, 9", salad, "No Blue"	$20.00 – 25.00	Casserole, "Thick Rim," w/recessed knob lid	$50.00 – 55.00
Row 3: Creamer, tankard	$16.00 – 20.00	Drip jar, "Thick Rim"	$40.00 – 45.00
Crab shell	$18.00 – 20.00	Teapot, Aladdin	$180.00 – 200.00
Sugar packet holder, #716	$18.00 – 20.00	Teapot, French	$120.00 – 140.00
Coffee pot, sunken cover, Washington	$65.00 – 85.00	Teapot, Parade	$250.00 – 285.00

Handled Shakers

Round Ashtray

"Rayed" Cookie Jar

Pretzel Jar

No. 641 Vase

Flared Ashtray

Bird on Nest Soup

Cylindrical Mug

Barrel Mug

Chocolate Tumbler

Ketchup Condiment Jar

Cream Bottle

"Norse" Sugar and Creamer

No. 193 Empire Creamer

Round Tea Tile

Bellvue Creamer

No. 142 Sauce Boat

Rectangular Baker

Petite Marmite

Side Handled French Casserole

Kitchenware	Value
Row 1: Shaker, handled (embossed letters)	$18.00 – 20.00
Ashtray, round	$22.00 – 27.00
Cookie jar, "Rayed"	$250.00 – 295.00
Pretzel jar	$200.00 – 225.00
Vase, #641	$25.00 – 30.00
Row 2: Ashtray, flared	$22.00 – 27.00
Soup, Bird on Nest	$40.00 – 45.00
Ketchup jar	$100.00 – 125.00
Cream bottle	$18.00 – 20.00
Mug, cylindrical	$14.00 – 16.00
Mug, round	$14.00 –16.00
Tumbler, chocolate	$20.00 – 22.00

Kitchenware	Value
Row 3: Creamer, "Norse"	$15.00 – 17.00
Sugar and lid, "Norse"	$22.00 – 27.00
Tea tile, round	$22.00 – 27.00
Creamer, Bellvue	$22.00 – 25.00
Creamer, #193, Empire	$22.00 – 25.00
Row 4: Baker, rectangular	$100.00 – 125.00
Petite marmite	$30.00 – 35.00
Casserole, side handle, French	$45.00 – 55.00
Sauce boat, #142	$16.00 – 20.00

RX Decoration

Hall pieces with the Rx decoration were used as premium items for pharmacists by the Owens-Illinois Corporation. The piece most often seen is the electric percolator. The New York shape teapot has proven elusive and is finally shown in the photo. Other items made by Hall are also illustrated. Dinnerware with this decoration was made by Taylor, Smith and Taylor. Matching glass tumblers in three sizes and stainless with this decoration may also be found.

Rx Kitchenware	Value
Butter, ¼ pound	$22.00 – 25.00
Casserole	$22.00 – 27.00
Cup	$2.00 – 4.00
Gravy boat and underplate	$15.00 – 18.00
Mug, Irish coffee	$6.00 – 8.00
Percolator, electric	$45.00 – 55.00
Saucer	$1.00 – 1.50
Shaker, ea.	$4.00 – 5.00
Teapot, New York	$100.00 – 110.00

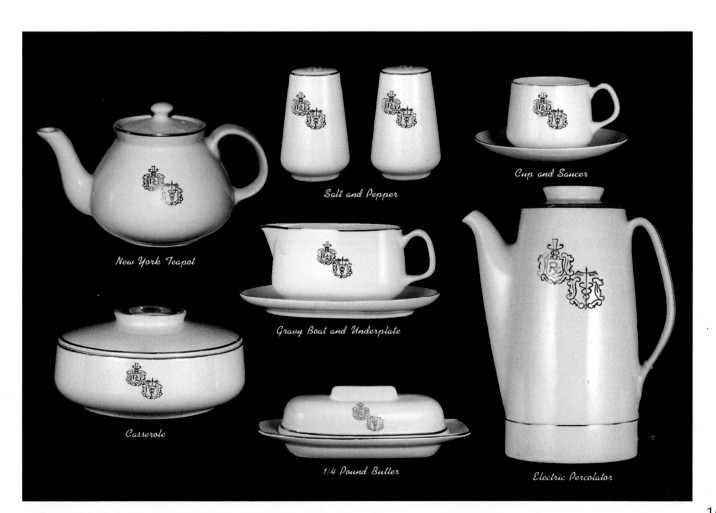

New York Teapot

Salt and Pepper

Cup and Saucer

Gravy Boat and Underplate

Casserole

1/4 Pound Butter

Electric Percolator

Two-Tone Cooking China

The listing below for Hall's Two-Tone Cooking China was compiled from a mid-1950s catalog listing. The illustration on the next page features the Citron and Mahogany color combination. Notice a pair of handled shakers consists of one of each color. In addition these pieces may also be found in a green and yellow color combination. See the examples in the photograph below. The prices listed below are for Citron and Mahogany. Price the green and yellow combination about 20% higher.

Two-Tone Cooking China	Value
Baker, #710, 40 oz., deep	$11.00 – 13.00
Baker, #711, 58 oz., deep	$12.00 – 15.00
Bean pot, New England, 5 pint	$40.00 – 45.00
Bean pot, New England, 6 pint	$40.00 – 45.00
Bowl, 24 oz., salad	$7.00 – 9.00
Bowl, 4 pint, salad	$16.00 – 18.00
Bowl, 4 quart, salad	$18.00 – 22.00
Bowl, 2 gallon, salad	$25.00 – 30.00
Bowl, 2 pint, "Thin Rim"	$8.00 – 10.00
Bowl, 3½ pint, "Thin Rim"	$12.00 – 14.00
Bowl, 2⅔ quart, "Thin Rim"	$15.00 – 18.00
Casserole, 2 pint, round, handled	$12.00 – 14.00
Casserole, 3½ pint, round, handled	$13.00 – 15.00
Casserole, 6 pint, round, handled	$18.00 – 20.00
Casserole, 3½ pint, oval, handled	$13.00 – 15.00
Casserole, 5 pint, oval, handled	$16.00 – 19.00
Casserole, 7 pint, oval, handled	$20.00 – 24.00
Casserole, side handle, French, 8 oz.	$18.00 – 22.00
Casserole, side handle, French, 4 pint	$22.00 – 27.00
Casserole, side handle, French 7, pint	$25.00 – 30.00
Coffee pot, French Coffee Biggin, 4, 6 cup	$50.00 – 60.00
Coffee pot, French Coffee Biggin, 10 cup	$60.00 – 70.00

Two-Tone Cooking China	Value
Creamer, #321, Boston	$11.00 – 13.00
Custard, #352	$4.50 – 5.50
Dish, shirred egg, 7, 12 oz.	$6.00 – 8.00
Jar, 4 oz., horseradish	$25.00 – 35.00
Jar, 4 oz., mustard	$25.00 – 35.00
Jug, "Five Band," 1½ pint	$18.00 – 20.00
Jug, 2 quart, Princeton	$40.00 – 50.00
Marmite, 2, 3 pint	$11.00 – 13.00
Marmite, 4 pint	$12.00 – 15.00
Mug, #536, 8 oz.	$5.00 – 7.00
Onion soup, 8 oz., French	$8.00 – 10.00
Onion soup, 1 pint, French	$12.00 – 14.00
Pot pie, #391, 8 oz.	$9.00 – 11.00
Rarebit, 8, 15 oz., Welsh	$8.00 – 10.00
Shaker, handled	$8.00 – 10.00
Souffle, 8, 10, 12 oz.	$8.00 – 10.00
Souffle, 2, 2½, 3 pint, French	$12.00 – 14.00
Souffle, oval fluted, 4, 5, 7½ oz.	$8.00 – 10.00
Stackette set, 4-piece	$40.00 – 50.00
Sugar and cover, #320 Boston	$15.00 – 18.00
Teapot, Boston	$60.00 – 70.00

New England Bean Pot

Stack Set

Round Handled Casserole

French Baker

White Bake Ware

Hall produced a wide variety of shapes of white bakeware that was designed primarily for institutional use. The pieces shown in the catalog reprint to the right date from the mid-1950s. Today many collectors are searching for this durable china to use in their kitchens.

White Bake Ware	Value
Ashtray, 4½"	$4.00 – 6.00
Bean pot, New England, ½ pint, no cover	$12.00 – 14.00
Bean pot, New England, 5 pint	$20.00 – 25.00
Bean pot, New England, 6 pint	$20.00 – 25.00
Bowl, 24 oz., salad	$10.00 – 12.00
Bowl, 4 pint, salad	$12.00 – 14.00
Bowl, 4 quart, salad	$15.00 – 18.00
Bowl, 2 gallon, salad	$22.00 – 27.00
Casserole, 16 oz., round	$8.00 – 10.00
Casserole, 2 pint, round, handled	$11.00 – 13.00
Casserole, 3½ pint, round, handled	$12.00 – 14.00
Casserole, 5, 6 pint, round, handled	$14.00 – 18.00
Casserole, 2, 3½ pint, oval, handled	$12.00 – 14.00
Casserole, 5 pint, oval, handled	$14.00 – 18.00
Casserole, 7 pint, oval, handled	$18.00 – 22.00
Casserole, French, side handle, 8, 12 oz.	$18.00 – 20.00
Casserole, French, side handle, 1½, 2½, 4 pint	$22.00 – 27.00
Casserole, French, side handle, 6, 7, 8 pint	$25.00 – 32.00
Casserole, rnd, shallow, hndl Casserole, side handle, French, 8 oz.	$16.00 – 18.00
Casserole, side handle, French, 4 pint	$18.00 – 22.00
Casserole, side handle, French, 7 pint	$25.00 – 30.00
Coffee pot, French Coffee Biggin, 3, 4, 6 cup	$40.00 – 50.00
Coffee pot, French Coffee Biggin, 10 cup	$55.00 – 65.00
Coffee pot, Washington, 15 cup	$37.00 – 47.00
Coffee pot, #3322, 24 oz., demi	$20.00 – 25.00
Creamer, #321, Boston	$10.00 – 12.00
Creamer, #1395, morning set	$10.00 – 12.00
Creamer, #3324, demi coffee set	$10.00 – 12.00
Cup, 5 oz., hndl, Turkish coffee	$7.00 – 9.00
Custard, #382	$4.00 – 5.00
Custard, fluted 3½, 5, 7 oz.	$4.00 – 5.00

White Bake Ware	Value
Dish, 20 oz., serving	$8.00 – 10.00
Dish, 40, 60 oz., serving	$16.00 – 20.00
Dish, #1149, 9", fondue	$18.00 – 20.00
Dish, shirred egg, 7, 8, 12, 14 oz.	$8.00 – 12.00
Jar, 4 oz., horseradish	$16.00 – 18.00
Jar, 4 oz., mustard	$16.00 – 18.00
Jug, #247, 5 pint	$20.00 – 25.00
Jug, #625, 3 pint	$18.00 – 22.00
Jug, "Five Band," 1½ pint	$14.00 – 16.00
Jug, 2 quart Princeton	$22.00 – 27.00
Jug, #2633, 4¾ pint	$20.00 – 24.00
Marmite, 1½ pint	$6.00 – 8.00
Marmite, 2, 3 pint	$8.00 – 12.00
Mug, #535, 8 oz.	$5.00 – 7.00
Mug, #1272, 7 oz. hndl coffee	$5.00 – 7.00
Mug, #1273, 10 oz. hndl coffee	$6.00 – 8.00
Mug, #1310, 9 oz. conic	$5.00 – 7.00
Onion soup, 8, 14 oz., French	$6.00 – 9.00
Ramekin, fluted, 2, 2¾, 3, 4½, 6 oz.	$4.00 – 5.00
Ramekin, 4 oz., scalloped	$4.00 – 5.00
Rarebit, 8, 12, 15 oz., Welsh	$5.00 – 8.00
Rarebit, 30 oz., Welsh	$11.00 – 13.00
Shaker, handled	$4.00 – 6.00
Shell, baking, 2½ oz.	$4.00 – 5.00
Shell, baking, 4½, 5½ oz.	$4.00 – 5.00
Souffle, 8, 10, 12 oz.	$6.00 – 8.00
Souffle, 1, 1½, 2, 2½, 3 pint	$10.00 – 12.00
Souffle, 2, 3 quart	$12.00 – 14.00
Souffle, 2½, 3 pint, French	$10.00 – 12.00
Souffle, 2, 3 quart, French	$12.00 – 14.00
Souffle, oval fluted, 4, 5, 7½ oz.	$8.00 – 10.00
Sugar and cover, #320, Boston	$12.00 – 14.00
Sugar #1394, morning set	$10.00 – 12.00
Sugar, #3323, demi coffee set	$10.00 – 12.00
Teapot, #1393, morning set	$25.00 – 30.00
Teapot, Aladdin	$40.00 – 45.00
Tumbler, 343, handled chocolate	$6.00 – 8.00

HALL CHINA *Famous White Bake Ware*

75 to 78 ROUND CASSEROLE (Handled)

No.	Capacity	Diam.	Height	Net Wt. Lbs. Doz.
75	2 pts.	7⅜	3	34¼
76	3½ pts.	8¼	3⅜	43
77	5 pts.	9	3¾	55
78	6 pts.	10	4⅛	78

84 to 86 FRENCH DRIP COFFEE BIGGIN

No.	Capacity	Net Wt. Lbs. Doz.
84	16 oz.- 3 cup	19
84½	24 oz.- 4 cup	29¾
85	32 oz.- 6 cup	39
86	50 oz.-10 cup	46

99 to 103 OVAL CASSEROLE (Handled)

No.	Capacity	Length	Width	Height	Net Wt. Lbs. Doz.
99	2 pts.	7½	5½	3¾	29
100	3½ pts.	8½	6¼	4	34¼
101	5 pts.	9½	7	4⅞	48½
102	7 pts.	10¼	7½	5	62
103	7 pts.	11¼	8⅞	4	67½

106 to 108 MARMITE CASSEROLE

No.	Capacity	Diam.	Height	Net Wt. Lbs. Doz.
106	1½ pts.	6⅝	3	24
107	2 pts.	7⅝	3⅛	27
108	3 pts.	8⅝	3¼	28

228 to 230 BAKING SHELL

No.	Capacity	Length	Width	Height	Net Wt. Lbs. Doz.
228	2½ oz.	4	4⅜	1¼	4
229	4¼ oz.	4⅞	4⅝	1⅜	6¼
230	5½ oz.	5	5⅜	1½	7

432 to 435 FRENCH SHIRRED EGG DISH (Round)

No.	Capacity	Diam.	Height	Net Wt. Lbs. Doz.
432	7 oz.	5¼	⅞	6
433	8 oz.	5⅞	1	7½
434	12 oz.	6½	1⅛	9½
435	14 oz.	7	1¼	13½

477-479 FRENCH ONION SOUP

No.	Capacity	Height	Diam.	Net Wt. Lbs. Doz.
477	8 oz.	3¼	4¼	12
479	14 oz.	3⅞	5	15

498 to 507 SOUFFLE

No.	Capacity	Diam.	Height	Net Wt. Lbs. Doz.
498	8 oz.	4	2	5½
499	10 oz.	4½	2	5
500	12 oz.	4½	2⅛	5½
501	1 pt.	5	2¼	8
502	1½ pts.	6	2¼	10¼
503	2 pts.	6½	2⅜	12¾
504	2½ pts.	7	2⅜	18½
505	3 pts.	7¾	2⅝	22½
506	2 qts.	8¾	3⅛	33
507	3 qts.	9½	3¾	44¼

527 to 531 FRENCH WELSH RAREBIT

No.	Capacity	Length	Width	Height	Net Wt. Lbs. Doz.
527	8 oz.	8¼	4¼	1⅛	6¼
528	12 oz.	9⅛	4⅞	1⅜	8½
529	15 oz.	10¼	5½	1½	10¾
531	30 oz.	12½	6¾	1⅝	19¼

644 to 651 FRENCH CASSEROLE (Side Handled)

No.	Capacity	Diam.	Height	Net Wt. Lbs. Doz.
644	8 oz.	4¼	2	13¾
645	12 oz.	5¼	2¼	20½
646	1½ pts.	6¼	2½	31¼
647	2½ pts.	7¼	3	41
648	4 pts.	8¼	3¾	55
649	6 pts.	9¼	3⅝	74
650	7 pts.	10¼	4	94½
651	8 pts.	11¼	4⅛	126

780 to 783 NEW ENGLAND BEANPOT (Handled)

No.	Capacity	Height	Diam. Top	Net Wt. Lbs. Doz.
780—No Cover	½ pt.	3	2¾	6¾
782—With Cover	5 pts.	6	5⅜	57
783—With Cover	6 pts.	6½	5⅜	67

831 SCALLOPED RAMEKIN

No.	Capacity	Diam.	Height	Net Wt. Lbs. Doz.
831	4 oz.	3¼	1⅝	2½

842 to 845 FLUTED RAMEKIN

No.	Capacity	Diam.	Height	Net Wt. Lbs. Doz.
842	½ oz.	1⅝	1	¾
843	1 oz.	2¼	1¼	1¾
844	2 oz.	2¾	1⅛	2
844½	3 oz.	3⅛	1⅜	2¾
845	4½ oz.	3½	1½	3

848 to 850 FLUTED CUSTARD

No.	Capacity	Diam.	Height	Net Wt. Lbs. Doz.
848	3½ oz.	2⅞	2¼	3
849	5 oz.	3⅜	2⅜	3¼
850	7 oz.	3¾	2½	4½

1272-1273 COFFEE MUG (Handled)

No.	Capacity	Height	Net Wt. Lbs. Doz.
1272	7 oz.	5½	9¾
1273	10 oz.	6	10

1280 to 1284 SALAD BOWL

No.	Capacity	Diam.	Height	Net Wt. Lbs. Doz.
1280	24 oz.	7¼	2¼	15
1282	4 pts.	9¾	3	27
1283	4 qts.	12	4⅛	81
1284	2 gal.	15¾	4¾	122¼

Zeisel Kitchenware

In addition to the dinnerware lines which have been discussed previously, Eva Zeisel designed a kitchenware shape for Hall during the 1950s. Two patterns — Casual Living and Tri-Tone — are available.

Casual Living pieces are Seal brown and white with a decoration of pastel brushstrokes and dots in the white area.

Tri-Tone pieces have a three-color decoration — pink, turquoise, and gray over a white body. The pink and turquoise areas overlap to form gray triangles and the knobs of lids are also gray.

The cookie jar and the bean pot are similar in shape. The cookie jar has a flared collar into which the lid fits and the bottom is a little fatter than the bean pot bottom. The bean pot has no collar.

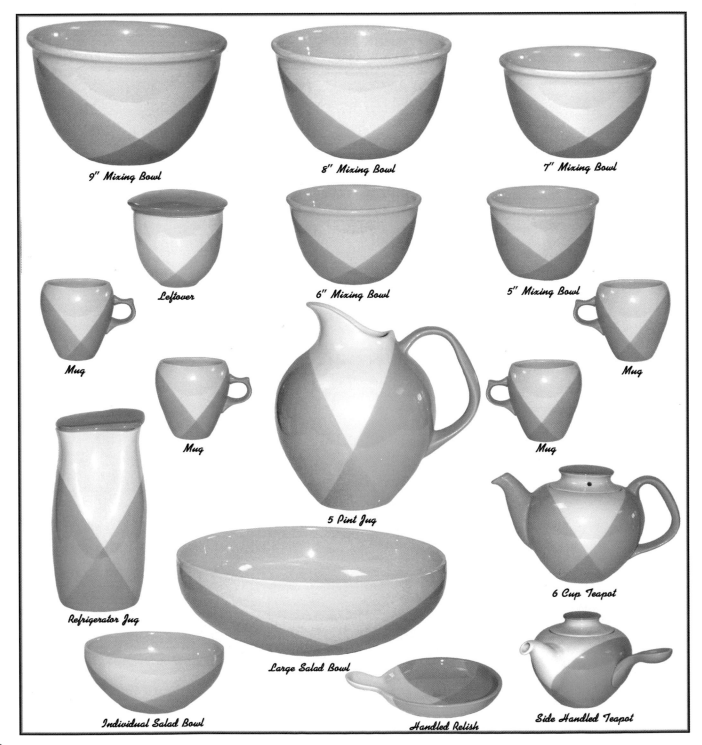

9" Mixing Bowl

8" Mixing Bowl

7" Mixing Bowl

Leftover

6" Mixing Bowl

5" Mixing Bowl

Mug

Mug

Mug

Mug

5 Pint Jug

Refrigerator Jug

6 Cup Teapot

Large Salad Bowl

Individual Salad Bowl

Handled Relish

Side Handled Teapot

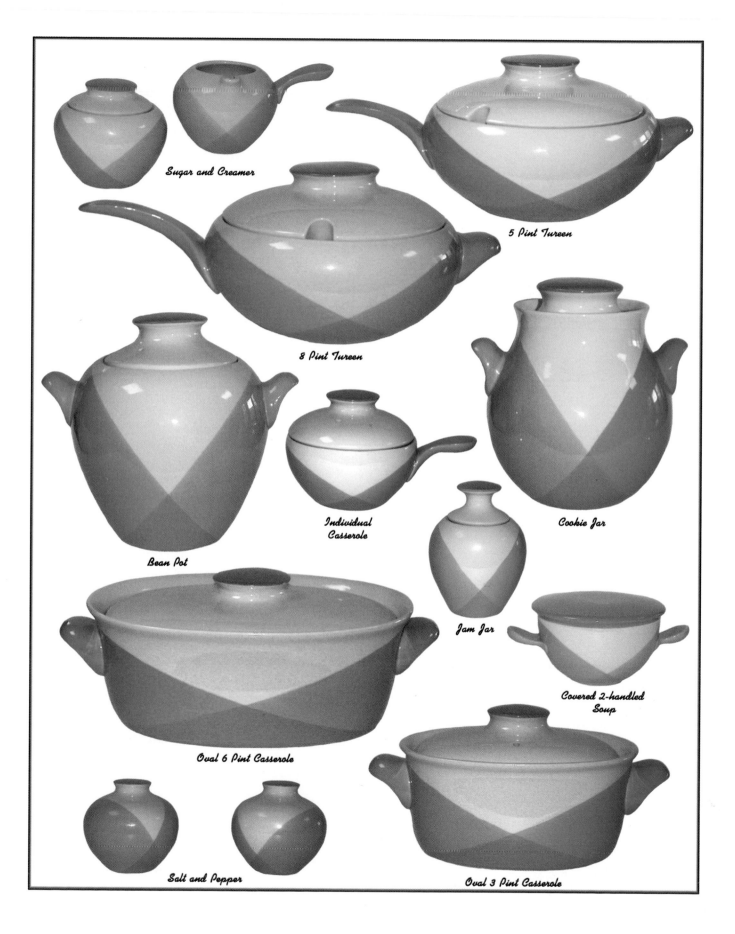

Sugar and Creamer

5 Pint Tureen

8 Pint Tureen

Individual
Casserole

Cookie Jar

Bean Pot

Jam Jar

Covered 2-handled
Soup

Oval 6 Pint Casserole

Salt and Pepper

Oval 3 Pint Casserole

Handled Relish

6-cup Teapot

5 Pint Jug

8 Pint Tureen

Jam Jar

Creamer

Sugar and Lid

Kitchenware	Casual Living	Tri-Tone
Bean pot	$75.00 – 90.00	$250.00 – 285.00
Bowl, covered, 2-H soup	$22.00 – 25.00	$75.00 – 85.00
Bowl, individual salad	$7.00 – 9.00	$35.00 – 40.00
Bowl, large salad	$20.00 – 25.00	$70.00 – 85.00
Bowl, 5"		$27.00 – 30.00
Bowl, 6"		$30.00 – 35.00
Bowl, 7"		$40.00 – 45.00
Bowl, 8"		$50.00 – 55.00
Bowl, 9"		$65.00 – 75.00
Casserole, individual	$18.00 – 22.00	$110.00 – 125.00
Casserole, oval, 3 pt.	$20.00 – 25.00	$110.00 – 125.00
Casserole, oval, 6 pt.	$25.00 – 32.00	$130.00 – 145.00
Cookie jar	$70.00 – 90.00	$250.00 – 285.00
Creamer	$12.00 – 14.00	$27.00 – 30.00
Jam jar	$22.00 – 27.00	$90.00 – 110.00
Jug, 5 pt.	$50.00 – 65.00	$220.00 – 250.00
Jug, refrigerator	$60.00 – 70.00	$180.00 – 210.00
Leftover and cover	$22.00 – 27.00	$85.00 – 110.00
Mug	$18.00 – 22.00	$50.00 – 60.00
Relish, 1-handle	$12.00 – 16.00	$32.00 – 37.00
Shakers, ea.	$14.00 – 16.00	$30.00 – 35.00
Sugar and lid	$16.00 – 18.00	$45.00 – 55.00
Teapot, 6-cup	$70.00 – 90.00	$220.00 – 250.00
Teapot, side-handled	$85.00 – 100.00	$290.00 – 320.00
Tureen, 5 pt.	$25.00 – 32.00	$120.00 – 135.00
Tureen, 8 pt.	$40.00 – 50.00	$175.00 – 190.00

Miscellaneous Kitchenware

New England #4 Bean Pot

Handled 4-piece Shaker Set

SALT PEPPER SUGAR FLOUR

"Novelty Radiance" Salt & Pepper

SALT PEPPER

New England #4 Bean Pot

Mustard

Feather 9 1/2" Salad Bowl

6" Bowl

5" Bowl

Side Handle French Casserole

Feather 7 3/4" Plate

"Thick Rim" 8 1/2" Bowl

"Thick Rim" 7 1/2" Bowl

"Thick Rim" 6" Bowl

Drip Jar

Kitchenware	Value
Row 1: Bean pot, New England, #4, ivory with red stripe	$140.00 – 160.00
Shaker, handled, ivory with red stripes	$150.00 – 180.00
Row 2: Salt and pepper, "Novelty Radiance," art glaze blue	$120.00 – 135.00
Bean pot, New England, #4	$125.00 – 140.00
Mustard pot, light blue	$40.00 – 60.00
Feather 9½", salad bowl	$30.00 – 40.00

Kitchenware	Value
Row 3: Bowl, 6", maroon	$8.00 – 10.00
Bowl, 5", green	$7.00 – 10.00
Casserole, side handle, French	
Feather, 7¾", salad plate	$12.00 – 14.00
Row 4: Bowl, "Thick Rim," 8½"	$22.00 – 25.00
Bowl, "Thick Rim," 7½"	$16.00 – 18.00
Bowl, "Thick Rim," 6"	$14.00 – 16.00
Drip jar, gold iridescent decoration	$60.00 – 80.00

KITCHENWARE DECAL PATTERNS
Acacia and "Autumn Flowers"

Acacia is a 1940s pattern that is not easy to find. Many of the pieces which have been turning up are in the "Radiance" shape. The appearance of the all-china drip coffee pot, the "Radiance" teapot, stack set, and covered jugs has generated renewed interest in this pattern among collectors. All the dinnerware found to date in this pattern has been made by Taylor, Smith and Taylor. Hall purists may not find a mixture acceptable, but the different styles of pottery look nice together.

The decal decoration shown at the bottom of the photo on the next page has been named "Autumn Flowers" by collectors. Pieces with this decal are found infrequently. Thus far discoveries have been limited to a few different shapes. The most interesting pieces for collectors are the pretzel jar and the New England bean pot. Notice the decal appears on an ivory body except for the buffet casserole which has an eggshell body.

Kitchenware	Acacia	Autumn Flowers
Bean pot, New England, #4	$140.00 – 180.00	$100.00 – 130.00
Bowl, 9½", salad	$20.00 – 25.00	
Bowl, 6", "Radiance"	$18.00 –22.00	$16.00 – 18.00
Bowl, 7½", "Radiance"	$20.00 – 25.00	$20.00 – 22.00
Bowl, 9", "Radiance"	$25.00 – 32.00	$22.00 – 27.00
Bowl, 10", "Radiance"	$32.00 – 37.00	
Bowl, 6" "Thin Rim"	$18.00 – 22.00	
Bowl, 7¼", "Thin Rim"	$22.00 – 27.00	
Bowl, 8½", "Thin Rim"	$25.00 – 32.00	
Casserole, buffet		$50.00 – 60.00
Casserole, "Medallion"	$35.00 – 45.00	
Casserole, "Radiance"	$35.00 – 45.00	
Custard, "Radiance"	$18.00 – 22.00	
Coffee pot, "Baron"	$175.00 – 225.00	
Coffee pot, "Terrace"	$125.00 – 150.00	
Drip coffee pot, #691	$450.00 – 550.00	
Drip coffee pot, all-china, "Radiance"	$250.00 – 350.00	
Drip jar and lid, "Radiance"	$30.00 – 35.00	
*Jug, "Radiance," #1	$120.00 – 135.00	
*Jug, "Radiance," #2	$130.00 –155.00	
*Jug, "Radiance," #3, #4	$145.00 – 165.00	
*Jug, "Radiance," #5, #6	$160.00 – 185.00	
Leftover, rectangular		$45.00 – 55.00
Leftover, square		$80.00 – 100.00
Marmite and cover	$37.00 – 42.00	
Pretzel jar		$140.00 – 165.00
Ramekin, #844½, 3 ounce	$25.00 – 30.00	
Shakers, handled ea.	$20.00 – 24.00	
Stack set, "Radiance"	$100.00 – 145.00	
Teapot, "Radiance"	$200.00 – 225.00	
Tea set, Tea-for-Four	$300.00 – 350.00	

*With cover

Acacia

"Radiance" All-china Drip Coffee Pot

"Radiance" Teapot

Tea-for-Four Tea Set

#691 All-china Drip Coffee Pot

No. 3 "Radiance" Jug

No. 5 "Radiance" Jug

"Radiance" Custard

8 1/2" "Thin Rim" Bowl

7 1/4" "Thin Rim" Bowl

6" "Thin Rim" Bowl

SALT

PEPPER

Handled Salt & Pepper

New England No. 4 Bean Pot

Buffet Casserole

9" Salad Bowl

Marmite & Cover

Autumn Flowers

Pretzel Jar

7 1/2" "Radiance" Bowl

New England No. 4 Bean Pot

Beauty

The name "Beauty" will usually have a color associated with it as collectors attempt to distinguish the color background upon which the decal has been placed. For example, if the decal is on an item with a totally white background, the piece is referred to as "White Beauty." Pieces of "Black Beauty" will have parts with a Hi-black glaze. However, the colorful orange and black decal will appear on a portion which has a Hi-white glaze. Very few kitchenware pieces with this decal are being found and no dinnerware is known. Among the items most frequently seen are the "Radiance" casserole and the handled shakers with a white background. The casserole shown in the metal holder has the Foreman Brothers backstamp. The 12" round bowl shown at the bottom of the photo is unusual. It has a light yellow glaze with platinum trim.

The side handle casserole is shown with different color bodies. The "Novelty Radiance" style shakers, square leftover, and the shirred egg dish are interesting additions to the listing.

Beauty	*Value*
Baker, French	$35.00 – 45.00
Bean pot, New England, #2	$130.00 – 145.00
Bean pot, New England, #3	$130.00 – 145.00
Bean pot, New England, #4	$120.00 – 140.00
Bowl, 9½", salad	$25.00 – 27.00
Bowl, 12", salad	$40.00 – 50.00
Bowl, 6", "Radiance"	$18.00 – 22.00
Bowl, 7½", "Radiance"	$22.00 – 25.00
Bowl, 9", "Radiance"	$27.00 – 32.00
Bowl, 6" "Thin Rim"	$18.00 – 22.00
Bowl, 7¼", "Thin Rim"	$22.00 – 27.00
Bowl, 8½", "Thin Rim"	$27.00 – 32.00
Casserole (Forman), 2-handled	$45.00 – 50.00
Casserole, "Radiance"	$35.00 – 45.00
Casserole, round knob handle	$40.00 – 45.00
Casserole, side handled	$65.00 – 85.00
Casserole, "Thick Rim"	$37.00 – 45.00
Custard	$20.00 – 22.00
Dish, shirred egg	$30.00 – 35.00
Drip coffee pot, all-china, #691	$300.00 – 350.00
Drip jar and lid, "Thick Rim"	$30.00 – 37.00
*Jug, "Radiance," #1	$100.00 – 125.00
*Jug, "Radiance," #2	$130.00 – 140.00
*Jug, "Radiance," #3, #4	$140.00 – 150.00
*Jug, "Radiance," #5, #6	$140.00 – 165.00
Leftover, square	$110.00 – 130.00
Marmite and cover	$37.00 – 42.00
Shaker, handled	$22.00 – 25.00
Shaker, "Novelty Radiance"	$40.00 – 60.00
Stack set, "Radiance"	$100.00 – 125.00
Teapot, "Radiance"	$250.00 – 280.00
Teapot, "Rutherford"	$225.00 – 265.00

*With cover

No. 5 "Radiance" Jug

"Rutherford" Teapot

No. 691 Drip Coffee Pot

Forman Brothers 2-handled Casserole

No. 4 "Radiance" Jug

Handled Salt & Pepper

Custard

Shirred Egg Dish

New England No. 2 Bean Pot

Side-handled Casserole

"Radiance" Stack Set

Side-handled Casserole

"Novelety Radiance" Salt & Pepper

7 1/4" "Thin Rim" Bowl

6" "Thin Rim" Bowl

French Fluted Baker

12" Salad Bowl

9 1/2" Salad Bowl

9 1/2" Salad Bowl

Blue Blossom

Blue Blossom is a blue-body decal kitchenware line which was introduced in 1939. The decal consists of an elongated green leaf tipped with a colorful red, yellow, and white iris-like flower. A Blue Blossom morning set tea service has been found advertised in a 1940s Blackwell-Wieland Company wholesale catalog. It is referred to in that catalog as an "Apple Blossom" pattern. The wholesale price for the entire set — teapot, sugar, creamer, and lids — was $2.60. Notice the teapot and creamer are the same shape as the No. 1 tea set teapot and creamer. However, the sugar to the Blue Blossom set has handles and a lid. The sugar to the No. 1 tea set is handleless and has no lid. Also, no cups, saucers, or plates have been found with the Blue Blossom set.

Although new shapes with this decal are still being uncovered, the flood of reports of new items has dwindled to a mere trickle. The rectangular baker pictured on the opposite page and the Baltimore teapot are the only items new to the current listing. Significant additions to any collection would include canisters and matching shakers, the Airflow teapot, the #691 all-china drip coffee pot, and the "Zephyr" style butter and leftover. Other interesting pieces which are difficult to find are the Streamline teapot, and the "Sundial" coffee server, batter bowl, and cookie jar. Notice the decal on the shirred egg dish is on the white interior area. The handled shakers are comprised of a four-piece set and four different sizes of ball jugs may be found.

Considering the relatively high price of the more desirable pieces of this pattern, collector interest is almost unbelievable. New collectors are aggressively competing with seasoned veterans for the limited supply and the prices are gradually rising.

Kitchenware	Value
Baker, rectangular	$225.00 – 250.00
Ball jug, #1	$145.00 – 165.00
Ball jug, #2	$145.00 – 165.00
Ball jug, #3	$120.00 – 150.00
Ball jug, #4	$145.00 – 185.00
Batter jug, "Sundial"	$290.00 – 320.00
Bean pot, New England, #4	$185.00 – 225.00
Bowl, 6", "Thick Rim"	$30.00 – 32.00
Bowl, 7½", "Thick Rim"	$32.00 – 37.00
Bowl, 8½", "Thick Rim"	$35.00 – 42.00
Butter, 1 lb., "Zephyr"-style	$600.00 – 700.00
Canister, "Radiance"	$350.00 – 400.00
Casserole, #76, round	$55.00 – 65.00
Casserole, #77, round	$60.00 – 65.00
Casserole, #100, oval	$65.00 – 70.00
Casserole, "Five Band"	$60.00 – 65.00
Casserole, "Sundial," #1	$50.00 – 60.00
Casserole, "Sundial," #4	$40.00 – 55.00
Casserole, "Thick Rim"	$50.00 – 60.00
Coffee pot, French coffee biggin	$300.00 – 400.00
Coffee server, "Sundial"	$500.00 – 650.00
Cookie jar, "Five Band"	$250.00 – 300.00
Cookie jar, "Sundial"	$350.00 – 400.00
Creamer, morning set	$45.00 – 55.00
Creamer, New York	$40.00 – 45.00
Custard, "Thick Rim"	$25.00 – 28.00

Kitchenware	Value
Drip coffee pot, #691	$450.00 – 550.00
Drip jar, #1188, open	$55.00 – 65.00
Drip jar and cover, "Thick Rim"	$90.00 – 100.00
Jug, Donut	$250.00 – 300.00
Jug, 1½ pt., "Five Band"	$80.00 – 100.00
Jug, 2 qt., "Five Band"	$125.00 – 150.00
Jug, loop handle	$175.00 – 200.00
Leftover, loop handle	$130.00 – 150.00
Leftover, "Zephyr"-style	$180.00 – 225.00
Shakers, "Five Band," ea.	$30.00 – 37.00
Shakers, handled, ea. (4)	$35.00 – 40.00
Shakers, "Radiance," canister style, ea.	$90.00 – 100.00
Shirred egg dish	$55.00 – 65.00
Sugar and lid, morning set	$70.00 – 80.00
Sugar and lid, New York	$60.00 – 70.00
Syrup, "Sundial"	$195.00 – 225.00
Teapot, Airflow	$700.00 – 900.00
Teapot, Baltimore	UND
Teapot, Hook Cover	$280.00 – 320.00
Teapot, morning set	$260.00 – 315.00
Teapot, New York	$300.00 – 375.00
Teapot, "Sundial"	$300.00 – 375.00
Teapot, Streamline	$280.00 – 325.00
Water bottle, "Zephyr"	$600.00 – 800.00

"Radiance" Canisters

"Radiance" Canister-style Salt & Pepper

Shirred Egg Dish

New England No. 4 Bean Pot

Hook Cover Teapot

"Five Band" Cookie Jar

"Five Band" Salt & Pepper

"Five Band" 1 1/2 Pint Jug

Rectangular Baker

New York Teapot

Streamline Teapot

"Five Band" 2 Quart Jug

"Zephyr" Leftover

"Zephyr" Butter

Handled Salt & Pepper

Handled Sugar Shaker

"Sundial" Coffee Server

No. 691 All-china Drip
Coffee Pot

Morning Set Teapot

Morning Set Creamer

Morning Set Sugar

"Sundial" No. 1 Casserole

"Sundial" Teapot

"Thick Rim" Custard

"Sundial" Syrup

"Sundial" Cookie Jar

Donut Jug

Loop Handle Jug

Loop Handle Leftover

No. 77 Round Casserole

"Sundial" Batter Jug

No. 4 Ball Jug

No. 3 Ball Jug

No. 2 Ball Jug

No. 1 Ball Jug

"Blue Crocus" and "Blue Floral"

"Blue Crocus" is a kitchenware pattern which uses the crocus decal with pieces having a cadet blue body. Currently, only a few bowls, a casserole, and the handled shakers have been found in this pattern.

"Blue Crocus"	Value
Bowl, 6", straight sided	$25.00 – 28.00
Bowl, 7½", straight sided	$27.00 – 32.00
Bowl, 9", straight-sided	$35.00 – 40.00
Bowl, 6", "Thick Rim"	$25.00 – 30.00
Bowl, 7½", "Thick Rim"	$30.00 – 33.00
Bowl, 8½", "Thick Rim"	$30.00 – 35.00
Casserole, "Thick Rim"	$60.00 – 70.00
Shakers, handled, ea.	$27.00 – 32.00

Blue Crocus

6" Straight-sided Bowl   7 1/2" Straight-sided Bowl   Handled Shakers

"Blue Floral"

2-quart Casserole

WILL HAVE THESE ITEMS AVAILABLE HIS NEXT TRIP!

2 - QUART CASSEROLE
Covered casserole for simplified cooking and serving. Guaranteed against heat breakage. Cooks evenly. Makes an attractive help-yourself serving dish. Hall Ovenware . . . Cadet Blue pattern.

$3.50

3 - PIECE BOWL SET
A nest of one, two, and three-quart bowls. Ideal for mixing, baking, serving, storing. Guaranteed against heat breakage. Cadet Blue pattern — blue on the outside with dainty floral pattern on the inside rim.

$2.00

The "Blue Floral" pattern consists of a set of three mixing bowls and a casserole. The bowls have cadet blue exteriors and white interiors with a tiny floral sprig decoration. The casserole has a cadet blue base and a white lid with a large blue knob. The floral decoration of the casserole is on the white part of the lid. This pattern was made for the Jewel Tea Company during the mid-1940s. The casserole retailed for $2.00 and the three-piece bowl set was $3.50.

"Blue Floral"	Value
Bowl, 6¼"	$18.00 – 22.00
Bowl, 7¾"	$22.00 – 24.00
Bowl, 9"	$26.00 – 30.00
Casserole	$45.00 – 50.00

Blue Garden

Blue Garden is a kitchenware pattern employing a floral decal on a cobalt body. The delicate white flowers and green leaves are not as colorful as the decoration of the Blue Blossom pattern, but they are still attractive enough to perk collector interest. Also, prize pieces such as the "Sundial" coffee server, "Zephyr"-style water bottle, butter, or leftover are bound to attract a lot of attention in any collection. Some veteran Hall collectors, who had previously thought Blue Garden contained an insignificant number of pieces, are now looking at this pattern again. Both old and new collectors are finding the search for these pieces is not effortless. The only item anyone is finding in abundance is the "Sundial" #4 casserole. Most other pieces are scarce, but the list of known items continues to grow and so does the number of collectors.

Donut Jug

New England No. 4 Bean Pot

"Five Band" 1 1/2 Pint Jug

"Zephyr" Leftover

"Zephyr" Butter

"Zephyr" Water Bottle

"Five Band" Casserole

Handled Shakers

"Thick Rim" Custard

Kitchenware	Value	Kitchenware	Value
Ball jug, #1	$125.00 – 145.00	Drip jar, #1188, open	$45.00 – 55.00
Ball jug, #2	$125.00 – 145.00	Drip jar and cover, "Thick Rim"	$65.00 – 75.00
Ball jug, #3	$110.00 – 125.00	Jug, Donut	$220.00 – 255.00
Ball jug, #4	$115.00 – 130.00	Jug, 1½ pt., "Five Band"	$50.00 – 55.00
Batter jug, "Sundial"	$265.00 – 310.00	Jug, 2 qt., "Five Band"	$80.00 – 100.00
Bean pot, New England, #4	$175.00 – 195.00	Jug, loop handle	$120.00 – 145.00
Bowl, 6", "Radiance"	$23.00 – 27.00	Leftover, loop handle	$115.00 – 135.00
Bowl, 7½", "Radiance"	$28.00 – 32.00	Leftover, "Zephyr"	$140.00 – 160.00
Bowl, 9", "Radiance"	$32.00 – 37.00	Shakers, canister style, ea.	$65.00 – 85.00
Bowl, 6", "Thick Rim"	$22.00 – 25.00	Shakers, handled, ea. (4)	$25.00 – 30.00
Bowl, 7½", "Thick Rim"	$27.00 – 30.00	Sugar and lid, morning set	$60.00 – 68.00
Bowl, 8½", "Thick Rim"	$32.00 – 37.00	Sugar and lid, New York	$55.00 – 65.00
Butter, 1 lb., "Zephyr"	$550.00 – 650.00	Syrup, "Sundial"	$150.00 – 175.00
Canister, "Radiance"	$270.00 – 350.00	Teapot, Airflow	$700.00 – 900.00
Casserole, "Sundial," #1	$45.00 – 55.00	Teapot, Aladdin	$1,200.00 – 1,400.00
Casserole, "Sundial," #4	$28.00 – 35.00	Teapot, Donut	$1,200.00 – 1,400.00
Coffee server, "Sundial"	$475.00 – 525.00	Teapot, morning set	$250.00 – 325.00
Cookie jar, "Five Band"	$220.00 – 260.00	Teapot, New York	$300.00 – 350.00
Cookie jar, "Sundial"	$325.00 – 370.00	Teapot, "Sundial"	$300.00 – 350.00
Creamer, morning set	$45.00 – 55.00	Teapot, Streamline	$285.00 – 325.00
Creamer, New York	$27.00 – 32.00	Water bottle, "Zephyr"	$550.00 – 575.00
Custard, "Thick Rim"	$20.00 – 24.00		

Airflow Teapot

Aladdin Teapot

Washington Coffee Pot

Donut Teapot

"Radiance" Canister Set

"Sundial" Syrup

Streamline Teapot

No. 2 Ball Jug

"Sundial" Teapot

"Sundial" Coffee Server

Morning Set Sugar

Morning Set Creamer

Morning Set Teapot

"Sundial" Cookie Jar

Loop Handle Jug

"Sundial" Batter Jug

No. 4 Ball Jug

"Thick Rim" Casserole

"Thick Rim" Drip Jar

Loop Handle Leftover

"Thick Rim" 6" Bowl

Boston 4-cup Teapot   Boston 4-cup Teapot   Boston 2-cup Teapot   Chinese Tea Cup

7 1/2" Casserole   6" Shallow Bowl   Chinese Tea Cup   Philadelphia 4-cup Teapot

Boston 4-cup Teapot

4" Shallow Finger Bowl   4" Shallow Finger Bowl   5" Casserole   Ash Tray

The Blue Willow decal is only being found on a few shapes and the reports of collectors finding pieces of this pattern are infrequent. Perhaps the most exciting news to teapot collectors is the existence of this decoration on three different size Boston teapots. Notice in the photo that three different Oriental scenes may be found. Examples of the three different decals are depicted on the four-cup Boston teapots shown in the picture.

The casserole will be found in two sizes. Both the 5" and 7½" sizes are pictured. The lid features the Blue Willow pattern, is gently domed, and has a knob handle.

Although most of Hall's Blue Willow which collectors have been finding appears to date to the twenties, an ashtray has been made recently. It has the new backstamp which would place it in the post 1970 era. Also, the decal lacks the quality and fine detail of the decals on the earlier pieces. This ashtray is pictured at the bottom right in the photo.

Kitchenware	Value
Ashtray	$25.00 – 35.00
Bowl, 4", finger	$32.00 – 40.00
Bowl, 6", plum pudding	$40.00 – 50.00
Bowl, 5¼" x 7½"	$40.00 – 50.00
Casserole, 5"	$75.00 – 85.00
Casserole, 7½"	$95.00 – 125.00
Teacup, Chinese (2-styles)	$28.00 – 32.00
Teapot, 2-cup, Boston	$250.00 – 300.00
Teapot, 4-cup, Boston	$250.00 – 300.00
Teapot, 6-cup, Boston	$245.00 – 290.00
Teapot, 5-cup, Philadelphia	$400.00 – 450.00

Cactus

According to an article in the trade magazine *China, Glass and Lamps*, Hall introduced the Cactus pattern to retailers at trade shows in January 1937. The article described the pattern as "blending shades of green, yellow, red, orange, blue, brown, and gray." The decal appeared on a new Hall kitchenware shape which was also being introduced in various solid colors. The new shape was not named in the article but the illustration pictures the shape we are calling "Five Band." Items with the Cactus decal originally introduced on the "Five Band" shape were as follows: cookie jar, covered syrup, shakers, two sizes of jugs, three sizes of mixing bowls, a casserole, and a batter bowl.

Hall also used the Cactus decal on other shapes. One of the most commonly found items is the "Viking" Drip-O-lator coffee pot which was made for the Enterprise Aluminum Company of Massilon, Ohio. Enterprise supplied the aluminum dripper and marketed the finished product under its Drip-O-lator trademark. A covered sugar and creamer in this shape may also be found with diligent searching.

Kitchenware	Value
Ball jug, #3	$225.00 – 255.00
Batter bowl, "Five Band"	$95.00 – 125.00
Bowl, 6", "Five Band"	$20.00 – 25.00
Bowl, 7¼", "Five Band"	$25.00 – 30.00
Bowl, 8¾", "Five Band"	$32.00 – 37.00
Bowl, 6", "Radiance"	$20.00 – 25.00
Bowl, 7½", "Radiance"	$25.00 – 30.00
Bowl, 9", "Radiance"	$32.00 – 37.00
Bowl, 10", "Radiance"	$40.00 – 50.00
Casserole, "Five Band"	$45.00 – 55.00
Casserole, "Radiance"	$45.00 – 55.00
Coffee pot, "Five Band"	$60.00 – 70.00
Coffee pot, "Viking" Drip-O-lator	$35.00 – 45.00
Cookie jar, "Five Band"	$300.00 – 350.00
Creamer, New York	$30.00 – 35.00

Kitchenware	Value
Creamer, "Viking"	$30.00 –35.00
Custard, "Radiance"	$22.00 – 24.00
Jug, 1½ pt., "Five Band"	$60.00 – 70.00
Jug, 2 qt., "Five Band"	$90.00 – 110.00
Onion soup, individual	$50.00 – 60.00
Shakers, "Five Band," ea.	$20.00 – 22.00
Shakers, handled, ea.	$22.00 – 25.00
Stack set, "Radiance"	$115.00 – 130.00
Sugar and lid, New York	$40.00 – 50.00
Sugar and lid, "Viking"	$40.00 – 50.00
Syrup, "Five Band"	$95.00 – 125.00
Teapot, French (6 or 8 cup)	$200.00 – 250.00
Teapot, "Rutherford"	$300.00 –350.00
Teapot, Streamline	$350.00 – 400.00

"Five Band" Cookie Jar — "Viking" Coffee Pot — French Teapot — 2 Quart "Five Band" Jug — "Radiance" Stack Set — Individual Onion Soup — "Five Band" Salt & Pepper — PEPPER SALT — Handled Salt & Pepper — 1 1/2 Pint "Five Band" Jug — New York Sugar & Creamer — "Five Band" Batter Bowl — No. 3 Ball Jug — "Viking" Sugar & Creamer — "Five Band" Syrup — "Five Band" Casserole — "Radiance" 9" Bowl — "Five Band" 8 3/4" Bowl

Carrot and Golden Carrot

Although it is possible to assemble a collection of Hall's Carrot pattern, much diligent searching will be required to find many of the pieces. The Carrot/Golden Carrot kitchenware listing has turned out to be more extensive than many collectors originally anticipated. However, the number of items with gold decoration is still quite limited. Only the Windshield teapot, the Zeisel cookie jar, the #65, #68, #70, #95¾ casseroles, the 12½" Welsh rarebit, and the three-piece "Thick Rim" bowl set have been reported with gold trim. Of these pieces, the teapot is found most frequently, but it is also the most desirable item, which keeps the price relatively high.

Notice there are two different styles of custard cups in this pattern.

Kitchenware	Value	Kitchenware	Value
Ball jug, #3	$250.00 – 295.00	Casserole, 10", #70, rnd.	$60.00 – 75.00
Batter bowl, "Five Band"	$90.00 – 125.00	Casserole, 11½", oval	$85.00 – 95.00
Bean pot, New England, #4	$180.00 – 200.00	Casserole, "Radiance"	$45.00 – 55.00
Bean pot, New England, #2	$180.00 – 200.00	Cookie jar, "Five Band"	$300.00 – 350.00
Bowl, 6", "Five Band"	$22.00 – 25.00	Cookie jar, Zeisel	$350.00 – 400.00
Bowl, 7¼", "Five Band"	$28.00 – 32.00	Custard, #351½	$22.00 – 25.00
Bowl, 8¾", "Five Band"	$32.00 – 37.00	Custard, "Radiance"	$22.00 – 25.00
Bowl, 6", "Radiance"	$22.00 – 25.00	Dish, 12½", Welsh rarebit	$70.00 – 95.00
Bowl, 7½", "Radiance"	$28.00 – 32.00	Jug, #5, "Radiance"	$65.00 – 80.00
Bowl, 9", "Radiance"	$32.00 – 37.00	Shaker, "Five Band," ea.	$20.00 – 24.00
Bowl, 10", "Radiance"	$40.00 – 50.00	Shaker, handled, ea.	$22.00 – 25.00
Bowl, 6", "Thick Rim"	$22.00 – 28.00	Shaker, "Novelty Radiance," ea.	$45.00 – 55.00
Bowl, 7½", "Thick Rim"	$28.00 – 32.00	Stack set, "Radiance"	$110.00 – 135.00
Bowl, 8½", "Thick Rim"	$32.00 – 37.00	Syrup, "Five Band"	$95.00 – 125.00
Casserole, 5¾", #65, rnd.	$40.00 – 47.00	Teapot, "Radiance"	$300.00 – 350.00
Casserole, 8¼", #68, rnd.	$55.00 – 65.00	Teapot, Windshield	$195.00 – 225.00

New England No. 4 Bean Pot • New England No. 2 Bean Pot • No. 3 Ball Jug • No 68 Round Casserole • Zeisel-style Cookie Jar • "Radiance" Custard • No. 351 1/2 Custard • Handled Salt & Pepper • Windshield Teapot • No. 65 Round Casserole • 11 1/2" Oval Casserole • "Radiance" Casserole • 12 1/2" Welsh Rarebit • No. 70 Round Casserole • "Novelty Radiance" Salt & Pepper

Clover and Golden Clover

The Clover decal is a very stylized and colorful red, blue, and green decal. Items with this decal will be found both with and without gold decoration. Pieces which are gold encrusted are called Golden Clover. According to Hall ads, the Golden Clover line consists of the Windshield teapot, the #68 round casserole, the "big-eared" Zeisel cookie jar, and the three-piece "Thick Rim" mixing bowl set. However, as may be seen from the photo, other pieces with gold decoration may be found. Other sizes of round casseroles, the "Five Band" jug, and the stack set may be found with gold decoration. The handled shakers may be found as a four-piece set.

Kitchenware	Value
Ball jug, #3	$200.00 –220.00
Batter bowl, "Five Band"	$95.00 – 125.00
Bean pot, New England, #4	$185.00 – 200.00
Bowl, 6", "Radiance"	$22.00 – 28.00
Bowl, 7½", "Radiance"	$25.00 – 32.00
Bowl, 9", "Radiance"	$32.00 – 38.00
Bowl, 10", "Radiance"	$42.00 – 50.00
Bowl, 6", "Thick Rim"	$22.00 – 26.00
Bowl, 7½", "Thick Rim"	$28.00 – 32.00
Bowl, 8½", "Thick Rim"	$32.00 – 35.00
Casserole, 5¾", #65, rnd.	$42.00 – 50.00
Casserole, 8¼", #68, rnd.	$55.00 – 65.00
Casserole, 10", #70, rnd.	$95.00 – 110.00

Kitchenware	Value
Casserole, "Radiance"	$47.00 – 52.00
Casserole, "Thick Rim"	$45.00 – 55.00
Cookie jar, "Five Band"	$280.00 – 300.00
Cookie jar, Zeisel-style	$275.00 – 320.00
Jug, 1½ pt., "Five Band"	$55.00 – 65.00
Jug/cover, #1, "Radiance"	$95.00 – 115.00
Jug, #5, "Radiance"	$52.00 – 57.00
Shaker, salt or pepper, handled, ea.	$22.00 – 28.00
Shaker, flour or sugar, handled, ea	$40.00 – 45.00
Shaker, "Novelty Radiance," ea.	$52.00 – 60.00
Stack set	$110.00 – 135.00
Teapot, Windshield	$245.00 – 295.00

Stack Set

Zeisel-style Cookie Jar

"Five Band" Cookie Jar

"Five Band" 1 1/2 Pint Jug

Handled 4-piece Shaker Set

"Radiance" No. 1 Covered Jug

Windshield Teapot

Clover (Pink)

Very few different shapes of this Pink Clover design are showing up. In addition to the pieces pictured, "Radiance" canisters, "Thick Rim" bowls, several casseroles, a jug, and a round baker have been found.

No. 761 Oval Casserole

"Medallion" Jug

No. 503 Round Baker

Kitchenware	Value
Baker, #503, 6", round	$18.00 – 22.00
Bowl, 6", "Thick Rim"	$18.00 – 22.00
Bowl, 7½", "Thick Rim"	$22.00 – 25.00
Bowl, 8½", "Thick Rim"	$30.00 – 35.00

Kitchenware	Value
Canister, "Radiance"	$285.00 – 300.00
Casserole, "Radiance"	$40.00 – 60.00
Casserole, #761, 10", oval	$55.00 – 65.00
Jug, "Medallion"	$50.00 – 60.00

Daisy

This dainty red and black floral decal is sometimes confused with the Red Poppy decal by novice collectors. However, closer examination reveals the two patterns are really quite different. Only a handful of different shapes with this decal have surfaced. The cookie jar and canisters are prizes for any collector. The "Cathedral" coffee pot was made for Drip-O-lator and is one of the more commonly found pieces with this decal.

Kitchenware	Value
Baker, French	$18.00 – 22.00
Ball jug, #3	$125.00 – 150.00
Batter bowl, "Five Band"	$45.00 – 55.00
Bowl, 6", "Five Band"	$18.00 – 22.00
Bowl, 7½", "Five Band"	$20.00 – 25.00
Bowl, 8¾", "Five Band"	$25.00 – 30.00
Canister, "Radiance"	$250.00 – 300.00
Cookie jar, "Five Band"	$100.00 – 125.00
Coffee pot, "Cathedral"	$45.00 – 55.00
Shaker, handled	$20.00 – 24.00

"Cathedral" Coffee Pot

"Five Band" Cookie Jar

"Radiance" Canister

"Five Band" Batter Bowl

French Fluted Baker

"Five Band" 8 3/4" Bowl

"Five Band" 7 1/4" Bowl

Handled Shakers

Elena

The Elena pattern incorporates numerous Eva Zeisel design pieces into a Hostessware set. Most pieces have a gold color "Hostessware" backstamp. This pattern is new to this edition of the book and more pieces are sure to surface. The price list below includes the pieces we have seen.

Hostessware	Value	Hostessware	Value
Bean pot	$145.00 – 185.00	Dish, 6½", shirred egg	$12.00 – 14.00
Bowl, 2-handle soup	$27.00 – 32.00	Dish, 8½", shirred egg	$16.00 – 18.00
Bowl, #619, 6"	$12.00 – 14.00	Jug, 5-pint	$110.00 – 125.00
Bowl, large salad	$22.00 – 25.00	Jug, refrigerator	$120.00 – 145.00
Casserole, 3-pint, handled	$50.00 – 60.00	Mug, 7 oz.	$20.00 – 25.00
Casserole, 3-pint, oval	$40.00 – 50.00	Plate, 9"	$18.00 – 20.00
Creamer	$16.00 – 18.00	Shaker, ea.	$10.00 – 11.00
Dish, 5¼", shirred egg	$12.00 – 14.00	Sugar and lid	$22.00 – 27.00

5 Pint Jug

6" No. 619 Bowl

Elena Hostessware Backstamp

Elena

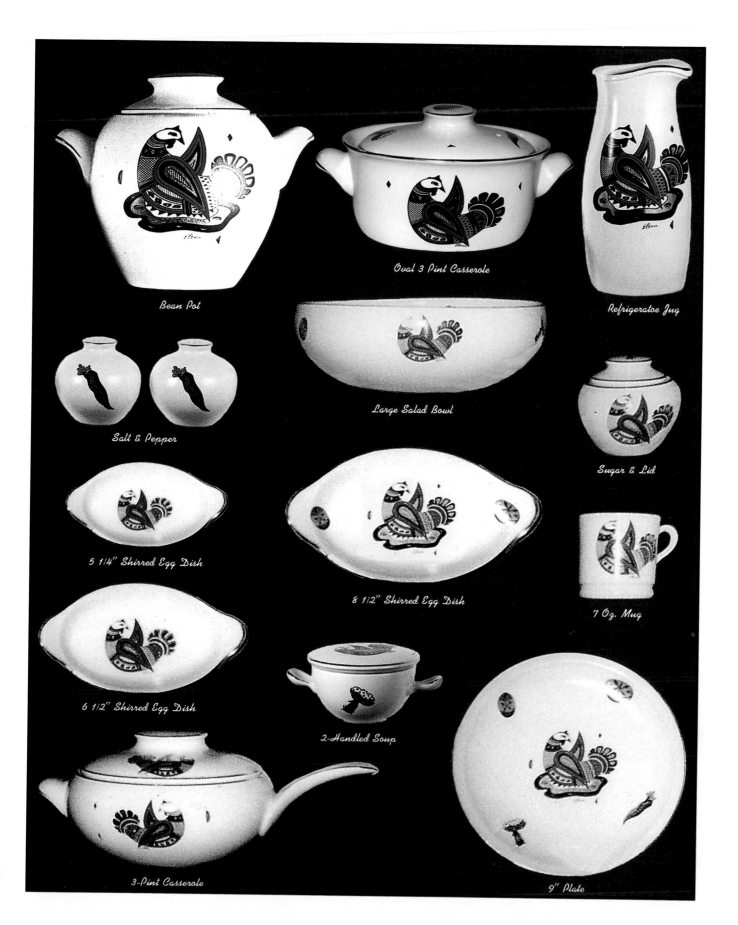

Bean Pot

Oval 3 Pint Casserole

Refrigeratoe Jug

Salt & Pepper

Large Salad Bowl

Sugar & Lid

5 1/4" Shirred Egg Dish

8 1/2" Shirred Egg Dish

7 Oz. Mug

6 1/2" Shirred Egg Dish

2-Handled Soup

3-Pint Casserole

9" Plate

Fantasy

Fantasy is a very colorful — almost gaudy — floral decal which is found infrequently. Most pieces are also neatly trimmed with a narrow red band. The only commonly found pieces are the handled shakers and all styles of casseroles. Special finds would include the "Sundial" coffee server, loop handle leftover, and the morning tea set. Finding a Streamline teapot in Fantasy would send most any teapot collector to dreamland.

Additional items of interest which are pictured for the first time include the morning set teapot and the "Zephyr" leftover. The appearance of the "Zephyr" leftover would indicate that a "Zephyr" shape butter should also exist.

Kitchenware	Value
Baker, rectangular	$150.00 – 190.00
Ball jug, #1	$150.00 – 175.00
Ball jug, #2	$150.00 – 175.00
Ball jug, #3	$130.00 – 160.00
Ball jug, #4	$160.00 – 185.00
Batter bowl, "Five Band"	$250.00 – 275.00
Batter jug, "Sundial"	$350.00 – 450.00
Bean pot, New England, #4	$195.00 – 230.00
Bowl, 6", "Thick Rim"	$25.00 – 30.00
Bowl, 7½", "Thick Rim"	$30.00 – 35.00
Bowl, 8½", "Thick Rim"	$35.00 – 42.00
Casserole, "Radiance"	$75.00 – 85.00
Casserole, "Sundial," #1	$55.00 – 65.00
Casserole, "Sundial," #4	$55.00 – 65.00
Casserole, "Thick Rim"	$55.00 – 65.00
Coffee server, "Sundial"	$450.00 – 550.00
Cookie jar, "Five Band"	$255.00 – 285.00
Cookie jar, "Sundial"	$340.00 – 360.00

Kitchenware	Value
Creamer, morning set	$35.00 – 40.00
Creamer, New York	$40.00 – 45.00
Custard, "Thick Rim"	$27.00 – 32.00
Drip jar, #1188, open	$55.00 – 65.00
Drip jar and cover, "Thick Rim"	$80.00 – 95.00
Jug, 5", "Five Band"	$60.00 – 80.00
Jug, 6¾" "Five Band"	$125.00 – 145.00
Jug, Donut	$200.00 – 225.00
Leftover, loop handle	$140.00 – 160.00
Leftover, "Zephyr"	$180.00 – 200.00
Shakers, handled, ea.	$28.00 – 30.00
Sugar and lid, morning set	$45.00 – 52.00
Sugar and lid, New York	$47.00 – 55.00
Syrup, "Five Band"	$120.00 – 150.00
Syrup, "Sundial"	$180.00 – 200.00
Teapot, morning set	$300.00 – 350.00
Teapot, Streamline	$350.00 – 425.00
Teapot, "Sundial"	$380.00 – 435.00

"Sundial" No. 4 Casserole

"Sundial" No. 1 Casserole

Streamline Teapot

Handled Salt and Pepper

Zephyr Leftover

Loop Handled Leftover

Morning Set Teapot

Morning Set Sugar

No. 3 Ball Jug

"Five Band" Cookie Jar

Morning Set Creamer

"Thick Rim" Casserole

Donut Jug

"Sundial" Teapot

"Sundial" Batter Jug

No. 1 Ball Jug

New England No. 4 Bean Pot

Rectangular Baker

No. 2 Ball Jug

"Five Band" 1 1/2 Pint Jug

Flamingo

The Flamingo decal was originally found on the "Viking" Drip-O-lator coffee pot that Hall made for the Enterprise Aluminum Company. Other pieces with this decal have been found in the last few years.

Collectors will find this decal more commonly on the "Five Band" batter bowl and the "Viking" Drip-O-lator coffee pot. Interesting, but hard-to-find pieces, are the #691 drip coffee pot, the Streamline teapot, and the "Five Band" cookie jar. Any Streamline teapots appearing on the market are eagerly snatched by teapot collectors.

There have been reports to us over the years that the birds depicted in this decal are actually not flamingos. While this may be the case, it is probably too late to change the name of this pattern in order to be ornithologically correct.

Kitchenware	Value
Ball jug, #3	$350.00 – 450.00
Batter bowl, "Five Band"	$95.00 – 105.00
Casserole, "Five Band"	$65.00 – 75.00
Casserole, "Radiance"	$65.00 – 75.00
Coffee pot, "Viking" Drip-O-lator	$55.00 – 65.00
Cookie jar, "Five Band"	$260.00 – 280.00
Creamer, "Viking"	$30.00 – 35.00
Drip coffee pot, #691	$500.00 – 625.00
Shaker, "Five Band," ea.	$38.00 – 42.00
Shaker, handled, ea.	$45.00 – 55.00
Sugar and lid, "Viking"	$40.00 – 47.00
Syrup, "Five Band"	$140.00 – 165.00
Teapot, Streamline	$550.00 – 650.00

"Five Band" Cookie Jar

No. 691 Drip Coffee Pot

"Viking" Coffee Pot

"Five Band" Casserole

"Five Band" Salt & Pepper

"Five Band" Batter Bowl

Handled Salt & Pepper

"Viking" Creamer, Sugar & Lid

"Five Band" Syrup

Floral Lattice

The Floral Lattice kitchenware has a decal which consists of a vine-like potted flower that is intertwined in a lattice framework. This mini-floral decal may be frequently spotted on the "Five Band" batter bowl and syrup. Other pieces in this pattern are not easily found. Notice some pieces are trimmed in red while others are trimmed with platinum bands.

Kitchenware	Value
Ball jug, #3	$180.00 – 225.00
Batter bowl, "Five Band"	$75.00 – 95.00
Bowl, 6", "Five Band"	$20.00 – 25.00
Bowl, 7¼", "Five Band"	$28.00 – 32.00
Bowl, 8¾", "Five Band"	$40.00 – 47.00
Canister, "Radiance"	$250.00 – 350.00
Casserole, #99, oval	$65.00 – 75.00
Casserole, #76, round	$60.00 – 70.00
Casserole, #101, round	$65.00 – 75.00
Coffee pot, "Viking," Drip-O-lator	$40.00 – 50.00
Cookie jar, "Five Band"	$225.00 – 250.00
Drip coffee pot, "Kadota"	$250.00 – 350.00
Onion soup, individual	$35.00 – 45.00
Shaker, canister style, ea.	$90.00 – 125.00
Shaker, handled, ea.	$32.00 – 38.00
Syrup, "Five Band"	$85.00 – 100.00
Tea tile, 6", round	$65.00 – 75.00

"Radiance" Canister Set

"Radiance" Canister-style Salt & Pepper

"Five Band" Syrup

"Five Band" Cookie Jar

No. 99 Oval Casserole

French Drip Coffee Biggin Teapot Bottom

Individual Onion Soup

"Five Band" Batter Bowl

Kadota All-china Coffee Pot

Meadow Flower

"Radiance" Canisters

Handled Salt & Pepper

No. 3 Ball Jug

"Thick Rim" Custard

8 1/2" "Thick Rim" Bowl

New England No. 4 Bean Pot

1 1/2 Pint "Five Band" Jug

7 1/2" "Thick Rim" Bowl

Streamline Teapot

Hall's use of the Meadow Flower decal dates to the late 1930s. Many collectors find these red-trimmed pieces with their colorful variegated floral decals quite attractive. Although the list of known shapes with this decal is gradually increasing, none of the pieces is easy to find. The most significant discoveries have been a canister set and the Streamline teapot. The existence of the canisters means the canister-style shakers should exist, but to date no one has reported finding them.

Kitchenware	Value
Ball jug, #1	$160.00 – 195.00
Ball jug, #2	$160.00 – 195.00
Ball jug, #3	$140.00 – 180.00
Ball jug, #4	$155.00 – 190.00
Bean pot, New England, #4	$220.00 – 265.00
Bowl, 6", "Thick Rim"	$22.00 – 28.00
Bowl, 7½", "Thick Rim"	$28.00 – 32.00
Bowl, 8½", "Thick Rim"	$40.00 – 47.00
Canister, "Radiance"	$425.00 – 500.00
Casserole, "Radiance"	$60.00 – 70.00

Kitchenware	Value
Casserole, "Sundial," #4	$55.00 – 65.00
Casserole, "Thick Rim"	$50.00 – 60.00
Cookie jar, "Five Band"	$280.00 – 320.00
Custard, "Thick Rim"	$28.00 – 32.00
Drip jar, #1188, open	$55.00 – 65.00
Drip jar and cover, "Thick Rim"	$75.00 – 90.00
Jug, "Five Band"	$60.00 – 70.00
Shakers, handled, ea.	$40.00 – 55.00
Teapot, Streamline	$750.00 – 900.00

Morning Glory

Straight-sided 6" Bowl

Aladdin Teapot

Straight-sided 7 1/2" Bowl

All-china Drip Coffee Pot

Straight-sided 5" Bowl

"Thick Rim" Casserole

"Thick Rim" 8 1/2" Bowl

Straight-sided 9" Bowl

The Morning Glory kitchenware line was produced by Hall during the 1940s to coordinate with the Wildwood dinnerware pattern of the Jewel Company. Morning Glory, like Autumn Leaf, was a decal which was reserved exclusively for use on pieces produced for the Jewel Tea Company of Barrington, Illinois. The pieces have a cadet body with contrasting Hi-white areas which contain the Morning Glory decal.

Since the number of available pieces in this decal is limited, many collectors mix these items with other cadet-colored patterns such as Rose Parade and Royal Rose. All the patterns with cadet bodies go well together to create an interesting and useful collection.

"Thick Rim" bowls and casseroles have been found. This shape bowl is not as plentiful as the straight-sided bowl. The casseroles have a white lid which contains the pattern and a blue bottom which has no pattern.

Morning Glory Kitchenware	Value	Morning Glory Kitchenware	Value
Bowl, 4⅜", straight-sided	$16.00 – 18.00	Bowl, 7½", "Thick Rim"	$25.00 – 30.00
Bowl, 5", straight-sided	$18.00 – 20.00	Bowl, 8½", "Thick Rim"	$30.00 – 35.00
Bowl, 6", straight-sided	$18.00 – 20.00	Casserole, "Thick Rim"	$37.00 – 45.00
Bowl, 7½", straight-sided	$24.00 – 28.00	Custard, 3½", straight-sided	$22.00 – 25.00
Bowl, 9", straight-sided	$30.00 – 35.00	Drip coffee pot, all-china	$225.00 – 245.00
Bowl, 6", "Thick Rim"	$20.00 – 25.00	Teapot, Aladdin	$170.00 – 200.00

Rose Parade

Rose Parade kitchenware has a cadet blue body with contrasting white trim. The areas of white trim are accented by a petite pastel floral decal. The most commonly found color of flower is pink. However, other colors including blue and yellow may also be found. This line dates to the 1940s and has become very popular with collectors again today. See the photo below for examples of decal differences.

Although sets of Rose Parade are generally relatively easy to assemble, collectors seem to be having problems finding the fluted baker, salad bowl, and custards. Notice there are two different styles of mixing bowls — straight-sided and Sani-Grid. Sani-Grid bowls are shaped like the straight-sided bowls, but have a series of rings on the inside near the top edge.

A few rarities have been reported by collectors. A lid to the sugar is shown in the photo to the right. Several lids have been found over the last few years and more are sure to exist. Another Rose Parade item still missing from many collections is the "Jordan" style all-china coffee pot. A spoon with this decal has also been found. These pieces are rare prizes for enthusiastic collectors.

Some collectors have trouble distinguishing between this pattern and another pattern with a similar pink flower on a blue body with white trim called Royal Rose. Identification has been made somewhat easier by Hall, since the majority of Rose Parade pieces contain the backstamp with the identifying words "Rose Parade." To identify pieces which may have escaped the backstamp, the Royal Rose line has silver trim and the Rose Parade pieces lack this trim.

Rose Parade	Value	Rose Parade	Value
Baker, French, fluted	$40.00 – 52.00	Drip coffee pot, "Jordan"	$700.00 – 900.00
Bean pot, tab-handled	$115.00 – 135.00	Drip jar and cover, tab-handled	$32.00 – 37.00
Bowl, 9", salad	$30.00 – 35.00	Jug, 5", Sani-Grid	$40.00 – 45.00
Bowl, 6", Sani-Grid	$27.00 – 32.00	Jug, 6½", Sani-Grid	$50.00 – 55.00
Bowl, 7½", Sani-Grid	$30.00 – 35.00	Jug, 7½", Sani-Grid	$55.00 – 65.00
Bowl, 8¾", Sani-Grid	$37.00 – 42.00	Salt box	UND
Bowl, 6", straight-sided	$22.00 – 25.00	Shaker, Sani-Grid, ea.	$20.00 – 22.00
Bowl, 7½", straight-sided	$28.00 – 32.00	Spoon	UND
Bowl, 9", straight-sided	$35.00 – 40.00	Sugar, Sani-Grid	$20.00 – 22.00
Casserole, tab-handled	$40.00 – 45.00	Sugar lid, Sani-Grid	$300.00 – 400.00
Creamer, Sani-Grid	$20.00 – 22.00	Teapot, 3-cup, Sani-Grid	$55.00 – 65.00
Custard, straight-sided	$27.00 – 30.00	Teapot, 6-cup, Sani-Grid	$70.00 – 85.00

Pink Flower

Pink & White Floral Sprig

Pink & Blue Flower

Rose Parade Spoon

Rose Parade Salt Box
Sample Courtesy of Hall China

Sani-Grid 7 1/2" Jug

Sani-Grid 6 1/2" Jug

Sani-Grid 5" Jug

Tab-handled Bean Pot

Sani-Grid 3-cup Teapot

Sani-Grid 6-cup Teapot

Tab-handled Drip Jar

Straight-sided Custard

Tab-handled Casserole

Sani-Grid Sugar and Lid

Sani-Grid Creamer

Sani-Grid Open Sugar

French Fluted Baker

Sani-Grid Salt and Pepper

9" Salad Bowl

Straight-sided 9" Bowl

Staight-sided 7 1/2" Bowl

Sani-Grid 6" Bowl

Rose White

The Rose White kitchenware pattern features a pink rose decal on a Hi-white body with silver trim. This rose decal is the same as the decal used on blue-bodied Royal Rose pieces. However, the shape of the body of the Rose White items is the same as that in Rose Parade. The listing of Rose White pieces is not extensive, and with few exceptions, a complete set is not difficult to obtain.

The hardest pieces to find are the "Medallion" bowls, the fluted baker, the small custard, and the sugar and creamer. Items easiest to acquire appear to be the teapots, shakers, drip jar, and casserole.

In addition to the normal straight-sided mixing bowl set, a set of bowls in the "Medallion" shape has been found with the Rose White decal. An example of the "Medallion" style bowl is shown in the top right corner of the photo. The bottom of the bean pot will be found both with and without the rose decal. The most commonly found jugs only have the decal on the handle, but examples have also been found with a decal near the spout. Some salt and pepper shakers are only decorated on the handle. Others have both a handle decoration and a decal on the side.

There have been no reports of a sugar lid in this pattern, but since one exists in Rose Parade, one might also be found for this pattern.

Rose White	Value
Baker, French, fluted	$35.00 – 40.00
Bean pot, tab-handled	$85.00 – 95.00
Bowl, 6", "Medallion"	$40.00 – 45.00
Bowl, 7¼", "Medallion"	$45.00 – 50.00
Bowl, 8½", "Medallion"	$50.00 – 55.00
Bowl, 6" Sani-Grid	$20.00 – 22.00
Bowl, 7½" Sani-Grid	$22.00 – 27.00
Bowl, 9", Sani-Grid	$30.00 – 35.00
Bowl, 6", straight-sided	$18.00 – 22.00
Bowl, 7½", straight-sided	$22.00 – 25.00
Bowl, 9", straight-sided	$27.00 – 32.00
Bowl, 9", salad	$20.00 – 25.00
Casserole, tab-handled	$27.00 – 32.00
Creamer, Sani-Grid	$14.00 – 16.00
Custard, straight-sided	$22.00 – 25.00
Drip jar and cover, tab-handled	$24.00 – 27.00
Jug, 5", Sani-Grid	$37.00 – 42.00
Jug, 6½", Sani-Grid	$40.00 – 50.00
Jug, 7½", Sani-Grid	$50.00 – 60.00
Shaker, Sani-Grid, ea.	$12.00 – 14.00
Sugar, Sani-Grid	$14.00 – 16.00
Teapot, 3-cup, "Pert"	$40.00 – 50.00
Teapot, 6-cup, "Pert"	$50.00 – 60.00

Sani-Grid 6-cup Teapot

Sani-Grid 3-cup Teapot

"Medallion" 8 1/2" Bowl

Tab Handle Bean Pot

Tab Handle Bean Pot

Sani-Grid 7 1/2" Jug

Tab Handle Casserole

Sani-Grid 6 1/2" Jug

Sani-Grid 5" Jug

Sani-Grid Salt & Pepper

Tab Handle Drip Jar

Sani-Grid Shaker

Royal Rose

Ball Jug

Aladdin Teapot

French Teapot

Salad Bowl

Handled Salt

"Thick Rim" Drip Jar

Handled Pepper

7 1/2" "Thick Rim" Bowl

8 1/2" "Thick Rim" Bowl

Casserole

Royal Rose kitchenware has a cadet body with contrasting Hi-white features. The decoration consists of a pink rose decal and silver trim. Many people confuse this pattern with the similar blue-bodied pattern — Rose Parade. However, Royal Rose pieces are accented with silver trim and the shapes are different from those used in the Rose Parade pattern.

The Aladdin teapot is the most difficult item to find in Royal Rose. Also, the 9" salad bowl is not easily found.

Royal Rose	Value
Ball jug, #3	$90.00 – 100.00
Bowl, 9", salad	$25.00 – 30.00
Bowl, 5¼" straight-sided	$20.00 – 22.00
Bowl, 6", straight-sided	$20.00 – 25.00
Bowl, 7½", straight-sided	$26.00 – 30.00
Bowl, 9", straight-sided	$37.00 – 42.00
Bowl, 6", "Thick Rim"	$20.00 – 25.00
Bowl, 7½", "Thick Rim"	$22.00 – 27.00
Bowl, 8½", "Thick Rim"	$35.00 – 42.00
Casserole, "Thick Rim"	$37.00 – 42.00
Custard, straight-sided	$32.00 – 37.00
Drip jar and cover, "Thick Rim"	$30.00 – 35.00
Shaker, handled, ea.	$16.00 – 18.00
Teapot, Aladdin	$140.00 – 160.00
Teapot, French	$125.00 – 145.00

HALL KITCHENWARE

SECRET PROCESS FIREPROOF CHINA

NO. 05 KITCHENWARE ASSORTMENT

CADET AND WHITE
ROYAL ROSE DECORATION

Quantity	Item	Capacity	Height Inches	Diam. Top Inches
2 only	**3 Piece Bake Bowl Set**			
	1376—Bowl	2 pts.	3¼"	6⅜"
	1377—Bowl	3 ½ pts.	3⅞"	7½"
	1378—Bowl	2 ½ qts.	4½"	8⅝"
2 only	**3 Piece Range Set**			
	1186—Salt	8 oz.	4¾"	
	1187—Pepper	8 oz.	4¾"	
	988—Grease Pot	16 oz.	2½"	5⅜"
2 only	**398—Casserole**	3 pts.	3⅛"	8¼"
2 only	**3078—Salad or Bake Dish**	4 pts.	3⅛"	9⅛"
2 only	**1411 Aladdin Teapot**	6 cup	6½"	
2 only	**633—Jug**	2 qts.	7"	

Shipping Weight of Assortment—50 pounds
Guaranteed against breakage in oven heat

Guaranteed by Good Housekeeping

"Shaggy Tulip"

"Radiance" Stack Set

Pretzel Jar

Casserole

New England #4 Bean Pot

5 1/4" Shirred Egg Dish

SUGAR

Handled Shaker

"Radiance" Condiment Jar   "Radiance" Coffee Pot Bottom   "Kadota" All-China Drip Coffee Pot   6 1/2" Shirred Egg Dish

"Shaggy Tulip" is a colorful floral decal line dating from the mid-thirties. Not much new information concerning "Shaggy Tulip" has been uncovered in the past few years. However, the discovery of the "Radiance" all-china coffee pot and the "Radiance" condiment jar have perked interest in this pattern. Add these pieces to the canisters and the "Radiance" teapot and you have a very exciting collection. Collectors should be aware that the "Kadota" all-china drip coffee pot is one of the most common pieces of this pattern. The "Radiance" shape jug will be found with or without a cover. Keep in mind the covers are scarce and those jugs having covers are worth more than double the value of those without.

Remember, the rolling pin, pie lifter, spoon, fork, and dinnerware which are sometimes found with this decal are not Hall items, but were made by Harker. However many enthusiasts find these are also very attractive items to display.

"Shaggy Tulip"	Value	"Shaggy Tulip"	Value
Bean pot, New England, #4	$185.00 – 220.00	Drip coffee pot, "Radiance," all-china	$290.00 – 350.00
Bowl, 6", "Radiance"	$22.00 – 27.00	Drip jar and cover, "Radiance"	$30.00 – 35.00
Bowl, 7½", "Radiance"	$27.00 – 32.00	Jug and cover, "Radiance," #2, #3	$120.00 – 150.00
Bowl, 9", "Radiance"	$35.00 – 42.00	Jug and cover, "Radiance," #4, #5, #6	$135.00 – 180.00
Canister, "Radiance"	$300.00 – 350.00	Pretzel jar	$175.00 – 195.00
Casserole, Buffet	$55.00 – 65.00	Shakers, handled, ea. (4)	$20.00 – 24.00
Casserole, "Radiance"	$40.00 – 50.00	Shakers, "Radiance Novelty," ea.	$55.00 – 60.00
Coffee pot, "Perk"	$65.00 – 75.00	Shirred egg dish, 5¼"	$25.00 – 30.00
Condiment jar, "Radiance"	$300.00 – 350.00	Shirred egg dish, 6½"	$25.00 – 30.00
Custard, "Radiance"	$18.00 – 22.00	Stack set, "Radiance"	$90.00 – 110.00
Drip coffee pot, "Kadota," all-china	$95.00 – 115.00	Teapot, "Radiance"	$245.00 – 270.00

"Stonewall"

"Radiance" #5 Jug & Cover

Square Leftover

"Radiance" Casserole

"Medallion" Juicer

"Thin Rim" 7 1/4" Bowl

'Radiance" #2 Jug & Cover

SALT PEPPER

"Novelty Radiance" Salt & Pepper

SALT PEPPER FLOUR SUGAR

Handled Shakers Set of Four

The "Stonewall" decal consists of green vertical bars which look like an inverted wooden fence slat. These green bars have a white zigzag line running along each side. Positioned between the bars will be one or more green baskets of pink and orange flowers. Although most of the items in this pattern are being found with an ivory body, a few pieces have been found with an eggshell body.

The number of pieces in this listing has expanded phenomenally since the first book. However, none of these pieces is easy to find and anyone who chooses to collect this pattern is undertaking a considerable challenge. The "Medallion" juicer has proven to be almost nonexistent. Other pieces that are challenging for collectors to acquire are the stack set, leftovers, the "Kadota" coffee pot, and the "Novelty Radiance" shakers.

The "Radiance" jugs are sometimes found without covers. Consider the bottoms worth about half to two-thirds less than the indicated values.

"Stonewall"	Value
Bean pot, New England, #2	$185.00 – 225.00
Bowl, 6", "Radiance"	$25.00 – 30.00
Bowl, 7½", "Radiance"	$30.00 – 35.00
Bowl, 9", "Radiance"	$35.00 – 40.00
Bowl, 10", "Radiance"	$45.00 – 55.00
Bowl, 6", "Thin Rim"	$22.00 – 27.00
Bowl, 7¼", "Thin Rim"	$27.00 – 32.00
Bowl, 8½", "Thin Rim"	$32.00 – 37.00
Casserole, "Radiance"	$40.00 – 50.00
Custard, "Radiance"	$22.00 – 27.00
Drip jar, #1188, open	$40.00 – 45.00
Drip coffee pot, "Kadota," all-china	$475.00 – 550.00
Jug and cover, #1, #2, "Radiance"	$90.00 – 125.00
Jug and cover, #4, #5, "Radiance"	$105.00 – 135.00
Jug and cover, #6, "Radiance"	$125.00 – 155.00
Juicer, "Medallion"	$550.00 – 650.00
Leftover, rectangular	$90.00 – 110.00
Leftover, square	$120.00 – 150.00
Shakers, handled, ea. (4)	$30.00 – 35.00
Shakers, "Novelty Radiance," ea.	$75.00 – 85.00
Stack set, "Radiance"	$115.00 – 130.00
Teapot, "Radiance"	$325.00 – 370.00

"Wild Poppy"

The "Wild Poppy" decal first appeared in the late 1930s. It combines a rust-colored poppy-like flower with a sprig of wheat. This pattern was sold by Macy's, which probably explains why many of the more unusual pieces are being found in the New York area. Many items have been added to the list of known pieces in the last few years. Some of the more interesting are a number of all-china coffee pots. These may be seen in the photographs.

Items of significant rarity that have been found since the last book include the "Zephyr" water bottle and the Baltimore teapot. Other items in this pattern that are not often seen include the "Radiance" condiment jar, mustard with spoon lid, "Zephyr" leftover, "Zephyr" butter, rectangular baker, and ball jug #3.

"Radiance" mixing bowls with colored interiors also exist. Some have been found with maroon interiors and others have green glaze on the inside. An abundance of casseroles and other ovenware items were also produced in this pattern. The French drip Coffee Biggin has been found in two, four, six, and eight cup sizes. Notice the French teapot in the photo with the infusor. A French teapot with an infusor is unusual in a decal pattern. The "Radiance" custard will be found with and without the wheat sprig.

"Radiance" Canister Set

"Medallion" Square Leftover

Handled 4-piece Shaker Set

New England #4 Bean Pot

New England #3 Bean Pot

Novelty Radiance" Salt & Pepper

"Radiance" Canister-style Salt Shaker

"Wild Poppy"	Value	*"Wild Poppy"*	Value
Baker, oval	$95.00 – 125.00	Drip coffee pot, French Coffee	
Baker, rectangular	$185.00 – 225.00	Biggin	$390.00 – 450.00
Ball jug, #3	$140.00 – 165.00	Drip coffee pot, "Radiance"	$370.00 – 420.00
Bean pot, New England, #3	$250.00 – 270.00	Drip coffee pot, sm., "Terrace"	$350.00 – 400.00
Bean pot, New England, #4	$220.00 – 255.00	Drip jar, #1188, open	$65.00 – 75.00
Bowl, 5¼", "Radiance"	$24.00 – 28.00	Jug and cover, #1, #2, "Radiance"	$120.00 – 145.00
Bowl, 6", "Radiance"	$22.00 – 25.00	Jug and cover, #3, #4, #5, "Radiance"	$120.00 – 150.00
Bowl, 7½", "Radiance"	$27.00 – 32.00	Jug and cover, #6, "Radiance"	$140.00 – 165.00
Bowl, 9", "Radiance"	$32.00 – 37.00	Leftover, sq.	$135.00 – 165.00
Bowl, 10", "Radiance"	$40.00 – 45.00	Leftover, "Zephyr"	$200.00 – 225.00
Butter dish, 1 lb., "Zephyr"	$600.00 – 800.00	Mustard, spoon lid	$250.00 – 295.00
Canister, "Radiance"	$195.00 – 220.00	Onion soup, individual	$60.00 – 75.00
Casserole, #101, oval	$90.00 – 110.00	Shakers, handled, ea. (4)	$40.00 – 55.00
Casserole, #103, oval	$115.00 – 140.00	Shakers, "Novelty Radiance," ea.	$60.00 – 75.00
Casserole, 8", round, 2-H	$40.00 – 50.00	Shakers, "Radiance," canister style, ea.	$85.00 – 95.00
Casserole, 10½", round, #76	$70.00 – 80.00	Shirred egg dish, 5¼"	$27.00 – 30.00
Casserole, "Radiance"	$40.00 – 47.00	Shirred egg dish, 6½"	$27.00 – 30.00
Casserole, "Sundial," #1	$65.00 – 75.00	Stack set, "Radiance"	$160.00 – 180.00
Casserole, "Sundial," #4	$50.00 – 60.00	Sugar and lid, Hollywood	$45.00 – 55.00
Casserole, "Thick Rim"	$45.00 – 55.00	Sugar and lid, New York	$40.00 – 50.00
Cocotte, handled	$85.00 – 95.00	Teapot, Baltimore	UND
Coffee pot, 2-cup, Washington	$170.00 – 200.00	Teapot, French	$300.00 – 345.00
Coffee pot, 12-cup, Washington	$175.00 – 225.00	Teapot, New York, 2- or 4-cup	$320.00 – 355.00
Cookie jar, "Five Band"	$225.00 – 265.00	Teapot, New York, 6-cup	$285.00 – 325.00
Cookie jar, "Sundial"	$550.00 – 650.00	Teapot, New York, 8-cup	$290.00 – 340.00
Condiment jar, "Radiance"	$400.00 – 500.00	Teapot, "Radiance"	$325.00 – 345.00
Creamer, Hollywood	$35.00 – 40.00	Teapot, Tea for Two set	$500.00 – 600.00
Creamer, New York	$27.00 – 32.00	Teapot, Tea for Four set	$550.00 – 650.00
Custard, "Radiance"	$20.00 – 25.00	Tea tile, 6"	$90.00 – 120.00
Drip coffee pot, #691, all-china	$395.00 – 420.00	Water bottle, "Zephyr"	$800.00 – 950.00

"Radiance" #4 Covered Jug

"Radiance" #5 Covered Jug

"Radiance" #6 Covered Jug

"Five Band" Cookie Jar

6" Tea Tile

"Radiance" #3 Jug

"Radiance" #2 Covered Jug

"Radiance" #1 Covered Jug

Mustard w/Spoon Lid

"Zephyr" 1# Butter

Covered Onion Soup

5 1/4" Shirred Egg Dish

Baltimore Teapot

"Radiance" Stack Set

207

#691 Drip Coffee Pot

"Radiance" All-china Drip Coffee Pot

New York Sugar & Lid

New York Creamer

French Drip Coffee Biggin--6-cup

New York 6-cup Teapot

"Radiance" Teapot

French Drip Coffee Biggin--2-cup Bottom

French Teapot with Infusor

Small Terrace All-china Coffee Pot

"Sundial" #1 Casserole

French Drip Coffee Biggin 4-cup Bottom

#101 9 1/2" Oval Casserole

New York 4-cup Teapot

Washington 12-cup Coffee Pot

"Zephyr" Water Bottle

"Radiance" Casserole

#93 11 1/2" Oval Casserole

#76 10 1/2" Round Casserole

Miscellaneous Hall Decal Kitchenware

The pieces shown in these photos represent patterns about which very little is known at this time. In all of these patterns we have seen less than a half dozen different pieces, and in most even, fewer. Some patterns have been named by researchers or collectors. We will use those names whenever possible and continue to search for answers to questions about the history of these patterns.

Kitchenware	Value
1. Green Poppy "Rutherford" teapot	$150.00 – 175.00
2. Green Poppy "Medallion" coffee	$130.00 – 150.00
3. Floral Sprig Boston 2-cup teapot	$225.00 – 250.00
4. Floral Sprig No. 3 Ball jug	$225.00 – 270.00
5. Red floral handled shakers, pr.	$40.00 – 45.00
6. Green Poppy Boston teapot	$200.00 – 225.00
7. Devon coffee pot with red and white floral decal	$110.00 – 130.00
8. Devon coffee pot with pink and yellow floral decal	$110.00 – 130.00

Kitchenware	Value
9. "Piggly Wiggly" handled shakers, pr.	$50.00 – 60.00
10. Floral spray "Radiance" teapot	$175.00 – 200.00
11. Shaggy floral "Radiance" teapot	$200.00 – 250.00
12. Floral bouquet "Radiance" covered jug	$100.00 – 125.00
13. Large lavender and white floral "Radiance" bowl	$20.00 – 25.00
14. Irish Setter French baker	$75.00 – 95.00
15. Pink floral handled shakers	$27.00 – 32.00
16. Floral Chain "Radiance" casserole	$30.00 – 35.00

Refrigerator Ware

The popularity of the modern electric refrigerator in the late 1930s resulted in the production of numerous types of cold storage units from glass and china. Hall China made items for retail sale as well as exclusive designs for Westinghouse, General Electric, Sears, Hotpoint, and Montgomery Ward. Premium type refrigerator items were also an important part of the production of the era. The accompanying McCormick ad reprint illustrates an example of one such premium.

Three basic items are included in the Hall refrigerator line. There are water bottles or water servers, leftovers or refrigerator boxes, and covered butters.

The water containers are covered pieces intended to be placed in the refrigerator for water storage. Closure is achieved with either a cork-encased china stopper or with a china lid. Leftovers are deep dishes with a shallow or flat china lid. The butter dishes have a flat bottom and a deep lid.

Today the popularity of Hall refrigerator ware is astounding. Many people are again using these items in their refrigerators and the water servers are especially popular. The renewed interest in Hall water servers may have been partly responsible for Hall's re-introduction of the Streamline and "Nora" shapes for the retail market during the early 1980s.

General Electric

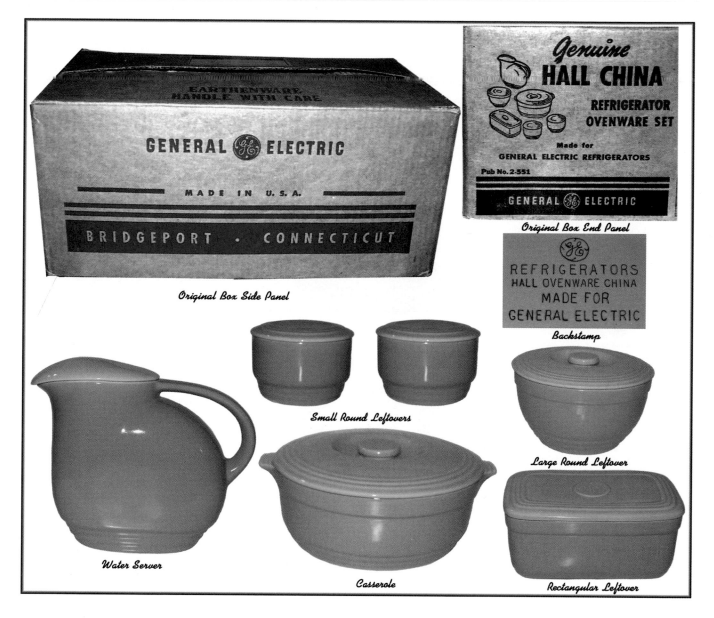

Original Box Side Panel

Original Box End Panel

Backstamp

Small Round Leftovers

Large Round Leftover

Water Server

Casserole

Rectangular Leftover

Hall supplied a combination refrigerator ovenware set for customers that purchased General Electric refrigerators. The GE logo was used on the lids of all pieces except the water server. The bodies of the pieces were a gray color called addison and the lids were were a yellow daffodil color. The set is shown in the photo along with panels from an original box. Included in the set were two small round leftovers, a larger round leftover, a rectangu-lar leftover, a round covered casserole, and a covered water server. This water server, rectangular leftover, and small round leftovers may also be found with other color bodies. These were produced for Westinghouse with a daffodil lid and a light blue bottom. The water server was also a part of the general line in stock brown with a daffodil lid.

Refrigerator Ware	Value
Casserole	$37.00 – 42.00
Leftover, rect.	$22.00 – 25.00
Leftover, 4", round	$10.00 – 12.00

Refrigerator Ware	Value
Leftover, 7", round	$27.00 – 32.00
Water server	$55.00 – 65.00

Hotpoint

Water Server

4 3/4" Square Leftover

8 3/4" Round Leftover

4" Square Leftover

7 3/4" Round Leftover

Rectangular Leftover

6 3/4" Square Leftover

6 3/4" Round Leftover

8 1/2" Square Leftover

Bright colored leftovers were included in a refrigerator ware line which Hall produced for Hotpoint. The line consisted of a water server, three sizes of round leftovers, five different sizes of square leftovers, and a rectangular leftover. The Dresden blue water servers with the cork encased china stoppers are not easily found. Some sizes of the square leftovers and the rectangular leftover are also proving hard to find. Some of the leftovers have been found in more than one color. The small 4" square leftover comes in Indian Red and Chinese Red. Both colors are especially popular among collectors. The refrigerator items are priced below in some of the more commonly found colors. Colors other than those listed have been reported and may occasionally be found.

Refrigerator Ware	Color	Value	Refrigerator Ware	Color	Value
Leftover, rect.	Sandust	$22.00 – 25.00	Leftover, 4¾", sq.	Light/Dark Gray	$30.00 – 35.00
Leftover, 6¾", round	Maroon	$22.00 – 25.00	Leftover, 5¾", sq.	Green Luster	$30.00 – 35.00
Leftover, 7¾", round	Green	$30.00 – 35.00	Leftover, 6¾", sq.	Daffodil/Maroon	$37.00 – 42.00
Leftover, 8¾", round	Warm Yellow	$47.00 – 52.00	Leftover, 8½", sq.	Warm Yellow	$47.00 – 55.00
Leftover, 4", sq.	Chinese/Indian Red	$37.00 – 42.00	Water server	Dresden	$55.00 – 65.00

Montgomery Ward, Sears, and Solar

Montgomery Ward

6" Covered Bowl · 7" Covered Bowl · Water Server · Rectangular Leftover · 8" Covered Bowl

Sears

Leftover Set · Leftover

Solar

Water Server

Hall produced a line of refrigerator ware for Montgomery Ward in the early 1940s. The color usually seen is delphinium, but pieces can also be found in Hall's Hi-white color. There are two styles of rectangular leftovers. The larger 5¼" x 8½" leftover with the V-shape lid is not easy to find. Also included in the set are three sizes of round covered bowls with raised elongated handles, a rectangular leftover, and a water server. Collectors have also reported the existence of a rectangular open baker.

Refrigerator Ware	Value
Bowl, 6", covered	$18.00 – 22.00
Bowl, 7", covered	$22.00 – 27.00
Bowl, 8", covered	$25.00 – 30.00
Bowl, knob handle	$22.00 – 28.00

Refrigerator Ware	Value
Baker, 6½" x 10½"	$20.00 – 25.00
Leftover, rect.	$20.00 – 25.00
Leftover, lg., rect.	$25.00 – 45.00
Water server	$45.00 – 55.00

Hall made one piece of refrigerator ware for Sears. It is a three-part leftover which is normally found in the cadet and Hi-white colors. The center piece is solid cadet and the end pieces have cadet bases and Hi-white lids. There have been several reports of another color combination being found. This set has a solid Hi-black center piece and Hi-white end pieces which have Hi-black lids. An example of the end section is shown in the photo above.

Refrigerator Ware	Value
Sears' leftover, 3-part	$70.00 – 90.00

A cobalt water server was made for Solar Refrigerators. The shape is the same as the Phoenix design produced for Westinghouse in several other colors. The backstamp of this water server reads: "Made Exclusively for Solar Refrigerators by The Hall China Company." We have not seen any other refrigerator accessories with this backstamp.

Refrigerator Ware	Value
Water server, cobalt	$100.00 – 125.00

Westinghouse

The "Hercules" shape was offered as "Peasant Ware" by Westinghouse in 1940 and 1941. A set consisted of a rectangular butter, a water server, and two leftovers. Cobalt is the most common color of the water server, but it may also be found in tan with the Westinghouse backstamp. Later, this mold was used to produce water servers for Toucan Enterprises of Chicago. The colors of these water servers were cobalt, tan, brown, and ivory. Most of these will have the "TOUCAN ENTERPRISES, CHICAGO" backstamp. Beginning in 1984, Hall began producing this covered water server in several colors as part of the Hall American line. To identify the new pieces look for the new square backstamp. In addition to the regular split-lid shape water server another style has been found. The second shape, which has a full-length, detached, semi-hinged lid is shown in the photo on the next page. Three-piece sets have surfaced in turquoise. A set is comprised of a water server, a butter, and a leftover.

The "General" design was offered in 1939, as an accessory to Westinghouse refrigerators. Sets were comprised of a water server, two leftovers, and a butter. The water server is found frequently in delphinium, and has been showing up with some regularity in garden green. The butter and leftovers are seen in garden, sunset, delphinium, and yellow.

"Phoenix" was the earliest line of Hall refrigerator ware used by Westinghouse. This line was introduced in 1938, and consisted of a water server, a leftover, and a butter. The most commonly found color is delphinium, but all three pieces are also found occasionally in lettuce green. There have also been reports of a cobalt water server.

The "Adonis" line in blue and daffodil was offered by Westinghouse in 1952. A set consisted of a water server, four small round leftovers, and two rectangular leftovers. Two styles of ovenware sets were offered at the same time. These ovenware pieces are shown in the photo below. Each set was comprised of three pieces — two covered casseroles and one open baker. The "Ridged" line came in canary and the "Plain" line was made in delphinium. Some of the bakers and casseroles have been found with metal holders. An example of one style of holder is shown in the photo below.

Refrigerator Ware	"Hercules"	"General"	"Phoenix"	"Adonis"
Butter	$45.00 – 55.00	$40.00 – 50.00	$50.00 – 60.00	
Leftover, rect.	$18.00 – 22.00	$20.00 – 25.00	$20.00 – 24.00	$20.00 – 25.00
Leftover, round				$10.00 – 12.00
Water server	$95.00 – 115.00	$55.00 – 65.00 *	$55.00 – 65.00 **	$50.00 – 60.00
Water server, hinged lid	$125.00 – 145.00			
*Green water server	$85.00 – 100.00			
**Green water server	$95.00 – 110.00			
Bakeware	"Ridged"	"Plain"		
Casserole, covered	$20.00 – 25.00	$20.00 – 25.00		
Baker, open	$12.00 – 15.00	$18.00 – 22.00		

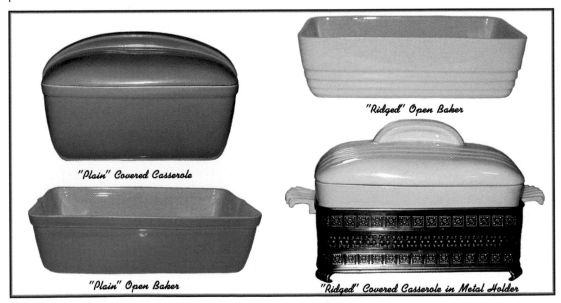

"Plain" Covered Casserole

"Ridged" Open Baker

"Plain" Open Baker

"Ridged" Covered Casserole in Metal Holder

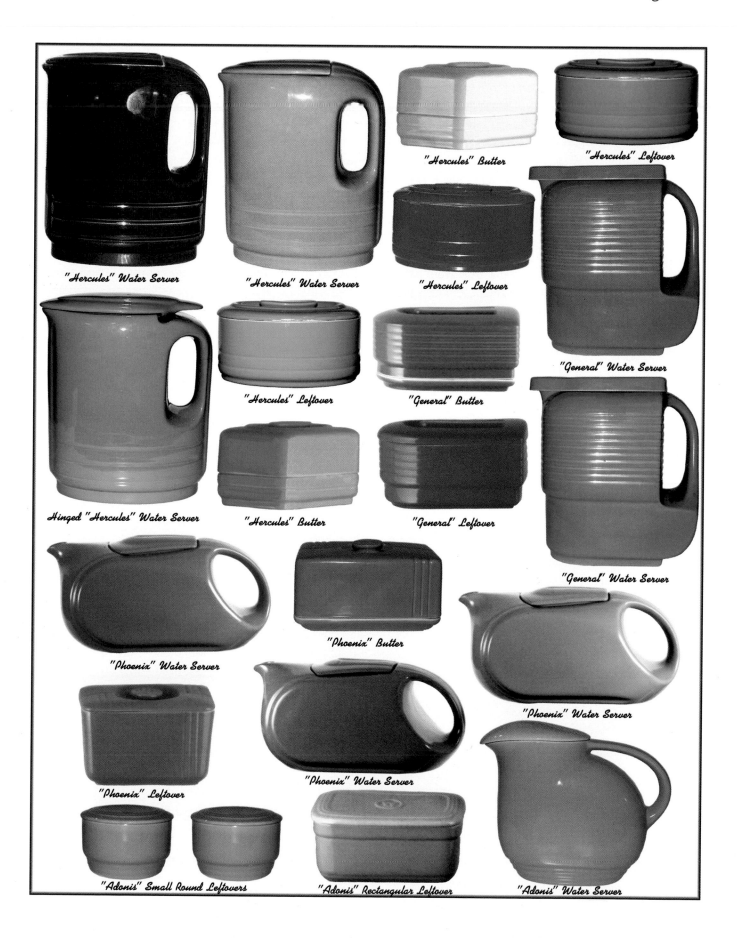

"Hercules" Water Server

"Hercules" Water Server

"Hercules" Butter

"Hercules" Leftover

"Hercules" Leftover

"General" Water Server

Hinged "Hercules" Water Server

"Hercules" Leftover

"General" Butter

"Hercules" Butter

"General" Leftover

"General" Water Server

"Phoenix" Water Server

"Phoenix" Butter

"Phoenix" Water Server

"Phoenix" Leftover

"Phoenix" Water Server

"Adonis" Small Round Leftovers

"Adonis" Rectangular Leftover

"Adonis" Water Server

Miscellaneous Refrigerator Ware

Hall made numerous shapes of refrigerator ware for the retail market. The large-size loop handle and Streamline jugs were reissued in the 1980s as part of the Hall American line. These items were produced for department stores and gift shops and bear the rectangular Hall backstamp.

The loop handle jug was introduced in the thirties and is still available in the general line. It was made in two sizes: 9-cup and 7-cup. It is found in many different solid colors and in a few of the decal lines. The smaller size appears to be harder to find than the larger size.

The Plaza water server may be found with a cork encased china stopper, but so many of these jugs are more commonly found without stoppers that they were probably issued without them in some promotion. Although the jug was produced from the thirties to the sixties, not many are found today. The red water server is pictured with its original stopper. Also, notice the Plaza water server in the unusual Citrus color shown in the photo.

The "Zephyr" line consists of two sizes of stoppered water bottles, a covered one-pound butter, and a covered rectangular leftover. The line dates to the late thirties and will be found predominantly in the Chinese red color. However, pieces do exist in several other colors and in a few of the decal lines. Notice the blue water bottle and the brown butter in the picture. The two sizes of water bottles are shown in the photo to the right. The smaller bottle is 7" tall, holds 27 ounces, and has a single wide grouping of vertical lines at the center of the bottle. The larger bottle is 7½" tall, holds 48 ounces, and has two narrower rows of vertical ridges.

The Streamline jug was selected for reissue in the Hall American line. The older jugs are not easy to find and date to the thirties. New pieces will bear the square backstamp.

The #628 water server has been found in numerous colors. It was introduced in the late thirties, but is no longer in production.

Refrigerator Ware	Green/Brown/Light Blues	Red/Cobalt
Butter, "Zephyr"	$125.00 – 150.00	$180.00 – 210.00
Jug, loop handle, large	$60.00 – 75.00	$70.00 – 85.00
Jug, loop handle, small	$60.00 – 75.00	$70.00 – 85.00
Jug, Streamline	$75.00 – 85.00	$125.00 – 145.00
Leftover, "Zephyr"	$65.00 – 85.00	$85.00 – 95.00
Water bottle, "Zephyr," large	$290.00 – 325.00	$270.00 – 320.00
Water bottle, "Zephyr," small	$275.00 – 320.00	$275.00 – 325.00
Water server, #628	$65.00 – 75.00	$85.00 – 115.00
*Water server, Plaza	$75.00 – 85.00	$110.00 – 125.00
*With china stopper	$250.00 – 350.00	

9-cup Loop Handle Jug

9-cup Loop Handle Jug

7-cup Loop Handle Jug

Plaza Water Server with
China Stopper

Plaza Water Server

Plaza Water Server

Small-size
"Zephyr" Water Bottle

"Zephyr" Leftover

"Zephyr" Butter

"Zephyr" Butter

Large-size
"Zephyr" Water Bottle

Streamline Jug

Streamline Jug

No. 628 Water Server

"Stork Club"   Gold "Sunburst" Decoration   "Rockwell" Silver Overlay

French Flower Decoration   Emerald   Gold "Grape & Vine" Decoration

The Ball jug was introduced in 1938, and quickly became a best seller for Hall. It may be found in numerous solid colors and is in virtually all the decal lines. It is available in four different sizes — 1½ pint, 2⅓ pint, 2 quart, and 5¼ pint. The #3 size, 2 quart, is the most commonly found. Although this shape was not chosen for reissue in the Hall American line, new Ball jugs in stock green, stock brown, and other colors are available in the institutional line. These later Ball jugs are marked with the rectangular backstamp. A few Ball jugs with interesting decorations are pictured in the photo above. A matte black jug with a gold decorated white handle is shown on page 145. Another Ball jug with the gold French Flower decoration is pictured on page 152.

Common Solid Colors	*Light Blues/Emerald/Canary*	*Red/Cobalt*	*Stock Brown/Green*
Ball jug, #1, 5¼"	$40.00 – 50.00	$65.00 – 75.00	$22.00 – 27.00
Ball jug, #2, 5¾"	$38.00 – 45.00	$65.00 – 70.00	$22.00 – 27.00
Ball jug, #3, 7"	$35.00 – 40.00	$60.00 – 70.00	$20.00 – 24.00
Ball jug, #4, 7½"	$42.00 – 52.00	$65.00 – 75.00	$25.00 – 30.00

Special Solid Colors	*Value*
Old Rose	$65.00 – 85.00
Orchid	$200.00 – 225.00

Photo Above:

Decorated Ball Jugs	*Value*
Black "Stork Club"	$1,000.00 – 1,200.00
Canary with Gold "Sunburst"	$150.00 – 175.00
Ivory with Rockwell Silver Overlay	$200.00 – 250.00
Cadet with Gold French Flower	$150.00 – 170.00
Canary with Gold "Grape & Vine"	$190.00 – 210.00

Tankard-style Pitcher   Tankard-style Pitcher   Tankard-style Pitcher

Large-size Donut Jug   Large-size Donut Jug   Small-size Donut Jug

The Donut jug was introduced in the late thirties and is still in the institutional line. The old Donut jug may be found in two sizes and a variety of solid colors. It has also been found in a few of the decal lines and some have been appearing with gold decoration. One of the more commonly found decorations is the gold French Flower decoration. These pieces also have a gold encrusted handle and gold around the lip. Gold decorated examples are pictured on page 152. The large-size jug was reissued in 1984, in numerous colors as a part of Hall's re-entry into the retail market. These later jugs have a rectangular backstamp.

Tankard pitchers are usually found with decals and are generally part of a beer set — see page 346 for examples. Although most of the pitchers found without decals are undecorated, a few gold decorated examples like the one in the photo have turned up. Hall is still making this shape pitcher. Pitchers with the new backstamp have been found in red. They are especially attractive in this color even though they are new.

Refrigerator Ware	Green/Brown/Light Blues	Maroon/Canary	Red/Cobalt
Jug, Donut, large	$45.00 – 55.00	$50.00 – 65.00	$70.00 – 75.00
Jug, Donut, small	$45.00 – 55.00	$47.00 – 55.00	$65.00 – 70.00
Tankard pitcher (solid colors)	$120.00 – 150.00		$200.00 – 250.00
Tankard pitcher (decorated)	$170.00 – 200.00		

Flip-top Jug   Room Service   Princeton Jug

Rivera Jug   "Nora" Jug   Princeton Jug

"Nora" water servers came with and without china lids. They were a covered water server available in Hall's general line and also a premium item for McCormick Tea in their lidless form. See the reprint from a 1955 magazine at the front of this section. New covered jugs in this shape were produced as part of the Hall American line beginning in 1984. The bottoms of these later jugs bear the rectangular Hall backstamp, however, the lids are not marked.

The Princeton jug has been a part of the institutional line for many years. It is usually found in stock brown or stock green, but may also be found in some more interesting colors. This shape jug is also shown in Oyster White with red trim on page 161.

The Riviera jug may be found in new colors with the square Hall mark. Prices below are for the older jugs. New jugs appear to be selling for about half the price of an older jug in a comparable color.

Refrigerator Ware	Green/Brown/Light Blues	Red/Cobalt
Jug, Flip-top	$100.00 – 125.00	
Jug, Princeton	$45.00 – 65.00	$100.00 – 125.00
Jug, Riviera	$45.00 – 55.00	$80.00 – 90.00
Jug , Room Service	$25.00 – 35.00	$65.00 – 85.00
Water server, "Nora"	$35.00 – 42.00	

TEAPOTS AND COFFEE POTS

The first Hall teapots were part of the institutional line. The early colors were stock brown, stock green, and white. In 1920, the Boston, New York, and French shapes were selected for a store promotion. These teapots were decorated with gold and Hall's Gold Decorated Teapot line was born. The new line was very successful and many new shapes were added over the next few decades. These new shapes were combined with a rainbow of new colors to catapult Hall China into prominence as the leading producer of teapots in the world.

Many of Hall's teapots, which are collectible today, are part of the Gold Decorated line. The backstamp on these teapots will usually include a gold code number which was used for reordering purposes. Each shape teapot will have a standard gold design, although some experimentation in the early years has resulted in different gold designs on some of the older teapots. Also, on some shapes there is a gold decoration which collectors refer to as "special." "Specials" have the standard gold design for their shape. In addition, they also will have gold encrusted handles, spouts, and knobs. The gold mark on the backstamp will usually be followed by an "S."

Undecorated teapots will usually have the #5 backstamp, red teapots have the #6 kitchenware backstamp, and teapots made in the twenties or early thirties have the #4 backstamp.

In the thirties, six teapots were selected for decal decoration. The shapes chosen were the Baltimore, French, Los Angeles, Newport, New York, and Philadelphia. Sales of these teapots with the decal decorations were not very good. Therefore, most of them are difficult for collectors to find.

In the early forties Hall introduced a series of six teapots which has become known as the Victorian line. Although several of these teapots have been found in two colors, they were essentially only offered in one basic color. Later, gold decoration was added in an attempt to increase sales. However, this line was never very popular, and it was discontinued by the end of the decade.

Also in the forties, another series of six teapots, called the Brilliant Series, was designed by J. Palin Thorley. These teapots were made in several colors, but each style has a single color in which it will be found most often. Decorations included rhinestones, decals, and gold, but many of these teapots will also be found undecorated. This line was offered sporadically through the late sixties.

In the late fifties, Hall brought out a new line of teapots call Gold Label. These teapots were very gaudy — almost covered with gold decoration. The shapes of the teapots were selected from among those used earlier No new shapes were introduced. This new line of teapots was sold along with several other matching kitchenware accessories. Gold Label decorated teapots may be identified through the letters "GL" which follow the gold code number on the bottom of the teapots.

In the 1960s another attempt was made to revive the interest in teapots through the use of decals. The six teapots chosen and their decorations are as follows:

Teapot	Decoration
Boston	gold fruit decal
French	gold rose decal
Hollywood	gold leaf decal
Los Angeles	green and yellow leaf decal
Philadelphia	black hearth scene decal
Windshield	green, white, and brown floral band

In 1984, Hall began offering teapots to the public again through retail outlets via their Hall American line. The Airflow, Rhythm, and square T-Ball teapots were marketed through major department stores and specialty shops across the country. Today, many of these later teapots may be found at flea markets, resale shops, and antique malls throughout the country. To identify these new issues look for the square backstamp.

Hall produced many different coffee pots. Many of these pots were used in the decal lines and will be identified there. However, some were sold to other companies such as Enterprise, Tricolator, and Westinghouse. These companies then added the metal parts and marketed the finished product. Some, but not all of the coffee pots will bear a Hall backstamp.

To help with identification, the coffee pots and teapots in the following photographs will have both their shape name and color name. In some cases recognition of the colors may still be difficult, since some colors do not print the exact shade. Since color is such an important factor in the price of the teapots, an attempt will be made to note the hard-to-find colors for each shape. The price guide has been divided into as many categories as practical to aid collectors in their attempt to distinguish between common and unusual teapots.

Airflow Teapots

The Airflow teapot was introduced in 1940, and was produced in eight-cup and six-cup sizes. Today, the larger eight-cup size is much harder to find than the smaller version. The Airflow will be found in a variety of solid colors. The most commonly found colors are cobalt, canary, and Chinese red. In addition, a standard gold decoration and several variations of the standard decoration will be found. The standard decoration consists of a large single rose on the center of each side of the teapot and multiple gold leaf sprigs around the opening. The foot, handle, and lid are accented with gold lines. A variation of the gold decoration includes a "special" which may be seen on the cobalt and ivory teapots in the center row of the photo on the next page. This decoration consists of a gold encrusted handle and spout used in combination with the standard decoration. Other variations are achieved by deleting a part of the standard decoration. One version omits the large center rose on the sides of the teapot. Another style omits both the flowers and leaves, leaving only the thin gold highlighting lines. Examples of Airflow teapots with decals are shown with the Blue Blossom and Blue Garden patterns

The Ivy decorated teapot shown below was marketed by Thornberry's of Ohio during the 1970s. The Airflow teapot was one of the items Hall chose to re-introduce in 1985, when the retail business was re-established. New Airflow teapots will be found, but all should have the square backstamp which has been in use since the seventies. Also, new decal versions of this teapot are being marketed by China Specialties.

Airflow Teapot	Solid Color	Standard Gold	Gold Special
Black	$45.00 – 55.00	$37.00 – 42.00	$50.00 – 65.00
Cadet	$67.00 – 75.00	$55.00 – 65.00	
Canary	$65.00 – 75.00	$60.00 – 65.00	$125.00 –150.00
Chinese Red	$125.00 – 135.00		
Citrus	$175.00 – 225.00		
Cobalt	$75.00 – 100.00	$55.00 – 65.00	$125.00 – 150.00
Dresden	$65.00 – 75.00	$65.00 – 75.00	
Emerald	$85.00 – 110.00	$75.00 – 100.00	
Golden Glo	$150.00 – 180.00		
Indian Red	$125.00 – 150.00		
Ivory	$45.00 – 65.00	$65.00 – 75.00	$110.00 – 130.00
Marine	$125.00 – 135.00	$125.00 – 135.00	
Maroon	$75.00 – 100.00	$100.00 – 125.00	
Orchid	$250.00 – 300.00		
Pink	$75.00 – 100.00		
Rose	$75.00 – 100.00	$100.00 – 125.00	
Silver Luster	$100.00 – 150.00		
Turquoise	$65.00 – 75.00	$75.00 – 85.00	$145.00 – 165.00
Warm Yellow	$65.00 – 75.00	$75.00 – 85.00	$140.00 – 160.00
Black satin	$80.00 – 90.00		
Ivory with Silver Overlay	$250.00 – 300.00		
Ivory with Thornberry Ivy decal	$65.00 – 85.00		

6-cup
Silver Luster

6-cup Thornberry
White with Ivy Trellis Decoration

6-cup
Golden Glo

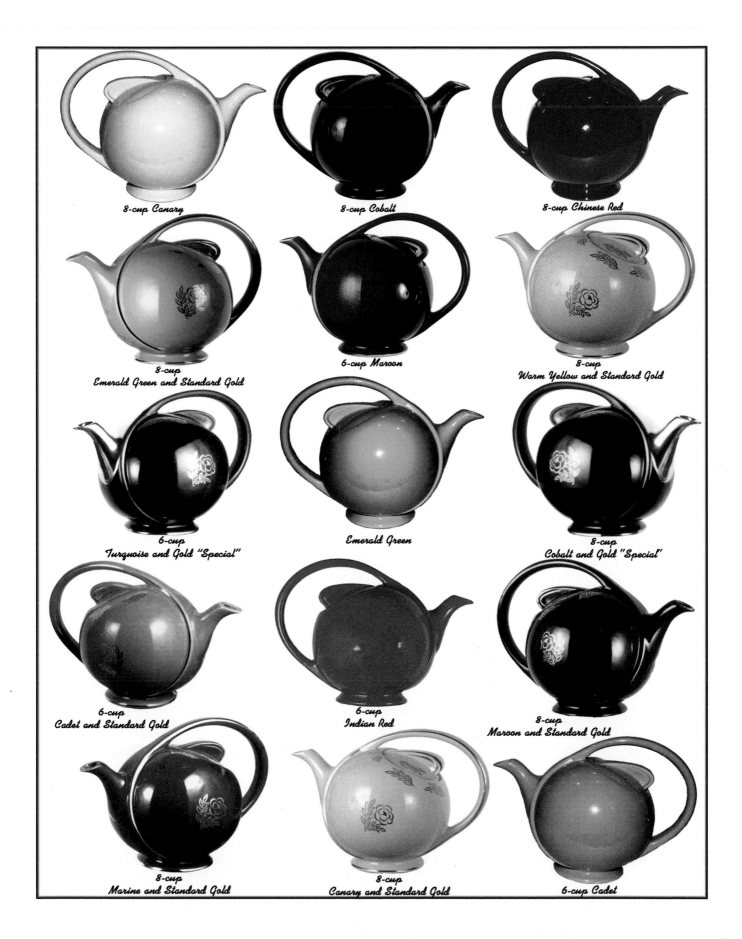

8-cup Canary

8-cup Cobalt

8-cup Chinese Red

8-cup
Emerald Green and Standard Gold

6-cup Maroon

8-cup
Warm Yellow and Standard Gold

6-cup
Turquoise and Gold "Special"

Emerald Green

8-cup
Cobalt and Gold "Special"

6-cup
Cadet and Standard Gold

6-cup
Indian Red

8-cup
Maroon and Standard Gold

8-cup
Marine and Standard Gold

8-cup
Canary and Standard Gold

6-cup Cadet

Aladdin Teapots

The original narrow body Aladdin teapot with the round opening was introduced in 1939. In 1940, an optional infuser was offered. A few years later Hall experimented with an Aladdin teapot with an oval opening and an oval lid and infuser. However, by the end of World War II, the teapot with the round opening was re-instated. In 1942, a modified wide-bodied version of the Aladdin teapot was introduced to be used with Jewel's Autumn and Morning Glory patterns. For the most part, very few other patterns or decorations will be found on this style of teapot, however, there are some exceptions as can be seen in the photo on page 227. Other wide body Aladdin teapots may be found with various hand-painted decorations. Generally, these teapots were decorated by independent artists and lack the Hall backstamp. Floral decorations, especially roses were popular subjects with these artists. Examples of these decorated teapots are shown on page 159.

Undecorated Aladdin teapots may be found in almost any Hall color. There are several variations of gold decorated Aladdin teapots. The simplest decoration consists of thin gold lines highlighting the handle, spout, lid opening, lid base, and knob. Examples may be seen on the canary, marine, and cadet teapots on the next page. The yellow teapot on the top row is an example of a Gold Label decoration called Squiggle. Colors available in this pattern are daffodil and ivory. For other matching pieces in this pattern see page 153. The heavily gold encrusted teapots at the bottom of the photo are also part of the Gold Label line. The design on these teapots is called Swag. The most commonly found colors with this design include ivory, pink, and maroon.

The yellow teapot with gold splatter, shown in the photo on page 227, appears to have been decorated with a sponge. This is one of the more gaudy and unusually decorated Aladdin teapots. The turquoise teapot on page 227 with the gold handle and the gold knob on the lid is what is referred to as a "special." A variation of these "specials" will be found with a gold encrusted spout. This teapot also features the much scarcer oval opening. Notice the accompanying sugar and creamer in the Boston shape which completes this set.

Advertisements have confirmed Aladdin teapots in various colors were sold by Grand Union during the mid-1950s. Teapots with infusors retailed for $3.25 each.

A multitude of regular-style Aladdin teapots will be found with decals. Some of the more common ones are in the Blue Bouquet, Red Poppy, and Wildfire patterns. Other patterns where the Aladdin teapot is a rarity include Crocus, Blue Garden, and Brown-eyed Susan. For more information on the availability and prices of Aladdin teapots with decals, see the individual dinnerware and kitchenware listings.

The narrow body Aladdin teapots with both shapes of openings were were sold with or without infusors. The shape and size of the oval lid varies. Lids used with teapots without infusors are larger and have a flared flange that does not fit into the infusor. The smaller lids with the straight flange are designed to fit into the infusors. Examples of the two styles of oval lids are shown in the photo below.

Styles of Oval Teapot Lids

Oval Lid For Infusor   Oval Lid For Teapot Bottom

Orchid Gold Label with Swag Design

Aladdin Teapots

Black with "Ming Cha" Tea Label

Closeup of Metal Tag from Teapot on Left

Daffodil with Gold Label Squiggle Decoration

Marine with Standard Gold

Cobalt

Cadet Blue with Standard Gold

Chinese Red with Oval Lid

Warm Yellow with Matching Infusor

Canary with Standard Gold

White with Standard Gold

Marine with Gold Label Swag Design

Cadet Blue Gold Label with Swag Design

Ivory Gold Label with Swag Design

Camellia Gold Label with Swag Design

Pink Gold Label with Swag Design

Aladdin Teapot	Solid Color	Standard Gold	Gold Label
Black	$40.00 – 50.00	$55.00 – 65.00	
Blue Turquoise	$100.00 – 125.00	$100.00 – 125.00	
Cadet	$60.00 – 75.00	$75.00 – 85.00	$200.00 – 225.00
Canary	$50.00 – 60.00	$65.00 – 85.00	$185.00 – 200.00
Chartreuse	$65.00 – 85.00	$65.00 – 85.00	
Chinese Red	$165.00 – 180.00		
Citrus	$300.00 – 350.00		
Cobalt	$100.00 – 125.00	$125.00 – 150.00	
Dresden	$90.00 – 100.00	$100.00 – 125.00	$185.00 – 200.00
Emerald	$75.00 – 85.00	$85.00 – 90.00	
Golden Glo	$180.00 – 225.00		
Gray	$60.00 – 75.00		
Indian Red	$225.00 – 250.00		
Ivory	$50.00 – 65.00	$65.00 – 75.00	$150.00 – 165.00
Marine	$75.00 – 90.00	$75.00 – 90.00	$185.00 – 225.00
Maroon	$75.00 – 85.00	$75.00 – 85.00	$185.00 – 225.00
Orchid	$350.00 – 450.00		$800.00 – 1000.00
Pink	$65.00 – 75.00	$75.00 – 80.00	$180.00 – 220.00
Rose	$85.00 – 110.00	$85.00 – 110.00	
Silver Luster	$185.00 – 200.00		
Turquoise	$90.00 – 100.00	$90.00 – 110.00	
Warm Yellow	$75.00 – 85.00	$75.00 – 85.00	

Special Decorations

Canary with Gold Spatter $250.00 – 300.00

Canary with French Flower $225.00 – 275.00

Ivory with Floral decal $200.00 – 250.00

Ivory with Floral Basket decal $200.00 – 250.00

Ivory with Floral Sprig decal $200.00 – 250.00

Mini Fleurette decoration $225.00 – 250.00

Ivory with Floral Decal   *Silver Luster*

Maroon

Black with Gold Mini Fleurette Decoration

Camellia

Chartreuse with Standard Gold

Chinese Red with White Infusor

Golden Glo

Pink with White Infusor

Canary with Gold Spatter Design

Emerald Green

Canary with "French Flower" Design

Turquoise with Special Gold and Matching Boston Sugar and Creamer

Decorated Wide Body Aladdin Teapots

Ivory with Floral Basket Design

Ivory with Floral Sprig Design

Ivory with Iridescence and Gold Mini Fleurette Design

HALL TEAPOTS

SECRET PROCESS FIREPROOF CHINA

1411½
ALADDIN INFUSER
CANARY—#0679R

1411½
ALADDIN INFUSER
GRAY—#00663R

1411½
ALADDIN INFUSER
MAROON—#0673R

1411½
ALADDIN INFUSER
CADET—#0669R

1411½
ALADDIN INFUSER
MARINE—#0676R

1411½
ALADDIN INFUSER
CHARTREUSE—#00662R

1411½ GOLD DECORATED GROUP WITH INFUSER
1411 GOLD DECORATED GROUP WITHOUT INFUSER

1411½ GROUP SHIPPING WEIGHT 23 POUNDS • 1411 GROUP SHIPPING WEIGHT 18 POUNDS
PACKED 6 TO CARTON

Guaranteed by
Good Housekeeping

Albany Teapots

The six-cup Albany teapot was introduced in the early 1930s. It will be found undecorated and with three different gold decorations. The color seen most frequently with the standard decoration is turquoise.

The three different styles of gold decorations are shown in the photograph on page 230. The cadet, turquoise, warm yellow, and emerald teapots depict the standard Albany gold decoration. The "special" gold decoration is illustrated by the cobalt and maroon teapots on the top row. This includes the standard decoration and a gold encrusted handle, spout, and knob on the lid. A vari-ation of the "special" gold design is illustrated by the maroon teapot at the right side of the second row. The teapots in the center vertical row are examples of the two colors associated with the Gold Label Line. The pattern of this decoration is called "Reflection."

The more common and less collectible colors are all greens, all browns, pink, black, ivory, turquoise, and most lighter blues.

Unusual and more collectible colors include cobalt, rose, warm yellow, canary, maroon, orchid, and gray.

Albany Teapots	Solid Color	Standard Gold	Gold Special	Gold Label
Black	$35.00 – 45.00	$50.00 – 60.00		
Blue Turquoise	$50.00 – 60.00	$65.00 – 75.00		$150.00 – 175.00
Cadet	$45.00 – 55.00	$55.00 – 60.00		
Canary	$60.00 – 70.00			
Chinese Red	$225.00 – 250.00			
Cobalt	$50.00 – 65.00	$65.00 – 70.00	$75.00 – 85.00	
Dresden	$45.00 – 55.00	$65.00 – 75.00		
Emerald	$50.00 – 60.00	$55.00 – 65.00		
Ivory		$45.00 – 55.00		$95.00 – 110.00
Mahogany		$45.00 – 55.00		$50.00 – 65.00
Marine		$85.00 – 90.00		
Maroon	$45.00 – 55.00	$65.00 – 75.00	$90.00 – 125.00	$90.00 – 125.00
Pink				$150.00 – 175.00
Turquoise	$45.00 – 55.00	$65.00 – 75.00		
Warm Yellow	$45.00 – 55.00	$65.00 – 75.00		

Maroon gold "special" with variant gold decoration $200.00 – 225.00

Warm Yellow Marine Chinese Red

Maroon and Gold "Special"

Ivory Gold Label
with Reflection Design

Cobalt and Gold "Special"

Emerald Green with Standard Gold

Blue Turquiose Gold Label
with Reflections Design

Maroon Gold Special Variant

Celadon and Gold "Special"

Pink Gold Label
with Reflection Design

Turquoise with Standard Gold

Warm Yellow with Standard Gold

Mahogany Gold Label
With Reflections Design

Cadet with Standard Gold

Art Deco Teapots

The teapots shown below are from what appears to be a three teapot series which collectors are calling "Deco." Researchers have assigned the names "Adele," "Damascus," and "Danielle" to these three teapots. The colors which are being found are olive green, light blue, maroon, and yellow. Each one turns up most often in one basic color, but all have been found in more than one of the above colors.

Teapot	Blue	Green	Maroon	Yellow
"Adele"	$200.00 – 250.00	$175.00 – 200.00	$225.00 – 250.00	$200.00 – 225.00
"Damascus"	$200.00 – 250.00	$190.00 – 210.00	$225.00 – 250.00	$200.00 – 250.00
"Danielle"	$150.00 – 185.00	$145.00 – 165.00	$185.00 – 200.00	$150.00 – 185.00

"Danielle"

"Adele"

"Damascus"

Baltimore Teapots

The Baltimore teapot holds six cups and first appeared in the early 1930s. It may be found undecorated, with several styles of gold decorations, or with different decals. Colors which are easiest to find include maroon, emerald, and marine. The cadet and emerald teapots in the picture are examples of the standard gold decoration. The maroon and ivory teapots are from the Gold Label Line. The Baltimore teapot has recently been found with the No. 488 and Wild Poppy decals. This shape teapot has been found with several other interesting decals. One decal, shown in the picture, features multiple pink roses on an ivory body. Another decal usually found on an ivory body consists of a colorful floral arrangement in a flower pot. A third decal, Minuet, is usually found on a warm yellow teapot. An example of this decal may be seen in the picture. Another confirmed decal is called "Leaf and Vines."

Notice prices of many of the standard gold decorated teapots are about the same as the same color undecorated teapots.

Common and less collectible colors include most greens, most lighter blues, yellows, black, maroon, pink, and ivory. Unusual and more collectible colors are rose, orchid, red, and cobalt.

Baltimore Teapot	Solid Color	Standard Gold	Gold Label
Black	$35.00 – 45.00	$45.00 – 55.00	
Cadet	$55.00 – 65.00	$75.00 – 85.00	$95.00 – 125.00
Chinese Red	$250.00 – 300.00		
Emerald	$65.00 – 75.00	$90.00 – 110.00	
Ivory	$30.00 – 40.00	$45.00 – 55.00	$100.00 – 125.00
Marine		$90.00 – 110.00	
Maroon	$65.00 – 75.00	$90.00 – 100.00	$125.00 – 140.00
Orchid	$200.00 – 250.00		
Warm Yellow	$55.00 – 65.00	$60.00 – 75.00	

Decal Decorations		
Blue with Leaf and Vine Decal	$200.00 – 250.00	
Ivory with Flower Pot Decal	$225.00 – 250.00	
Ivory with Pink Rose Decal	$200.00 – 225.00	
Mahogany with gold decoration	$100.00 – 150.00	
Warm Yellow with Minuet Decal	$200.00 – 225.00	

Emerald with Standard Gold

Cadet with Standard Gold

Maroon Gold Label with Nova Design

Ivory with Flower Pot Decal

Warm Yellow with Minuet Decal

Mahogany and Gold

Ivory with Pink Rose Decal

Red

Marine with Standard Gold

Ivory Gold Label with Nova Design

Bellevue Teapots and Coffee Pots

Chinese Red Teapot

Light Blue Teapot

Orchid Teapot

Chinese Red 2" Creamer

Cobalt Teapot with Gold Insignia

Green and White Teapot with Black Trim

Chinese Red Sugar and Lid

Chinese Red Creamer

Green and White Coffee Pot with Black Trim

Cobalt Coffee Pot with Gold Trim

Cobalt Coffee Pot with Gold Insignia

Cobalt Coffee Pot

Nickle Clad Teapot

Nickle Clad Sugar and Lid

Nickle Clad Creamer

Nickle Clad Coffee Pot

Interest in the Bellevue teapot among collectors has been minimal. The teapot introduced in the 1920s will be found in at least six different sizes and is still being made in some colors. It is most commonly found in stock brown and stock green, but as can be seen in the photo, it will occasionally be found in attractive colors and with gold decoration. It has been found in one decal dinnerware line in the two-cup size — Orange Poppy — and attracts great interest among those interested in that pattern.

Bellevue	Common Solid Colors	Red	Cobalt	Gold Decorated
Coffee pot	$25.00 – 35.00	$55.00 – 65.00	$50.00 – 55.00	$65.00 – 75.00
Creamer	$15.00 – 18.00	$20.00 – 25.00	$20.00 – 22.00	$22.00 – 25.00
Sugar and lid	$18.00 – 22.00	$22.00 – 27.00	$22.00 – 25.00	$27.00 – 30.00
Teapot, 2, 4-cup	$25.00 – 35.00	$35.00 – 45.00	$35.00 – 45.00	$40.00 – 50.00
Teapot, 6, 10-cup	$45.00 – 55.00	$65.00 – 75.00		
Teapot, 2-cup orchid	$200.00 – 250.00			
Teapot/coffee pot, small green & white	$45.00 – 55.00			

Nickel clad items add 25% to common color prices.

Boston Teapots

The Boston shape teapot was one of the original four teapots selected for Hall's venture into the retail markets in 1920. During the 1920s several different styles of gold decoration were used. These decorations are not easy to find and are seen most often on teapots with a stock brown, stock green, or cobalt body. Look for the embossed HALL mark used in combination with the #4 backstamp to help identify these early teapots.

Two-cup teapots are shown in the photo below. The decoration shown on the cadet and chartreuse teapots is the one normally found on this shape teapot produced for the Gold Decorated Line. These teapots will be found in sizes ranging from one cup to eight cups.

The cobalt teapot is from the Gold Label Line. These teapots are decorated with an allover fleur-de-lis pattern and have golden handles, spouts, and knobs. The stock brown teapot with the Trailing Astor decoration is an example of an Old Gold decoration from the mid-1920s. The teapots with the metal handles and lids were made for the Detroit Athletic Club.

1 – 3 cup Boston Teapot	Solid Color	Standard Gold	Gold Label	Old Gold Design
Black	$20.00 – 25.00	$25.00 – 30.00		
Cadet	$30.00 – 35.00	$35.00 – 45.00		
Canary	$25.00 – 30.00	$35.00 – 45.00		
Chartreuse	$20.00 – 30.00	$40.00 – 45.00		
Chinese Red	$100.00 – 125.00			
Cobalt	$33.00 – 40.00	$55.00 – 60.00	$75.00 – 85.00	$100.00 – 125.00
Dresden	$30.00 – 35.00	$40.00 – 45.00		
Emerald	$40.00 – 45.00	$55.00 – 65.00		
Green Luster	$35.00 – 45.00	$40.00 – 50.00	$55.00 – 65.00	
Ivory	$20.00 – 25.00	$35.00 – 45.00	$55.00 – 60.00	
Marine	$35.00 – 40.00	$50.00 – 55.00		
Maroon	$30.00 – 35.00	$35.00 – 45.00		
Orchid	$200.00 – 225.00			
Pink	$25.00 – 30.00	$40.00 – 45.00		
Rose	$30.00 – 35.00	$50.00 – 55.00		
Stock Brown/Green	$20.00 – 25.00	$25.00 – 35.00		$45.00 – 55.00
Turquoise	$35.00 – 40.00	$45.00 – 50.00		
Warm Yellow	$35.00 – 40.00	$45.00 – 55.00		

Detroit Athletic Club: Stock Brown/Green, $85.00 – 95.00; Cobalt, $100.00 – 125.00
Add 15% to above prices for one-cup teapots.

2-cup Teapots

Cadet with Standard Gold

Chartreuse with Standard Gold

Stock Brown with Trailing Astor Design

Cobalt Gold Label with Fleur-de-lis

Pink

Nickle Clad

Cobalt Detroit Athletic Club

Stock Brown Detroit Athletic Club

Boston teapots have been found advertised in the following sizes: 1 cup, 1½ cup, 2 cup, 3 cup, 4 cup, 5 cup, 6 cup, and 8 cup.

The cobalt, gray, Old Rose, and black teapots are examples of early gold decorations. The design on the Old Rose teapot is referred to as "Trailing Astor." The black teapot utilizes the same gold floral decoration which is normally found on the French shape teapots. This design is usually called French Flower. Notice the handle and spout of this teapot are gold encrusted. Boston shape teapots "in blue, green, and brown glaze with gold stamped decoration" were advertised in the five-cup size in a 1925 Butler Brothers catalog at $1.50 each.

Teapots shown in the second row illustrate the Boston standard gold decorated line. Examples in the third row depict the fleur-de-lis Gold Label decoration.

The gold coated set is from Hall's Golden Glo line. The bright gold glaze has been applied over a Hi-white base. The Golden Glo line is quite extensive and many of these pieces were made as early as the forties. However, some pieces are still in production. For more information about the items available in this line, see the Golden Glo listing under kitchenware.

The Boston shape has been subjected to various decal applications. Hall developed a retail teapot line during the 1960s, in which a Boston teapot with a decal was used. The body of this teapot was green and it contained a golden fruit decal in a band around the center. This shape teapot has also been used in some of the regular decal dinnerware and kitchenware lines.

Common and less collectible colors include all greens, all browns, most lighter blues, yellows, black, maroon, pink, ivory, and gray. Unusual and more collectible colors are red, cobalt, rose, orchid, and turquoise.

Matching sugar and creamer sets were also sometimes sold with the Boston teapots. In addition this shape sugar and creamer were also decorated and sold to match teapots of other shapes such as the Aladdin and Philadelphia.

The white teapots at the bottom of the photo were marketed by Thornberry's of Ohio during the 1970s.

4 – 8-cup Boston Teapot	Solid Color	Standard Gold	Gold Label	Old Gold Design
Black	$20.00 – 25.00	$45.00 – 50.00		$35.00 – 45.00
Cadet	$30.00 – 35.00	$45.00 – 55.00		
Canary	$25.00 – 30.00	$45.00 – 55.00		
Chartreuse	$30.00 – 35.00	$45.00 – 50.00		
Chinese Red	$200.00 – 225.00			
Cobalt	$40.00 – 45.00	$55.00 – 60.00	$85.00 – 95.00	$200.00 – 225.00
Dresden	$30.00 – 35.00	$45.00 – 55.00	$90.00 – 115.00	
Emerald	$40.00 – 45.00	$55.00 – 65.00		
Gray	$20.00 – 25.00	$35.00 – 45.00		
Green Luster	$35.00 – 45.00	$40.00 – 50.00	$95.00 – 115.00	
Ivory	$20.00 – 25.00	$35.00 – 45.00	$60.00 – 65.00	
Marine	$35.00 – 45.00	$55.00 – 60.00		
Maroon	$35.00 – 40.00	$45.00 – 55.00		
Orchid	$220.00 – 250.00			
Pink	$30.00 – 35.00	$45.00 – 50.00		
Rose	$30.00 – 35.00	$50.00 – 60.00		
Stock Brown/Green	$20.00 – 25.00	$30.00 – 40.00		$45.00 – 75.00
Turquoise	$35.00 – 40.00	$45.00 – 55.00		
Warm Yellow	$35.00 – 40.00	$50.00 – 55.00		

Golden Glo teapot, $150.00 – 175.00; sugar and lid, $20.00 – 25.00; creamer, $12.00 – 15.00

Thornberry decal, $75.00 – 95.00; Sears decal, $90.00 – 115.00

Black with French Flower decoration, $125.00 – 150.00

Old Rose with Trailing Astor decoration, $200.00 – 250.00

Add 20% to above prices for 8-cup teapots.

6-cup
Cobalt with Old Gold Band Design

6-cup
Old Rose with Trailing Astor Design

6-cup
Gray with Black Marble Design

6-cup
Pink with Standard Gold

6-cup
Ivory with Standard Gold

6-cup
Cobalt with Standard Gold

6-cup
Green Luster Gold Label with Fleur-de-lis

6-cup
Ivory Gold Label with Fleur-de-lis

6-cup
Dresden Gold Label with Fleur-de-lis

4-cup
Canary with Standard Gold

4-cup
Black with French Flower Design

6-cup
Green with Sear's Golden Fruit Decal

6-cup
Golden Glo

6-cup
Thornberry's Summer Song Design

6-cup
Thornberry's Flower Garden Design

Golden Glo Sugar and Creamer

Old Rose Creamer with French Flower Design

Cobalt Sugar and Creamer with Palm Leaf Design

Cobalt Creamer with Old Gold Design

Cleveland Teapots

Chinese Red

Emerald Green with Standard Gold

Warm Yellow

Turquoise with Standard Gold

Cobalt with Standard Gold

Warm Yellow with Standard Gold

The Cleveland is a six-cup teapot which was introduced in the late thirties. It is most commonly found in emerald with gold decoration, but is also available in other colors with and without gold decoration. The standard gold decoration is shown on the four gold decorated teapots in the picture. Those collectors who are seeking undecorated teapots will have to be more patient than those looking for gold decorated ones. However, prices for both types are currently about the same for equivalent colors.

Common and less collectible colors are turquoise, all yellows, and all greens.

Unusual and more collectible colors include most blues, red, and cobalt.

Cleveland Teapots	Solid Color	Standard Gold
Black		$60.00 – 75.00
Cadet	$35.00 – 45.00	$75.00 – 85.00
Chinese Red	$225.00 – 250.00	
Cobalt	$90.00 – 125.00	$90.00 – 125.00
Emerald	$45.00 – 55.00	$70.00 – 80.00
Ivory	$25.00 – 30.00	$75.00 – 85.00
Turquoise	$45.00 – 55.00	$75.00 – 85.00
Warm Yellow	$45.00 – 55.00	$75.00 – 85.00

French Teapots

The French teapot was one of the earliest to be added to the Gold Decorated line. This style teapot is a perfect example of Hall's decorating diversity. The gold decorations on some of the early teapots exhibit excellent craftsmanship. A prime example is the cobalt teapot with the gold palm leaf decoration which is shown in the photograph on page 241. Another interesting early gold decoration is called "Sycamore." Some of the early teapots dating from the 1920s, such as the cobalt ones with the French Flower, Palm Leaf, and Nouveau shown in the photos will be found with infusors. Later French teapots do not have infusors. The two most frequently found gold decorations are the "daisy" from the Gold Label line and the gold "French Flower" decoration. These two decorations are found on all sizes of French teapots ranging from the one-cup size to the 12-cup size. The various sizes of the French teapot which have been found are 1, 1½, 2,

3, 4, 6, 8, 10, and 12-cups. The 6 and 8-cup sizes of French teapots are the most common. The 6-cup teapot will also be found in numerous colors with Lipton Tea embossed in the bottom. Boston shape sugars and creamers will also be found to match these teapots in some colors. For more information about the teapots made for Lipton see page 331.

The matte black 6-cup teapot with the gold rose decal to the right center of the photo on page 241 is from Hall's 1960s decal line. This teapot has been found advertised in Sears' catalogs from this era. The warm yellow teapot with the Minuet decal is from a decal line of six teapots that Hall produced during the 1930s.

French teapots have also been found with several different hand-painted decorations. An example decorated with acorns and oak leaves is shown in the photo on page 241.

6-cup Ivory with
Embossed Gold Band Design

6-cup Cobalt Special
with French Flower Design

6-cup "No-blue"

2-cup Old Rose
with French Flower Design

2-cup Chartreuse
with French Flower Design

2-cup Canary
with French Flower Design

2-cup Cadet Gold Label
with Daisy Design

4-cup Ivory with
Green Nouveau Design

10-cup Addison Gold Label
with Daisy Design

2-cup Black with
Sears' Gold Flower Design

French Teapots

1 – 3-cup French Teapots	Solid Color	Standard Gold	Gold Label
Black	$20.00 – 25.00	$30.00 – 35.00	$35.00 – 40.00
Blue Turquoise	$30.00 – 35.00	$55.00 – 65.00	$65.00 – 75.00
Cadet	$30.00 – 35.00	$45.00 – 50.00	$55.00 – 60.00
Canary	$30.00 – 35.00	$45.00 – 50.00	$55.00 – 60.00
Chartreuse	$30.00 – 35.00	$35.00 – 42.00	
Chinese Red	$150.00 – 175.00		
Cobalt	$35.00 – 45.00	$45.00 – 55.00	$55.00 – 65.00
Dresden	$30.00 – 35.00	$45.00 – 50.00	$55.00 – 60.00
Emerald	$35.00 – 45.00	$45.00 – 55.00	$55.00 – 65.00
Gray	$25.00 – 35.00	$35.00 – 45.00	$65.00 – 75.00
Ivory	$20.00 – 25.00	$35.00 – 40.00	$45.00 – 50.00
Marine	$35.00 – 45.00	$45.00 – 55.00	
Maroon	$30.00 – 35.00	$45.00 – 55.00	
Pink	$30.00 – 35.00	$45.00 – 50.00	$55.00 – 60.00
Rose	$30.00 – 35.00	$45.00 – 55.00	
Stock Brn/Gn	$20.00 – 25.00	$30.00 – 35.00	
Turquoise	$35.00 – 45.00	$45.00 – 60.00	
Warm Yellow	$30.00 – 35.00	$45.00 – 50.00	

4 – 8-cup French Teapots	Solid Color	Standard Gold	Gold Label
Black	$25.00 – 30.00	$35.00 – 40.00	$35.00 – 40.00
Blue Turquoise	$35.00 – 40.00	$55.00 – 65.00	$65.00 – 75.00
Cadet	$30.00 – 40.00	$45.00 – 55.00	$55.00 – 65.00
Canary	$35.00 – 40.00	$45.00 – 55.00	$55.00 – 65.00
Chartreuse	$30.00 – 35.00	$35.00 – 45.00	
Chinese Red	$140.00 – 165.00		
Cobalt	$35.00 – 45.00	$45.00 – 60.00	$60.00 – 70.00
Dresden	$30.00 – 40.00	$45.00 – 55.00	$55.00 – 65.00
Emerald	$35.00 – 45.00	$45.00 – 60.00	$60.00 – 70.00
Gray	$25.00 – 35.00	$35.00 – 45.00	$65.00 – 75.00
Ivory	$20.00 – 25.00	$35.00 – 45.00	$45.00 – 55.00
Marine	$35.00 – 45.00	$45.00 – 55.00	
Maroon	$40.00 – 45.00	$50.00 – 65.00	
Pink	$35.00 – 40.00	$45.00 – 55.00	$55.00 – 60.00
Rose	$30.00 – 40.00	$50.00 – 60.00	
Stock Brn/Gn	$20.00 – 25.00	$35.00 – 45.00	
Turquoise	$35.00 – 45.00	$45.00 – 60.00	
Warm Yellow	$30.00 – 35.00	$45.00 – 50.00	

Special Decorations

Acorn and Oak Leaf decoration, $200.00 – 250.00

Hand-painted decorations, $200.00 – 250.00

Gold Leaf and Purple Flower, $250.00 – 325.00

Nouveau decoration, $100.00 – 175.00

Sycamore decoration, $150.00 – 185.00

Minuet decal, $125.00 – 150.00

Black with gold band, $70.00 – 85.00

Matte Black with Gold Flower, $100.00 – 125.00

Silver luster, $100.00 – 125.00

Palm Leaf decoration, $250.00 – 350.00

Stock green with gold mini floral band, $125.00 – 150.00

6-cup French Teapots

Old Rose with Sycamore Design

Cobalt with Sycamore Design

Ivory with Gold Leaf and Purple

Cobalt with Special Nouveau Design and Monogram

Stock Green Special with Gold Mini Floral Band

Cobalt with Palm Leaf Design

Black with Gold Band Decoration

Warm Yellow with Minuet Decal

Black with Gold Rose (Sears)

Ivory Hand Painted with Acorns and Oak Leaves

Chinese Red

Cadet with French Flower Design

Silver Luster

Ivory Gold Label with Daisy Design

Pink Gold Label with Daisy Design

10 – 12-cup French Teapots	Solid Color	Standard Gold	Gold Label
Black	$27.00 – 32.00	$37.00 – 42.00	$37.00 – 42.00
Blue Turquoise	$45.00 – 50.00	$57.00 – 65.00	$67.00 – 75.00
Cadet	$35.00 – 45.00	$50.00 – 60.00	$65.00 – 70.00
Canary	$35.00 – 45.00	$50.00 – 60.00	$65.00 – 70.00
Chartreuse	$40.00 – 45.00	$35.00 – 45.00	
Chinese Red	$180.00 – 225.00		
Cobalt	$55.00 – 65.00	$65.00 – 70.00	$70.00 – 80.00
Dresden	$35.00 – 45.00	$50.00 – 60.00	$65.00 – 70.00
Emerald	$45.00 – 55.00	$55.00 – 60.00	$70.00 – 75.00
Gray	$35.00 – 40.00	$35.00 – 45.00	$65.00 – 75.00
Ivory	$27.00 – 32.00	$35.00 – 45.00	$50.00 – 55.00
Marine	$45.00 – 55.00	$55.00 – 60.00	
Maroon	$45.00 – 55.00	$55.00 – 65.00	
Pink	$35.00 – 45.00	$50.00 – 60.00	$65.00 – 75.00
Rose	$40.00 – 50.00	$50.00 – 60.00	
Stock Brn/Gn	$20.00 – 25.00	$35.00 – 45.00	
Turquoise	$45.00 – 50.00	$55.00 – 60.00	
Warm Yellow	$35.00 – 45.00	$50.00 – 60.00	

Globe Teapots

The six-cup Globe teapot was made with two different shapes of spouts. The No-Drip spout Globe shown on the top row has a different standard gold decoration than the regular Globe pictured on the second row.

Both teapots are found more often with gold decoration than without. Both styles are hard to find, but the No-Drip version appears to be a little more available than the other style.

Globe Teapots	Solid Color	Standard Gold
Cadet	$75.00 – 100.00	$100.00 – 125.00
Camellia	$45.00 – 55.00	$60.00 – 75.00
Canary	$75.00 – 100.00	$100.00 – 125.00
Chartreuse	$40.00 – 45.00	$100.00 – 125.00
Chinese Red	$375.00 – 425.00	
Cobalt	$200.00 – 250.00	
Emerald	$100.00 – 150.00	
Ivory	$40.00 – 45.00	
Marine	$150.00 – 175.00	$100.00 – 125.00
Rose	$45.00 – 55.00	$60.00 – 75.00

No-Drip Teapots	Solid Color	Standard Gold
Addison	$35.00 – 45.00	$50.00 – 60.00
Camellia	$45.00 – 55.00	$50.00 – 65.00
Cadet	$40.00 – 50.00	$50.00 – 60.00
Canary	$50.00 – 55.00	$50.00 – 60.00
Chartreuse	$40.00 – 45.00	$45.00 – 55.00
Rose	$45.00 – 55.00	$55.00 – 65.00
Turquoise	$45.00 – 55.00	$60.00 – 75.00

Globe
Regular Spout

Chinese Red

Camellia with Standard Gold

Chartreuse with Standard Gold

Canary with Standard Gold

Cobalt

Cadet with Standard Gold

Camellia with Standard Gold

Chartreuse with Standard Gold

Addison with Standard Gold

Globe
No-Drip

Cadet with Standard Gold

Turquoise with Standard Gold

243

Hollywood Teapots

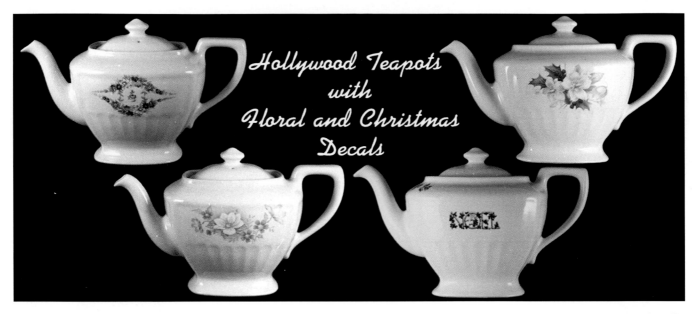

Hollywood Teapots
with
Floral and Christmas
Decals

The Hollywood teapot first appeared in the late 1920s. It may be found in a five-cup size in addition to the three sizes illustrated here — four-cup, six-cup, and eight-cup. There is also a matching sugar and creamer available for some decorations. The standard decoration is shown on several teapots at the right side of the photo. The chartreuse teapot at the top right is an example of the Gold Label "Grid" decoration. A more commonly found color with this decoration is pink.

The pearlized-color teapot shown in the center of the pic-

ture is uncommon. The "special" gold treatment of the handle and spout add to the appeal of this teapot. Several other shapes of teapots with this unusual color glaze have been found. These are highly desirable additions to the collections of teapot lovers. The mahogany teapot with the gold flower decoration is from a decal line Hall produced during the 1960s.

The Hollywood teapot is often found in maroon and in a variety of greens and the lighter blue colors. Also, the six-cup size is the most common of the four sizes.

Hollywood Teapots	Solid Color	Standard Gold	Gold Special	Gold Label
Black	$35.00 – 40.00	$50.00 – 55.00		$85.00 – 95.00
Blue Turquoise	$45.00 – 55.00			
Cadet	$40.00 – 50.00	$55.00 – 65.00		
Canary	$40.00 – 50.00	$55.00 – 60.00		
Chartreuse	$40.00 – 45.00	$55.00 – 60.00		$90.00 – 11.00
Chinese Red	$185.00 – 225.00			
Cobalt	$50.00 – 60 00	$60.00 – 80.00		
Emerald	$40.00 – 45.00	$60.00 – 65.00		
Ivory	$35.00 – 40.00	$45.00 – 55.00		$80.00 – 95.00
Marine	$50.00 – 60.00	$80.00 – 95.00		$100.00 – 125.00
Maroon	$40.00 – 45.00	$50.00 – 60.00	$100.00 – 125.00	
Pink	$40.00 – 45.00	$60.00 – 75.00		
Stock Brn/Gn	$30.00 – 40.00			
Warm Yellow	$40.00 – 45.00	$50.00 – 65.00		

Special Decorations

Christmas decals	$175.00 – 225.00
Pearlized glaze	$175.00 – 210.00
Creamer	$20.00 – 30.00
Sugar	$35.00 – 45.00
Floral decals	$100.00 – 125.00

6-cup Warm Yellow

4-Cup Marine with Standard Gold

6-Cup Chartreuse Gold Label with Grid Design

6-cup Indian Red

6-cup Golden Glo

8-cup Maroon with Standard Gold

6-cup Mahogany with Gold Flower Design

8-cup Ivory "Special" with Pearl Finish

4-cup Emerald with Standard Gold

8-cup Black Gold Label with Grid Design

6-cup Chinese Red

4-cup Pink with Standard Gold

Red and Ivory Sugar and Creamer with Gold Trim

4-cup Pink

4-cup Chartreuse with Standard Gold

Black Gold Special Sugar and Creamer

6-cup Maroon Gold Special

Maroon Gold Special Sugar and Creamer

Hook Cover Teapots

The Hook Cover is a six-cup teapot which was introduced in 1940. It derives its name from the small hook on the body over which an opening in the lid fits to lock it into place. Colors usually found are cadet and delphinium. The standard gold decoration consists of a large gold flower along with four gold sprigs on each side of the body and gold trim on the foot, spout, handle, and around the lid and lid opening. Another gold decorated version of this teapot has been turning up. This style of decoration has gold lines on the handle, spout, and lid

similar to the standard gold version, but the large gold flower and gold sprigs are lacking.

The Gold Label version of the Hook Cover is covered with gold stars and sports a gold encrusted handle and spout. The ivory and cadet teapots to the top right of the photo are examples of this style of gold decoration

An elusive gold decorated teapot is shown in the middle of the second row. This teapot has a gold encrusted spout and handle and the body is decorated with the mini fleurette pattern.

Hook Cover Teapots	Solid Color	Standard Gold	Gold Label	Gold Line Design
Black	$40.00 – 45.00	$50.00 – 60.00		$55.00 – 65.00
Cadet	$40.00 – 45.00	$40.00 – 50.00	$50.00 – 60.00	
Canary	$40.00 – 50.00	$50.00 – 55.00		
Chinese Red	$200.00 – 225.00			
Cobalt	$75.00 – 85.00	$75.00 – 85.00		$75.00 – 85.00
Delphinium	$40.00 – 45.00	$40.00 – 50.00		
Emerald	$65.00 – 75.00	$65.00 – 80.00		
Ivory			$60.00 – 70.00	
Maroon	$45.00 – 50.00	$45.00 – 55.00		
Orchid	$250.00 – 300.00			
Turquoise	$50.00 – 60.00	$65.00 – 75.00		
Warm Yellow	$60.00 – 70.00			

Special Gold Decoration
Turquoise with Mini Fleurette decoration, $200.00 – 250.00

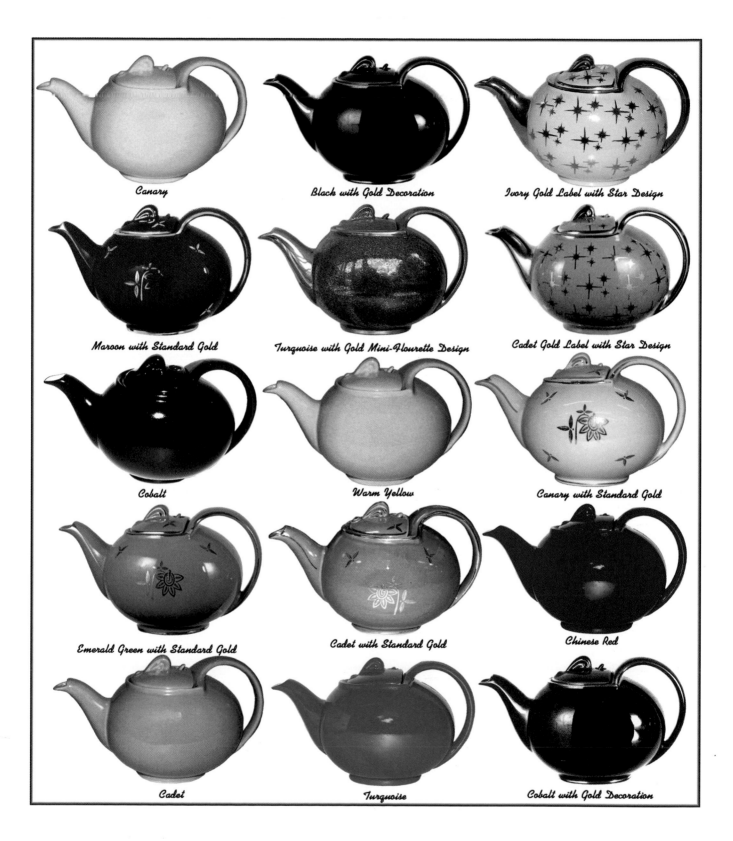

Canary

Black with Gold Decoration

Ivory Gold Label with Star Design

Maroon with Standard Gold

Turquoise with Gold Mini-Flourette Design

Cadet Gold Label with Star Design

Cobalt

Warm Yellow

Canary with Standard Gold

Emerald Green with Standard Gold

Cadet with Standard Gold

Chinese Red

Cadet

Turquoise

Cobalt with Gold Decoration

Illinois, Indiana, and Kansas Teapots

The Illinois is a very hard-to-find six-cup teapot which dates to the 1930s. This teapot has been found in solid colors and with two different gold decorations. The decoration seen most often has a gold band with a floral design around the top of the teapot. The lid also has a matching floral band. The second decoration consists of gold spirals which form a series of circles near the top of the teapot. The colors found most readily are cobalt and maroon.

The Kansas and Indiana are two teapots which are still lacking from many collections. Both will be found with gold decoration more often than without. The usual gold decorations may be seen in the photograph. The Kansas teapot will also be found with platinum trim.

Illinois Teapots	Solid Color	Standard Gold	Gold Nebula
Black	$150.00 – 170.00	$165.00 – 190.00	
Canary	$155.00 – 175.00	$175.00 – 200.00	$175.00 – 200.00
Chinese Red	$450.00 – 500.00		
Cobalt	$200.00 – 225.00	$200.00 – 250.00	
Maroon	$175.00 –195.00	$190.00 – 220.00	$200.00 – 230.00
Pink	$155.00 – 175.00		$180.00 – 200.00
Stock Brown	$100.00 – 125.00	$140.00 – 160.00	
Stock Green	$100.00 – 125.00	$140.00 – 160.00	

Indiana Teapot	Solid Color	Standard Gold
Chinese Red	$500.00 – 550.00	
Cobalt	$400.00 – 500.00	$450.00 – 550.00
Ivory	$200.00 – 250.00	$250.00 – 275.00
Maroon	$300.00 – 350.00	$350.00 – 450.00
Orchid		$600.00 – 800.00
Warm Yellow	$300.00 – 400.00	$350.00 – 450.00

Kansas Teapot	Solid Color	Standard Gold	Platinum Trim
Chinese Red	$550.00 – 600.00		
Emerald Green	$400.00 – 500.00		$400.00 – 500.00
Ivory	$200.00 – 250.00	$350.00 – 400.00	
Maroon	$300.00 – 350.00	$400.00 – 500.00	

Illinois

Cobalt

Chinese Red

Maroon with
Standard Gold

Maroon with
Gold Nebula Design

Pink with Gold Nebula Design

Cobalt with
Standard Gold

Kansas

Emerald Green with Standard Platinum

Ivory

Maroon with Standard Gold

Ivory with
Standard Gold

Warm Yellow with Standard Gold

Maroon with Standard Gold

Indiana

Orchid with Standard Gold

249

Los Angeles Teapots

The Los Angeles teapot may be found in three sizes — eight-cup, six-cup, and four-cup. Of the three sizes, the six-cup is the most common. This teapot first appeared in the mid-twenties and was subjected to a number of different decorations during its many years of production. The standard gold decoration is illustrated on the teapots in the top row.

The Gold Label version is shown on the teapots in the third row of the picture. The Gold Label decoration on this teapot is called "Medallion." The most frequently found colors — cobalt, Monterey, and pink — are shown in the picture.

In addition to gold decoration, decals were also applied to this shape teapot. A 1930s floral band decal is shown circling the upper body on the eight-cup teapot pictured in the center of the bottom row. A band of green leaves is often found in this same position on a mustard color teapot which was produced during the 1960s.

The more unusual colors for the Los Angeles include red, and blue turquoise.

Los Angeles 6-cup

Teapots	Solid Color	Standard Gold	Gold Label
Black	$40.00 – 45.00	$45.00 – 50.00	
Blue Turquoise	$55.00 – 60.00		$85.00 – 95.00
Cadet	$45.00 – 50.00	$50.00 – 55.00	
Canary	$45.00 – 50.00	$50.00 – 55.00	
Chinese Red	$200.00 – 225.00		
Cobalt	$50.00 – 55.00	$55.00 – 65.00	
Dresden	$45.00 – 50.00	$50.00 – 55.00	
Emerald	$50.00 – 60.00	$55.00 – 65.00	$75.00 – 85.00
Maroon	$50.00 – 55.00	$55.00 – 65.00	
Monterey			$85.00 – 95.00
Pink	$45.00 – 55.00	$55.00 – 60.00	$75.00 – 85.00
Stock Brown	$30.00 – 35.00		
Stock Green	$30.00 – 35.00		
Warm Yellow	$35.00 – 45.00	$40.00 – 50.00	

Special Decorations
Milky Blue with Flower Band decoration, $15.00 – 150.00
Mustard with green Leaf Band decoration, $80.00 – 90.00

Emerald 6-cup with Standard Gold

Cadet 4-cup with Standard Gold

Cobalt 6-cup with Standard Gold

Chinese Red 6-cup

Cobalt 8-cup

Canary 4-cup

Cobalt 6-cup Gold Label

Monterey 6-cup Gold Label

Pink 6-cup Gold Label

Warm Yellow 6-cup with Standard Gold

Milky Blue Glaze 6-cup
with Flower Band Decal

Blue Turquoise 6-cup Gold Label

Los Angeles 4 & 8-cup Teapots	*Solid Color*	*Standard Gold*
Black	$40.00 – 45.00	$45.00 – 50.00
Blue Turquoise	$60.00 – 65.00	
Cadet	$45.00 – 50.00	$50.00 – 55.00
Canary	$45.00 – 50.00	$50.00 – 55.00
Chinese Red	$220.00 – 275.00	
Cobalt	$50.00 – 55.00	$75.00 – 85.00
Dresden	$45.00 – 50.00	$55.00 – 60.00
Emerald	$50.00 – 60.00	$65.00 – 75.00
Maroon	$55.00 – 60.00	$65.00 – 75.00
Pink	$45.00 – 55.00	$55.00 – 60.00
Stock Brown	$30.00 – 35.00	
Stock Green	$30.00 – 35.00	
Warm Yellow	$35.00 – 45.00	$50.00 – 55.00

Manhattan Teapots

The side-handled Manhattan teapot is usually found in the small two-cup size. It is most frequently seen in stock brown, stock green, maroon, and cobalt. We have not seen this teapot with gold decoration.

Manhattan Teapot	*Value*	*Manhattan Teapot*	*Value*
Chinese Red	$175.00 – 200.00	Maroon	$95.00 – 120.00
Cobalt	$160.00 – 180.00	Stock Brown	$35.00 – 40.00
Ivory	$40.00 – 45.00	Stock Green	$35.00 – 40.00

Stock Brown   *Cobalt*   *Maroon*   *Stock Green*

Melody Teapots

The Melody teapot was first produced in 1939. It is a six-cup teapot which may be found with gold decoration; although it is probably found more frequently without decoration. The standard gold design on the body is three rings close to the base and three more rings inside the white collar in addition to trim on the handle and around the top edge. The lid is also decorated with a gold ring. The Melody is also found in ivory decorated with the Orange Poppy decal.

Although this teapot is somewhat elusive, most collectors will not encounter great difficulty in adding an example to their collection if they are willing to pay the price this attractive shape commands. The more frequently found colors include red, cobalt, and turquoise.

A miniature version of this teapot is sometimes seen decorated with decals familiar to Hall collectors. China Specialties is marketing this relatively new item that is called a "Baby Melody." For more information see the Reissues section in the back of this book.

Melody Teapots	Solid Color	Standard Gold
Black	$110.00 – 150.00	$125.00 –155.00
Cadet	$200.00 – 220.00	$220.00 – 250.00
Canary	$150.00 – 175.00	$210.00 – 230.00
Chinese Red	$250.00 – 275.00	
Cobalt	$220.00 – 260.00	
Emerald	$200.00 – 225.00	$220.00 – 250.00
Ivory	$75.00 – 85.00	$150.00 – 175.00
Marine	$200.00 – 240.00	$240.00 – 270.00
Maroon	$185.00 – 200.00	$200.00 – 225.00
Turquoise	$190.00 – 210.00	$220.00 – 235.00
Warm Yellow	$150.00 – 185.00	$190.00 – 220.00

Ivory with Platinum Trim

Canary with Gold Trim

Cobalt

Maroon

Emerald

Chinese Red

Turquoise with Gold Trim

Cobalt with Gold Trim

Maroon with Gold Trim

Moderne Teapots

The Moderne teapot has a six-cup capacity. It is commonly found in ivory, canary, and cadet, and is usually seen without gold decoration. The standard gold application is limited to the knob of the lid, the very inside tip of the spout, and the foot. The plain design of this teapot has caused many common color Moderne teapots to be left on dealer's tables begging for homes.

However, the discovery of the Moderne teapot in several unusual colors and with some exotic decorations has piqued collector interest. Notice especially the orchid color and the teapots with extensive gold decoration in the picture. Many teapot collectors are eagerly seeking these Moderne specimens.

Moderne Teapots	Solid Color	Standard Gold
Black	$30.00 – 35.00	$45.00 – 50.00
Cadet	$45.00 – 55.00	$60.00 – 70.00
Canary	$45.00 – 55.00	$60.00 – 70.00
Chinese Red	$125.00 – 145.00	
Cobalt	$55.00 – 65.00	$65.00 – 75.00
Delphinium	$45.00 – 55.00	$60.00 – 70.00
Dresden	$45.00 – 55.00	$60.00 – 70.00
Emerald	$50.00 – 60.00	$55.00 – 65.00
Indian Red	$125.00 – 145.00	$175.00 – 195.00
Ivory	$30.00 – 40.00	$40.00 – 45.00
Marine	$45.00 – 55.00	$55.00 – 65.00
Maroon	$50.00 – 60.00	$60.00 – 70.00
Orchid	$200.00 – 250.00	
Pink	$45.00 – 55.00	$60.00 – 70.00
Warm Yellow	$45.00 – 55.00	$60.00 – 70.00

Special Gold Decorations
Gold & silver Art Deco, $400.00 – 500.00
Ivory with Gold floral design, $250.00 – 300.00
Canary with gold floral design, $275.00 – 325.00

Cobalt with Standard Gold

Orchid with Tea Tile

Silver and Gold Art Deco

Warm Yellow and Standard Gold

Marine with Tea Tile

Maroon and Standard Gold

Emerald and Standard Gold

Indian Red and Standard Gold

Ivory with Gold Floral Design

Cadet

Emerald with Tea Tile

Canary

Ivory with Standard Gold

Chinese Red with Tea Tile

Cobalt

Morning Tea Sets

Chinese Red Morning Tea Set

Marine Blue Morning Tea Set

Hall's Morning Tea Set is comprised of a 21 ounce covered teapot, a covered sugar, and a creamer. The set is found most often in Chinese Red, but was also made in other solid colors. Decal versions of this set exist in a few of the kitchenware patterns and several sets have been found with the Autumn Leaf decal. For more information on the decal sets see the Autumn Leaf, Blue Blossom, Blue Garden, and Fantasy sections of this book.

The teapot and creamer were also used with the No. 1 Tea Set shown on page 272.

Color	Morning Set Teapot	Sugar and Lid	Creamer
Chinese Red	$225.00 – 250.00	$45.00 – 55.00	$30.00 – 35.00
Cobalt	$200.00 – 250.00	$40.00 – 50.00	$30.00 – 35.00
Marine	$200.00 – 250.00	$40.00 – 50.00	$30.00 – 35.00

Musical Teapots

Hall produced a six-cup musical teapot in the mid-fifties. The teapot was advertised in Montgomery Ward catalogs from 1951 through 1954. Retail price varied from $6.95 to $7.25 in these catalogs. The teapot has been found most often in the cadet blue color shown in the picture to the right, but other colors may be found as well. Notice the unusual iridized ivory teapot with red trim in the photo. Musical teapots have a cavity on the under side into which the wind-up music box fits. The original music box was made by Thoren's, Inc., and is held in place by a metal band. Appropriately, the music box plays "Tea for Two." Numerous teapots are found with their music boxes missing. Musical teapots without music boxes or with new replacement music boxes bring significantly less than teapots with original working parts.

Musical Teapot	Value	Musical Teapot	Value
Cadet	$155.00 – 170.00	Iridized Ivory/red trim	$200.00 – 250.00
Canary	$155.00 – 170.00		

Musical Teapots

Ivory Pearl with Red Trim

Closeup of Original Thoren's Inc. Music Box Label

Cadet

Canary

Photo of Music Box

[11] HALL CHINA MUSICAL TEAPOT. As you pour, this nicely designed cadet blue china teapot tinkles forth with strains of "Tea for Two." A 22-note Helvetic movement is concealed in the base of the pot. Heavy china holds heat well. Capacity is about six (five-ounce) cups.
53 C 5481—Shipping weight 4 lbs............7.25

Ad From 1951 Montgomery Wards Catalog

Nautilus Teapots

The Nautilus is a sea shell-shaped six-cup teapot which first appeared in 1939. This teapot is hard to find and commands a respectable price. This teapot may be found in solid colors, with a standard gold decoration, and with a gold special decoration. Normal gold decoration is limited to a few simple lines as may be seen on several teapots in the photo. The gold special decoration consists of the standard gold decoration with the addition of a gold encrusted handle and spout on the body of the teapot. Additional gold is also found on the knob of the lid.

Nautilus Teapots	Solid Color	Standard Gold	Gold Special
Cadet	$200.00 – 250.00	$225.00 – 250.00	
Canary	$140.00 – 160.00	$180.00 – 200.00	$260.00 – 300.00
Chinese Red	$450.00 – 500.00		
Cobalt	$300.00 – 350.00	$340.00 – 365.00	$350.00 – 400.00
Emerald	$225.00 – 255.00	$260.00 – 285.00	
Maroon	$225.00 – 260.00	$275.00 – 300.00	
Turquoise	$210.00 – 235.00	$240.00 – 260.00	
Warm Yellow	$200.00 – 235.00	$240.00 – 260.00	

Cobalt and Gold Special

Cadet Blue

Turquoise

Turquoise with Standard Gold

Warm Yellow with Standard Gold

Chinese Red

Warm Yellow

Maroon

Maroon with Standard Gold

Canary with Standard Gold

Cobalt with Standard Gold

Cobalt

Newport Teapots

The Newport teapot was introduced in the 1930s. It will be found in both seven-cup and five-cup sizes. This teapot was used in the Autumn Leaf pattern and is most commonly found with that decal in the seven-cup size. In addition, the Newport will be found in several solid colors and with gold, silver, and decal decorations. The standard gold decoration consists of a narrow gold bubble band on the shoulder of the teapot and on the lid.

The handle and spout are also trimmed with gold lines. Two decal decorations for the Newport are pictured. The decal decoration pictured on the pink teapot at the top right is from the 1930s and features a bouquet of multi-colored flowers in a black urn. The handle, spout, and lid are also accented with black trim. A decal with berries is shown on a gold decorated teapot at the left of the photo.

Newport Teapot	Solid Color	Standard Gold	Decal Decoration
Chinese Red	$350.00 – 395.00		
Ivory	$30.00 – 35.00		
Pink	$45.00 – 55.00	$55.00 – 65.00	$145.00 – 175.00
Stock Brown	$30.00 – 35.00		
Stock Green	$30.00 – 35.00		
Warm Yellow	$50.00 – 60.00	$70.00 – 90.00	

Special Decorations
  Pink with gold Posey decoration, $250.00 – 275.00
  Pink with silver Flowers in the Breeze
    decoration, $250.00 – 275.00

Pink with Floral Decal

Pink With Silver Flowers in the Breeze Decoration

Pink with Flower Pot Decal

Warm Yellow with Gold Bubble Design

Pink with Gold Posey Decoration

Newport Teapots

Stock Green

New York Teapots

The New York teapot was added to the Gold Decorated line from the institutional line in 1920. In the ensuing years it became one of the most successful of all Hall teapots. It will be found in more colors, sizes, and decorations than any other Hall teapot. The New York shape was also used in many of the decal lines and was the teapot shape selected by the National Autumn Leaf Collectors Club for their first limited edition piece produced by Hall. The New York teapot is still being produced for the institutional line. To identify the newer teapots, look for the square Hall backstamp.

Nine different sizes — 1, 1½, 2, 3, 4, 6, 8, 10, and 12-cup — of the New York teapot have been produced. Today collectors are finding the four, six, and eight-cup sizes most often. The other larger and smaller sizes appear less frequently. The standard gold decoration is best seen on the Dresden teapot with the matching sugar and creamer on page 264.

The older New York teapots are appearing primarily in cobalt, stock brown, and stock green colors. These teapots are generally identified by their non-standard gold decorations and their early backstamp. The early backstamp used on the teapots during the 1920s is like the #4 backstamp shown in the identification section or may be a slight variation. In the variations, the "Made in U.S.A." is missing or is outside the circle.

The cobalt teapot at the top left of the photo on page 264 is referred to as a "special." It has the standard gold decoration along with a gold encrusted handle and spout. The teapot shown on the right side of the bottom row of the photo on page 263 is very unusual. The decoration consists of an all-over paisley floral pattern and extensive gold embellishment. Hand-painted gold and enamel decorations also consist of a palm leaf design similar to the ones seen on the French and Philadelphia shape teapots. Another interesting decoration is the Burbick design pictured on the bottom row on page 263. This teapot has been found advertised in a 1928 Sears catalog with a matching sugar and creamer. The set sold for $3.75.

Three different combinations of game bird decals consisting of ducks, pheasants, or grouse have been found by collectors. These decals have been found on two-cup teapots, but could also exist on other sizes. Examples of these teapots are pictured with the "Game Birds" pattern located in the dinnerware section of this book.

The silver teapot shown in the photo below is an example of a metal clad teapot. These teapots were coated with a special metal alloy to resist chipping. Shown in the picture on the next page are various sizes and colors of the New York teapot with the Gold Label decoration.

In addition, the New York shape has been found with the same multicolored floral and black urn decal which is pictured on the Newport teapot shown on page 260. This decal dates to the 1930s, and is not commonly found today.

Some of the common or less collectible colors include lighter blues, all greens, all browns, all yellows, ivory, pink, and black. Unusual or more collectible colors are red, cobalt, blue turquoise, rose, and orchid.

2-cup
Chinese Red

2-cup Metal-clad

2-cup Black
with Gold Trim

4-cup Maroon

4-cup Warm Yellow

2-cup Ivory
with Gold Dot Design

1 – 4-cup

New York Teapot	Solid Color	Standard Gold	Gold Label
Black	$20.00 – 25.00	$25.00 – 30.00	
Blue Turquoise	$30.00 – 35.00		$85.00 – 95.00
Cadet	$30.00 – 35.00	$35.00 – 45.00	$50.00 – 60.00
Canary	$25.00 – 30.00	$35.00 – 45.00	
Chartreuse	$20.00 – 30.00	$40.00 – 45.00	
Chinese Red	$100.00 – 125.00		
Cobalt	$33.00 – 40.00	$55.00 – 60.00	
Dresden	$30.00 – 35.00	$40.00 – 45.00	
Emerald	$40.00 – 45.00	$55.00 – 65.00	
Ivory	$20.00 – 25.00	$35.00 – 45.00	$55.00 – 65.00
Marine	$35.00 – 40.00	$50.00 – 55.00	
Maroon	$30.00 – 35.00	$35.00 – 45.00	
Orchid	$200.00 – 250.00		$250.00 – 275.00
Pink	$25.00 – 30.00	$40.00 – 45.00	$45.00 – 55.00
Rose	$30.00 – 35.00	$50.00 – 55.00	
Stock Brown/Green	$20.00 – 25.00	$25.00 – 35.00	
Turquoise	$35.00 – 40.00	$45.00 – 50.00	
Warm Yellow	$35.00 – 40.00	$45.00 – 55.00	$65.00 – 75.00

Special Decorations

Ivory with Gold Dot, $125.00 – 150.00

Stock Green miniature, $50.00 – 65.00

Metal clad, $90.00 – 110.00

Dresden creamer, sugar and lid, $40.00 – 50.00

*12-cup Turquoise Blue
Gold Label with Gold Flower*

*10-cup Warm Yellow
Gold Label with Gold Flower*

*8-cup Pink Gold Label
with Gold Flower*

*6-cup Matte Finish Orchid
Gold Label with Gold Flower*

*4-cup Ivory
Gold Label with Gold Flower*

*2-cup Cadet Gold Label
with Gold Flower*

6 and 8-cup

New York Teapot	Solid Color	Standard Gold	Gold Label	Gold Special
Black	$22.00 – 27.00	$27.00 – 32.00		
Blue Turquoise	$35.00 – 40.00		$85.00 95.00	
Cadet	$32.00 – 37.00	$37.00 –47.00	$50.00 – 60.00	
Canary	$25.00 – 30.00	$35.00 –45.00		
Chartreuse	$25.00 – 30.00	$40.00 – 45.00		
Chinese Red	$120.00 – 145.00			
Cobalt	$35.00 – 45.00	$55.00 – 60.00		$100.00 – 125.00
Dresden	$30.00 – 35.00	$40.00 – 45.00		
Emerald	$40.00 – 45.00	$55.00 – 65.00		
Ivory	$22.00 – 27.00	$35.00 – 45.00	$55.00 – 65.00	
Marine	$40.00 – 45.00	$50.00 – 55.00		
Maroon	$35.00 – 40.00	$45.00 – 50.00		
Orchid	$200.00 – 250.00		$250.00 – 275.00	
Pink	$25.00 – 30.00	$40.00 – 45.00	$45.00 – 55.00	
Rose	$35.00 – 40.00	$50.00 – 55.00		
Stock Brown/Green	$20.00 – 25.00	$25.00 – 35.00		
Turquoise	$35.00 – 40.00	$45.00 – 50.00		
Warm Yellow	$35.00 – 40.00	$45.00 – 55.00	$65.00 – 75.00	

Special Decorations

Burbick decoration, $400.00 – 500.00   French Flower, $200.00 – 250.00
Gold Band, $45.00 – 55.00   Paisley, $400.00 – 450.00
Gold Palm Leaf, $400.00 – 450.00   Silver Band, $45.00 – 55.00

6-cup Stock Brown
with French Flower Design

6-cup Canary
with Wide Gold Band

6-cup Light Blue
with Wide Gold Band

6-cup Cobalt
with Burbick Decoration

6-cup Stock Green
with Burbick Decoration

6-cup Paisley Decorated
with Gold

10 and 12-cup

New York Teapot	Solid Color	Standard Gold	Gold Label
Black	$25.00 – 30.00	$30.00 – 35.00	
Blue Turquoise	$40.00 – 50.00		$95.00 – 110.00
Cadet	$35.00 – 40.00	$40.00 – 50.00	$55.00 – 65.00
Canary	$35.00 – 40.00	$45.00 – 50.00	
Chartreuse	$30.00 – 40.00	$40.00 – 50.00	
Chinese Red	$180.00 –200.00		
Cobalt	$55.00 – 60.00	$65.00 – 70.00	
Dresden	$35.00 – 45.00	$40.00 – 50.00	
Emerald	$45.00 – 50.00	$50.00 – 60.00	
Ivory	$25.00 – 30.00	$35.00 – 45.00	$65.00 – 70.00
Marine	$40.00 – 45.00	$50.00 – 60.00	
Maroon	$45.00 – 50.00	$50.00 – 60.00	
Orchid	$250.00 – 300.00		$250.00 – 275.00
Pink	$35.00 – 40.00	$40.00 – 45.00	$60.00 – 70.00
Rose	$35.00 – 40.00	$50.00 – 55.00	
Stock Brown/Green	$25.00 – 30.00	$25.00 – 35.00	
Turquoise	$45.00 – 50.00	$45.00 – 50.00	
Warm Yellow	$45.00 – 50.00	$45.00 – 55.00	$75.00 – 85.00

6-cup Cobalt Gold "Special"

Chinese Red

6-cup Ivory with Standard Gold

4-cup Canary with Standard Gold

8-cup Dresden with Standard Gold

4-cup Blue Turquoise with Standard Gold

Stock Green Miniature with Standard Gold

2-cup Maroon with Standard Gold

Dresden Sugar and Lid

Dresden Creamer

Novelty Teapots — Automobile

Hall's Novelty Teapot Group consists of six uniquely shaped teapots introduced in 1938 and produced until the end of 1941 when production priorities shifted to the war effort. The shapes associated with this group include the automobile, basket, basketball, birdcage, donut, and football.

The automobile is a six-cup novelty teapot which was introduced in 1938. The unique styling of this teapot continuously amazes spectators at glass and pottery shows today. Even unenlightened browsers are impressed by the lines of this unusual teapot, and that is even before they find out the price. The automobile may be found in a number of solid colors. Red, cobalt, maroon, canary, and turquoise appear to be most common. Also, it may be found in many of these same colors with either gold or platinum trim. The decorated teapots usually have an encrusted spout, solid decoration on the raised areas of the lid, and highlighted wheels, fenders, and door hinges and handles. However, some teapots will be found with a decoration which consists of merely a few simple gold or platinum lines. Collectors need to be aware this teapot was reissued in 1993, as a limited edition collectible. Also, China Specialties has utilized this design in a number of their decal lines. For more detailed information see the Reissues section in the back of this book.

Automobile Teapots	Solid Color	Standard Decoration	Special Decoration
Black	$330.00 – 370.00	$350.00 – 400.00	
Cadet	$400.00 – 450.00	$500.00 – 550.00	
Canary	$375.00 – 425.00	$450.00 – 500.00	
Chinese Red	$600.00 – 650.00		
Cobalt	$550.00 – 600.00	$600.00 – 650.00	
Delphinium	$400.00 – 450.00	$500.00 – 550.00	
Dresden	$400.00 – 450.00	$500.00 – 550.00	
Emerald	$475.00 – 525.00	$550.00 – 575.00	
Indian Red	$650.00 – 750.00		
Ivory	$250.00 – 300.00	$300.00 – 350.00	
Marine	$475.00 – 525.00	$550.00 – 575.00	
Maroon	$475.00 – 525.00	$540.00 – 580.00	
Orchid	$800.00 – 900.00		
Turquoise	$500.00 – 550.00	$540.00 – 585.00	
Warm Yellow	$400.00 – 450.00	$450.00 – 500.00	$500.00 – 550.00
Art Glaze Blue	$450.00 – 500.00		

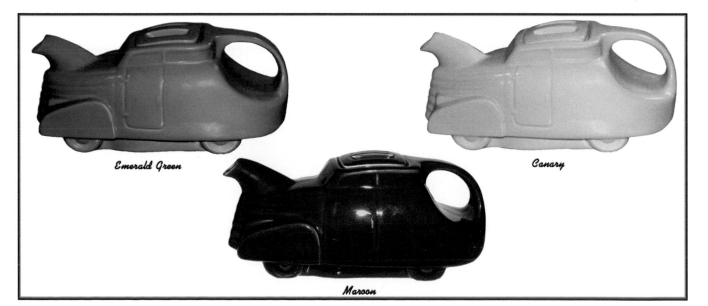

Emerald Green

Canary

Maroon

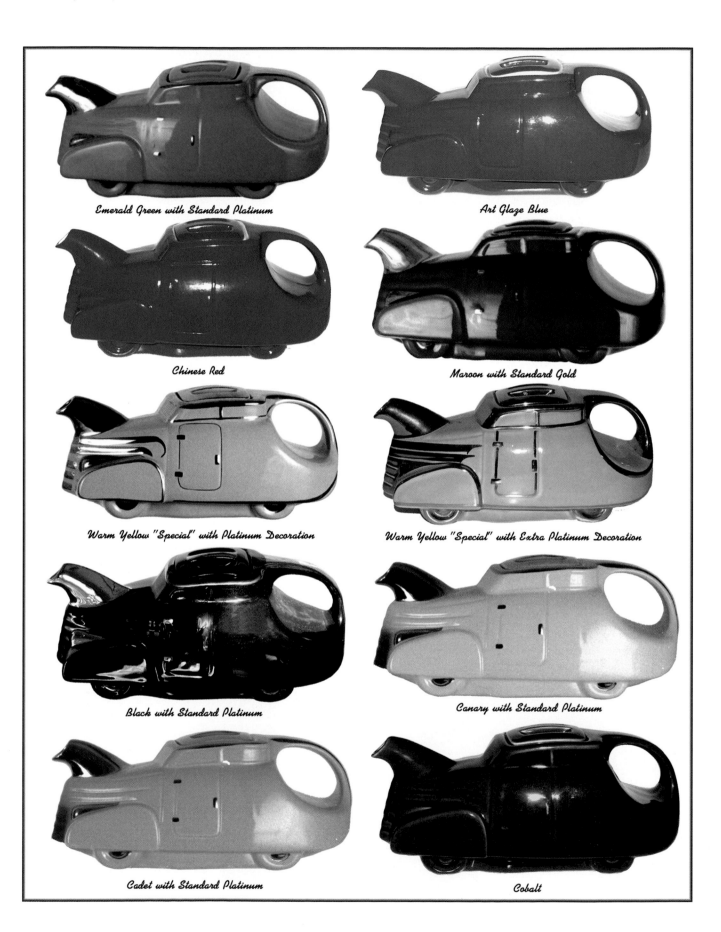

Emerald Green with Standard Platinum

Art Glaze Blue

Chinese Red

Maroon with Standard Gold

Warm Yellow "Special" with Platinum Decoration

Warm Yellow "Special" with Extra Platinum Decoration

Black with Standard Platinum

Canary with Standard Platinum

Cadet with Standard Platinum

Cobalt

Novelty Teapots — Basket

The basket is a six-cup teapot which was first made in 1938. It is the easiest to find of all the novelty teapots. Baskets are usually found in canary and will be commonly decorated with a few platinum lines. The most easily found undecorated colors are Chinese red and canary. The basket will also be found in other colors, but these are rather unusual.

Basket Teapot	Solid Color	Standard Decoration	Basket Teapot	Solid Color	Standard Decoration
Black	$120.00 – 150.00		Indian Red	$250.00 – 275.00	
Cadet	$120.00 – 140.00	$140.00 – 160.00	Ivory	$95.00 – 125.00	
Canary	$110.00 – 125.00	$120.00 – 140.00	Marine	$200.00 – 225.00	
Chinese Red	$250.00 – 275.00		Maroon	$140.00 – 180.00	$185.00 – 210.00
Citrus	$250.00 – 300.00		Turquoise	$140.00 – 180.00	$175.00 – 200.00
Cobalt	$225.00 – 245.00		Warm Yellow	$150.00 – 175.00	$160.00 – 190.00
Emerald	$130.00 – 160.00	$160.00 – 195.00			

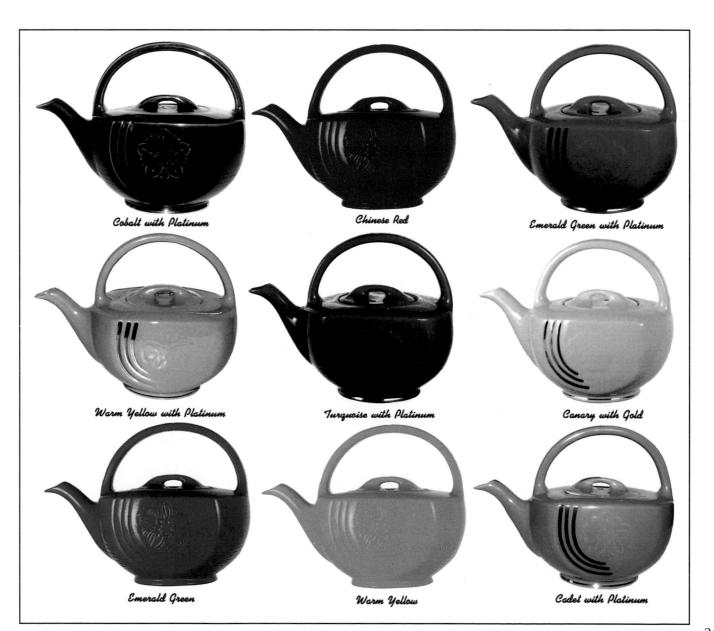

Cobalt with Platinum Chinese Red Emerald Green with Platinum

Warm Yellow with Platinum Turquoise with Platinum Canary with Gold

Emerald Green Warm Yellow Cadet with Platinum

Novelty Teapots — Basketball

The basketball has consistently proven to be the hardest to find of the novelty teapots. It is a six-cup teapot which first made its appearance in 1938. However, it has not surpassed the football or automobile in desirability or price. The most commonly found colors are undecorated Chinese red and decorated turquoise. The gold decorated turquoise basketball in the top row of the picture is what collectors call a "special" since it has a gold encrusted handle and spout in addition to the standard decoration.

Basketball Teapot	Solid Color	Standard Decoration	Special Decoration
Cadet	$400.00 – 450.00	$500.00 – 550.00	$525.00 – 575.00
Canary	$400.00 – 450.00	$470.00 – 525.00	$525.00 – 575.00
Chinese Red	$600.00 – 650.00		
Cobalt	$575.00 – 625.00	$600.00 – 650.00	
Emerald	$575.00 – 625.00	$600.00 – 650.00	
Indian Red	$700.00 – 750.00		
Ivory	$200.00 – 250.00	$400.00 – 450.00	
Marine	$575.00 – 625.00	$600.00 – 650.00	
Maroon	$450.00 – 500.00	$525.00 – 575.00	
Turquoise	$450.00 – 500.00	$525.00 – 575.00	$575.00 – 625.00
Warm Yellow	$450.00 – 500.00	$520.00 – 570.00	$525.00 – 575.00

Turquoise with Gold "Special"   Cobalt   Warm Yellow with Standard Gold

Warm Yellow   Chinese Red   Turquoise

Novelty Teapots — Birdcage

The birdcage is a hard-to-find novelty teapot which was introduced in 1938. It will be found in solid colors and with gold decoration. Gold decoration consists of highlighting lines on the cage and gold decoration on the embossed birds. Examples of gold special birdcages are the cadet teapot in the center of the top row and the canary teapot shown in the second row of the photo. The most commonly found undecorated colors are Chinese red and maroon. Decorated birdcages are turning up most often in maroon and cadet blue.

Birdcage Teapot	Solid Color	Standard Decoration	Special Decoration
Cadet	$350.00 – 400.00	$400.00 – 450.00	$450.00 –500.00
Canary	$325.00 – 375.00	$375.00 – 425.00	$425.00 – 475.00
Chinese Red	$550.00 – 600.00		
Cobalt	$600.00 – 650.00	$620.00 – 670.00	$650.00 – 700.00
Emerald	$600.00 – 650.00	$620.00 – 670.00	
Indian Red	$750.00 – 850.00		
Ivory	$225.00 – 250.00	$275.00 – 325.00	
Marine	$450.00 – 500.00	$500.00 – 550.00	
Maroon	$300.00 – 350.00	$350.00 – 400.00	$450.00 –500.00
Turquoise	$500.00 – 550.00	$525.00 – 575.00	
Warm Yellow	$450.00 – 500.00		

Maroon with Standard Gold

Cadet with Gold "Special"

Turquoise

Chinese Red

Cobalt

Canary with Gold " Special"

Maroon

Turquoise with Standard Gold

Chinese Red with Standard Gold

Cadet

Novelty Teapots — Donut

The donut, which first appeared in 1938, is one of the easiest to find of all the novelty teapots. However, phenomenal collector demand has kept the price high and the supply low. Gold decoration consists of a few simple lines accenting the handle, spout, and lid. The donut is found in a variety of solid colors and is the only novelty teapot which has been found in the dinnerware decal patterns. It is found most often with the Orange Poppy decal and is also know to exist in the Crocus pattern.

New teapots were produced during the 1980s in several colors for Naomi's Antiques of San Francisco. Hall has also made Donut teapots in Autumn Leaf for the NALCC. Check the backstamp before buying.

Donut Teapot	Solid Color	Standard Decoration	Donut Teapot	Solid Color	Standard Decoration
Black	$120.00 – 150.00	$150.00 – 175.00	Indian Red	$450.00 – 500.00	
Cadet	$300.00 – 350.00	$350.00 – 400.00	Ivory	$120.00 – 150.00	$150.00 – 175.00
Canary	$300.00 – 350.00	$350.00 – 400.00	Marine	$350.00 – 400.00	$400.00 – 450.00
Chinese Red	$350.00 – 400.00		Maroon	$350.00 – 400.00	$400.00 – 450.00
Citrus	$500.00 – 600.00		Orchid	$850.00 – 950.00	
Cobalt	$350.00 – 400.00	$400.00 – 450.00	Turquoise	$320.00 – 380.00	$370.00 – 420.00
Delphinium	$300.00 – 350.00	$350.00 – 400.00	Warm Yellow	$420.00 – 450.00	
Emerald	$350.00 – 400.00	$400.00 – 450.00			

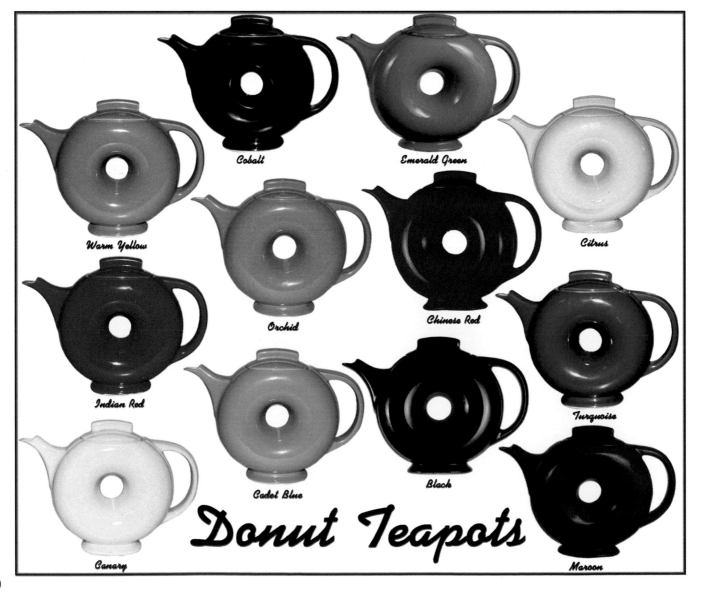

Cobalt · Emerald Green · Warm Yellow · Orchid · Chinese Red · Citrus · Indian Red · Turquoise · Cadet Blue · Black · Canary · Maroon

Donut Teapots

Novelty Teapots — Football

The football seems to be appearing more frequently lately than it has in the past. Maybe its high price is forcing some out of attics. However, collector enthusiasm for these teapots is keeping the price high and the supply of mint condition teapots is being quickly absorbed into collections. The football has been found in numerous solid colors. Of these red, cobalt, maroon, and turquoise are probably the most common. Gold decoration normally consists of a few simple lines on the handle, lid, and side of the teapot. However, a variation dubbed a "special" will be found having a gold encrusted handle and spout in addition to the standard gold lines. Beginning in 1993, Hall re introduced the football teapot as part of a limited edition series for a private company. The new teapot has been produced in several colors and with a few new decals. See the Reissues section of this book for details.

Football Teapot	Solid Color	Standard Decoration	Football Teapot	Solid Color	Standard Decoration
Black	$400.00 – 500.00	$500.00 – 550.00	Emerald	$650.00 – 700.00	$700.00 – 750.00
Cadet	$500.00 – 600.00	$500.00 – 600.00	Indian Red	$750.00 – 800.00	
Canary	$500.00 – 600.00	$500.00 – 600.00	Ivory	$400.00 – 450.00	$400.00 – 450.00
Chinese Red	$700.00 – 750.00		Marine	$650.00 – 700.00	$700.00 – 750.00
Citrus	$750.00 – 850.00		Maroon	$500.00 – 600.00	$500.00 – 600.00
Cobalt	$650.00 – 700.00	$700.00 – 750.00	Turquoise	$500.00 – 600.00	$500.00 – 600.00
Delphinium	$500.00 – 600.00	$500.00 – 600.00	Warm Yellow	$650.00 – 700.00	$700.00 – 750.00
Dresden	$500.00 – 600.00	$500.00 – 600.00			

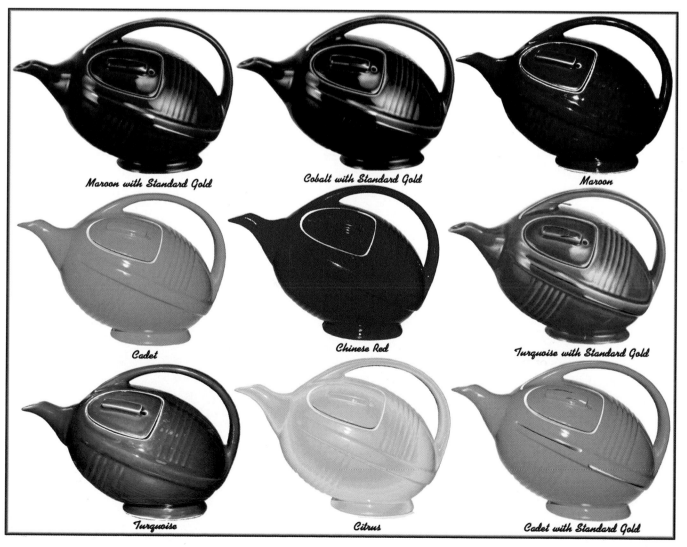

Maroon with Standard Gold   Cobalt with Standard Gold   Maroon

Cadet   Chinese Red   Turquoise with Standard Gold

Turquoise   Citrus   Cadet with Standard Gold

No. 2 Coffee Set

No. 1 Tea Set

The No. 1 Tea Set and No. 2 Coffee Set were both introduced in the early 1950s. Both the Coffee Set and Tea Set came in two colors and with three different floral decorations. The yellow color is called Buttercup and the light blue color is Blue Belle. The three decorations are 80-B, a blue flower; 80-Y, a yellow flower; and 80-P, a pink flower. Both sets are trimmed with gold lines.

The Tea Set uses the morning set teapot and creamer shapes. However, the similarity between the two sets ends there. The shape of the sugar is different and a cup and party plate have been added. The morning set sugar has handles and a lid. The No. 1 Tea Set sugar is open and has no handles. Also the morning set does not have cups and saucers. The party plates have an off-center ring upon which the teacup fits. The party plates to the Tea Set are round while the plates to the Coffee Set are scalloped.

The No. 2 Coffee Set has an open sugar with a ruffled top and a tall creamer with a handle and general shape that matches the coffee pot. This coffee pot shape is also used in the Golden Glo line, and a larger version which bears the Drip-O-lator backstamp may be found decorated with a floral decal.

The Blue Belle Coffee Set and the Buttercup Tea Set have been found advertised in a 1952 Jewel Tea Company catalog.

Item	Coffee Set	Tea Set
Coffee pot	$85.00 – 110.00	
Creamer	$16.00 – 18.00	$16.00 –18.00
Cup	$10.00 –12.00	$10.00 – 12.00
Plate	$7.00 – 9.00	$7.00 – 9.00
Sugar	$16.00 – 18.00	$16.00 – 18.00
Teapot	$95.00 – 125.00	

Ohio Teapots

Cobalt with Standard Gold   Maroon with Standard Gold   Stock Brown with Standard Gold

Daffodil with Gold Dot Design   Pink with Gold Dot Design   Ivory with Gold Dot Design

The Ohio teapot has been found in solid colors and with two different styles of gold decorations. These gold decorations are illustrated in the photo above. None of these teapots is easily found. The standard gold decoration is found most often on early colors such as stock brown, stock green, and cobalt. The Gold Dot decoration is usually found on canary, pink, or maroon teapots.

Ohio Teapot	Solid Color	Standard Gold	Gold Dot
Black	$150.00 – 170.00	$200.00 – 225.00	
Canary	$200.00 – 225.00		$250.00 – 300.00
Chinese Red	$500.00 – 600.00		
Cobalt	$300.00 – 320.00	$350.00 – 400.00	
Maroon	$200.00 – 225.00	$250.00 – 300.00	$250.00 – 300.00
Pink	$180.00 – 200.00		$250.00 – 300.00
Stock Brown	$120.00 – 140.00	$170.00 – 190.00	
Stock Green	$120.00 – 140.00	$170.00 – 190.00	

Parade Teapots

The Parade is a six-cup teapot which is usually found in canary. The standard gold decoration is illustrated in the photograph in emerald canary and cobalt. Finding colors such as red, maroon, or cobalt is a challenge, but not an impossible task. The Parade teapot is also part of the Gold Label line. The most commonly found color of the Gold Label teapot is also canary and the gold design is called Squiggle. Unusual gold decorations for this shape include French Flower and mini-Fleurette which are also illustrated in the picture.

Parade Teapot	Solid Color	Standard Gold	Gold Label
Black	$30.00 – 35.00	$37.00 – 42.00	
Cadet	$50.00 – 55.00	$57.00 – 62.00	
Canary	$30.00 – 35.00	$37.00 – 42.00	$40.00 – 45.00
Chinese Red	$300.00 – 350.00		
Cobalt	$70.00 – 85.00	$65.00 – 75.00	
Delphinium	$50.00 – 55.00	$57.00 – 62.00	
Emerald	$70.00 – 85.00	$65.00 – 75.00	
Ivory	$25.00 – 30.00	$37.00 – 42.00	$40.00 – 45.00
Marine	$70.00 – 85.00	$65.00 – 75.00	
Maroon	$60.00 – 70.00	$65.00 – 75.00	
Mustard	$50.00 – 55.00		
Turquoise	$60.00 – 70.00	$65.00 – 75.00	
Warm Yellow	$60.00 – 70.00		
Special Decoration			
French Flower	$180.00 – 200.00	Golden Glo	$170.00 – 190.00
Mini Fleurette	$250.00 – 300.00	Silver Luster	$170.00 – 190.00

Emerald with Standard Gold　　*Cadet Blue with Standard Gold*　　*Canary with Standard Gold*

Chinese Red

Ivory Gold Label

Canary Gold Label

Canary with French Flower Decoration

Silver Luster

Delphinium

Maroon with Standard Gold

Cobalt with Standard Gold

Warm Yellow

Cobalt

Golden Glo

Cobalt with Mini Fleurette Decoration

NATIONALLY *Hall* ADVERTISED

SUPERIOR QUALITY
DECORATED TEAPOTS
AND COOKING CHINA

Aladdin Infuser Teapot

Star Teapot

Hook Cover Teapot

Sani-Grid Teapot

Parade Teapot

Airflow Teapot

Windshield Teapot

Moderne Teapot

Mrs. America's Favorite Teapots Combine Beauty and Utility . . .

★

BEAUTIFUL SHAPES . . . from traditional, perennially popular styles to most modern functional designs that match newest home furnishings ideas.

LOVELY COLORS . . . a rainbow variety of underglaze shades, all of which permanently retain their full brilliance.

GLEAMING DECORATIONS . . . genuine Hall gold decorations make these famous teapots favorites of all lovers of distinguished chinaware.

SECRET PROCESS . . . the only china made by our single-firing process which inseparably fuses body, color, and glaze, producing a ware that is crazeproof, stainproof, and absorption-proof.

THE HALL CHINA COMPANY
EAST LIVERPOOL · OHIO
*World's Largest Manufacturer of
Decorated Teapots and Cooking China*

FOR VICTORY
BUY
UNITED STATES
WAR
BONDS
AND
STAMPS

Philadelphia Teapots

The Philadelphia teapot was produced in the 1½, 3, 4, 5, 6, 7, and 10-cup sizes. The Philadelphia shape was one of the first to be added to the Gold Decorated line in the early 1920s. Due to this early introduction, and as a result of its success, this shape was treated to a number of different gold and decal decorations.

One of the earlier gold designs is illustrated by the teapots at the bottom of the photo on page 279. These teapots have an allover "Gold Loop" design and the handle, spout, and lid opening are trimmed with gold. This design teapot along with a matching sugar and creamer was advertised in a 1928 Sears catalog. Other early gold designs are shown on the remainder of the teapots in the same picture. The decoration on the maroon teapot at the top right is being called "Nouveau." The cobalt and Old Rose teapots in the second row are examples of the "Bubble" design.

The teapots on the bottom row of the picture on page 281 are from the Gold Label line of the mid-1950s. The basket design is commonly found on a pink body and less often in the other colors. Matching kitchenware accessories will also be found with this decoration. For more information see the Gold Label pattern in the kitchenware section.

The pink teapot at the bottom left of the photo on page 280 illustrates the Minuet decal. This decal is also found on the Baltimore teapot and a Drip-O-lator coffee pot. Other decals will also be found on Philadelphia teapots. In the 1930s, a large colorful floral decal was used. Decal decoration in the 1960s featured a black hearth scene, usually on a teapot with a blue body. A teapot with this decal is illustrated in the picture on page 280.

The teapots on the top two rows of the picture on page 281 are examples of the standard gold decoration for the Philadelphia shape. The teapots below illustrate the mother-of-pearl glaze. Notice many of these teapots were sold with a matching sugar and creamer. The sugar and creamer was not always the Philadelphia style. The beauty of these sets is further enhanced through extensive gold decoration.

Two different styles of gold band decoration are shown in the picture on page 282. The two end teapots have a wider gold band than the teapot in the center.

Pearlized Philadelphia Tea Sets

6-cup Teapot   *6-cup Teapot*   *6-cup Teapot*

"Norse" Covered Sugar and Creamer   *Philadelphia Covered Sugar & Creamer*

Philadelphia Teapots

1 – 4-cup

Philadelphia Teapot	Solid Color	Standard Gold	Gold Label	Gold Loop Design
Black	$20.00 – 25.00	$27.00 – 32.00		$37.00 – 42.00
Blue Turquoise	$37.00 – 42.00	$45.00 – 50.00	$47.00 – 57.00	
Cadet	$30.00 – 35.00	$37.00 – 42.00		
Canary	$27.00 – 35.00	$35.00 – 40.00		
Chinese Red	$135.00 – 150.00			
Cobalt	$52.00 – 57.00	$60.00 – 65.00		$60.00 – 65.00
Delphinium	$32.00 – 37.00	$40.00 – 45.00		
Dresden	$32.00 – 37.00	$40.00 – 45.00		
Emerald	$32.00 – 37.00	$40.00 – 45.00		
Gray	$27.00 – 35.00	$35.00 – 40.00		
Indian Red	$165.00 – 190.00			
Ivory	$20.00 – 25.00	$27.00 – 32.00	$37.00 – 42.00	
Marine	$52.00 – 57.00	$60.00 – 65.00		
Maroon	$32.00 – 37.00	$40.00 – 45.00		
Old Rose	$32.00 – 37.00	$40.00 – 45.00		
Pink	$27.00 – 35.00	$35.00 – 40.00	$37.00 – 42.00	
Stock Brown	$20.00 – 25.00	$27.00 – 32.00		$37.00 – 42.00
Stock Green	$20.00 – 25.00	$27.00 – 32.00		$37.00 – 42.00
Turquoise	$32.00 – 37.00	$40.00 – 45.00		
Warm Yellow	$27.00 – 35.00	$35.00 – 40.00		

Special Decoration

Gold Band	$40.00 – 50.00
Nouveau	$90.00 – 110.00
Pearlized Ivory	$145.00 – 165.00
Tiny "Bubble"	$75.00 – 85.00
Trailing Aster	$120.00 – 140.00
Minuet Decal	$130.00 – 150.00
Palm Leaf	$200.00 – 225.00
Silver Luster	$160.00 – 180.00

6-cup Canary
Standard Gold

4-cup Stock Green
Gold "Bubble" Decoration

4-cup Stock Green
Gold Nouveau Decoration

6-cup White
Thornberry Antique Rose Decoration

Black with
Gold "Daisy Sprig" Decoration

10-cup Old Rose
Gold Palm Decoration

5-cup Maroon
Gold Nouveau Decoration

5-cup Old Rose
Gold "Bubble" Decoration

6-cup Cobalt
Gold "Bubble" Decoration

6-cup Stock Green
Gold "Loop" Decoration

6-cup Cobalt
"Gold Loop" Decoration

5-cup Emerald
Gold "Loop" Decoration

6-cup Stock Brown
Gold "Loop" Decoration

5-cup Maroon
Gold "Loop" Decoration

5-cup Marine
Gold "Loop" Decoration

Covered Sugar & Creamer, Pearlized with Gold "Loop" Decoration

5 – 7-cup

Philadelphia Teapot	Solid Color	Standard Gold	Gold Label	Gold Loop Design
Black	$25.00 – 30.00	$30.00 – 35.00		$40.00 – 45.00
Blue Turquoise	$40.00 – 45.00	$45.00 – 50.00	$55.00 – 60.00	
Cadet	$35.00 – 40.00	$40.00 – 52.00		
Canary	$32.00 – 37.00	$37.00 – 45.00		
Chinese Red	$155.00 – 180.00			
Cobalt	$62.00 – 77.00	$70.00 – 80.00		$80.00 – 95.00
Delphinium	$35.00 – 40.00	$40.00 – 52.00		
Dresden	$35.00 – 40.00	$40.00 – 52.00		
Emerald	$40.00 – 47.00	$50.00 – 55.00		
Gray	$35.00 – 40.00	$37.00 – 42.00		
Indian Red	$195.00 – 220.00			
Ivory	$25.00 – 30.00	$32.00 – 37.00	$42.00 – 50.00	
Marine	$52.00 – 57.00	$60.00 – 65.00		
Maroon	$42.00 – 47.00	$50.00 – 55.00		
Old Rose	$42.00 – 47.00	$50.00 – 55.00		
Pink	$30.00 – 35.00	$37.00 – 45.00	$47.00 – 52.00	
Stock Brown	$25.00 – 30.00	$27.00 – 32.00		$42.00 – 47.00
Stock Green	$20.00 – 25.00	$27.00 – 32.00		$42.00 – 47.00
Turquoise	$32.00 – 37.00	$40.00 – 45.00	$47.00 – 52.00	
Warm Yellow	$32.00 – 37.00	$35.00 – 40.00		

Special Decoration

Blue Willow	$400.00 – 450.00	Burbick decoration	$250.00 – 300.00
Gold Band	$40.00 – 50.00	Mayflower decal	$120.00 – 140.00
Minuet Decal	$140.00 – 160.00	Nouveau	$90.00 – 110.00
Palm Leaf	$220.00 – 250.00	Pearlized Ivory	$150.00 – 170.00
Silver Luster	$160.00 – 180.00	"Bubble"	$75.00 – 90.00
Trailing Aster	$120.00 – 140.00		

4-cup Pink
Minuet Decal Decoration

6-cup Blue
Hearth Scene Decoration

4-cup Cobalt
Burbick Decoration

6-cup Turquoise
Standard Gold

8-cup Ivory
Standard Gold

6-cup Maroon
Standard Gold

5-cup Camellia
Standard Gold

6-cup Cobalt
Standard Gold

5-cup Chinese Red

6-cup Art Glaze Blue

6-cup Chinese Red

6-cup Silver Lustre

6-cup Pink
Gold Label Basket Decoration

6-cup Turquoise
Gold Label Basket Decoration

6-cup Blue Turquoise
Gold Label Basket Decoration

Philadelphia Teapots

10-cup

Philadelphia Teapot	Solid Color	Standard Gold	Gold Label	Gold Loop Design
Black	$32.00 – 35.00	$35.00 – 40.00		$45.00 – 50.00
Blue Turquoise	$40.00 – 45.00	$50.00 – 55.00	$65.00 – 70.00	
Cadet	$40.00 – 45.00	$45.00 – 52.00		
Canary	$32.00 – 37.00	$37.00 – 45.00		
Chinese Red	$175.00 – 220.00			
Cobalt	$67.00 – 77.00	$70.00 – 80.00		$85.00 – 100.00
Delphinium	$40.00 – 45.00	$45.00 – 52.00		
Dresden	$40.00 – 45.00	$45.00 – 52.00		
Emerald	$45.00 – 50.00	$52.00 – 57.00		
Gray	$37.00 – 40.00	$40.00 – 45.00		
Indian Red	$215.00 – 230.00			
Ivory	$27.00 – 32.00	$35.00 – 40.00	$42.00 – 50.00	
Marine	$52.00 – 57.00	$60.00 – 65.00		
Maroon	$45.00 – 50.00	$52.00 – 57.00		
Old Rose	$45.00 – 50.00	$52.00 – 57.00		
Pink	$35.00 – 40.00	$37.00 – 45.00	$50.00 – 55.00	
Stock Brown	$27.00 – 32.00	$30.00 – 35.00		$42.00 – 47.00
Stock Green	$27.00 – 32.00	$30.00 – 35.00		$42.00 – 47.00
Turquoise	$35.00 – 40.00	$40.00 – 45.00	$50.00 – 55.00	
Warm Yellow	$32.00 – 37.00	$40.00 – 45.00		

Special Decoration

Gold Band	$40.00 – 60.00	Minuet Decal	$150.00 – 170.00
Nouveau	$125.00 – 150.00	Palm Leaf	$275.00 – 300.00
Pearlized Ivory	$160.00 – 190.00	Silver Luster	$170.00 – 190.00
"Bubble"	$100.00 – 120.00	Trailing Aster	$145.00 – 160.00

6-cup Canary
Wide Gold Band

6-cup Rose
Medium Gold Band

6-cup Ivory
Wide Gold Band

Rhythm Teapots

The Rhythm is a six-cup teapot which was introduced in 1939. Due to the design of the teapot, it is very difficult to find this shape of teapot with a good lid. The standard gold decoration is pictured below. The easiest color to find is canary in both solid color and gold decorated. Other colors which are usually found include Chinese Red, cobalt, emerald, and turquoise. Finding other colors is not easy.

Rhythm Teapot	Solid Color	Standard Gold
Black	$90.00 – 110.00	$100.00 – 125.00
Cadet	$120.00 – 140.00	$150.00 – 190.00
Canary	$100.00 – 120.00	$140.00 – 160.00
Chinese Red	$220.00 – 250.00	
Cobalt	$160.00 – 180.00	$160.00 – 180.00
Emerald	$100.00 – 120.00	$150.00 – 190.00
Ivory	$60.00 – 80.00	$100.00 – 125.00
Maroon	$120.00 – 140.00	$150.00 – 190.00
Turquoise	$120.00 – 140.00	$150.00 – 190.00
Warm Yellow	$125.00 – 150.00	

Canary

Chinese Red

Maroon with Standard Gold

Emerald with Standard Gold

"Rutherford" Teapots

Chinese Red   Green Band with Silver Trim   Chinese Red "Ribbed"

Red Band with Black Trim   Matte White with Blue Dots   Matte White with Red Dots

The "Rutherford" teapot is the same shape as the "Ribbed" teapot from the basic kitchenware shapes. The smooth version is shown here in Chinese Red and in white with various decorations. It will also be found with decals in some of the dinnerware lines. The matte white teapots with colored dots are from the Eggshell Buffet Service. Another teapot from that line may be found decorated with the "Swag" design. An example is shown on page 146.

"Rutherford" Teapot	Value
Chinese Red	$325.00 – 350.00
Ivory with green and silver trim	$300.00 – 325.00
Matte white with red and black trim	$300.00 – 325.00
Matte white with blue dots	$285.00 – 300.00
Matte white with red dots	$220.00 – 250.00

Sani-Grid Teapots

Sani-Grid teapots are a part of the kitchenware line. This shape teapot is more commonly associated with some of the decal lines, but gold decorated teapots in this shape also exist. They are usually found in cadet or yellow with gold decoration on the handle, spout, and around the lid opening. Undecorated teapots are found most often with a Chinese red body and a Hi-white handle. An example of this color teapot may be found in the Kitchenware section on page 141. A Golden Glo Sani-Grid teapot with a matching sugar and creamer is pictured on the bottom row of the photo below. The pearlized ivory teapot with gold decoration is an unusual finish for this shape. A few hand painted Sani-Grid teapots have also been found. See page 159 for examples.

Sani-Grid Teapots	Solid Color	Standard Decoration
Cadet	$18.00 – 20.00	$65.00 – 75.00
Canary	$32.00 – 37.00	$75.00 – 85.00
Chinese Red	$47.00 – 52.00	
Golden Glo	$125.00 – 140.00	
Pearlized Ivory		$125.00 – 135.00
Golden Glo sugar/creamer	$32.00 – 40.00	

Pearlized Ivory with Gold Trim   Cadet with Platinum Decoration   Canary with Gold Decoration

Golden Glo Tea Set

Star Teapots

The Star teapot has been named for its style of standard gold decoration. This teapot was introduced in 1939, and is only available in the six-cup size. Turquoise and cobalt are the only common colors. Other decorated colors will be found with diligent searching. Also, undecorated versions of this teapot were made. Again, the most abundant undecorated colors are turquoise and cobalt.

The 1939 and 1940 New York World's Fair backstamp "A GENUINE HALL TEAPOT — MADE IN U.S.A. — SOLD EXCLUSIVELY AT THE NEW YORK WORLD'S FAIR — 1940" will appear on the bottom of some cobalt Star teapots. Either date may be found and the World's Fair trylon and perisphere will be found on the side of these cobalt teapots. The 1939 date is the hardest to find, but both of these teapots are unusual.

Other Star teapots with special decorations include several styles of Sterling silver overlay. These overlays have been found on several different color teapots. Another interesting gold decoration is the "Sprig" design pictured in the photo below. This decoration is unusual on this shape of teapot.

Star Teapot	Solid Color	Standard Gold	Gold Special	Silver Overlay
Cadet	$90.00 – 105.00	$110.00 – 125.00		
Canary	$100.00 – 115.00	$120.00 – 135.00	$140.00 – 170.00	
Chinese Red	$450.00 – 550.00			
Cobalt	$140.00 – 160.00	$90.00 – 115.00		$500.00 – 600.00
Delphinium	$90.00 – 105.00	$110.00 – 125.00		
Emerald	$90.00 – 105.00	$110.00 – 125.00		
Indian Red	$450.00 – 550.00			
Ivory	$80.00 – 90.00	$90.00 – 100.00		$400.00 – 500.00
Marine	$140.00 – 160.00	$150.00 – 175.00		
Maroon	$80.00 – 95.00	$100.00 – 110.00		
Orchid	$550.00 – 650.00			
Pink	$90.00 – 105.00	$110.00 – 125.00		
Turquoise	$60.00 – 75.00	$60.00 – 70.00		
Warm Yellow	$80.00 – 95.00	$100.00 – 110.00		

Special Decorations				
Gold Sprig		$250.00 – 300.00		
World's Fair		$750.00 – 950.00		

Turquoise Star Teapot
with
Unusual Gold "Sprig" Decoration

Cadet with Standard Gold

Chinese Red

Emerald Green with Standard Gold

Canary with Standard Gold

Cobalt with Standard Gold

Turquoise with Standard Gold

Cobalt with Silver Overlay

Ivory with Silver Decoration

Ivory with Silver Decoration

Maroon with Standard Gold

Emerald Green

Cobalt with Gold World's Fair Decoration

Streamline Teapots

The Streamline is a six-cup teapot which first appeared in 1937. It is commonly found in canary, delphinium, and Chinese red. Gold decoration most often consists of a few narrow lines outlining the lid opening, handle, spout, lid, and knob. However, a "special" gold decoration exists which features a gold encrusted handle, spout, and knob. This may be seen on the warm yellow teapot in the photo. A platinum decoration has also been found on some canary teapots. The platinum bands are much wider and more gaudy than the standard gold lines. The Streamline shape is also used in a number of the decal lines. Some examples of these elusive teapots with decals are shown in the Crocus, Fantasy, Meadow Flowers, and Wildfire patterns.

Streamline Teapot	Solid Color	Standard Gold	Gold Special	Platinum Decoration
Black	$40.00 – 50.00	$45.00 – 55.00		
Cadet	$60.00 – 65.00	$75.00 – 85.00		
Canary	$60.00 – 65.00			$95.00 – 115.00
Chinese Red	$115.00 – 135.00			
Cobalt	$110.00 – 125.00	$115.00 – 135.00		
Delphinium	$60.00 – 65.00	$75.00 – 85.00		
Dresden	$60.00 – 65.00	$75.00 – 85.00		
Emerald	$65.00 –70.00	$75.00 – 85.00		
Indian Red	$225.00 – 250.00			
Ivory	$40.00 – 45.00	$55.00 – 65.00		
Marine	$110.00 – 125.00	$115.00 – 135.00		
Maroon	$80.00 – 95.00	$115.00 – 125.00		
Orchid	$300.00 – 400.00			
Pink	$65.00 –70.00			
Turquoise	$60.00 – 75.00	$75.00 – 85.00		
Warm Yellow	$70.00 – 80.00	$85.00 – 95.00	$115.00 – 135.00	

Special Color				
Art Glaze Blue	$125.00 – 150.00			
No Blue	$120.00 – 140.00			

Warm Yellow with Special Gold Decoration

Chinese Red

Emerald Green

Black

Orchid

Art Glaze Blue

Maroon with Standard Gold

Delphinium with Standard Gold

Turquoise with Standard Gold

Canary with Heavy Platinum Trim

No Blue

Citrus

"Sundial" Teapots

The "Sundial" teapot is most often seen in canary. The standard gold decoration is shown on the decorated teapots in the picture. If a gold special decoration exists for this shape teapot, we have not seen one. The "Sundial" shape teapot is a basic part of one of Hall's major kitchenware shapes and will also be found with several decal decorations. The "Sundial" teapot was also made in the 8 ounce and 10 ounce individual sizes. These sizes are still being made in stock green and stock brown.

Sundial Teapots	Solid Color	Standard Gold
Black	$50.00 – 60.00	$60.00 – 70.00
Cadet	$65.00 – 75.00	$85.00 – 95.00
Canary	$55.00 – 65.00	$60.00 – 70.00
Chinese Red	$160.00 – 180.00	
Citrus	$250.00 – 290.00	
Cobalt	$70.00 – 80.00	$85.00 – 95.00
Dresden	$65.00 – 75.00	$85.00 – 95.00
Emerald	$65.00 – 75.00	$85.00 – 95.00
Indian Red	$250.00 – 270.00	
Ivory	$45.00 – 55.00	$55.00 – 65.00
Marine	$70.00 – 80.00	$90.00 – 110.00
Maroon	$80.00 – 90.00	$100.00 – 125.00
Stock Brown	$45.00 – 55.00	
Stock Green	$45.00 – 55.00	
Turquoise	$80.00 – 90.00	$100.00 – 125.00
Warm Yellow	$80.00 – 90.00	$100.00 – 125.00
Special Color		
Art Glaze Blue	$170.00 – 190.00	

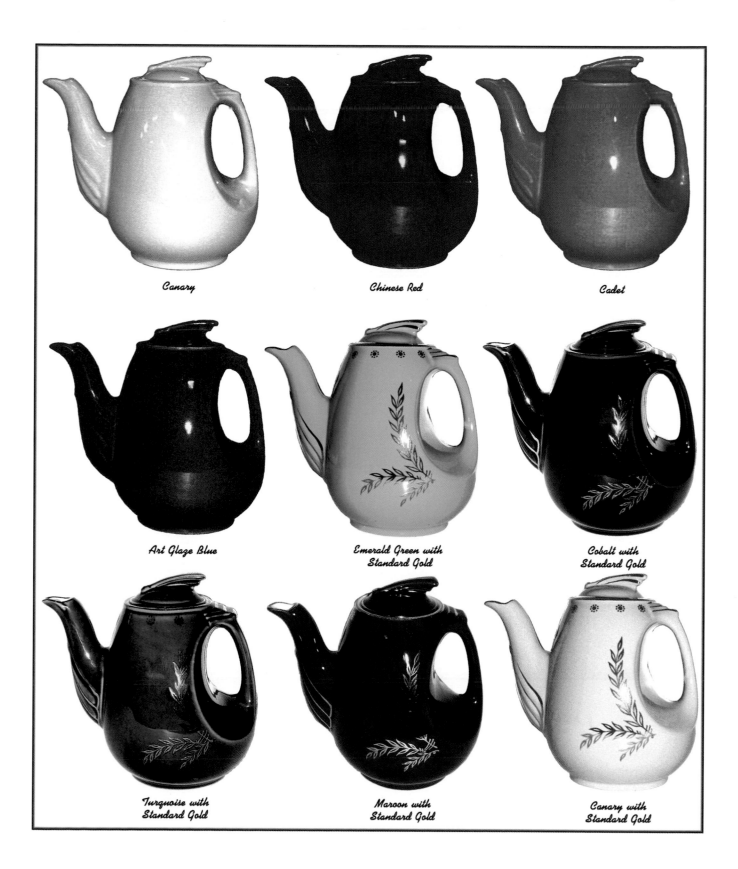

Canary

Chinese Red

Cadet

Art Glaze Blue

Emerald Green with
Standard Gold

Cobalt with
Standard Gold

Turquoise with
Standard Gold

Maroon with
Standard Gold

Canary with
Standard Gold

Surfside Teapots

The Surfside teapot has a six-cup capacity and was introduced in 1937. It is usually found with the standard gold decoration shown on the canary teapot in the picture. However, it may also be found in various solid colors without decoration or with the "special" gold decoration as seen on the emerald green teapot in the photo. "Special" teapots such as this were often sold in sets with an accompanying sugar and creamer. In this case the matching sugar and creamer set is the Boston shape. The most readily found colors are emerald and canary. Unusual colors include black, all blues, red, and orchid. The Surfside has not been found in any of the decal patterns.

Surfside Teapot	Solid Color	Standard Gold	Gold Special
Black	$110.00 – 130.00	$130.00 – 150.00	
Cadet	$140.00 – 160.00	$180.00 – 200.00	
Canary	$130.00 – 150.00	$160.00 – 180.00	$200.00 – 220.00
Chinese Red	$220.00 – 245.00		
Cobalt	$190.00 – 210.00	$200.00 – 225.00	
Delphinium	$140.00 – 160.00	$180.00 – 200.00	
Dresden	$140.00 – 160.00	$180.00 – 200.00	
Emerald	$180.00 – 200.00	$200.00 – 220.00	$220.00 – 240.00
Indian Red	$245.00 – 260.00		
Ivory	$120.00 – 140.00	$135.00 – 155.00	
Maroon	$180.00 – 200.00	$200.00 – 220.00	
Turquoise	$180.00 – 200.00	$200.00 – 220.00	
Warm Yellow	$170.00 – 185.00	$180.00 – 200.00	

Turquoise with
Standard Gold

New York
Sugar & Lid

Chinese Red

Canary with
Standard Gold

New York
Creamer

Emerald Green with
Special Gold

Cobalt with Standard Gold

Warm Yellow with Standard Gold

Tea-for-Two and Tea-for-Four Teapots

Both Tea-for-Two and Tea-for-Four sets are comprised of two pots and a matching tray. One pot is used for hot tea and the other pot is for storage of extra hot water.

These sets differ from the Twin-Tee sets shown on page 299 in several ways. The tops of the Tea-for-Two and Tea-for-Four pots are angled rather than straight and the trays do not have the full-length center division like the Twin-Tee trays.

Sets in both sizes may be found in solid colors, with gold trim and with a variety of decal decorations. Tea-for-Four sets have proven to be much harder to find than their smaller counterpart.

Collectors should be aware new Tea-for-Two sets are available in many solid colors. Check for an old back-stamp to determine the vintage of a set before paying a high price.

Tea-for-Two Set	Solid Color	Illinois Gold Design
Black	$40.00 – 50.00	
Cadet	$80.00 – 100.00	$120.00 – 140.00
Canary	$85.00 – 95.00	
Chinese Red	$220.00 – 250.00	
Cobalt	$110.00 – 130.00	$160.00 – 180.00
Emerald	$80.00 – 100.00	
Ivory	$40.00 – 50.00	$110.00 – 130.00
Marine	$85.00 – 100.00	$130.00 – 150.00
Maroon	$85.00 – 95.00	$140.00 – 160.00
Pink	$60.00 – 65.00	$130.00 – 150.00
Rose	$65.00 – 75.00	$140.00 – 160.00

Decal Decoration		
Floral	$160.00 – 180.00	
Other	$140.00 – 160.00	

Tea-for-Four Set	Solid Color	Illinois Gold Design
Black	$60.00 – 70.00	
Cadet	$100.00 – 120.00	$180.00 – 200.00
Canary	$100.00 – 120.00	
Chinese Red	$350.00 – 390.00	
Cobalt	$140.00 – 160.00	$200.00 – 220.00
Emerald	$140.00 – 160.00	
Ivory	$100.00 – 120.00	$140.00 – 160.00
Marine	$125.00 – 150.00	$150.00 – 170.00
Maroon	$125.00 – 150.00	$150.00 – 170.00
Pink	$100.00 – 125.00	$140.00 – 160.00
Rose	$115.00 – 135.00	$150.00 – 170.00

Decal Decoration		
Daisy and Poppy	$290.00 – 325.00	
Tulip and Carnation	$290.00 – 325.00	

Tea for Two

Pink with Gold
Illinois Decoration

Cadet with Gold
Illinois Decoration

Chinese Red

Tea
for
Four

White and Gold and Tulip and Carnation Decoration

Marine with Gold Illinois Decoration

Old Rose with Gold Illinois Decoration

White with Gold and Daisy and Poppy Decoration

Thorley Teapots

A series of six new teapots which collectors call "Thorley Teapots" was introduced in the early 1950s. These teapots were designed by the noted J. Palin Thorley and were probably intended to replace the Victorian series teapots which had been discontinued due to lackluster sales. These teapots are officially know as the "Brilliant Series Group 120 Teapots."

Although the Thorley teapots are sometimes found plain, they are most often found with gaudy gold decoration. Some have glass rhinestones imbedded in small pockets formed in the body. Collectors are most interested in the teapots with rhinestones. This line, like the earlier Victorian series, was not highly successful, but these teapots still remained in the catalogs as late as 1968. At that time the wholesale cost was $4.95 each.

The "Grape" design teapot was also made with the Classic pattern Bouquet decal. This teapot has also been found with the Game Bird decal. In addition, several pieces of kitchenware were produced in the matching "Grape" pattern. These include a set of three mixing bowls, a round handled casserole, and a cookie jar. These are usually found in yellow, but were also made in ivory.

The "Grape" teapot is the easiest to find. The "Apple" has been the most difficult acquisition for most collectors, but the other four teapots are becoming very hard to find.

Teapot	Apple Green	Black	Cobalt	Ivory	Maroon
"Apple"		$80.00 – 90.00	$120.00 – 130.00	$70.00 – 85.00	
"Grape"			$80.00 – 100.00	$40.00 – 50.00	
"Regal"	$90.00 – 100.00				$100.00 – 110.00
"Royal"				$60.00 – 70.00	
"Starlight"				$40.00 – 50.00	
"Windcrest"				$45.00 – 55.00	

Teapot	Pink	Sky Blue	Yellow	Standard Gold	Gold and Rhinestones
"Apple"		$90.00 – 110.00		Add 20%	Add 30%
"Grape"			$40.00 – 50.00	Add 10%	Add 30%
"Regal"				Add 30%	Add 40%
"Royal"			$70.00 – 80.00	Add 30%	Add 40%
"Starlight"	$45.00 – 55.00		$45.00 – 55.00	Add 30%	Add 40%
"Windcrest"			$45.00 – 55.00	Add 20%	Add 30%

Special Decoration

Grape with Gold Band	$60.00 – 70.00
Grape with Special Gold	$220.00 – 250.00

Kitchenware	Yellow or Ivory
Bowl, 6"	$8.00 – 10.00
Bowl, 7½"	$10.00 – 12.00
Bowl, 8¾"	$12.00 – 14.00
Casserole	$27.00 – 32.00
Cookie jar	$35.00 – 45.00

Cookie Jar   6" Bowl   Casserole

Gold Decorated
Sky Blue "Apple"

Gold Decorated
Black "Apple"

Gold Decorated
Ivory "Apple"

Ivory "Grape" Gold Decorated
with Rhinestones

Cobalt "Grape"
Gold Decorated

Yellow "Grape" with Gold Band

Maroon "Regal"

Apple Green "Regal"
Gold Decorated

Gold Decorated "Royal"

Lemon Yellow "Starlight"

Pink "Starlight"
Gold Decorated

Lemon Yellow "Windcrest" Gold Decorated

Twin-Tee Teapots

The Twin-Tee sets consist of a hot water pot (short spout) and a pot for holding the brewed tea (long spout). There is also a matching divided tray which serves as a trivet for the hot pots. The Twin-Tee sets were introduced in 1926, and may be found in numerous colors. Collectors like these small sets because of the different decals and interesting gold decorations which have been applied to them.

Notice these sets were only made in one size and differ from the Tea-for-Two sets shown on page 295.

Twin-Tee Set	Solid Color*	Illinois Gold Design
Black	$40.00 – 50.00	
Cadet	$80.00 – 100.00	$120.00 – 140.00
Canary	$85.00 – 95.00	
Chinese Red	$260.00 – 290.00	
Cobalt	$110.00 – 130.00	$160.00 – 180.00
Emerald	$80.00 – 100.00	
Ivory	$40.00 – 50.00	$110.00 – 130.00
Marine	$85.00 – 100.00	$130.00 – 150.00
Maroon	$85.00 – 95.00	$140.00 – 160.00
Pink	$60.00 – 65.00	$130.00 – 150.00
Rose	$65.00 – 75.00	
Stock Brown	$40.00 – 50.00	
Stock Green	$40.00 – 50.00	

*Black trim, add 15%.

Other Decorations	
Black Garden	$220.00 – 250.00
Floral Garden	$220.00 – 250.00
Gold Flowers in the Breeze	$160.00 – 180.00
Gold Nouveau	$220.00 – 250.00
Gold Posey	$175.00 – 190.00
Pansy	$180.00 – 200.00

Twin Tee Sets

White with Floral Garden Decoration and Black Trim

Rose with Gold Illinois Decoration

Rose Backstamp

White with Gold Art Nouveau Design

Stock Green with Gold "Posey" Decoration

White with Pansy Decoration

Pansy Backstamp

Stock Brown with Gold "Posey" Decoration

Cobalt

Blue with Black Trim

Pink with Gold Flowers
in the Breeze Decoration

White with Black Garden
Decoration and Black Trim

Green Art Glaze

Very Early Gold Decorated Teapots

The teapots shown on this page are from an early gold decorated line which probably dates to the mid-twenties. These teapots are all very elusive. Many veteran Hall teapot collectors are still lacking examples of these teapots.

The ten-sided cobalt "Columbia" teapot shown in the photo has the #4 backstamp with the numbers 15-80 in place of "MADE IN U.S.A." The "Columbia" has been found in several different colors and with three different gold decorations.

The "Johnson" teapot is an elegantly designed piece with liberal gold decoration. The long spout and gently rounded handle add grace and balance to the finished teapot. We have seen this teapot in stock green and cobalt. Both colors had the same Gold Medallion decoration.

The "Naomi" teapot has six paneled sides. Each panel has a gold decorated emblem and the panels are outlined with a gold border.

A new teapot, the "Bartow," has been discovered in this series. This new teapot is six-sided and has the same Gold Medallion decoration as the "Johnson." We have only seen this teapot in turquoise, but other colors were probably made.

Teapot	Value
"Bartow"	$500.00 – 600.00
"Columbia," cobalt/gold lavaliere	$600.00 – 700.00
"Columbia," Old Rose/gold medallion	$600.00 – 700.00
"Columbia," stock brown/gold floral	$400.00 – 500.00
"Columbia," stock green/gold lavaliere	$400.00 – 500.00
"Johnson	$500.00 – 600.00
"Naomi"	$450.00 – 500.00

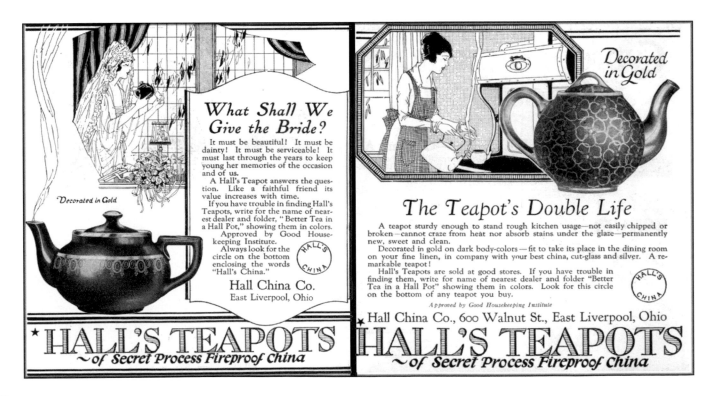

Decorated in Gold

What Shall We Give the Bride?

It must be beautiful! It must be dainty! It must be serviceable! It must last through the years to keep young her memories of the occasion and of us.

A Hall's Teapot answers the question. Like a faithful friend its value increases with time.

If you have trouble in finding Hall's Teapots, write for the name of nearest dealer and folder, "Better Tea in a Hall Pot," showing them in colors.

Approved by Good Housekeeping Institute.

Always look for the circle on the bottom enclosing the words "Hall's China."

Hall China Co.
East Liverpool, Ohio

★ **HALL'S TEAPOTS**
~of Secret Process Fireproof China

Decorated in Gold

The Teapot's Double Life

A teapot sturdy enough to stand rough kitchen usage—not easily chipped or broken—cannot craze from heat nor absorb stains under the glaze—permanently new, sweet and clean.

Decorated in gold on dark body-colors—fit to take its place in the dining room on your fine linen, in company with your best china, cut-glass and silver. A remarkable teapot!

Hall's Teapots are sold at good stores. If you have trouble in finding them, write for name of nearest dealer and folder "Better Tea in a Hall Pot" showing them in colors. Look for this circle on the bottom of any teapot you buy.

Approved by Good Housekeeping Institute

★ Hall China Co., 600 Walnut St., East Liverpool, Ohio

HALL'S TEAPOTS
~of Secret Process Fireproof China

300

Cobalt Naomi with
Gold Illinois Decoration

Old Rose "Columbia" with
Gold Medallion Decoration

Cobalt Columbia with
Gold Lavaliere Decoration

Turquoise "Barlow"
with Gold Medallion Decoration

Stock Green Columbia with
Gold Lavaliere Decoration

Stock Brown Columbia with
Gold Floral Decoration

Stock Green Johnson with
Gold Medallion Decoration

Victorian Style Teapots

Six Victorian style six-cup teapots were introduced in the early 1940s. This was not a dramatically successful line and gold decoration was later added to help stimulate sales. However, success was not attained and the line was dropped by the end of the decade. As a result, although undecorated teapots are available in sufficient quantity, collectors are finding great difficulty in obtaining gold decorated teapots.

An ad to the right from a 1947 catalog illustrates that two of these teapots — the "Plume" and "Birch" — were sold by Jewel for $1.75 each.

For the most part, each teapot is only available in a single color. The "Plume" and "Bowknot" are pink, and the "Birch" is pastel blue. The "Benjamin" and "Connie" are usually found in light green. However, an occasional teapot may be found in an odd color. Some examples are shown in the photo to the right. The "Benjamin" and The "Connie" are occasionally seen in yellow. The "Murphy" has also been seen in a steel gray color.

The amount of gold decoration varies considerably among the different shapes. The "Benjamin," "Birch," and "Connie" feature generous gold decoration. They each have gold encrusted handles, and spouts along with liberal use of gold on the teapot body. The "Bowknot" and "Murphy" display a conservative use of gold. The "Plume" has been found with two styles of gold decoration. Both styles are illustrated in the photograph.

Teapot	Green	Yellow	Gold Decorated
"Benjamin"	$45.00 – 55.00	$125.00 – 145.00	$180.00 – 220.00
"Connie"	$35.00 – 45.00	$120.00 – 140.00	$155.00 – 190.00

Teapot	Blue	Pink	Gold Decorated
"Birch"	$30.00 – 35.00		$150.00 – 175.00
"Bowknot"		$75.00 – 95.00	$140.00 – 155.00
"Murphy"	$35.00 – 45.00		$120.00 – 145.00
"Plume"		$30.00 – 40.00	$120.00 – 140.00*

*with gold floral decoration $200.00 – 225.00

Green "Connie"

Yellow "Connie"

Green "Connie"
with Gold Decoration

Green "Benjamin"

Green "Benjamin" with Gold Decoration

Yellow "Benjamin"

Pink "Plume" with Gold Decoration

Pink "Plume"

Blue "Birch"

Pink "Plume" with Gold Decoration

Blue "Murphy"

Blue "Birch"
with Gold Decoration

Victorian Teapots

Pink "Bowknot" with Gold Decoration

Pink "Bowknot"

Windshield Teapots

The six-cup Windshield teapot was first offered in 1941. The colors easiest to find are camellia, maroon, and the ivory Gold Label with polka dots. Hard-to-find colors include black, all blues, and all greens. This style teapot is available both with and without gold decoration and will also be found in some of the decal patterns. The standard Windshield gold floral decoration is shown on the teapots in the center of the picture. The Gold Label teapot also has matching kitchenware accessories which include a cookie jar, casserole, coffee pot, and three-piece bowl set. The yellow teapot with the green and white floral decal is from a decal line Hall experimented with in the 1960s. Several game bird decals will be found on ivory Windshield teapots. These include scenes with ducks, pheasants, and grouse. For more information see the "Game Birds" dinnerware page.

Windshield Teapot	Solid Color	Standard Gold	Gold Label
Black	$35.00 – 45.00	$45.00 – 52.00	
Cadet	$45.00 – 55.00	$50.00 – 55.00	
Camellia	$50.00 – 60.00	$55.00 – 65.00	$60.00 – 70.00
Canary	$45.00 – 55.00	$65.00 – 75.00	
Chinese Red	$225.00 – 250.00		
Cobalt	$65.00 – 75.00	$65 00 – 75.00	
Dresden	$50.00 – 60.00	$50.00 – 60.00	
Emerald	$60.00 – 65.00	$60.00 – 70.00	
Indian Red	$200.00 – 250.00		
Ivory	$25.00 – 30.00	$40.00 – 50.00	$50.00 – 60.00
Marine	$60.00 – 65.00		
Maroon	$50.00 – 60.00	$60.00 – 70.00	
Turquoise	$45.00 – 55.00	$50.00 – 60.00	
Warm Yellow	$40.00 – 45.00	$45.00 – 55.00	

Special Decorations:
Maroon with enameled white flowers, $100.00 – 125.00
Mustard with green & white floral band, $90.00 – 110.00

Chinese Red

Camellia Gold Label

Ivory Gold Label

Emerald Green with
Standard Gold

Cadet with
Standard Gold

Camellia with
Standard Gold

Maroon with
Standard Gold

Cobalt with
Standard Gold

Canary with
Standard Gold

Yellow with Green
Brown & White Floral Band

Maroon with
White Enameled Flowers

Turquoise with
Standard Gold

Miscellaneous Teapots

The "Bowling Ball," a teapot from the late thirties, was very successful at disguising its existence until a few years ago. After its initial confirmation as a Hall teapot, a virtual avalanche of "Bowling Balls" appeared. Recently, it seems as if this teapot has gone back into hiding again and really may be as scarce as was once thought. The usual color it is found in is turquoise. We have seen one in cobalt and have not heard of the "Bowling Ball" being found in any other color or with any gold decoration.

The canary and cobalt teapots on the top row are examples of the elusive "Philbe" teapot. The tip of the spout was designed with an unusual flared collar to prevent dripping. The cobalt teapot is decorated with the Gold Label style "Daisy" design. The original source for this teapot confirmed it was made by Hall and recently "Philbe" teapots have been found with the #5 backstamp. Other recent discoveries have included gold decorated teapots in cadet and canary.

The green "Dodecagon" teapot to the left in the third row is embossed "HALL" on the bottom. Collectors are more familiar with the Forman Brothers version of the ten-sided Dodecagon teapot. This teapot is usually found with a

decaled ivory body and a chrome lid. However, some of these teapots have appeared in solid colors with a china lid and a Hall backstamp.

The French drip Coffee Biggin is actually a coffee pot with its dripper in place. However, it can also be used as a teapot with the dripper removed. It may be found in numerous colors and in sizes ranging from two-cup to eight-cup. We have not seen it with gold decoration. Common colors are stock brown, stock green, and canary. This teapot has also been found in a few of the decal lines.

The Red Coach and similar Detroit Athletic Club teapots pictured on page 235 have a china liner that is fitted into a pewter handle.

Sherlock Holmes is a very large teapot that Hall was commissioned to produce for a private company. Ronald Reagan was made during the term of his presidency and was subsequently sold for a number of years at the Hall Closet.

The early brown teapot pictured below has a hole in the center of the knob through which a chain is inserted that is attached to a large meal tea leaf holder. The chain can be adjusted to conveniently lower the tea leaves or to hold them in a raised position.

Teapot	Common Color	Unusual Color
"Bowling Ball"	$500.00 – 550.00	
Dodecagon	$55.00 – 65.00	
French drip Coffee Biggin	$60.00 – 80.00	$185.00 – 210.00
"Philbe"	$1,200.00 – 1,500.00	UND
Reagan	$100.00 – 125.00	
Red Coach	$85.00 – 95.00	
Sherlock Holmes	$200.00 – 225.00	
Super Ceram "Raised Panel"	$25.00 – 30.00	
Zeisel-shape, gold Mini Fluerette	$200.00 – 250.00	
Zeisel-shape, hand painted	$125.00 – 150.00	
Teapot below: "Tea Slider"	$125.00 – 155.00	

Early Hall Teapot with Wooden Finial and Metal Tea Leaf Holder

"Philbe"

"Philbe" with French Teapot
Gold Label "Daisy" Decoration

"Bowling Ball"

Zeisel-shape
with Hand Painted Flowers

Zeisel-shape with Gold Mini Fleurette

French Coffee Biggin

Dodecagon

Sherlock Holmes

French Coffee Biggin Bottom

Red Coach

Super Ceram "Raised Panel"

French Coffee Biggin Bottom

French Coffee Biggin Dripper

Reagan

Coffee Pots

The Washington coffee pot was introduced in 1919. The retail price of a nine-cup Washington was $1.89 in the Montgomery Ward catalog from that year. This coffee pot is still being made and it has appeared in many different colors and with numerous decorations over the long span of production. Sizes of the Washington coffee pot include 1, 1½, 2, 6, 10, 12, and 15-cup.

Researchers have christened the large red and white teapot on the second row "Deca-flip." It is usually found in this color combination, but may on occasion be found with the color pattern reversed. This inverse version has been found in an original box that indicates it was a premium for the Cook Coffee Company.

The "Baron" is seen most often in Chinese red, but may also be found in other colors. It is not easy to find.

The green "Alcony" coffee pot almost appears to be a large version of the short-spout "Carraway" that was made for Tricolator. The lid and handle on the two coffee pots appear identical in design. The "Alcony" at the bottom right of the next page has the #5 backstamp.

The "Perk" coffee pot is similar in design and has the same decal as a coffee pot produced by Frauenfelter. However, the Frauenfelter coffee pot is 12-sided.

The maroon "Big Boy" coffee pot was also sold as an electric percolator with a glass dripper. The side panels from an original box are shown in the photo below.

The "Carrie" is an elusive coffee pot that has also been found as an electric percolator with a china dripper. See the Blue Bouquet pattern on page 53.

Coffee Pot	Common Color	Unusual Color	Coffee Pot	Common Color	Unusual Color
"Alcony"	$60.00 – 75.00		"Terrace," large-size	$45.00 – 55.00	
"Arthur"	$75.00 – 85.00		"Terrace," small-size	$45.00 – 55.00**	
"Baron"	$50.00 – 70.00	$120.00 – 150.00	Washington,		
*"Big Boy"	$35.00 – 45.00		1 to 2-cup	$25.00 – 32.00	$40.00 – 45.00
"Carrie"	$65.00 – 70.00	$90.00 – 125.00	Washington,		
"Corrie"	$50.00 – 65.00	$150.00 – 225.00	6-cup	$25.00 – 35.00	$50.00 – 60.00
"Deca-flip"	$75.00 – 85.00		Washington,		
Inverse "Deca-flip"	$80.00 – 95.00		12 and 15-cup	$35.00 – 40.00	$115.00 – 145.00
"Meltdown"	$50.00 – 60.00				
"Perk"	$45.00 – 55.00		*electric percolator with glass dripper $75.00 – 95.00		
"Ritz"	$55.00 – 65.00	$100.00 – 125.00	**with china dripper $100.00 – 125.00		

"Carrie"

Washington

"Big Boy"

Washington

Washington

Electromatic Coffeemaker

SUREST METHOD YOU EVER TRIED...FOR THE GRANDEST COFFEE YOU EVER TASTED

PAT. NO. 2272471 OTHER PATS. PEND.

THE NEW, REVOLUTIONARY *Electromatic Coffeemaker*

HEATS WATER UNIFORMLY-- EACH DROP PASSES THROUGH THE COFFEE AT PROPER BREWING TEMPERATURE.

PREHEATS COFFEE GROUNDS-- RELEASES MORE FLAVOR

ECONOMICAL--GIVES MORE COFFEE PER POUND.

FULLY AUTOMATIC--NO GUESSING; NO WATCHING

Large-size "Terrace"

Small-size "Terrace"

"Perk"

...Here's how simple, quick and easy it is to make delicious coffee... this better way.

"Baron"

Inverse "Deca-flip"

"Deca-flip"

"Meltdown"

"Corrie"

"Corrie"

"Ritz" with Trivet

"Arthur"

"Alcony"

Drip Coffee Pot Shapes

A number of different shapes of all-china drip coffee pots were produced by Hall. The complete coffee pot is comprised of four pieces. There is the base, a china dripper, a china spreader which fits inside the dripper, and a lid. Most of these shapes were used in the decal lines. The more common shapes are pictured to help with identification and for ease of comparison.

The #691 coffee is usually found in solid colors or decorated with a color band and silver trim. The colors may vary, as we have seen red, blue, yellow, and green bands.

The middle coffee pot on the top row in the photo below is unusual in that it has an electric warmer base made of metal. The design on the one in the picture is the only one we have seen on this shape.

The "Jordan" drip coffee pot is most commonly associated with the Autumn Leaf pattern. It is not common, but it has also been seen in cadet with a Hi-white handle and lid or with colored ribs. The distinguishing feature of this coffee pot is its vertical panels which are separated by distinct vertical ribs.

The "Kadota" coffee pot has a smooth body. We have only seen this in ivory in various decal patterns. Usually the backstamp is the Drip-O-lator mark.

The distinctive feature of the "Radiance" coffee pot is the series of rays which separate the body into vertical panels. This coffee pot may be found in solid colors and is used in the decal patterns.

The E-style coffee pot was only made in a single pattern — Mount Vernon. This pattern was designed by J. Palin Thorley and was sold by Sears from the 1940s through the 1950s.

Prices are only for the colors and decorations indicated. The decal pattern coffee pots are priced with their respective patterns.

"Jordan: Drip Coffee Pot with Red Trim

"Jordan" style Drip Coffee Pot with Electric Heating Element

"Kadota" Drip Coffee Pot with Serenade Decal

Terrace Coffee Pot with China Dripper

"Medallion" Drip Coffee Pot Chinese Red

E-style Drip Coffee Pot with Mt. Vernon Decal

No. 691 All-china Drip Coffee Pots with Color Band

No. 691 Drip Coffee Pot with Beauty Decal

No. 691 Drip Coffee Pot Chinese Red

No. 691 Drip Coffee Pot with Flamingo Decal

No. 691 Coffee Pot with Red Dot Decoration

"Radiance" Drip Coffee Pot Art Glaze Blue

"Radiance" Drip Coffee Pot with Acacia Decal

"Radiance" Drip Coffee Pot with No. 488 Decal

"Radiance Drip Coffee Pot Chinese Red

Drip Coffee Pot	Value	Drip Coffee Pot	Value
#691, solid color	$200.00 – 220.00	Metal base, "Jordan" style	$100.00 – 125.00
#691, color band	$220.00 – 240.00	"Jordan"	$250.00 – 300.00
"Medallion," solid color	$250.00 – 300.00	"Radiance," solid colors	$300.00 – 400.00

Electric Percolators

The most common shape of Hall electric percolators is the style used for the highly collectible percolator in the Autumn Leaf pattern. Today, this percolator with other decals is becoming more attractive to collectors.

Some of the numerous decals found on electric percolators will also be found on other accessory pieces. This has enabled collectors to put together matching mini-sets of certain decals.

Some of the more popular decals found on the percolators are the series of game bird decals. Other highly collectible accessory pieces found with the game bird decal are a New York teapot and a Windshield teapot. For more information see the "Game Bird" pattern in the dinnerware section of this book. Percolators in this shape with floral decal are seen less often than those with the game bird decals.

Another percolator with a gold Rx decoration is sometimes seen. The percolator is part of a set which was given as a premium to pharmacists. Other pieces are available with this decoration. For a more complete listing see the Rx listing in the Kitchenware section.

The percolator with the seal of the state of Ohio was found in its original box. This piece was marketed by Ernest Sohn of New York.

Another shape of electric percolators was made for the Forman Family. These usually have colored bodies, were a little taller than the "MJ" percolator, and have a series of vertical ribs near the top. A grouping of these colored percolators is shown in the photo to the right.

A third style of electric percolator is pictured. This style has a white body with vertical ribs. A matching sugar and creamer has also been found.

The photo below pictures two "MJ" style percolators. The one on the left with the coat-of-arms decal was found with eight matching handled mugs. The one with the "Gold Reindeer" decoration was bought with matching Tom & Jerry mugs.

Electric Percolator	Value
Bouquet decoration	$140.00 –165.00
Coat-of-arms decal	$75.00 – 85.00
Floral "Dogwood" decal	$75.00 – 85.00
Game Bird decal	$100.00 –120.00
Gold Deer	$60.00 – 70.00
Irish setter decal	$115.00 – 130.00
Rx decoration	$45.00 – 55.00
"Ribbed" Percolator	$65.00 – 85.00
Seal of Ohio	$80.00 – 90.00
Solid color (Forman)	$80.00 – 90.00
Gold Deer mug	$8.00 – 10.00
Coat-of-arms handled mug	$5.00 – 7.00

Coat of Arms with Mugs   *Deer Gold Decoration with Mugs*

MADE EXCLUSIVELY FOR
ERNEST SOHN CREATIONS
BY
THE HALL CHINA CO.
EAST LIVERPOOL, OHIO

Magnolia Electric Percolator

Bouquet Electric Percolator

Seal of Ohio Electric Percolator

Forman Electric Automatic Percolators in Pink, Blue, and Yellow

Ribbed Electric Percolator

Irish Setter Electric Percolator

Pheasants Electric Percolator

Geese Electric Percolator

Autumn Leaf Electric Percolator

COFFEE POTS, TEAPOTS, AND ACCESSORIES MADE FOR OTHER COMPANIES

Over the years, Hall has produced many items for other companies. In many cases these items have been an exclusive design for a particular company to market. Most often, Hall supplied a china part and the contracting company usually added a metal component to finish the product for the retail market. Coffee pots were usually fitted with metal drippers or lids and casseroles were placed into metal holders.

Among Hall's best customers for this type of arrange-ment were the Forman Family, Drip-O-lator, and the Tri-colator Company. Many of their products are shown in this chapter.

On occasion, some items were also made for other companies exclusively as a premium item and the company did not contribute to the manufacture of the product. Teapots made exclusively for Lipton, McCormick, and F. S. Martin are examples.

314

Bacharach Teapots

The round T-Ball was introduced in 1948. It was made by Hall for Bacharach of New York and has the following backstamp: "T-BALL TEAPOT – MADE FOR BACHARACH BY HALL CHINA COMPANY." A number of undecorated colors may be found, and a black teapot with gold decoration also exists. The black does not have the Bacharach backstamp. Instead it has a "HALL" mark and gold number (0850GL), with the letters "GL" possibly indicating this teapot was a part of the Gold Label line.

The square T-Ball was also made for Bacharach in the late 1940s. This teapot was re-introduced as part of the Hall American line in 1984. The old teapots will have the Bacharach backstamp. Both the round and square versions of the T-Ball have a side pocket on each side in which a tea bag may be placed.

Collectors should be aware there is another square teapot which also has side pockets. This teapot is sometimes confused with the Hall square T-Ball. However, this teapot lacks Hall's quality and does not have the Bacharach backstamp.

Color	T-Ball Round	T-Ball Square
Black	$60.00 – 70.00*	$50.00 – 62.00
Cadet	$90.00 – 125.00	$85.00 – 100.00
Canary	$90.00 – 125.00	$85.00 – 100.00
Chinese Red	$150.00 – 195.00	$150.00 – 195.00
Cobalt	$100.00 – 130.00	$100.00 –110.00
Emerald	$100.00 – 125.00	$90.00 – 110.00
Ivory	$45.00 – 55.00	$35.00 – 40.00
Marine	$95.00 – 110.00	$85.00 – 95.00
Maroon	$100.00 – 125.00	$90.00 – 110.00
Silver Luster	$125.00 – 150.00	$125.00 – 150.00
Stock Brown	$37.00 – 45.00	$35.00 – 40.00
Stock Green	$37.00 – 45.00	$35.00 – 40.00

*with gold decoration $185.00 – 200.00

Green Round T-Ball

Black Round T-Ball with Gold Decoration

Cobalt Round T-Ball

Silver Round T-Ball

Maroon Square T-Ball

Black Square T-Ball

Coffelator Coffee Pots

Hall produced the teapot pictured below for the Coffelator Company of Newark, New Jersey. The patent for the design of the coffee pot was owned by Coffelator; therefore, this shape pot was also made by other companies. Coffee pots produced by Hall have been found in Hall's distinctive glazes including Chinese Red, Delphinium, Indian Red, Ivory, Emerald, and Marine. Experienced Hall collectors will also be able to identify the coffee pots produced by Hall from the texture of the white underside of the pot.

Currently, there have been no reports of any of these coffee pots having been found with either gold or decal decoration.

Color	Value
Black	$60.00 – 75.00
Chinese Red	$155.00 – 200.00*
Cobalt	$150.00 – 190.00
Emerald	$140.00 – 170.00
Indian Red	$195.00 – 220.00
Ivory	$60.00 – 80.00

Chinese Red

Emerald

Marine

Indian Red

Cube Tea and Coffee Sets

The Cubes are tea and coffee sets made by Hall and several other companies under a British patent. Hall introduced the 12 oz. Cube teapot in the early 1930s and later in the decade expanded the line to include a 10 ounce coffee pot, open sugar, creamer, and tea tile. Older Hall teapots will have the Hall #5 backstamp, the patent numbers, and the following inscription on the bottom: "CUBE TEAPOTS, LIMITED, LEICESTER." The teapot was made for the institutional line for many years and is especially abundant in stock brown and stock green. Teapots produced after 1970 will have a square Hall backstamp.

Although the Cube-shape teapots have been found in numerous colors, very few have been found with gold decoration. An example of a gold decorated Cube with the French Flower design is shown on page 152.

Cube Teapot	Value
Black	$50.00 – 55.00
Chinese Red	$150.00 – 175.00
Delphinium	$90.00 – 100.00
Gray	$45.00 – 65.00
Marine	$90.00 – 110.00
Stock Brown	$40.00 – 50.00
Turquoise	$90.00 – 100.00

Cube Teapot	Value
Cadet	$90.00 – 100.00
Cobalt	$100.00 – 125.00
Emerald	$75.00 – 85.00
Indian Red	$175.00 – 225.00
Orchid	$200.00 – 250.00
Stock Green	$40.00 – 50.00

Cube Coffee Pot	Value		Value
Chinese Red	$175.00 – 200.00	Cobalt	$125.00 – 150.00
Stock Brown	$45.00 – 55.00	Stock Green	$45.00 – 55.00

Gray Cube Teapot

Indian Red Cube Teapot

Cobalt Cube Coffee Pot

Cadet Cube Teapot

Stock Green Cube Teapot

Orchid Cube Teapot

Dohrmann Teapots

Hall produced the teapot shown below for the Dohrmann Company. This company operated in the western states and most of the teapots will be found in that geographical area. The teapots have the following backstamp: "DOHRCO" and the HALL mark in a circle with "MADE IN U.S.A." underneath.

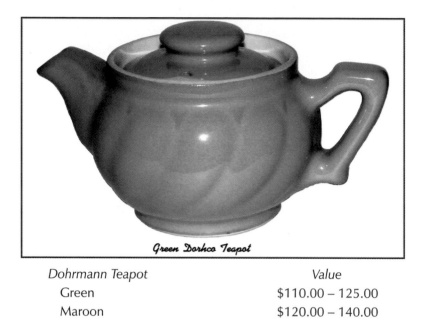

Green Dorhco Teapot

Dohrmann Teapot	Value
Green	$110.00 – 125.00
Maroon	$120.00 – 140.00

Drip-O-Lator Coffee Pots

Hall made coffee pot bodies for the Enterprise Aluminum Company of Massillon, Ohio. Enterprise supplied the aluminum dripper for these coffee pots and marketed the finished product. Some shapes will be found in more than one size. Although many shapes appear to be limited to a single decoration, there are a few coffee pot styles which will be found with numerous decorations. Other companies besides Hall also supplied china bases to the Enterprise Company. In some cases these bodies will bear the backstamp of the manufacturer, but the coffee pots produced by Hall will only have the Drip-O-lator mark. The coffee pot shapes known to be made by Hall will be illustrated and priced on the following pages. All the names of both the shapes and decorations have been contributed by researchers.

The "Trellis" is pictured in a solid color and with a V-shaped, multicolored floral decoration. The "Bauhaus" is usually found with the two floral decorations pictured. The "Waverly" is shown with two different style lids, and four different floral decals. The major differences between the "Waverly" and the "Wavelet" are the length of the spout and the size of the handle. The "Cathedral" coffee pot is available in two sizes and the same daisy-like decal is also found on a few kitchenware pieces. See the miscellaneous page in the kitchenware section. The "Sash" is found with both solid color bands and with a blue band with white stars. This coffee pot is known as the "Orb" with the colored, molded band smoothed over and replaced with a decal. The "Meltdown" is a shape which is very similar to a Drip-O-lator coffee pot produced by Frauenfelter. The biggest difference between the two is a slightly longer spout on the Hall coffee pot.

Drip-O-lator Coffee Pots

"Bauhaus" with Jonquil Decal

"Bauhaus" with Juneflower Decal

"Bricks & Ivy" with Squared Handle

No. 2 Coffee Set-shape Sugar

"Bricks & Ivy" with Rounded Handle

No. 2 Coffee Set-shape Creamer

"Dart" with Rose Decal

6-cup "Cathedral" with Daisy Decal

No. 2 Coffee Set-shape Coffee Pot

4-cup "Cathedral" with Daisy Decal

"Drape" with Mini-floral Decal

Drip-O-lator Coffee Pot	Value	Drip-O-lator Coffee Pot	Value
"Bauhaus" with Jonquil decal	$40.00 – 50.00	"Cathedral," 4-cup with Daisy decal	$40.00 – 45.00
"Bauhaus" with Juneflower decal	$40.00 – 50.00	Coffee Set coffee pot	$50.00 – 55.00
"Bricks and Ivy" with rounded handle	$37.00 – 42.00	Coffee Set creamer and sugar	$18.00 – 22.00
"Bricks and Ivy" with squared handle	$37.00 – 42.00	"Dart" with rose decal	$32.00 – 37.00
"Cathedral," 6-cup with Daisy decal	$40.00 – 45.00	"Drape" with mini floral decal	$40.00 – 45.00

Drip-O-lator Coffee Pots

"Jerry"

"Jerry" with "Floral Lattice" Decal

Kadota All-china Drip with "Wildflower" Decal

Lewis

Kadota Variation

Lotus with Impatiens Decal

Medallion with "Roses" Decal

Meltdown

Orb with Bird of Paradise Decal

Panel with Potted Flower Decal

Panel Sugar and Lid

Panel Creamer

Petal Small and Large

Drip-O-lator Coffee Pot	Value	Drip-O-lator Coffee Pot	Value
"Jerry," red and white	$50.00 – 55.00	"Medallion" creamer, sugar, and lid	$35.00 – 40.00
"Jerry," "Floral Lattice" decal	$55.00 – 65.00	Meltdown	$50.00 – 60.00
Kadota all-china, "Wildflower" decal	$90.00 – 110.00	Orb with Bird-of-Paradise decal	$50.00 – 60.00
Kadota variation	$40.00 – 45.00	Panel with Potted Flower decal	$45.00 – 55.00
Lewis	$40.00 – 45.00	Petal, large-size	$40.00 – 45.00
Lotus with Impatiens decal	$40.00 – 45.00	Petal, small-size	$40.00 – 45.00
"Medallion" with rose decal	$55.00 – 65.00		

"Rounded Terrace"
with Bouquet Decal

"Rounded Terrace"
with Pasture Rose Decal

"Rounded Terrace"
with Rambling Rose Decal

Blue "Sash" with Star Decoration

Red "Sash"

Green "Sash"

"Sweep"
with Modern Tulip Decal

"Target"
Dutch People Decal
On Front of Coffee Pot

"Scoop"
with Wildflower Decal

Drip-O-lator Coffee Pots

"Target" Windmill Decal on Backside

Drip-O-lator Coffee Pot	Value	Drip-O-lator Coffee Pot	Value
"Rounded Terrace," Bouquet decal	$45.00 – 50.00	"Sash," green	$60.00 – 65.00
"Rounded Terrace," Pasture Rose decal	$45.00 – 50.00	"Sash," red	$60.00 – 65.00
"Rounded Terrace," Rambling Rose decal	$45.00 – 50.00	"Sweep" with modern tulip decal	$40.00 – 50.00
		"Scoop" with Wildflower decal	$45.00 – 50.00
"Sash," blue with stars	$75.00 – 85.00	"Target" with Dutch decal	$40.00 – 45.00

"Trellis" with Floral Bouquet Decal

"Trellis"

"Trellis"

"Viking" with Cactus Decal

"Viking" with Floral Lattice Decal

"Viking" with Bird of Paradise Decal

"Viking" with Cactus Decal

"Waverly" with Yellow Rose Decal

Small "Wavelet" with Dome Lid and Minuet Decal

"Wavelet" Large-Size with Minuet Decal

"Waverly" with Iridized Mini-Fleurette Design

Drip-O-lator Coffee Pots

"Waverly" with Tulip Decal

"Wicker" with Mini Floral Decal

"Waverly" with Domed Lid and Jonquil Decal

"Waverly" with Jonquil Decal

"Waverly" with June Flower Decal

Examples of different styles of lids used with the same shape body are shown on the "Viking" Cactus and the "Waverly" Jonquil coffee pots. The "Viking coffee pot is found with either lid about equally. The "Waverly" coffee pot is found more frequently with the crest lid than with the domed lid.

Drip-O-lator Coffee Pot	Value
"Trellis" with floral bouquet decal	$45.00 – 55.00
"Trellis," red	$65.00 – 75.00
"Trellis," yellow	$55.00 – 65.00
"Viking" with Bird-of-Paradise decal	$45.00 – 50.00
"Viking" with Cactus decal	$60.00 – 65.00
"Viking" with Floral Lattice decal	$50.00 – 55.00
"Wavelet," large-size with Minuet decal	$50.00 – 55.00

Drip-O-lator Coffee Pot	Value
"Wavelet," small-size with Minuet decal	$50.00 – 55.00
"Waverly" with iridized Mini-Fleurette gold decoration	$100.00 – 125.00
"Waverly" with Jonquil decal	$40.00 – 45.00
"Waverly" with Juneflower decal	$40.00 – 45.00
"Waverly" with Tulip decal	$45.00 – 50.00
"Wicker" with mini-floral decal	$40.00 – 45.00

Forman Family Products

Forman Casseroles and Plates

MADE EXCLUSIVELY TO FORMAN FAMILY, INC. By THE HALL CHINA CO U.S.A.

Dodecagon Casserole Top View

Pie Plate with Chrysler Decal

Pink "Ribbed Buffet" Casserole

MADE EXCLUSIVELY FOR FORMAN BROS. Inc. By THE HALL CHINA CO.

Dodecagon Casserole with Chrysler Decal

MADE EXCLUSIVELY FOR FORMAN BROS. Inc. By THE HALL CHINA CO. HAND DECORATED

"Ribbed Buffet" Casserole with Floral Decal

Dodecagon Casserole with Floral Decal

Oval Casserole with Exotic Bird Decal

"Double Octagonal" Cassoerle with Eden Bird Decal

MADE EXCLUSIVELY FOR FORMAN BROS. Inc. By THE HALL CHINA CO. HAND DECORATED

Eden Bird Plate in Metal Holder

The Forman Family, Inc., was located in Brooklyn, New York. Products with the Forman Family backstamp represent the end result of a joint effort between Hall and Forman to produce useful articles from a combination of china and chrome. Teapots, coffee pots, casseroles, and electric percolators are the usual items which were finished by the Forman Family workers.

Decorated casseroles, pie plates, and plates are illustrated in the photo above. The "Ribbed Buffet" casserole may be found in two sizes in both the floral decal and solid color versions. The reprint on page 327 illustrates this casserole in three different colors.

Teapots, coffee pots, and other items assembled by the Forman Family are shown on the following pages.

Item	Value
Casserole, dodecagon, Chrysler decal	$45.00 – 55.00
Casserole, dodecagon, floral decal	$32.00 – 37.00
Casserole, "Double Octagon"	$40.00 – 55.00
Casserole, oval, Exotic Bird decal	$45.00 – 55.00
Casserole, floral decal, "Ribbed Buffet"	$47.00 – 57.00
Casserole, solid color, "Ribbed Buffet"	$45.00 – 55.00
Casserole, tab-handled lid with floral decal	$40.00 – 50.00
Pie plate with Chrysler decal	$45.00 – 55.00
Plate, metal holder, Eden Bird decal	$35.00 – 45.00

"Dutch" with "Christopher" Decal

"Dutch" with Eden Bird Decal and Metal Dripper

"Dutch" with Eden Bird Decal

DRIP-A-DROP COFFEE POT MADE BY FORMAN BROS Inc. BROOKLYN, N.Y. PATENT 1,792,218

Dodecagon with Inverted Crysler Decal

"Dutch" with Chrysler Decal

"Dutch" with "Orential Butterfly" Decal

"Edwards" with Blue-Trimmed Mother of Pearl Body

"Edwards" with Green-Trimmed Mother of Pearl Body

Forman Teapots

"Edwards" Backstamp

"Edwards" Backstamp

"Edwards" with Rust-Trimmed Mother of Pearl Body

The "Dutch" teapot is very similar to the "Diver" teapot that Hall produced for Tricolator. The lid of the "Dutch" fits over the top edge, but the lid of the "Diver" fits inside the rim. The shape of the two spout tips also differs slightly. The Dodecagon teapot has a metal lid with a tea strainer attached. Notice the backstamps and the new names associated with Forman teapots such as "DRIP-A-DROP" and "Adjusto Teapot." The Tip-Pot has two spouts, but only one internal chamber and is designed to fit into a metal holder with a candle warmer.

Forman Family Teapot	Value
Teapot, Adjusto with fruits decal	$185.00 – 210.00
Teapot, red Adjusto	$200.00 – 225.00
Teapot, yellow Adjusto	$140.00 – 160.00
Teapot, Dodecagon, Chrysler decal	$110.00 – 130.00
Teapot, "Dutch," "Christopher" decal	$65.00 – 75.00

Forman Family Teapot	Value
Teapot, "Dutch," Chrysler decal	$160.00 – 190.00
Teapot, "Dutch," Eden Bird decal	$75.00 – 85.00
Teapot, "Dutch," Oriental Butterfly	$85.00 – 95.00
Teapot, "Edwards"	$100.00 – 125.00
Tip-pot	$180.00 – 210.00

Forman Tip Pots and Adjusto Teapots

Ivory Tip-pot

Blue Tip-pot

Canary Adjusto Teapot

White Adjusto Teapot

Chinese Red Adjusto Teapot

White Adjusto Teapot with Fruit Decals

White Adjusto Teapot with Fruit Decals (Reverse Side)

Pink Cozy Hot Pot Shown
without Cover

Black Satin Cozy Hot Pot with
Gold Color Cover

Ivory Cozy Hot Pot with
Embossed Copper Color Cover

Light Blue Cozy Hot Pot with Chrome Cover and Sugar and Creamer on Original Tray

*Cozy Hot Pots
and
Accessories*

Blue Electric
Percolator

Yellow Electric
Percolator

Blue Buffet Casserole

Pink Buffet Casserole

Pink Electric Percolator

Yellow Buffet Casserole

The Forman version of the "Cozy Hot Pot" is shown in the photo above and in the catalog reprint on the next page. A similar "Cozy Hot Pot" in yellow with a slightly different handle was made by Hall for Lipton. See page 331 for an example of the Lipton style. Notice Forman also sold this teapot on a chrome tray with a matching sugar and creamer. Hall made an electric percolator for Forman in pink, blue, and yellow. These percolators have vertical ribs around the lower half of the body.

Forman Family Product	Value	Forman Family Product	Value
Casserole, "Ribbed Buffet," large	$45.00 – 55.00	Cozy sugar and creamer	$22.00 – 27.00
Casserole, "Ribbed Buffet," small	$30.00 – 35.00	Cozy "Hot Pot" set on tray	$90.00 – 110.00
Cozy "Hot Pot"	$45.00 – 55.00	Electric Percolator	$80.00 – 90.00

FORMAN 4 FAMILY

CoLOR
in harmony with your kitchen...

PERCOLATOR SETS
Listed below are the 3 color combinations available.

With the turquoise percolator, all the metal parts are finished in chromium.

With the yellow percolator, all the metal parts are finished in solid brass.

With the pink percolator, all the metal parts are finished in solid copper.

For further details, please refer to the copy shown on the right, underneath "percolator sets."

COMPLETELY AUTOMATIC
(A) PERCOLATOR

Enjoy coffee of the finest flavor—free of METALLIC taste—because it is made in vitrified china. Set it—forget it! Keeps continuously warm after shut-off. China by Hall, guaranteed heat-proof, and available in choice of the 3 most popular colors. Complete with cord set, cap. 4-8 cups, A.C. only, 110/115 volts, U.L. approved, shipping wt. 7½ lbs.

Cat. No. 6G-2123. Turquoise China.
Cat. No. 6G-2122. Yellow China.
Cat. No. 6G-2121. Pink China.
List Price 19.75.
DEALERS NET PRICE................ **13¹⁷**

COMPLETELY AUTOMATIC
(B) PERCOLATOR SETS. For gracious and elegant service—the percolator, as shown above, is combined with a sugar, creamer and tray to match. Available in any one of the 3 most popular colors, as described in copy at left. Each sugar and creamer is made of china with a slide-on slide-off metal cover. Tray 17½" x 10½" with embossed center. Shipping wt. 13 lbs.

Cat. No. 5G-2120. Turquoise/Chrome.
Cat. No. 5G-2119. Yellow/Brass.
Cat. No. 5G-2118. Pink/Copper.
List Price 34.95.
DEALERS NET PRICE................ **23³⁰**

CASSEROLE WITH CANDLE WARMER.
Bake in Pyrex—serve sizzling hot—from same dish. Preserves original flavor! Available in solid brass or copper, adding the warm Colonial touch. Cap. 3 pts. Ht. 8½", Shipping Wt. 4½ lbs. **Retail**

Cat. No. 6G-2117. Brass.
Cat. No. 6G-2116. Copper.
List Price 9.95.
DEALERS NET PRICE.... **6⁶³**

CHAFING DISH.
The hostess' delight for buffet and dinner parties! Makes entertaining a fascinating pleasure! Choice of solid copper or brass. Sterno heat for convenience. Cap. 2 qts., Ht. 10", Shipping wt. 5 lbs. **Retail**

6G-2112. Brass. 6G-2111. Copper
List Price 18.95.
DEALERS NET PRICE. **12⁶³**

CASSEROLE
A gourmet's surprise! A decorator's delight! China oven baking dishes surpass all. China available in the 3 most popular colors. Metal matched to harmonize. China by Hall, guaranteed heatproof, cap. 2 qts., Shipping wt. 6½ lbs. **Retail**

6G-2115. Turq./Chrome.
6G-2114. Yellow/Brass. } List 8.40.
6G-2113. Pink/Copper.
DEALERS NET PRICE............ **5⁶⁰**

COVER SLIDES-ON SLIDES-OFF

THE COZY HOT POT
The Continental touch! Brews tea and *KEEPS IT HOT*, ready to serve. Ideal for instant coffee, too! China in the 3 most popular colors. Insulated metal cover (to match) slides-on and slides-off to hold the heat. China by Hall, guaranteed heat-proof, cap. 6 cups, Shipping wt. 3¾ lbs.

Cat. No. 6G-2110. Turquoise/Chrome.
Cat. No. 6G-2109. Yellow/Brass.
Cat. No. 6G-2108. Pink/Copper.
List Price 7.95.
DEALERS NET PRICE.......................... **5³⁰**

PLEASE DO NOT DEDUCT 2% CASH DISCOUNT ON NET PRICES

PAGE A1

Forman Family Fuji Decal

"Dart" Coffee Pot

"Arch" Sugar and Lid   Arch Creamer   "Wide Panel" Electric Percolator   "Duce" Creamer   "Duse" Sugar and Lid

"Duse" Coffee Pot

Miscellaneous Forman Family

Golden Glo Teapot

Golden Glo Teapot Backstamp

Electric Warmer with Three Petite Marmites

Lettuce Green "Duse" Coffee Pot

The Fuji decal is one of Forman's more collectible patterns. The petite marmites that fit into the warmer were also decorated in this pattern.

The electric warmer holds three petite marmites and was designed to keep foods warm. In another application, ice could also be packed around the marmites to chill food.

Forman Family Product	Value
Coffee pot, "Dart" with Fuji decal	$65.00 – 75.00
Coffee Pot, "Duse" with Fuji decal	$70.00 – 80.00
Coffee Pot, "Duse," Lettuce Green	$35.00 – 45.00
Creamer, "Arch" with Fuji decal	$18.00 – 20.00
Creamer, "Duse," with Fuji decal	$18.00 – 20.00
Electric Percolator, "Wide Panel" with Fuji decal	$100.00 – 125.00

Forman Family Product	Value
Sugar and lid, "Arch" with Fuji decal	$20.00 – 25.00
Sugar and lid, "Duse" with Fuji decal	$20.00 – 25.00
Teapot, Golden Glo	$100.00 – 125.00
Warmer and 3 Petite Marmites with petite pink floral decal	$80.00 – 120.00
Warmer and 3 Petite Marmites with Fuji decal	$125.00 – 145.00

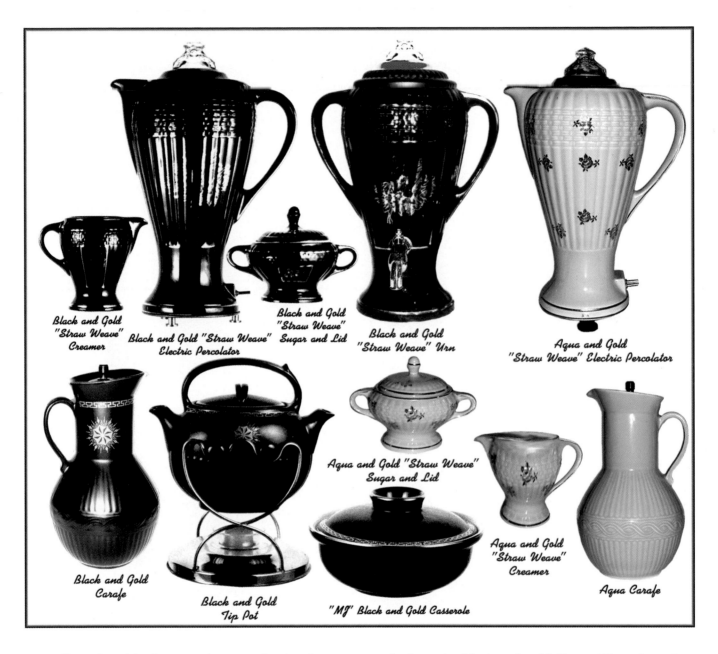

Black and Gold "Straw Weave" Creamer

Black and Gold "Straw Weave" Electric Percolator

Black and Gold "Straw Weave" Sugar and Lid

Black and Gold "Straw Weave" Urn

Aqua and Gold "Straw Weave" Electric Percolator

Black and Gold Carafe

Black and Gold Tip Pot

Aqua and Gold "Straw Weave" Sugar and Lid

"MJ" Black and Gold Casserole

Aqua and Gold "Straw Weave" Creamer

Aqua Carafe

Hall produced both urn and pour-style electric percolators for Forman in the "Straw Weave" pattern. A lamp made from the black and gold "Straw Weave" urn has also been spotted.

Forman Family Product	Value
Carafe, black and gold	$75.00 – 90.00
Carafe, aqua	$110.00 – 125.00
Casserole, "MJ" black and gold	$32.00 – 37.00
Creamer, black, gold, "Straw Weave"	$15.00 – 18.00
Creamer, blue, gold, "Straw Weave"	$18.00 – 20.00
Percolator, black, gold, "Straw Weave"	$140.00 – 160.00

Forman Family Product	Value
Percolator, blue, gold, "Straw Weave"	$130.00 – 155.00
Sugar and lid, black, gold, "Straw Weave"	$20.00 – 22.00
Sugar and lid, blue, gold "Straw Weave"	$22.00 – 27.00
Tip-pot, black and gold	$120.00 – 140.00
Urn, black, gold, "Straw Weave"	$130.00 – 150.00

Gardiner Coffee Pots

The coffee pot made for the Gardiner Company is a new addition to this book. A number of these coffee pots have been reported in a brown glaze which appears to be Swedish Brown. An ivory color coffee pot with silver trim is also shown in the picture. According to information stamped on the dripper, this coffee pot was made for the Gardiner Company of New Orleans, Louisiana. The patent date is August 30, 1921. Thus, this is an example of one of Hall's very early coffee pots.

Gardiner Coffee Pot	Value
Ivory with silver trim	$120.00 – 140.00
Swedish Brown	$125.00 – 150.00

Gardiner Drip Coffee Pot

Lipton Teapots

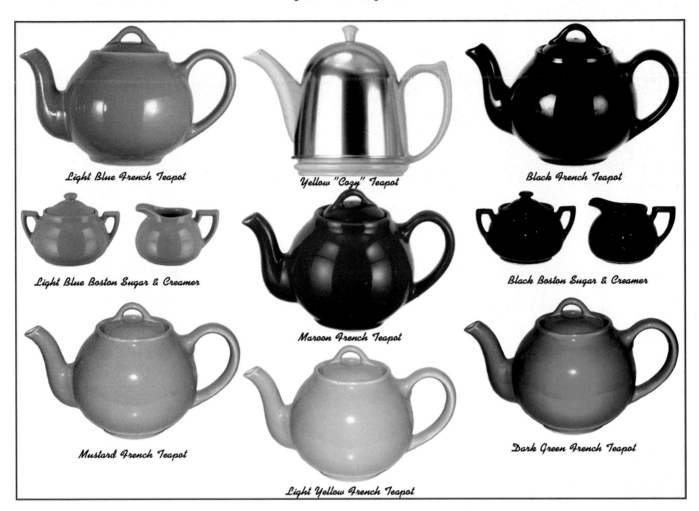

Light Blue French Teapot

Yellow "Cozy" Teapot

Black French Teapot

Light Blue Boston Sugar & Creamer

Black Boston Sugar & Creamer

Maroon French Teapot

Mustard French Teapot

Light Yellow French Teapot

Dark Green French Teapot

Beginning in 1935, Hall produced the French-shape teapot for Lipton in six different colors. The first teapots had a strainer on the inside at the start of the spout and were marked "Lipton Tea" on the bottom. Later teapots had no strainer and were marked "Lipton Tea Made in USA" on the bottom. The maroon color teapot has no matching sugar and creamer. The other five colors are dark green, light blue, mustard, black, and light yellow. These five colors all have matching color Boston-shape sugars and creamers.

Later, Lipton offered a "Cozy Cover" teapot as a premium. The teapot handles are shaped slightly different from the similar style teapot that Hall produced for Forman. Yellow has been the only color reported and these teapots are Marked "Hall" in a circle on the bottom. The ad to the right describes this new offer.

Lipton Teapot	Value
French-shape teapot	$40.00 – 65.00
"Cozy Cover" teapot	$35.00 – 45.00
Creamer, sugar, and lid	$35.00 – 45.00

Lipton Teapots

Hall produced large black institutional-size teapots with white embossed letters. Some of the lettering said "Lipton Tea" or "Lipton Iced Tea" as shown in the photo above. Also the embossed logos of other companies have been found on these teapots. Backstamps indicate these teapots were made for a long period. Teapots with older backstamps have been found in some long-established restaraunts and some with newer backstamps are still being used in some of the fast food chains.

Teapot	Value
Lipton embossed teapot	$300.00 – 350.00

London Teabob

Hall China produced a special teapot base for The American Teabob Company, maker of the "intelligent teapot." This teapot had a special metal tea basket, air tight float, and timing cup which allowed an individual to brew tea to a special taste.

In the first step the tea maker sets the time tube into the time cup for for an allowed steeping time of 3, 4, or 5 minutes. Then the tea leaves or tea bags are placed in the tea basket. The bobber is assembled and water is poured directly onto the tea leaves through the time cup. This allows the float to lift the tea basket and gauge the amount of water used. Next, the time cup is filled to submerge the tea basket. By infusion, the water steeps from the time cup through the time cup tube via the steep holes and into the perforated tea basket. As the water steeps from the time cup, the float bobs up and indicates when the tea is finished steeping.

An exact date of manufacture has not been determined. However, The American Teabob Company was founded in 1929 and indications are this teapot was produced between that date and the start of the Second World War. Colors of the teapot that have been found are stock brown and stock green.

London Teabob Teapot	Value
Stock Brown	$150.00 – 175.00
Stock Green	$150.00 – 175.00

London Teabob

Stock Green

Stock Brown

The Secret of Good Tea

London Teabob

AUTOMATICALLY BREWS PERFECT Tea

"As he brews
so shall he
drink"

TEA

"As You Like It"
ACT II. SCENE 1

AMERICAN TEABOB COMPANY
Sole Manufacturers
766-771 N. Water Street
MILWAUKEE, WISCONSIN

For Better Tea ～ THE LONDON TEABOB

WHAT IT IS

While the tea leaves are steeping the water flowing out of the time-cup measures the minutes—like the sand-glass of London Tea Tasters.

Just Start It

The hollow cylinder "A" is perforated, as indicated. An air-tight float "B" fits into the lower end of the cylinder "A" forming a tea-basket with a solid bottom and perforated sides and in this tea-basket the tea leaves are placed. The time-cup "C" is then fitted into the top of the tea-basket "A" and the three parts, thus joined in one, are inserted in the teapot.

How Much Tea?

In England, a level teaspoon of tea for each cup desired, is the rule. A famous food authority, Mr. Hutchinson, recommends: "One teaspoonful for each cup and one for the pot."

For the American taste the British measure may be too strong, but Britishers have often complained that Americans "do not put enough tea in the teapot" to make a good cup of tea.

In any event, with the LONDON TEABOB controlling the time of steeping and making it uniform—EVERY TIME—users find it easy to put in a quantity exactly suited to their taste.

Pour in the Boiling Water

As many cups of fresh boiling water as you wish to brew of tea are then poured directly onto the tea leaves, through the tube "D" in the center of the time-cup, letting the float lift the tea-basket, thus gauging the quantity of water poured in.

AND HOW IT WORKS

When the time-cup empties, the tea-basket rises automatically lifting the tea leaves out of the liquid and stopping the steeping.

Then fill the time-cup, which presses down the tea-basket and immerses the tea leaves. If the time-cup is filled first, it holds down the tea-basket and thus does not gauge the quantity of water poured in.

No Timing—No Watching

It will proceed to brew, BY INFUSION, the very best tea that can be made from the leaves, without requiring an instant's further attention from you.

In the bottom of the time-cup is a mathematically proportioned timing-vent, which controls the flow and allows the water in the time-cup to escape.

As long as any water remains in the cup, its weight holds the float at the bottom of the pot and keeps the leaves immersed and steeping in the near-boiling liquid.

At the instant of perfect infusion, the water has all escaped from the time-cup and the weight being removed, the float rises without any hand touching it—lifting the tea leaves out of the infusion and stopping the steeping.

To Serve—You Merely Pour

After the TEABOB rises, the tea is ready, and to serve, you merely pour, without removing the TEABOB, without bother of dripping tea-strainer, without need to time the steeping or to warm another teapot to pour off the liquid.

London Teabob Directions

*London Teabob
Showing Metal Accessories*

DIRECTIONS FOR USING

London Teabob

"The animated teamaker"

Nothing To Do But Start It. With the TEABOB you do not MAKE TEA — for the TEABOB makes tea for you. There is nothing to do but start it; and it is the simplest way of making the beverage perfectly. In fact cooking authorities call it a human impossibility to make the best tea ..., every time ... without the TEABOB.

Durability. The fireproof china ware will stand almost any heat, but pottery ware will crack or craze if exposed to heat more than that of boiling water.

Preventing Binding Its Action. The special shape of teapot in china or pottery tends to warp slightly in firing, so a metal collar keeps the tea-basket in vertical position for lifting freely. If not fitted so tightly it squeezes or binds the tea-basket and thus prevents it from lifting.

What It Is.

A perforated cylinder "A" with an air-float "B" fitting into the lower end, forms a tea-basket for the tea leaves. A timing-cup "C" at the top completes the tea-basket.

To Start It

Warm the teapot. Put a level teaspoonful of tea leaves into the tea-basket, as in (1), for each cup of tea. Join tea-basket with timing-cup, as in (2), and slip the joined parts into the teapot.

Pouring in the Boiling Water

As many cups of fresh, bubbling boiling water as you have allowed for are then poured into the timing-cup, as in (3), filling it, while the overflow runs thru the center tube "D" onto the tea leaves in basket.

To Measure the Water

If boiling water is poured from the kettle containing an unmeasured amount of water, pour it through center tube "D" as shown in (4), directly onto the tea leaves, gauging the quantity by the height the tea-basket rises before filling the timing-cup as in (3).

And How It Works

The TEABOB will brew, by infusion, the best tea that can be made from the tea leaves used, without requiring an instant's further attention from you for at the bottom of the timing-cup is a mathematically proportioned hole that allows the water in the timing-cup to escape. At the instant-of-Perfect-Infusion, the water has all escaped from the timing-cup and its weight being removed, the float rises lifting the tea leaves out of the liquid.

When to Serve

At any time after the tea-basket rises the tea is ready to pour, but if not served for five, ten or twenty minutes the infusion will remain the same well-balanced beverage. And each brewing will be of the same uniform flavor. No straining is required.

To Change the Timing

The center tube "D" of the time-cup "C" is tightly fitted onto the upturned rim in the bottom of the time-cup and need not be detached unless it is desired to change the timing from five minutes, at which it is first set, which is the time required to draw all the virtue from the leaf.

To reset, pull up the tube "D" to free it from the rim and replace it as shown in "5" so that the vent in the tube "D" registers with one of the vents in the rim of the time-cup, as indicated by the figures stamped opposite, i.e. 3-Min., 4-Min., 5-Min.

Cleansing

To clean, lift the tea-basket out of the teapot; slip the tea-cup and float out of the cylinder and place the cylinder and float under a faucet of running water, or otherwise wash off the tea leaves that cling to them. The parts may then be replaced in the teapot without drying them. Occasionally a little scouring powder may be lightly rubbed over the surface of the float and cylinder, which is all that is required to keep them clean.

(The tea trade, through long use of metal tea kettles, has found that new metal surfaces, before they become oxidized may affect flavor enough to be noticed by the most critical taste, but the third or fourth use as oxidizes the surface that it is completely immaterial and so remains if not scoured hard enough to scratch the oxidized surface.)

TEABOB, Inc., Sole Manufacturer, Milwaukee 3, Wisconsin

London Teabob Directions

333

Manning-Bowman Teapots

Hall produced an ivory, cobalt, and green vertical ribbed teapot for Manning-Bowman. The teapot was enclosed in a hinged chrome cover that slid over the top. The hinged top provided easy access to the lid and the chrome cover had areas cut out for the handle and spout. Examples of these metal covered teapots are not as easily found as the similar style Lipton or Forman Family teapots.

Manning-Bowman Teapot	Value
White teapot with chrome cover	$55.00 – 65.00
Green teapot with chrome cover	$60.00 – 70.00
Cobalt teapot with chrome cover	$70.00 – 80.00

Martin Million Dollar Coffee pots

Million Dollar Coffee Pot Backstamp

Hall produced the Million Dollar Coffee Pot exclusively for the F. S. Martin Company of Chicago, Illinois. The backstamp is illustrated in the photo above and indicates the coffee pot retailed for $1.95. Known colors include green, red, blue, black, and tan iridized with silver decoration.

Million Dollar Coffee Pot	*Value*
Black	$80.00 – 95.00
Blue	$150.00 – 180.00
Green	$140.00 – 160.00
Red	$200.00 – 225.00
Tan iridized with silver decoration	$182.00 – 210.00

The McCormick teapots were made by Hall China as a premium item for the McCormick Tea Company. Hall had a very long working relationship with McCormick. The first McCormick teapots were made in a dark brown color about 1916. A number of different McCormick teapots were made over the next 75 years. The last McCormick teapots made by Hall China were produced in the early 1990s. Recently, McCormick teapots have been made in China. These teapots are marked, "McCormick Tea and Spice Co. Made in China."

Early teapots, made before 1930, include a Mahogany teapot, Mahogany with gold decoration and a dark brown color with the gold French Flower design. The white base of these teapots is normally embossed "McCORMICK & Co. TEAS, BALTIMORE, MARYLAND."

In the early 1930s Hall introduced the No. 5106 (Bru-O-lator) McCormick infusor teapot. The earliest color was green and white with silver trim. Turquoise teapots were introduced in 1938 and cadet, maroon, and brown were made in the early 1940s. Pastel colors such as light blue, yellow, and pink were popular from the 1950s through the 1970s. Colors in the 1980s included white, light blue, and yellow. When production of this teapot ended in the early 1990s the colors in production were brown and cadet.

Other known colors for this teapot include, green, black, Golden Glo, and Coral Peach. The most commonly found colors are maroon, turquoise, light blue, and stock brown.

A few older McCormick teapots have been reported with a lid which locks into the infusor. In this teapot, the lid completely conceals the infusor when it is in place, and both the lid and infusor are removed from the teapot as one piece. The body of these teapots also differs slightly from a normal McCormick. There is a built-in strainer at the tip of the spout and the lid has a loop handle rather than a knob.

A two-cup size teapot with a large raised "Mc" on the side was made in 1950. Stock green and turquoise appear to be the usual colors. What appears to be a much earlier version of this teapot without the letters on the side has been found in a brown color.

Other teapots made by Hall for McCormick include the giant two gallon institutional teapots. These were made in several styles, in a few different colors and with several logo variations. Giant teapots have been found in black, maroon, brown, and cobalt. The most common logo is "McCormick" in large white letters on the side of the teapot. However, some of the brown teapots will have the "Banquet Tea" logo.

In 1982, Hall produced a white teapot with "YE OLD McCORMICK TEA HOUSE" pictured on the side of the teapot. Matching cups and saucers were also made.

McCormick Institutional Teapots	Value
Black with "McCormick" logo	$400.00 – 500.00
Cobalt with "McCormick" logo	$600.00 – 850.00

McCormick Institutional Teapots	Value
Maroon with "McCormick" logo	$500.00 – 650.00
Brown with "Banquet Tea" logo	$400.00 – 450.00

White Teapot with Green Band and Silver Trim

Golden Glo Teapot with White Infusor

White Teapot with Orchid Band and Silver Trim

Golden Glo Sugar & Lid

Golden Glo Creamer

Light Yellow Teapot with White Infusor

Mahogany Teapot with Gold Decoration

Light Blue Teapot with White Infusor

Turquoise 2-cup Teapot

Stock Green 2-cup Teapot

Swedish Brown 2-cup Teapot

McCormick Backstamp

1982 Cup & Saucer

1982 McCormick Teapot

McCormick 6-cup Teapots	Value	McCormick 6-cup Teapots	Value
Black	$40.00 – 45.00	White with green band	$45.00 – 55.00
Brown	$35.00 – 40.00	White with orchid band	$125.00 – 150.00
Mahogany with gold decoration	$85.00 – 95.00	Yellow	$85.00 – 95.00
Brown with gold French Flower		White	$30.00 – 35.00
decoration	$200.00 – 250.00	White with McCormick House decal	$130.00 – 150.00
Golden Glo	$140.00 – 160.00	**McCormick 2-cup Teapots**	*Value*
Light blue	$85.00 – 95.00	Brown without logo	$75.00 – 95.00
Maroon	$45.00 – 55.00	Stock green with logo	$120.00 – 150.00
Pink	$75.00 – 85.00	Turquoise with logo	$125.00 – 140.00
Turquoise	$40.00 – 50.00	Golden Glo creamer & sugar	$45.00 – 55.00

Teamaster Teapots

Different shapes of teapots which Hall produced for the Teamaster Company are shown in the photographs on the next page.

The Teataster is an oval, two-compartment teapot which was made for Teamaster in the forties. Most of the teapots are plain, but a few will be found with gold decoration. The backstamp states "TEAMASTER, MADE BY HALL IN U.S.A."

Twinspouts are round two-compartment teapots produced for the Teamaster Company. The teapots are usually marked "TWINSPOUT, TEAMASTER, Pat. No. 2135410." Twinspouts will be found with gold decoration

and some have been found with sterling silver overlay. The later teapots of this shape will be marked "INVENTO PRODUCTS."

Two different three-cup diamond-shape Twinspout teapots are pictured at the bottom of the photo. These are also two-compartment teapots. The Alma has a rounded handle and pointed pour spouts. The Irvine has a square handle and round pour spouts. Both were made for Teamaster and have the same backstamp as the Twinspouts above. We have not seen this teapot decorated.

Teataster Teapot	Solid Color	Gold Decorated	Twinspout Teapot	Solid Color	Gold Decorated
Black	$70.00 – 80.00	$90.00 – 100.00	Black	$60.00 – 70.00	$80.00 – 90.00
Cadet	$80.00 – 90.00	$100.00 – 120.00	Cadet	$70.00 – 80.00	$100.00 – 110.00
Canary	$80.00 – 90.00	$100.00 – 120.00	Canary	$70.00 – 80.00	$100.00 – 110.00
Chinese Red	$220.00 – 250.00		Chinese Red	$220.00 – 250.00	
Cobalt	$140.00 – 160.00	$160.00 – 180.00	Cobalt	$120.00 – 140.00	$130.00 – 150.00
Emerald	$110.00 – 120.00	$125.00 – 140.00	Emerald	$90.00 – 100.00	$115.00 – 125.00
Ivory	$40.00 – 50.00	$60.00 – 70.00	Ivory	$50.00 – 55.00	$50.00 – 60.00
Marine	$110.00 – 120.00	$160.00 – 180.00	Marine	$110.00 – 120.00	$120.00 – 140.00
Maroon	$110.00 – 120.00	$160.00 – 180.00	Maroon	$90.00 – 100.00	$120.00 – 130.00
Orchid		$350.00 – 400.00	Turquoise	$80.00 – 90.00	$100.00 – 120.00
Turquoise	$80.00 – 90.00	$100.00 – 120.00	Warm Yellow	$80.00 – 90.00	$100.00 – 120.00
Warm Yellow	$80.00 – 90.00	$100.00 – 120.00			

With Rockwell silver overlay, $220.00 – 250.00.
"Invento Products" backstamp, $40.00 – 45.00.

Alma 3-cup Teapot	Value	Irvine 3-cup Teapot	Value
Black	$180.00 – 200.00	Black	$180.00 – 200.00
Canary	$190.00 – 210.00	Canary	$200.00 – 220.00
Chinese Red	$280.00 – 320.00	Chinese Red	$280.00 – 320.00
Cobalt	$220.00 – 250.00	Cobalt	$220.00 – 250.00
Light Blue	$190.00 – 210.00	Light Blue	$200.00 – 220.00
Maroon	$200.00 – 220.00	Maroon	$210.00 – 230.00
Turquoise	$200.00 – 220.00	Turquoise	$210.00 – 230.00

Orchid Teataster

Turquoise Teataster

Canary Teataster with Gold Band

Cobalt Twinspout

Chinese Red Twinspout

Cobalt Twinspout with Silver Overlay

Ivory Twinspout

Canary Twinspout with Gold Band

Emerald Green Twinspout

Maroon Irvine

Turquoise Alma

Canary Alma

Warm Yellow Twinspout

Chinese Red Alma

Maroon Alma

Light Blue Alma

Tricolator Coffee Pots

POUR RIGHT
TRICOLATOR POT
U.S. Pat. No. 1663317

DEC T 148.

Emerald Green "Amory"

Cadet Blue "Amory"

Warm Yellow "Amory"

Art Glaze Yellow "Ansel"

Indian Red "Ansel"

Iridescent Tan "Blossom" with Silver Floral Decoration

Red "Blossom"

Orchid "Blossom"

Stock Green "Blossom"

Marine "Blossom"

Hall produced numerous pots for Tricolator. They may usually be identified through their backstamps. Many times "HALL" is embossed in the bottom in large block letters along with the words "Tricolator" or "Pour Right." Some of the shapes made for Tricolator are also being found with just the Hall mark.

Most of the Tricolator coffee pots are being found in more than one color and some have been found with decals. The Carraway has also been found in several sizes and with both a long and a short spout. It is pictured on the next page in different colors and with enamel decoration.

The coffee pot shape pictured on page 342 that most collectors have been calling "Coffee Queen," actually has different names depending upon the size of the pot. According to packing information enclosed with the coffee pots, the name of the four-cup size is Princess; the six-cup size is Coffee Queen; the eight-cup is Empress. All sizes may be found in seven colors.

The "Diver" has been found with several different decals. The shape of this teapot is very similar to the "Dutch" that Hall produced for the Forman Family.

Tricolator Coffee Pot	Value
"Amory"	$50.00 – 65.00
"Ansel"	$90.00 – 125.00
"Blossom," common color	$50.00 – 60.00

Tricolator Coffee Pot	Value
"Blossom," red or dark blue	$90.00 – 120.00
"Blossom," orchid	$220.00 – 250.00
"Blossom," tan iridized with silver	$120.00 – 140.00

"Buchanan" "Floral Spray" Decal

Marine "Buchanan" Showing Screw-lock Lid

Red "Buchanan"

Delphinium "Buchanan"

Warm Yellow Short Spout "Carraway"

Warm Yellow "Buchanan"

6 Cup Warm Yellow "Carraway"

Marine Long Spout "Carraway"

6 Cup Red "Carraway"

Warm Yellow Long Spout "Carraway"

Tricolator Coffee Pots and Teapots

Red Long Spout "Carraway

Marine Short Spout "Carraway"

"Carraway" with Hand Painted "Butterfly Garden" Design

Tricolator Coffee Pot	Value
"Buchanan" with "Floral Sprig" decal	$80.00 – 90.00
"Buchanan," solid color	$50.00 – 80.00
"Carraway," 4-cup red or blue	$100.00 – 120.00
"Carraway," 4-cup yellow	$70.00 – 80.00

Tricolator Coffee Pot	Value
"Carraway," 4-cup with hand-painted decoration	$140.00 – 160.00
"Carraway," 6-cup red or blue	$120.00 – 160.00
"Carraway," 6-cup yellow	$90.00 – 110.00

Coffee Empress

Tricolator Backstamp

Coffee Queen

Coffee Princess

Royal Family Series

Orginal packing information that came with this series of coffee pots referred to the four cup size as the Princess. The six cup size was the Coffee Queen. amd the eight cup size was called the Empress. All sizes came in seven different colors.

Crown Coffee Pots

Cobalt

Stock Green

Stock Brown

Tricolator Coffee Pot	Value	Tricolator Coffee Pot	Value
Photo Above:		"Diver," Floral Vase decal	$70.00 – 80.00
Coffee Empress, 8-cup	$40.00 – 50.00	"Diver," Rose Spray decal	$70.00 – 80.00
Coffee Queen, 6-cup	$30.00 – 40.00	"Hoyt," Floral Bouquet decal	$85.00 – 95.00
Coffee Princess, 4-cup	$30.00 – 40.00	"Hoyt," Oriental Bird decal	$140.00 – 160.00
Crown, cobalt	$50.00 – 60.00	"Hoyt," solid colors	$60.00 – 80.00
Crown, stock brown or green	$30.00 – 40.00	"Imperial," floral decals	$60.00 – 70.00
		"Imperial," bottom only	$45.00 – 55.00
Photo Next Page:		"Imperial," with china dripper	$200.00 – 250.00
"Dave"	$110.00 – 130.00	"Imperial," with metal dripper	$50.00 – 65.00
"Diver," Art Deco decoration	$110.00 – 125.00		

Marine "Dave"

"Dave" Screw-lock Lid

"Diver" with Floral Vine Decoration

"Diver" with Art Deco Decoration

Tricolator Coffee Pots

"Diver" with Rose Spray Decal

"Hoyt" with Floral Bouquet Decal

"Hoyt with Oriential Bird Decal

Warm Yellow "Hoyt"

Chinese Red "Imperial" All China Coffee Pot

Stock Green "Hoyt"

"Imperial" with Floral Decal

Yellow "Imperial" All China Coffee Pot

Marine "Imperial" Coffee Pot

Lettuce Green "Imperial" Coffe Pot with Metal Dripper and China Lid

Stock Green "Imperial" Coffee Pot

"Imperial" with Orange and Yellow Floral Spray Decal

343

Pink "Lincoln"   Warm Yellow "Lincoln"   Cadet "Lincoln"   Chinese Red "Ritz"

"Ritz" with Red and Silver "Panel and Rib" Decoration   Cobalt "Steve"   "Steve" Non-Drip Backstamp

"Ritz" with "Berries" Decal

"Ritz" with "Floral Sprig and Panel" Decoration   Green "Wellman"   Cadet "Steve" and Screw-lock Lid

Chinese Red "Wellman"   Cobalt "Wellman"   Stock Brown "Wilson"

Tricolator Coffee Pots

The "Ritz" coffee pot has been found with several different decal decorations and with combinations of colored and silver trim. This teapot is also sometimes found with just the "HALL" backstamp.

The "Wilson" coffee pot is very similar to the "Crown." The most obvious difference is the "Crown" has a scalloped base. Both coffee pots are found most often in stock brown and stock green. The "Crown" has also been found with the "HALL" backstamp with the gold French Flower decoration.

Tricolator Coffee Pot	Value
"Lincoln," cobalt or red	$90.00 – 110.00
"Lincoln," pastel colors	$55.00 – 65.00
"Ritz," Berries decal	$110.00 – 130.00
"Ritz," cobalt or red	$120.00 – 140.00
"Ritz," Floral Sprig and Panel decoration	$90.00 – 100.00
"Ritz," pastel colors	$50.00 – 60.00
"Ritz," Red and Silver Panel and Rib decoration	$95.00 – 110.00

Tricolator Coffee Pot	Value
"Steve," cobalt or red	$90.00 – 110.00
"Steve," pastel colors	$70.00 – 80.00
"Wellman," cobalt or red	$90.00 – 110.00
"Wellman," green or brown	$30.00 – 40.00
"Wilson," cobalt or red	$50.00 – 60.00
"Wilson," brown or green	$30.00 – 40.00

Westinghouse

"Hanging Vine" Urn   "Hanging Vine" Percolator   Cattail Percolator   Cattail Urn

"Hanging Vine" Sugar   Cattail Sugar   Cattail Creamer and Sugar

Westinghouse added the metal and electrical fixtures to the china percolator and coffee urn bodies produced by Hall. Two of the more successful patterns were Cattail and Hanging Vine. Today, the Cattail pattern is more desirable since it matches the popular Cattail dinnerware pattern produced by Universal.

Item	Value
Coffee urn, Cattail	$110.00 – 130.00
Coffee urn, Hanging Vine	$55.00 – 70.00
Creamer, Cattail	$22.00 – 25.00
Creamer, Hanging Vine	$9.00 – 11.00
Electric Percolator, Cattail	$110.00 – 130.00
Electric Percolator, Hanging Vine	$55.00 – 70.00
Sugar and lid, Cattail	$25.00 – 30.00
Sugar and lid, Hanging Vine	$12.00 – 15.00

Pretzel Jar

Flagon Mug

Abbey Meal Decal

Flagon Mug

Tankard Pitcher

Flagon Mug

Flagon Mug

Monk Decal

Tankard Pitcher

Pretzel Jar

Beer sets may be found in plain solid colors, with silver overlay, or with decals. Basic sets consist of a tankard and six matching mugs. Decal sets will have three right-handed and three left-handed mugs. The tankard is pictured here with the flagon shape mug. Another style, the barrel shape mug is sometimes found with these sets. The flagon is available in five sizes and the barrel mug comes in two sizes. Two different decals are shown — "Monk" and "Abbey Meal." Another decal depicting hunt scenes has been reported. A matching pretzel jar is also available for some decal sets.

Item	Solid colors	Decals
Tankard pitcher	$50.00 – 65.00	$125.00 – 140.00
Flagon, 8, 10, 12, 14, 16 oz.	$8.00 – 9.00	$30.00 – 35.00
Barrel mug, 8, 12 oz.	$7.00 – 9.00	
Pretzel jar	$60.00 – 75.00	$110.00 – 135.00

Punch Sets

No. 3046 Mug

Plum Pudding 8 Quart Tom & Jerry Bowl

Covered 5 Quart Tom & Jerry Bowl

No. 2044 Mug

5 Quart Covered Punch Bowl

No. 2044 Mug

Covered 5 Quart Tom & Jerry Bowl

Tom & Jerry

No. 3045 Mug

Footed 4 Quart Tom & Jerry Bowl

Old Crow Punch Set

The Old Crow punch set contains ten cups, a ladle, and a large elaborate advertising punch bowl. Initially these sets caused more excitement among collectors of advertising memorabilia than among Hall collectors. Some of the first sets were offered to collectors for as high as $450.00. However, the quantity of available sets has proven substantial. Therefore, prices of these sets have decreased to a reasonable level and more Hall collectors have become attracted to them.

Tom and Jerry sets were introduced in the thirties. They commonly had an ivory or Hi-black body, trimmed with gold. The covered bowls hold five quarts and were sold with the #2044 mug. The Plum Pudding bowl holds eight quarts and was sold with the No. 3046-7 oz. mugs. The footed bowl holds four quarts and was sold with the No. 3045-5 oz. mugs.

Bowl Style	Value
Plum Pudding, black or ivory	$60.00 – 75.00
Plum Pudding, Chinese Red	$180.00 – 200.00
Covered 5 quart, black or ivory	$90.00 – 110.00
Covered 5 quart, Chinese Red	$220.00 – 250.00
No. 2044 mug, black or ivory	$5.00 – 7.00
No. 2044 mug, Chinese Red	$9.00 – 11.00
No. 3045-5oz. mug, black or ivory	$6.00 – 8.00
No. 3046-7 oz mug, black or ivory	$6.00 – 8.00
No. 3046-7oz, mug, Chinese Red	$10.00 – 13.00
Old Crow punch bowl	$130.00 – 150.00
Old Crow Punch cup	$4.00 – 5.00
Old Crow punch set in original box	$180.00 – 210.00

AAA Mugs

The mugs at the top of the next page are examples of the style of mug that was made for the Ohio Automobile Association. These mugs were made from 1971 through 1981. Each year a different vintage auto was illustrated. With the exception of the 1975 mug, which was made by McCoy, all the mugs were made by Hall China.

Mug	Auto	Value
1971	1902 Ford Runabout	$7.00 – 9.00
1972	1903 Oldsmobile	$7.00 – 9.00
1973	1904 Packard Tunneau	$7.00 – 9.00
1974	1905 Prince Stanhope	$7.00 – 9.00
1975 (McCoy)	1906 White Limousine	$5.00 – 7.00
1976	1907 Studebaker Garford	$7.00 – 9.00
1977	1908 Cartercar Roadster	$7.00 – 9.00
1978	1909 White	$7.00 – 9.00
1979	1910 Hupmobile	$7.00 – 9.00
1980	1911 Empire	$7.00 – 9.00
1981	1912 Thomas	$7.00 – 9.00

Miscellaneous Mugs

Hall flagons, barrel, and tankard style mugs have been made for many years. Some may be found decorated with matching beer tankards. Others were made with advertising for various restaurants and clubs. The mugs in the center of the picture on the next page are examples of some of the different mugs produced.

Mug	Value
Flagon with Irish Setter	$20.00 – 25.00
Flagon with Bird Dog	$20.00 – 25.00
Flagon with Pheasant	$18.00 – 20.00
Tankard, red Fox and Hounds	$20.00 – 25.00
Flagon, German Polka	$18.00 – 22.00

Temperance Mugs

These four eight ounce pro-temperance mugs may have been produced for the Prohibition Party in 1934. All four mugs contain slogans denouncing the repeal of prohibition. The identity of two of the characters seems certain. One is Carry Nation, a noted temperance leader around the turn of the century. The mug with the caricature of Carry Nation asks the question, "Must I start all over again?" The figure with the mustache is probably Congressman Andrew Volstead of Minnesota who was instrumental in engineering the passage of the National Prohibition Act. His comment is, "They surely crabbed my act." The other two figures are still unidentified, although they may have been prominent members of the Prohibition Party. The figure in blue assures, "It will still be grape juice for me," and the smiling character in red admonishes, "I don't want it, you shouldn't have it."

Item	Value
Temperance Mug	UND

A number of different Hall lamps have been showing up. Identification of the lamps is difficult unless the paper label, which is usually in the shape of an Aladdin teapot, is still intact. Hall produced the china lamp bodies for other companies which added the metal bases and electrical fixtures.

Item	Value
Hall table lamp, solid color	$35.00 – 45.00
Hall table lamp, hand painted	$55.00 – 65.00
Hall table lamp, decal decoration	$45.00 – 55.00

Musical Little Brown Jug

According to the catalog information shown in the photo below, Hall made a musical little brown jug for Montgomery Ward in 1944. Although these jugs are not easily found at the present time, more may surface when collectors realize they exist and begin to look for them.

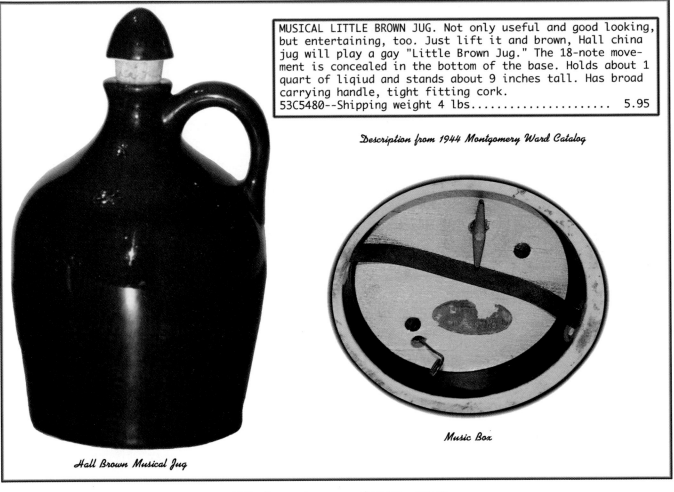

MUSICAL LITTLE BROWN JUG. Not only useful and good looking, but entertaining, too. Just lift it and brown, Hall china jug will play a gay "Little Brown Jug." The 18-note movement is concealed in the bottom of the base. Holds about 1 quart of liqiud and stands about 9 inches tall. Has broad carrying handle, tight fitting cork.
53C5480--Shipping weight 4 lbs..................... 5.95

Description from 1944 Montgomery Ward Catalog

Music Box

Hall Brown Musical Jug

Little Brown Jug $80.00 – 90.00

Watering Cans

The Hall watering can, which was produced in the early 1930s, is pictured here in some very striking colors. This early 1930s piece is very hard to find and information is not extensive at this time, but cadet is the color most frequently found. The citrus color appears to be the least common.

Cadet   *Orchid*   *Citrus*

Watering can $450.00 – 500.00

Children's Items

Hall produced a number of items with children's decals for use of small children. A cereal bowl and divided plate are shown in the picture below.

No. 391 1/2 Cereal Bowl

Square Divided Plate

Cereal bowl	$35.00 – 45.00
Divided plate	$120.00 – 150.00

Eljer Bathroom Set

Hall made a four-piece bath set for Eljer in the 1970s. We have seen these pieces in ivory and maroon, but other colors may have been made.

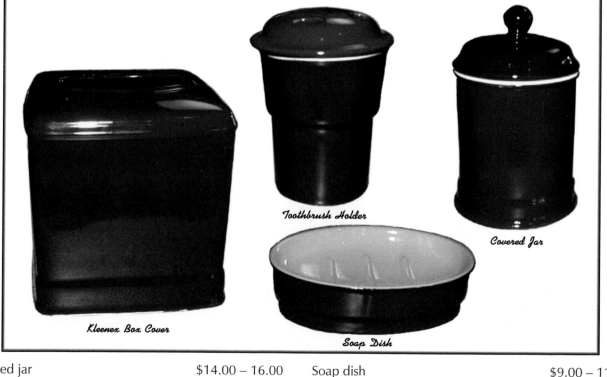

Toothbrush Holder

Covered Jar

Kleenex Box Cover

Soap Dish

Covered jar	$14.00 – 16.00	Soap dish	$9.00 – 11.00
Kleenex box cover	$20.00 – 25.00	Toothbrush holder	$12.00 – 15.00

Promotional Products

Hall China has produced many promotional pieces for private companies through the years. Since Hall China is primarily a hand operation, its facilities are easily adaptable to the special needs of its individual customers.

Therefore, many items of this nature are still being made. Collectors should be aware the Sanka set and several other promotional pieces which were originally produced by Hall have been reproduced in Japan.

Item	Value
Row 1:	
Jug, Riviera "Schenley"	$35.00 – 45.00
Jug, "Teacher's"	$25.00 – 30.00
Coffee pot, Washington "Dahlia Society"	$35.00 – 45.00
Teapot, Philadelphia "Ohio Music Association"	$40.00 – 45.00
Row 2:	
Jug, Seagram's	$22.00 – 27.00
Jug, Vat 69	$20.00 – 22.00
Coffee pot, Sanka	$20.00 – 25.00
Mug, Sanka	$5.00 – 7.00
Vase, Edgewater	$16.00 – 18.00

Item	Value
Row 3:	
Teapot, New York "21 Club"	$100.00 – 125.00
Bowl, Kraft Cheese with china lid*	$185.00 – 225.00
Decanter and display stand, "I. W. Harper"	$125.00 – 145.00
Teapot, Cube with advertisement	$55.00 – 65.00

*Without china lid, $20.00 – 25.00.

Miscellaneous Items

Hall produced a variety of items for airlines, hotels, and restaurants. Some of these items are shown on the next two pages.

Hotel Items	Value
Row 1: U. S. Grant ice bucket	$25.00 – 30.00
Palmer House ashtray	$15.00 – 20.00
U. S. Grant Tray	$15.00 – 18.00
Regency Hotel butter pat	$5.00 – 6.00
Palmer House ashtray	$12.00 – 14.00
Row 2: Brown Palace ashtray	$10.00 – 12.00
Ashtray	$12.00 – 15.00
Turquoise gold decorated spittoon	$25.00 – 35.00
Cobalt gold decorated spittoon	$30.00 – 40.00

Airline Items	Value
Pan American Ashtray	$27.00 – 32.00
United Airlines serving dish	$12.00 – 15.00
Braniff International mug	$5.50 – 6.50

Miscellaneous Vases	Value
Maroon trumpet vase	$18.00 – 20.00
Cadet trumpet vase	$15.00 – 18.00
Turquoise #641 advertising vase	$18.00 – 20.00
Daffodil bud vase	$12.00 – 14.00

Miscellaneous Ashtrays	Value
Row 1: Cobalt ashtray, #696	$7.00 – 8.00
Cobalt ashtray	$10.00 – 12.00
Ashtray with matchholder	$12.00 – 15.00
Row 2: Emerald ashtray with matchholder	$12.00 – 15.00
Cobalt ashtray with matchholder	$12.00 – 15.00
Cobalt ashtray with matchholder	$9.00 – 11.00
Row 3: Cadet round flared ashtray	$10.00 – 12.00
21 Club ashtray	$100.00 – 125.00
Warm Yellow #679 ashtray	$6.00 – 7.00

Miscellaneous Mugs	Value
Black satin #2274 footed mug	$6.00 – 8.00
Cadet #1270 Turkish coffee cup	$6.00 – 8.00
Chinese red #1314 cylindrical mug	$12.00 – 14.00
Chinese red 8 oz. barrel mug	$12.00 – 14.00

Items pictured on page 356	Value
Black coffee urn (Drip-O-lator)	$85.00 – 100.00
Maroon coffee urn (Drip-O-lator)	$100.00 – 125.00
Round 2-quart casserole with Red Riding Hood style decal	$35.00 – 45.00
Keen's Plum Pudding bowl with Red Riding Hood style decal	$35.00 – 45.00
Large black "The Long Expected Iced Tea" dispenser	$350.00 – 450.00

Items pictured on page 356	Value
Gold Dot carafe	$85.00 – 95.00
Gold Dot creamer	$15.00 – 18.00
Brown glaze 15½" bowl	$35.00 – 45.00
Swedish Brown hot pot prototype	UND
Gold clad Edgewater vase	$35.00 – 45.00

Hotel Items

US Grant Hotel Ice Bucket

Palmer House Ashtray

US Grant Tray

Regency Hotel

Palmer House Ashtray

Brown Palace Ashtray

Hotel Ashtray

Gold Decorated Spittoons

Airline Items

Serving Dish

Ashtray

Mug

Miscellaneous Ashtrays

Hard to Find 21 Club Ashtray

Miscellaneous Vases

Miscellaneous Mugs

Drip-O-lator Coffee Urns

Round Autumn Leaf Style Casserole

Keen's Small Advertising Bowl

Red Riding Hood Style Decal on Hall Items

Large Ice Tea Dispenser

The Long Expected ICED TEA

Gold Dot Carafe and Creamer

Bowl Backstamp

15 1/2" Large Bowl

Brown Glaze Hall

Prototype for Hall Hotpot

Gold Clad Edgewater Vase with Floral Decoration

REISSUES AND NEW PRODUCTS
Autumn Leaf Produced for Jewel

In 1976, Jewel discontinued the sale of Hall's Autumn Leaf to allow the Hall China Company to produce sufficient inventory to enable Jewel to fill orders on a timely basis. Production at Hall continued on the 13" platter, the 10" dinner plate, the 5½" fruit dish, the coupe soup bowl, the 7¼" salad plate, and the oval vegetable bowl. In 1978, Jewel announced plans for a major promotion involving those eight pieces which had remained in production and added four discontinued pieces. The additional pieces were the Newport teapot, the cake plate, the two-handle bean pot, and the three-piece mixing bowl set. All pieces made by Hall after August of 1978, were to have a new backstamp which included the "1978" date. However, all pieces of stock produced and stored in the warehouses prior to this date were to be sold in the promotion without the new mark. Old supplies of everything but the Newport teapot were on hand. However, production problems continued to plague Hall and the proposed special promotion was cancelled in mid-1979. Therefore, much of the production with both the old and new marks was disposed of by Jewel in the sale promoted by the poster below. Jewel is no longer selling Autumn Leaf china and the remaining stock was sold through the Hall Closet (Hall's outlet store at the factory location). Today, there is very little price difference between Autumn Leaf with the old or new mark.

Item	Jewel's Price in 1979
Bean pot	$17.00
Bowl set, 3-pc	$22.00
Bowl, 5½"	$2.00
Bowl, oval	$12.00
Cake plate	$12.00
Cup	$3.00
Plate, 10"	$5.00
Plate, 7¼"	$3.50
Saucer	$2.00

National Autumn Leaf Collectors Club Items

The Hall China Company also produced special pieces of china with the Autumn Leaf decal for members of the National Autumn Leaf Collectors Club. Members are entitled to buy these special club offerings, and the number produced is limited to the number ordered. Initially members were allowed to order two of the New York teapots. Then for a few years, issues were limited to one item per member. More recently, all members have been allowed to order five of the special club items. These pieces have a special backstamp which identifies them as items made for the NALCC. The following photos show many of the items which have been produced.

National Autumn Leaf Collectors Club Item	Number Produced	Original Price	Current Value
New York teapot (1986)	536	$23.00	$600.00 – 700.00
Edgewater vase (1987)	626	$16.00	$275.00 – 325.00
Candleholder, pr. (1989)	892 pr.	$21.00	$225.00 – 250.00
Philadelphia tea set (1990)	1,150	$60.00	$250.00 – 300.00
Tea-for-Two set (1990)	1,300	$45.00	$200.00 – 225.00
Sugar packet holder (1990)	1,712	Gift*	$95.00 – 110.00
Solo teapot (1991)	1,400	**	$100.00 – 125.00
Donut jug (1991)	1,400	**	$110.00 – 130.00
French teapot (1992)	1,500	***	$95.00 –110.00
Baby Ball jug (1992)	1,500	***	$85.00 – 100.00
Punch bowl, 12-cups (1992)	1,148	$160.00	$250.00 – 325.00
Donut teapot (1993)	2,008	$45.00	$125.00 – 150.00
Cream jug (1996)		****	

*These items were given free to members as a Christmas gift from the club.

**The large casserole, Solo teapot, and Donut jug were only offered to members as a set; $100.00 per set.

***The French teapot, Baby Ball jug, and a set of four chocolate mugs were included in a package that cost members $115.00 per set.

**** A free cream jug/toothpick holder was sent to every member of record as of January 1, 1996.

In addition to the items pictured, other items produced for the NALCC may find their way into collectors' hands. One item is an oyster cup which was made for members who attended the 1992 NALCC annual meeting. There were 360 of these oyster cups made. Other items which may surface are sample pieces which Hall provides to the club officers who ultimately decide whether to accept or reject the piece for official production for the membership.

Collectors who are interested in Autumn Leaf should consider becoming members of the National Autumn Leaf Collectors Club. Besides meeting and becoming friends with other members who are interested in the same collectible, other benefits include the opportunity to keep up with new developments and to buy, sell, and trade extra pieces. Currently membership is $20.00 per year. Checks should be made out to the NALCC and may be sent to Patti Byerly, 4514 Errington Road, Columbus, Ohio, 43227.

Donut Teapot

Solo Teapot

Donut Jug

Baby Ball Jug

Candlesticks

Philadelphia
Sugar
and Creamer

Philadelphia Teapot

Sugar Packet Holder

Punch Bowl
Shown with 6
of 12 Cups

Edgewater Vase

Tea for Two Set

French Teapot

New York Teapot

Creamer

*National
Autumn Leaf
Collectors Club
Items*

Bird Cage Teapot
5 Band Syrup
Chocolate Mug
Basketball Teapot
Handled Candlesticks
Large Oval Casserole
Nautilus Teapot

National Autumn Leaf Collectors Club Items

National Autumn Leaf Collectors Club Item	Number Produced	Original Price	Current Value
Candleholder, handled (1991)	2,100	Gift*	$110.00 – 125.00
Casserole (1991)	1,400	**	$120.00 – 145.00
Chocolate mug (1992)	1,500		$25.00 – 30.00
Nautilus teapot (1998)	4,375		$100.00 – 125.00
Basketball teapot (1998)			$120.00 – 150.00
Birdcage teapot (1995)		$60.00	$200.00 – 225.00
"Five Band" syrup (1994)			$90.00 – 100.00
Items Not Pictured			
Watering Can (1996)			$120.00 – 150.00
Espresso cups, 4 per set (1998), ea.			$20.00 – 25.00
Washington coffee pot (1999)			$100.00 – 125.00
T-ball square teapot (2000)			
Zepyhr water bottle (2000)			

*These items were given free to members as a Christmas gift from the club.
**Only offered to members as a set along with the Solo teapot and the Donut jug, $100.00 per set.

China Specialties Autumn Leaf Items

Another source of new Autumn Leaf items produced by Hall China is China Specialties. This private company has commissioned Hall and Libbey to produce limited edition items which were not made in the original production. With a few exceptions, all items are marked with a special backstamp which identifies their origin. The Airflow teapot was the first item produced for China Specialties and will not be found from the Jewel production era. The array of backstamps found on this teapot may result in some confusion among dealers and collectors. To our knowledge there are five different possibilities:

1. No backstamp.
2. Round Hall stamp under glaze in dark ink.
3. Square Hall stamp under glaze in dark ink.
4. Gold stamp "Hall Made in U.S.A."
5. Round Hall stamp in gold.

Other china pieces produced by Hall for China Specialties will generally have one of the following two backstamps:

1. Square Hall mark along with the year of manufacture.
2. Square Hall mark, the year of manufacture, and the words "China Specialties Exclusive Limited Edition."

A mistake was made at Hall China on the backstamps of some of the condiment sets produced for China Specialties in 1991. Some of the condiment jars were released with the following backstamp: "Made Especially for the Autumn Leaf Club by Hall China Company." Although an attempt was made to recall the jars with this mark, it was not entirely successful. None of the shakers which complete this set will have any identifying mark. Be aware that the teardrop shape shaker was not made by Hall for Jewel.

Batter Bowl (1996)

Clock (1996)

China Specialties Autumn Leaf Items

Hurrican Lamp (1994)

Memo Board (1992)

Demitasse Cup (1994)

Autumn Leaf Collectors Sign

China Specialties Autumn Leaf	Number Produced	Original Price	Current Value
Hurricane lamp (1994)		$27.50	$49.95
Memo board (1992)	615	*	$65.00
Batter bowl (1996)		$49.95	$69.95
Clock (1996)	1,699	$49.95	$89.95
Demitasse cup (1994)		$79.95 set of 4	$25.00
Display sign (1993)		$14.95	$18.95

*The memo board was offered with a deck of poker cards for $49.95 and with a deck of pinochle cards for $59.95.

361

China Specialties Autumn Leaf Photo Page 363:	Number Produced	Original Price	Current Value
Bean pot, 2½ pt. (1993)	1,550	$49.95	$175.00 – 200.00
Pretzel jar (1998)	1,500	$89.95	$89.95
Ashtray (1992)	200	Premium Gift	$125.00
Safety style ashtray (1992)	1,179	$30.00	$60.00 – 65.00
Spoon rest (1997)		$39.95	$39.95
Beer pitcher (1993)	1,500	$69.95	$300.00
Onion soup bowl (1992)	1,200	$25.00*	$40.00 – 50.00
Fort Pitt baker, 8 oz. (1993)		$16.95	$19.95
Display sign (1993)		$14.95	$18.95
Relish, 10½" (1993)	1,200	$22.00	$65.00
Shirley bell (1998)	1,200	$44.95	$89.95
Graeter shape bud vase (1995)	1,225	$27.50	$49.95
Prayer board** (1992)	1,000	$35.00	$35.00
Sherbet, set of 4 (1992)	1,400	$39.95	$125.00
Conic mug, set of 4 (1991)	600	$65.80	$180.00
Fluted shakers (1994)	1,650	$25.00	$39.95
Irish coffee mug (1991)	1,700	$22.50***	$45.00

*Could be purchased in a set of four for $89.95.

**The prayer board was originally offered in 1992 as a plain board along with a deck of playing cards.

***Could be purchased in a set of four for $79.95.

China Specialties Autumn Leaf Photo Page 364:	Number Produced	Original Price	Current Value
Airflow teapot (1990)	1,999	$49.95	$200.00 – 225.00
Automobile teapot (1993)	1,573	$79.95	$600.00 – 650.00
Windshield teapot (1999)		$89.95	$89.95
Hook Cover teapot (1994)	1,650	$49.95	$100.00 – 120.00
Baby Melody teapot (1995)	1,599	$39.95	$49.95
Boston sugar creamer & tray (1996)		$89.95	$89.95
Football teapot (1995)	1,399	$69.95	$99.95
Musical teapot (1998)	1,699	$89.95	$110.00 – 125.00
Reamer (1993)	1,550	$59.95	$250.00 – 300.00
Round butter (1995)	1,599	$49.95	$110.00 – 125.00
St. Louis chocolate pot (1994)	1,700	$39.95	$90.00 – 100.00
Condiment set, 3-pc. (1991)	1,500	$49.95	$100.00 – 125.00
Harriet candles (1997)		$49.95 pair	$49.95
Norris water jug (1991)	1,500	$69.95	$150.00
Giant ice tea dispenser (1995)	299	$695.00	$900.00 – 1,000.00
Bud vase (1991)	950	$30.00	$100.00

Items Not Pictured			
Utensil crock (1996)	900	$39.95	$130.00 – 150.00

One Handled Bean Pot (1993)

Pretzel Jar (1998)

Ashtray (1992)

Safety Style Ashtray (1992)

Spoon Rest (1997)

Beer Pitcher (1993)

Onion Soup (1992)

8 Oz. Fort Pit Baker (1993)

Shirley Bell (1998)

Genuine
Autumn Leaf
Hall

Autumn Leaf
Display Sign (1993)

10 1/2" Relish (1993)

Graeter Shape
Bud Vase (1995)

Autumn Leaf
Collector's Prayer

Bless this kitchen, Lord
It is the room I hold most dear
It is home to everything I love.
Bless all who enter here.

Know that each piece of Autumn Leaf
Isn't just a dish
But a memory of those I've loved
And a chance to reminisce.

Whenever I serve someone
From a piece of my Jewel Tea
It is my way of saying to them
"You are so very special to me."

Because, Lord, next to you
My family and each guest
This kitchen with its Autumn Leaf
Is the thing I love the best.

© Virginia Lee, 1992

Sherbet (1992)

Conic Mug (1991)

**China
Specialties
Items**

Colletor's Prayer Plaque (1992)

Fluted Top
Salt and Pepper
(1994)

Irish Coffee Mug (1991)

363

Airflow Teapot (1990)

Automoble Teapot (1993)

Windsheild Teapot (1999)

China Specialties Items

Baby Melody (1995)

Hookcover Teapot (1994)

Boston Sugar and Cremer
with Figural 8 Tray (1996)

Football (1995)

1993
CHINA SPECIALTIES
EXCLUSIVE
LIMITED EDITION
by Hall

Reamer (1993)

Butter (1995)

Musical (1998)

Condiment Set (1991)

St. Louis Chocolate Pot (1994)

Harriet Candles (1997)

Norris Water Jug (1991)

Ice Tea Dispenser (1995)

China Specialties Blue Blossom Items

Musical Teapot

Utensil Crock

Blue Blossom Collectors Sign

Reamer

Wall Clock

Baby Melody

Football Teapot

China Specialties Blue Blossom Items

Automobile Teapot

Batter Jug

China Specialties Blue Blossom	Number Produced	Original Price	Current Value
Automobile teapot (1995)	>500	$79.95	$125.00
Musical teapot (1998)		$89.95	$89.95
Utensil crock		$39.95	$79.95
Display sign		$14.95	$18.95
Reamer (1995)		$79.95	$125.00
Wall clock (1997)		$54.95	$54.95
Baby Melody teapot (1997)		$49.95	$125.00
Football teapot (1997)	100	$89.95	$125.00
Batter bowl (1997)		$54.95	$54.95
Giant ice tea dispenser (1996)	45	$695.00	$900.00 – 1000.00

China Specialties Blue Bouquet and Cameo Rose Items

Display Sign

Football Teapot

Automobile Teapot

China Specialties Cameo Rose Items

Hook Cover Teapot

Spoon Rest

Football Teapot

China Specialties Blue Bouquet Items

Batter Bowl

Reamer

Clock

China Specialties Blue Bouquet	Original Price	Current Value
Safety style ashtray (2000)	$39.95	$39.95
Spoon rest (2000)	$39.95	$39.95
Football teapot (2000)	$69.95	$89.95
Cameo Rose		
Display sign (1997)	$14.95	$18.95
Football teapot (2000)	$79.95	$79.95
Musical teapot	$89.95	$89.95
Automobile teapot (1999)	$99.95	$99.95
Hook Cover teapot (1998)	$54.95	$54.95
Batter bowl (1997)	$49.95	$49.95
Reamer (1997)	$59.95	$125.00
Wall clock (1997)	$54.95	$54.95
Items Not Pictured		
Cameo Rose Giant ice tea dispenser		$900.00 – 1000.00
Cameo Rose Shirley bell	$44.95	$44.95

China Specialties Cattail and Christmas Decal Items

China Specialties Cattail	Original Price	Current Value
Spoon rest (1999)	$39.95	$39.95
Reamer (1999)	$99.95	$99.95
Football teapot (1999)	$69.95	$69.95
Christmas Decal		
Automobile teapot (1997)	$79.95	$200.00
Musical teapot (1998)	$89.95	$95.00
Boston teapot, 16 oz. (1999)	$59.95	$59.95

China Specialties Crocus Items

Irish Coffee Mug

Ashtray

UTENSILS

Utensil Holder

Automobile Teapot

Iced Tea Dispenser

China Specialties Crocus	Number Produced	Original Price	Current Value
Photo Above:			
Irish coffee mug (1994)	sample		
Utensil crock (1996)	75	$39.95	$120.00
Safety style ashtray (1999)		$39.95	$39.95
Automobile teapot (1994)	600	$79.95	$295.00
Giant ice tea dispenser			$900.00 – 1,000.00
Total of 2000; sold in sets of four.			
Photo Page 369:			
Display sign (1995)		$14.95	$18.95
Spoon rest		$39.95	$39.95
Football teapot (1996)		$39.95	$225.00
Hook Cover teapot (1997)	600	$54.95	$69.95
Reamer (1995)		$59.95	$125.00
St. Louis chocolate pot (1997)	600	$39.95	$44.95
Bellevue teapot (2000)		$44.95	$44.95
Bellevue coffee pot (2000)		$34.95	$34.95
Hurricane lamp (1994)		$25.00	$49.95
Graeter bud vase (1994)		$25.00	$25.00
Shirley bell		$44.95	$44.95
Wall clock (1995)		$59.95	$79.95
Not Pictured			
Baby Melody teapot (1997)	125	$44.95	$125.00
Condiment jar (1994)		$25.00	$75.00

368

CROCUS, an art deco inspired "floral fantasy" design; was one of the few patterns Hall China made in the 1930's that was not produced analytically for one distributor. It was a "house pattern" and as such was applied to any shape a customer requested. Crocus has an extraordinary number of rare, unusual pieces because of this practice of short runs and special orders. In 1993, Hall China agreed to revive Crocus to produce an exclusive line of Limited Edition Collector's Items for China Specialties, not as reproductions, but as additions to the pattern using shapes never before decorated with this decal.

China Specialties   P.O. BOX 361280   Strongsville, OH 44136

Back of Crocus Sign

Crocus Sign

Spoon Rest

Automobile Teapot

Hook Cover Teapot

Reamer

St. Louis
Chocolate Pot

Bellevue Coffee Pot

Bellevue Teapot

Wall Clock

Shirley Bell

Hurricane Lamp

Graeter Bud Vase

China
Specialties
Crocus Items

369

China Specialties Orange Poppy Items

China Specialties Orange Poppy	Number Produced	Original Price	Current Value
Reamer		$79.95	$99.95
Spoon rest		$39.95	$39.95
Hook Cover teapot (1997)		$49.95	$79.95
St. Louis chocolate pot		$44.95	$44.95
Round butter (1998)		$54.95	$54.95
Display sign (1997)		$14.95	$18.95
Safety style ashtray (1999)		$39.95	$39.95
Utensil crock (1998)		$39.95	$39.95
Football teapot		$89.95	$89.95
Musical teapot (1997)		$89.95	$89.95
Automobile teapot			
Norris covered jug (1994)	sample		
Airflow teapot (1994)	sample		
Shirley bell (1998)		$44.95	$44.95
Items not pictured:			
Giant ice tea dispenser		$995.00	$995.00

Reamer

Spoon Rest

Hook Cover Teapot

St. Louis Chocolate Pot

Butter

Display Sign

Ashtray

UTENSILS

Football Teapot

Musical Teapot

Utensil Crock

Automobile Teapot

Norris Water Jug

Airflow Teapot

Shirley Bell

China Specialties
Orange Poppy Items

371

China Specialties Red Poppy Items

UTENSILS

Utensil Crock

Custard Cup

Hurrican Lamp

Spoon Rest

Shirley Bell

St. Louis
Chocolate Pot

*China Specialties
Red Poppy Items*

Red Poppy	Number Produced	Original Price	Current Value
Utensil crock (1996)	100	$39.95	$125.00
Hurricane lamp (1994)		$25.00	$49.95
Spoon rest		$39.95	$39.95
Ramekin/custard cup	sample		
Shirley bell		$44.95	$55.00
St. Louis chocolate pot (1997)	>450	$39.95	$59.95
Football teapot			$89.95
Display sign (1995)		$14.95	$18.95
Hook Cover teapot (1997)		$49.95	$69.95
Reamer (1993)	450	$59.95	$125.00
One handle bean pot (1994)	>500	$49.95	$195.00
Safety style ashtray (2000)		$39.95	$39.95
Automobile teapot (1995)		$89.95	$89.95
Bud vase (1993)	500	$25.00	$25.00
Musical teapot (1998)		$89.95	$89.95
Round butter (1995)		$49.95	$125.00
Batter bowl (1997)		$49.95	$110.00
Wall clock (1995)	>500	$49.95	$79.95
Items not pictured:			
Airflow teapot (1993)	400	$49.95	$125.00
Condiment jar (1993)	400	$25.00	$70.00
Giant ice tea dispenser	45	$695.00	$995.00

Display Sign

Football Teapot
showing back and front views

Hook Cover Teapot

Reamer

One Handled Bean Pot

Ashtray

Automobile Teapot

Bud Vase

Musical Teapot

Round Butter

China
Specialties
Red Poppy
Items

Batter Bowl

Wall Clock

373

China Specialties Silhouette Items

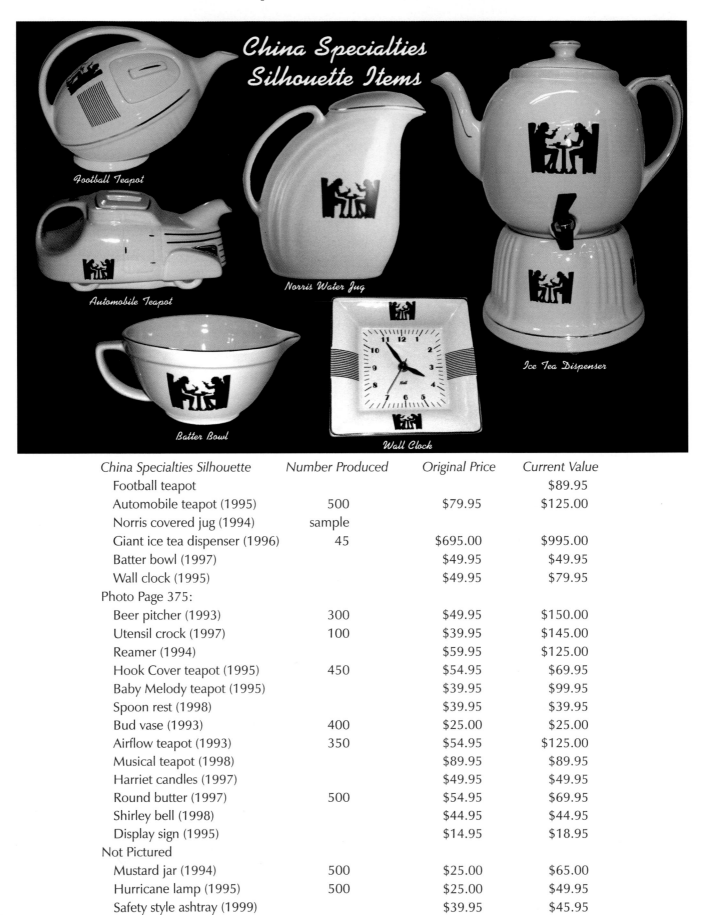

China Specialties Silhouette Items

Football Teapot

Automobile Teapot

Norris Water Jug

Ice Tea Dispenser

Batter Bowl

Wall Clock

China Specialties Silhouette	Number Produced	Original Price	Current Value
Football teapot			$89.95
Automobile teapot (1995)	500	$79.95	$125.00
Norris covered jug (1994)	sample		
Giant ice tea dispenser (1996)	45	$695.00	$995.00
Batter bowl (1997)		$49.95	$49.95
Wall clock (1995)		$49.95	$79.95
Photo Page 375:			
Beer pitcher (1993)	300	$49.95	$150.00
Utensil crock (1997)	100	$39.95	$145.00
Reamer (1994)		$59.95	$125.00
Hook Cover teapot (1995)	450	$54.95	$69.95
Baby Melody teapot (1995)		$39.95	$99.95
Spoon rest (1998)		$39.95	$39.95
Bud vase (1993)	400	$25.00	$25.00
Airflow teapot (1993)	350	$54.95	$125.00
Musical teapot (1998)		$89.95	$89.95
Harriet candles (1997)		$49.95	$49.95
Round butter (1997)	500	$54.95	$69.95
Shirley bell (1998)		$44.95	$44.95
Display sign (1995)		$14.95	$18.95
Not Pictured			
Mustard jar (1994)	500	$25.00	$65.00
Hurricane lamp (1995)	500	$25.00	$49.95
Safety style ashtray (1999)		$39.95	$45.95

Beer Pitcher

Utensil Crock

UTENSILS

Reamer

Baby Melody

Spoon Rest

Bud Vase

Hook Cover TEapot

Musical Teapot

Harriet Candlesticks

Airflow Teapot

Shirley Bell

Hall
Silhouette
Display Sign

China Specialties Silhouette Items

Round Butter

China Specialties Miscellaneous Decals Items

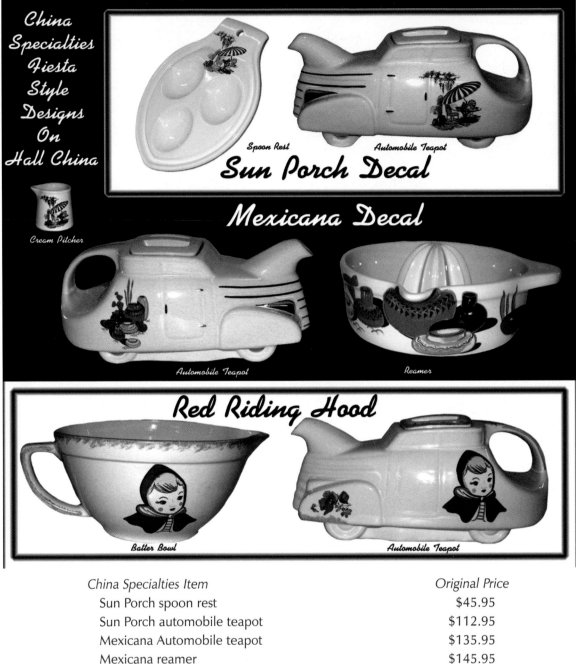

China Specialties Fiesta Style Designs On Hall China

Sun Porch Decal

Spoon Rest

Automobile Teapot

Cream Pitcher

Mexicana Decal

Automobile Teapot

Reamer

Red Riding Hood

Batter Bowl

Automobile Teapot

China Specialties Item	Original Price
Sun Porch spoon rest	$45.95
Sun Porch automobile teapot	$112.95
Mexicana Automobile teapot	$135.95
Mexicana reamer	$145.95
Red Riding Hood batter jug	$145.95
Red Riding Hood automobile	$125.95

China Specialties Novelty Teapots

Beginning in 1992, China Specialties commissioned Hall China to produce limited edition teapots. The shapes selected were from the Novelty Teapot Line which Hall China had produced originally in the late 1930s. Colors selected are those which are not believed to have been made originally, although some may appear similar to the old colors. All pieces are marked with a special back-stamp which indicates they are a limited edition reissue.

In a few instances, new teapots being represented as old have appeared on the resale market with their backstamp removed. Be suspicious of any automobile or football without a backstamp. Inspect the bottom carefully for scratches which may indicate the new mark has been removed. Also look at the spout. The hole in the spout of the new teapots is generally much smaller than in the earlier teapots.

China Specialties Novelty Teapots

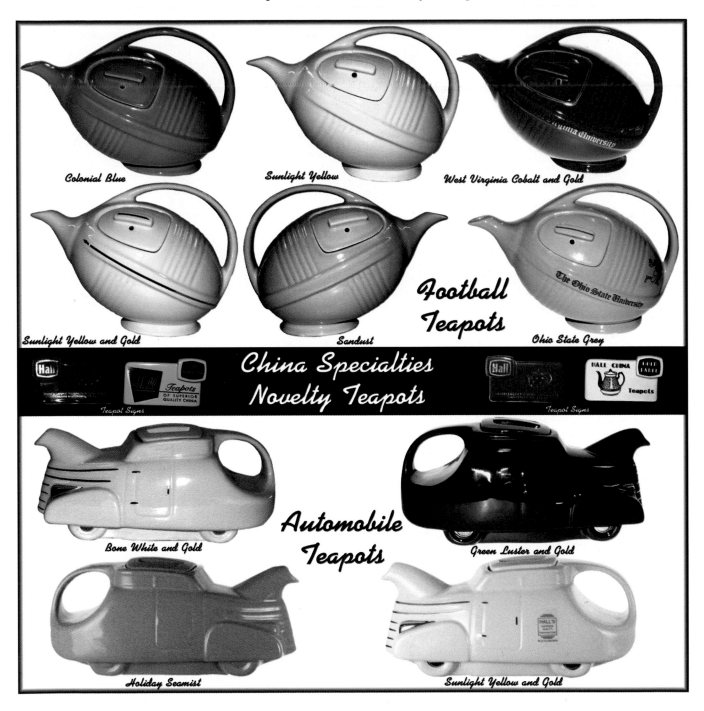

Colonial Blue

Sunlight Yellow

West Virginia Cobalt and Gold

Sunlight Yellow and Gold

Sandust

Football Teapots

Ohio State Grey

China Specialties Novelty Teapots

Teapot Signs

Teapot Signs

Bone White and Gold

Green Luster and Gold

Automobile Teapots

Holiday Seamist

Sunlight Yellow and Gold

Automobile Teapot

Color	No. Made	Original Price	Current Price
Bone white (1992)	300	$49.95	$100.00
Bone white/platinum (1992)	500	$59.95	$100.00
Green luster (1992)	100	$49.95	$85.00
Green luster/gold (1992)	200	$59.95	$85.00
Green luster/platinum (1992)	500	$69.95	$79.95
Sunlight yellow/gold (1993)	200	$69.95	$90.00
Sunlight yellow/platinum (1993)	300	$69.95	$79.95

Football Teapot

Color	No. Made	Original Price	Current Price
Sandust (1992)	350	$49.95	$100.00
Sandust/gold (1992)	150	$59.95	$150.00
Colonial blue (1992)	300	$49.95	$89.95
Colonial blue/gold (1992)	200	$69.95	$89.95
Sunlight yellow (1993)	300	$49.95	$69.95
Ohio State (1995)		$69.95	$69.95
West Virginia		$69.95	$69.95

China Specialties Non-Hall Items

China Specialties Non-Hall Items	Original Price	China Specialties Non-Hall Items	Original Price
Photo Above:		Thimble	$12.95
Child's starter set	$99.95	Canister set	$179.95
Child's covered casserole	*	Salad set	$29.95
Child's dinner plate	$10.00	Pilsner tumbler, Libbey	$29.95**
Child's platter	*	Water goblet, Libbey	$29.95**
Mini reamer	$22.95	Water tumbler, Libbey	$7.50
*Sold as a set with 2 plates for $59.95.		Ice tea tumbler, Libbey	$7.00*
Photo on Page 379:		Shot glass, Libbey	$5.00
"Rings" ¼ lb. butter	$39.95	Glass footedcandy	$24.95
Playing cards	$14.95	Glass ¼ lb. butter	$19.95
Wall pocket	$39.95	Rolling pin	$39.95
Flower pot with saucer	$19.95	Double switch plate	$35.00
Napkin ring	$39.95**	Single switch plate	$29.95
		* Autumn Leaf, $10.00	
		** Price for set of four.	

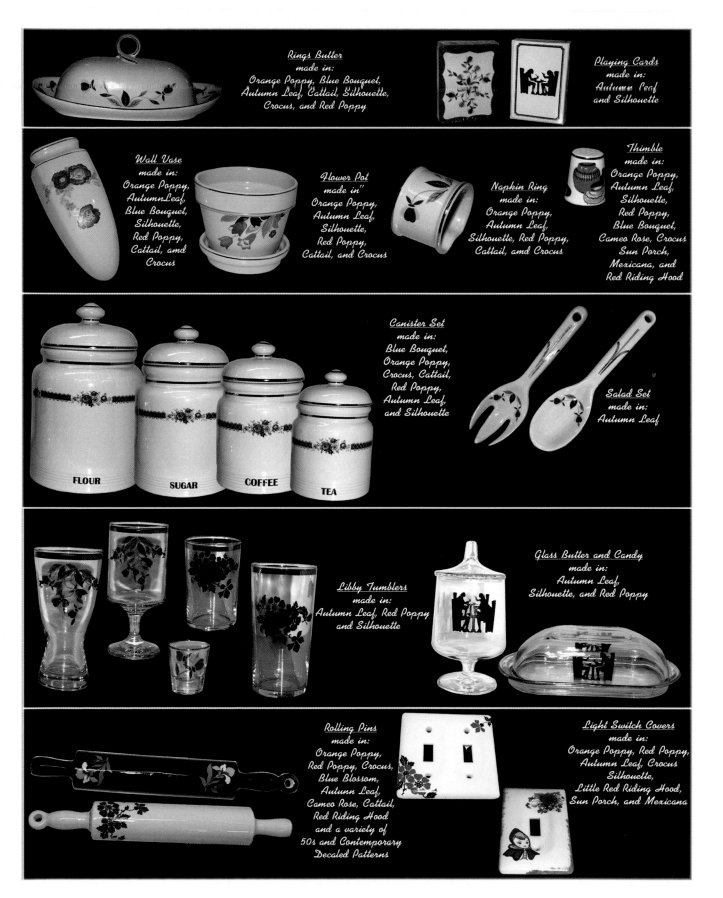

Rings Butter
made in:
Orange Poppy, Blue Bouquet,
Autumn Leaf, Cattail, Silhouette,
Crocus, and Red Poppy

Playing Cards
made in:
Autumn Leaf
and Silhouette

Wall Vase
made in:
Orange Poppy,
AutumnLeaf,
Blue Bouquet,
Silhouette,
Red Poppy,
Cattail, amd
Crocus

Flower Pot
made in"
Orange Poppy,
Autumn Leaf,
Silhouette,
Red Poppy,
Cattail, and Crocus

Napkin Ring
made in:
Orange Poppy,
Autumn Leaf,
Silhouette, Red Poppy,
Cattail, amd Crocus

Thimble
made in:
Orange Poppy,
Autumn Leaf,
Silhouette,
Red Poppy,
Blue Bouquet,
Cameo Rose, Crocus
Sun Porch,
Mexicana, and
Red Riding Hood

Canister Set
made in:
Blue Bouquet,
Orange Poppy,
Crocus, Cattail,
Red Poppy,
Autumn Leaf,
and Silhouette

Salad Set
made in:
Autumn Leaf

FLOUR   SUGAR   COFFEE   TEA

Libby Tumblers
made in:
Autumn Leaf, Red Poppy
and Silhouette

Glass Butter and Candy
made in:
Autumn Leaf,
Silhouette, and Red Poppy

Rolling Pins
made in:
Orange Poppy,
Red Poppy, Crocus,
Blue Blossom,
Autumn Leaf,
Cameo Rose, Cattail,
Red Riding Hood
and a variety of
50s and Contemporary
Decaled Patterns

Light Switch Covers
made in:
Orange Poppy, Red Poppy,
Autumn Leaf, Crocus
Silhouette,
Little Red Riding Hood,
Sun Porch, and Mexicana

Privately Produced Autumn Leaf

Stainless Steel Tableware

A four place stainless steel tableware service became available to collectors in late 1993. The tableware was produced for a private company by the International Silver Company using original dies which were used to make the silverplate issued by Jewel in 1958. Therefore, the shape of this issue is different from the shape of the stainless sold originally by Jewel in the early 1960s. This offering consists of a five place service — place fork, salad fork, place spoon, teaspoon, and place knife. Each piece is marked, "C & C Collectible® 93" on the back. A 20-piece service for four retails for $167.00.

Non-Hall Autumn Leaf

As with many other popular collectibles, there are numerous items resembling Autumn Leaf pieces which have been fashioned by industrious individuals. In many cases these attempts at imitating or adding to the original collectible has served a useful purpose and there has been no attempt by the maker to defraud the public or misrepresent the article. However, the problems with these articles occur when they reach the secondary market where people are unfamiliar with their origin. Novice collectors who find any unusual china piece, especially if it lacks the Jewel backstamp or shows few signs of age, would be well advised to check the authenticity of the piece with another knowledgeable collector or dealer before paying a high price for such an item. Some of the homemade non-china items are showing up at flea markets and collectors should be aware that these are recent creations which should not command the exorbitant prices reserved for truly rare items produced for Jewel by the Hall China Company. The following is a list of creations which we have been able to compile and their original prices where they were available.

Item	Original Price
Ceramic dinner bell on a wooden rack	$19.50
Ceramic bottle, pump soap	$27.50
Ceramic bud base	$10.50
Ceramic butter with dome shape ceramic lid	
Ceramic cabinet knobs	
Ceramic candleholder	$10.50
Ceramic footed candy dish	$25.20
Ceramic square ruffled candy and cover	$25.00
Ceramic candy scoop	$32.50
Ceramic child's set, four piece place setting	$100.00
Ceramic dresser box	
Ceramic egg cup	$10.50
Ceramic square hot plate	
Ceramic lamp	$100.00
Ceramic leftover, loop handle	
Ceramic napkin holder	$10.00
Ceramic napkin ring	
Ceramic picture frame	$43.75
Ceramic pie lifter	$7.00
Ceramic wall switch and outlet plates	$8.50
Ceramic large turkey platter	$38.50
Ceramic two-part reamer	$25.00

Item	Original Price
Ceramic rolling pin, 13" long	
Ceramic soap dish	$7.00
Ceramic soap dish, 2" x 5", oval	$24.50
Ceramic spoon rest	$7.00
Ceramic spooner	
Ceramic tissue box	$25.00
Ceramic toothpick holder	$5.00
Ceramic tureen, underplate, ladle	$38.50
Ceramic vase, 10"	
Clock made from a 10" dinner plate	$65.00
Glass cheese dome/wooden base and inlaid tile	$38.50
Coat rack, six peg oak	$28.50
Colander, white enamel	$38.95
Cutting board, 6" x 11", wooden	$23.95
Match safe, metal	
Paper towel holder, oak	$38.50
Place mats, oval 12" x 18", vinyl	
Quilt, homemade	
Salt/pepper, tall, wooden, hand painted	
Sifters, one and two cup metal	
Spice jars with rack	

In addition to the above, there are also reports of the existence of several hand-painted kitchen chairs. Clocks have also been fashioned from 9" plates and cake plates. Other items with the Autumn Leaf decal which have been offered for sale include wrist watches, afghans, napkins, and stationary. Needless to say, almost anything imaginable might be found with this popular decal. This section has been included to help enable you as a collector to make a knowledgeable decision about the origin of the various types of merchandise which may be offered to you. Be aware that new items are being produced constantly, and that this listing may not include all the new items you may encounter.

Hall American Line Reissues

In early 1985, Hall China announced a new retail line for department stores. Most of the 65 items targeted for this promotion were items already in production. These were primarily casseroles, bakers, bowls, and platters. The new items which were part of the reissue which concerned collectors the most were some teapot and water server shapes. The Airflow, Rhythm, and T-Ball square teapots, the Streamline and Donut jugs, and the "Hercules" and "Nora" shape water servers were included. Another piece which was made and caused some collector concern was the "Sundial" batter bowl. However, this piece was issued with a square base like the one used in the Autumn Leaf decal pattern. Identification of the new pieces is easy for anyone who is familiar with Hall's old color glazes. For others who are less experienced, the backstamp on the new items will be square; old items will have either the round backstamp or the "Superior Quality Kitchenware" mark.

NOMENCLATURE CROSS REFERENCE

Since Hall did not give names to every item produced, researchers have found it convenient to provide names to help with identification. In some cases more than one name has become associated with the same piece or shape. This listing will cross reference the multiple names for those collectors interested in using numerous references.

Names Used In This Reference	Other Names	Names Used In This Reference	Other Names
Adonis	Prince	Plume	Disraeli
Apple	Browning	Radiance	Sunshine
Baron	Big Boy	Rayed	J-Sunshine
Benjamin	Albert	Regal	Dickens
Birch	Darby	Ribbed	Flute
Bowknot	Gladstone	Rounded Terrace	Step-round
Bowling Ball	Pepper	Royal	Eliot
Cathedral	Arch	Rutherford	Alton
Connie	Victoria	Shaggy Tulip	Parrot Tulip
Coverlet	Cozy Cover	Silhouette	Taverne
Daniel	Rickson	Simplicity	Classic
Drape	Swathe	Starlight	Tennyson
Five Band	Banded	Stonewall	Banner 'n Basket
Floral Lattice	Flowerpot	Sundial	Saf-Handle
General	Emperor	Target	Bullseye
Grape	Darwin	Teardrop	Egg Drop
Great American	Golden Key	Terrace	Step-down
Hercules	Aristocrat	Thick Rim	Big Lip
Jerry	Monarch	Viking	Bell
Medallion	Colonial	Waverly	Crest
Murphy	Peel	Wild Poppy	Poppy & Wheat
Norse	Everson	Windcrest	Bronte
Novelty Radiance	Sunshine	Yellow Rose	Pastel Rose
Perk	Deca-plain	Zephyr	Bingo
Phoenix	Patrician		

BIBLIOGRAPHY

Autumn Leaf News. National Leaf Collectors Club: Austin, TX.

Barth, Harold. *History of Columbiana County, Vol. II.* Historical Publishing Co.: Topeka-Indianapolis, 1926.

China and Glass Red Book. China and Glass Tablewares, Commoner Publishing Company: New York.

Duke, Harvey. *Superior Quality Hall China: A Guide For Collectors.* ELO Books: U.S.A., 1977.

Duke, Harvey. *Hall 2.* ELO Books: U.S.A., 1985.

"History of the Hall China Company, East Liverpool, Ohio." Ceramic Abstracts and The Bulletin of the American Ceramic Society. August 15, 1945.

Jewel Home Shopping Service Catalogs. Jewel Home Shopping Service: Barrington, IL.

Sears, Roebuck and Co. Catalogs. Sears, Roebuck and Co.: Chicago, IL.

The Jewel News. Jewel Tea Co., Inc. Barrington, IL.

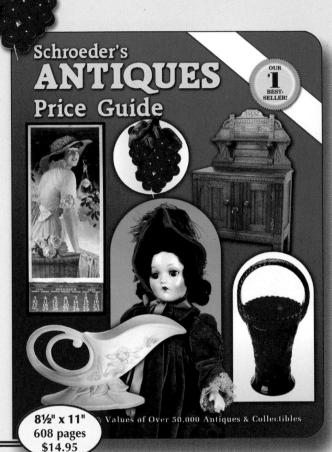